The publisher gratefully acknowledges
the generous support of the following:

The Music in America Endowment Fund of the
University of California Press Foundation, which
was established by a major gift from Sukey and
Gil Garcetti, Michael P. Roth, and the
Roth Family Foundation

The Constance and William Withey Endowment Fund
for History and Music of the
University of California Press Foundation

The Music Endowment Fund of the
University of California Press Foundation

Mingus Speaks

Mingus Speaks

JOHN F GOODMAN

With Photos by Sy Johnson

University of California Press

BERKELEY   LOS ANGELES   LONDON

University of California Press, one of the most distinguished university presses in the United States, enriches lives around the world by advancing scholarship in the humanities, social sciences, and natural sciences. Its activities are supported by the UC Press Foundation and by philanthropic contributions from individuals and institutions. For more information, visit www.ucpress.edu.

University of California Press
Berkeley and Los Angeles, California

University of California Press, Ltd.
London, England

Library of Congress Cataloging-in-Publication Data

Mingus, Charles, 1922–1979.
   Mingus speaks / [interviews by] John F Goodman.
      pages   cm
   Includes bibliographical references and index.
   ISBN 978-0-520-27523-2 (cloth : alk. paper)
   1. Mingus, Charles, 1922–1979—Interviews.   2. Jazz musicians—Interviews.   I. Goodman, John F, 1934–.
II. Title.
   ML418.M45A5   2013
   781.65092—dc23   2012044233

Manufactured in the United States of America

22 21 20 19 18 17 16 15 14 13
10 9 8 7 6 5 4 3 2 1

In keeping with a commitment to support environmentally responsible and sustainable printing practices, UC Press has printed this book on Rolland Enviro100, a 100% post-consumer fiber paper that is FSC certified, deinked, processed chlorine-free, and manufactured with renewable biogas energy. It is acid-free and EcoLogo certified.

Contents

Illustrations

Preface

This is not just another book on Mingus. This is the man speaking in his own voice. From the outset I did not want to write another critical study or an analysis of the music. It had to be basically a book of interviews, letting the man speak in his own headlong delivery, constructing his own verbal solos, punctuating with blasts fired off at musicians and critics who didn't measure up, with ramblings into paranoia and real pain. But I wasn't sure how to give it a form so that his voice would be heard—and heard accurately.

With all the stuff that's been written about him, there is very little in the way of extended interviews—and somehow he and I connected to make these happen.

Let me first give you some sense of who I am and where I came from— the bona fides in other words. I grew up in Chicago and its suburbs, fortunate to have parents who passed on to me their great love of music. As a toddler, I could identify the music in my father's big collection of 78-rpm records by the color and design of their labels: the Vocalions, Victors, and Columbias, the music of Duke and Lunceford, Paul Whiteman, Chick Webb and Ella (on blue-and-gold Decca), most of the major big bands, Glenn Miller, the Dorseys, a few small-group things, some show music, André Kostelanetz (yes), concert and symphonic music.

In high school, a group of us devoted ourselves to listening to and playing jazz, starting with Dixieland and small-group swing. We were early-'50s examples of what Norman Mailer later called white Negroes: we read Mezz Mezzrow (a Chicago guy);[1] aspired to be hip and cool; and made frequent weekend trips to the city to get drunk and hear some of the great old-timers—Baby Dodds, Henry "Red" Allen, Chicago veterans like George Brunis and Art Hodes, and of course the Ellington and Basie bands when they played the Blue Note. In 1954, a friend got us into the recording session for *Louis Armstrong Plays W. C. Handy*. We sang background on a tune or two.

My parents and another couple had given a celebrated party in 1950 featuring Armstrong's then-all-star group (with Jack Teagarden, Barney Bigard, Earl Hines, Arvell Shaw, Cozy Cole, and Velma Middleton). That event was talked about for years and still provokes pungent, sharp memories: Louis and Hines noodling at the piano; Jack T's famous trombone case with space for a clean shirt and a bottle of gin; my high-school friends sneaking by the cops and sitting on the lawn. There followed other musical functions—Oscar Peterson's trio at the Ambassador Hotel in Chicago, pianist Barbara Carroll in our living room, and a few more.

My father, who should have been a George Wein, promoted a series of country-club dance parties which featured the great bands of Duke Ellington, Les Brown, and Count Basie—dancing on the terrace, the saxes right in your face, loud and swinging. My mother had regular season tickets to the Chicago Symphony throughout the Fritz Reiner era and earlier, when the orchestra was finally achieving greatness. I had heard and studied the "standard repertoire," this orchestra's meat, but attending live performances in the acoustics of Orchestra Hall was to hear soloists like Rubenstein, Heifetz, and Dame Myra Hess in unforgettable explorations.

I finally discovered bebop and the new jazz as a freshman at Dartmouth in 1952, hearing one afternoon on a Boston radio station the sounds of Dizzy Gillespie, Charlie Parker, et al. The impact was stunning. Somehow I comprehended what they were doing, and my musical life changed henceforth. I wanted to play piano like Bud Powell.

Weekend trips to New York (and later Chicago, where I was in graduate school) brought me to the music of Miles, Monk, Mingus, Bud, Bird (heard once, on the stand at the Metropole, not playing well), and many other great musicians at a time when jazz was flowering. In 1965 I moved to New York to teach English at NYU and City College. And I became a music critic—first for the *New Leader*, a small but influential Leftish monthly which had a great arts section. Then I wrote album and concert reviews for *Playboy* for nine years, which gave me entrée to much of the music scene in New York—rock, classical, and jazz . . . Now we're finally getting close to Mingus.

Before New York, in 1962 (I think), I was auditioning his new *Oh Yeah!* album in a listening booth at a Madison, Wisconsin, record store, laughing and digging "Eat That Chicken," "Hog-Callin' Blues," and the rest. After some years of not paying much attention, I finally woke up to the raucous humor and formidable genius of Mingus and Roland Kirk playing together.

There has never been a record like *Oh Yeah!* and never a duo like Mingus and Kirk. I was lucky enough to get to know both of them, and their music changed my life.

Flash forward ten years, when I had left New York but was still writing for *Playboy.* There was news of an upcoming concert by Mingus, and I convinced Sheldon Wax, the magazine's managing editor and resident jazz lover, to let me cover it and possibly do a feature article on Mingus, who had recently emerged from a long, sad, and fallow period, during which he had been off-mike to all but a few close friends and associates. There was a story there.

This event was the first *Mingus and Friends* concert (there were two), and it happened in New York on February 4, 1972. Here's part of my some-what overbaked review of the concert, which had aroused a lot of interest in the New York music community.

> After much fanfare (e.g., Nat Hentoff's article in *The New York Times*) and expectation (this was Mingus's first concert in ten years), word had gone out that we were to witness a great comeback or another milestone in an already protean career.
>
> Most of the 2800 seats in Lincoln Center's Philharmonic Hall had been sold and were filled with a crowd, somewhat younger than we had expected, from the obviously higher reaches of hipdom—outlandishly fine chicks, studiously inelegant males, black saints and sinner ladies. They came to hear an 18-piece ensemble featuring Gene Ammons, Bobby Jones, Lee Konitz, Gerry Mulligan and Milt Hinton—for starters. Bill Cosby strove manfully and entertainingly as emcee. Teo Macero, who looks like a librarian, kept dropping the score but flailed away with the baton, assisted by Mingus from time to time. Dizzy Gillespie, James Moody and Randy Weston made brief appearances during a long jam session later in the program.
>
> . . . More like a rehearsal than a concert, its bright moments came inevitably when the band loosened up from the tight complexities of Mingus's earliest compositions or the structural requisites of some of the later ones: a classic blues solo by Gene Ammons on tenor, backed up by Mingus, which ended the first part of the concert; a couple of songs by Honey Gordon, who sounds like Duke Ellington's 1940s vocalist Joya Sherrill and Ella Fitzgerald combined; a piece written for Roy Eldridge and marvelously played by 18-year-old John Faddis on trumpet; and a few of the Mingus standards, such as "E's Flat Ah's Flat Too."
>
> The other good things were segments from the new Mingus album on Columbia, his first in eight years, *Let My Children Hear Music.* If what we heard of it that night is any indication, Charles is not jiving when he calls it "the best album I have ever made." Despite incredible setbacks in recent years and a sometimes disappointing concert, one of the great jazzmen of all time is back, making original, vital music again.[2]

That concert and *Children* marked a new beginning for Mingus, and they were the initial impetus for this book. When I first met him in 1972, Mingus was finally off the pills and out of the shadows, once again eating with a vengeance, blowing away people with insults, and talking. God, could he talk. I'd been around a lot of jazz people but had never heard anything like it.

In subsequent visits, I got to meet the Mingus family—Charles, Susan Graham Ungaro (not then his wife), arranger Sy Johnson, the musicians in his regular small band (Bobby Jones, Charles McPherson, and others)—many of whom will have something to say herein. I missed out on Dannie Richmond, the one I really should have talked with.

I quit writing about music in the 1980s in part because I could never resolve the critic's dilemma: you either limit yourself to readers versed in various kinds of technical talk and bore them with musicological maunderings, or you write your impressions. Neither approach alone is sufficient to render the sense of what's going on in music. On a deeper level, critics and musicians operate in different worlds, even when they intersect, as Julio Cortázar conveyed so well in his roman à clef of Charlie Parker's last years, "The Pursuer."[3] Unlike most other arts, music dances away when you reach out to it. The Mingus book also kept dancing away from me.

Part of my delay in getting it done at first was preoccupation with an increasingly messy personal life; part was owing to the need to raise a family and earn a living; part was avoidance of a project that I had endowed with a lot of emotional freight.

At one point a few years ago, my intention was to make these materials into a multimedia e-book production (à la Ken Burns but better) that I would self-publish with software like Adobe Acrobat. This would dramatically display Mingus the man, his music, his cohorts and friends, the works. Sy Johnson promised help and some photos; others contributed as well (see the acknowledgments). The New York Foundation for the Arts (NYFA) graciously sponsored the project in February 2008, and I worked for a year seeking funding.

When that wasn't forthcoming, I had to reevaluate. The project is now what I had originally conceived it to be—a book of interviews, and that's a better, much simpler solution, finally.

What Mingus and I did manage to get done was a twenty-hour series of taped interviews in 1972 and 1974 in Philadelphia and New York (see the chronology), an amateur recording of some fine music one night in Philly, and a number of revealing discussions with ten friends and associates, also interviewed by me and included here as chapter commentaries. I've placed these commentaries after the Mingus texts in their appropriate settings so as to give readers a different take on what Mingus and I talked about and, frequently, to add detail and perspective to things he brought up. My intention is to add a kind of counterpoint to the Mingus themes.

The interviews were first intended for a feature article, and later, when that miscarried, we continued the talks to develop a book-length publication, "my life in music," as Mingus put it. *Playboy* rejected my 1973 article submission; "too much of a fan-magazine tone," they said. In 1974, five years before he died, Mingus, Sue, and I met and talked with an editor from Doubleday about a book that never went beyond proposal stage. The year before, they had published Ellington's *Music Is My Mistress*, and Mingus had also talked for years about a book to cover his musical life—meaning all the stuff and substance that hadn't been given form in *Beneath the Underdog*, his 1971 autobiographical fantasy. The fact that Duke, whom Mingus worshipped, had done his "life in music" also must have influenced him. Our book would cover his musical development and progress, the important influences and contacts, his opinions on music and musicians, on life.

Mingus Speaks is not that book, but it provides clear glimpses into these areas, a few more pieces of the Mingus puzzle, and some new explanations as to how that wonderful music came together. There is much material here that has never been revealed before, and a side of Mingus that may come as a surprise to some. With minimal content editing, he talks directly about the subjects that were on his mind in 1972–74, one of his most creative and tumultuous periods.

Yet the technical editing and transcribing difficulties were considerable, given the man's rapid-fire, slurred manner of speaking. In most of these chapters, I've cut and pasted to keep the continuity; the reader will notice breaks in the text where these edits occurred. In other chapters, I decided to let the reader see how Mingus's mind worked, how one subject flowed into another without much prompting or direct questioning from me, how one association led to another. "Spontaneous composition" is what he called it in music.

There are only select references here to the Mingus literature and to unfamiliar names and events that might elude all but the most knowledgeable jazz person. My headnotes and comments are generally short; in a couple of instances, I've written more extended commentaries. The idea is to not distract the reader from Mingus, to amplify and explain only when necessary.[4]

Mingus allowed me to be his Boswell, I think, because we personally connected on a number of levels. He respected my background as a writer for some years on jazz and concert music, respected that I had been a "professor," that I worked at the time as a writer for *Playboy*. That last affiliation appealed both to his sense of humor and, one might say, his prurient interest: "You'd go right down in the heart of Tijuana and we'd go to this restaurant where they had the finest dancers—I mean bad, baby, bad. *Playboy*'d have trouble with this club. In fact, one broad I could tell I could have her without the money, one of the dancers. They weren't all whores."

Playboy had once made Mingus an offer to reprint and distribute some of his music (see chapter 6), which he foolishly rejected. And the magazine in the early 1970s still had considerable mystique in the world of jazz, having sponsored numerous festivals, conducting a highly regarded jazz poll, and booking jazz into its clubs. *Playboy* was also a somewhat fading though still central rallying point in American culture for promoting sexual freedom and "the good life," plus providing a forum for quality writing on racial issues and left-wing politics—all stuff that Mingus responded to.

In the interviews, we had conversations about the man's appetites, his fights and frustrations with Sue, his "extrasensory perceptions," as an early composition had it, the pains and the pleasures of living. Not to mention the music. The talk, the psychology, and the music were all of a piece with Charles. He was easily the most complex person I had ever met—and one of the most open. There weren't too many filters operating when Mingus talked, and I'm proud that he trusted me.

NOTES

1. Mezz Mezzrow and Bernard Wolfe, *Really the Blues* (New York: Random House, 1946).
2. "Acts and Entertainments," *Playboy*, May 1972, 24. I did other occasional reviews of Mingus music during my stint at *Playboy*. My signed obit for Mingus was published in the November 1979 issue, 60–62.
3. In *Blow-Up and Other Stories* (originally, *End of the Game and Other Stories*), trans. Paul Blackburn (New York: Pantheon, 1967), 182–247.
4. What Mingus said in these interviews was, of course, his own subjective truth, not always objective fact. Where I felt further explication was necessary, I've added chapter endnotes or in-text commentaries.

Introduction

"Don't take me for no
avant-garde, ready-born doctor."

Many people have tried to explain Mingus to the world. Finally, it's time for him to do the talking.

His music has been praised, anatomized, criticized, discographized. No longer jazz's angry man, he has achieved prominence as one of the great jazz composers, largely through the efforts of his wife Sue, who has done so much since his death to keep three bands going and let the public hear his music. Mingus is in the composer pantheon with Duke Ellington and a very few others. Wynton Marsalis loves him; he's part of the received jazz canon. Would he be proud of that? Dismissive? Both, probably.

For many critics and listeners, his music has been hard to fathom: is it traditional, free, or what? And yet, recent remarks of younger people in blogs, coming to his music for the first time, are revealing. (He always knew the kids would respond.) In *The Black Saint and the Sinner Lady*, one person heard "images of creeping hobos, fawning sophisticates, domestic loneliness, and a mind on fire." On YouTube, the audio track of "Solo Dancer" from *Black Saint* elicited this, among many comments: "So i'm 15 and this is the first time i heard this song AND IT'S FUCKING BRILLIANT. Can someone point me to a good place to start with Charles Mingus? Please?"[1]

His music is among the most personal of expressions in jazz. Filled with recurring recombinations of source material of all kinds (gospel, Dixieland, concert music, Spanish and Latin music, bebop, swing, New Orleans, R&B, free jazz, circus, and minstrel music), each piece is also a unique minibiography in sound. Not every one is fully realized, but each piece tells something about where Mingus has been. These are not generally Monkish or modernist-style compositions. They are personal statements.

For a man as verbal as Mingus was, a great frustration seemed to be his constant need to explain himself—in his music, to his audiences, in his book

Beneath the Underdog, in his essays, and finally in his talk here. The rush
of words, the abrupt shifts in subject (sometimes in mood) testify to this. I
usually understood what he was talking about and shared much of his taste
and affection for the music and its creators. We also came to share jokes,
drinks, and the latest political outrage.

Still, talking with Mingus? It was sometimes intimidating and, depending on his mood, now and again fraught with dense pauses and occasional
disconnects. After a time I learned not to try and fill the dead air. And it was
just a great privilege to hear him light up on a topic—as you will hear too.

Mingus, I came to think, felt forever on the outside of a world he repudi-
ated yet was very much part of. Outrage and joy were commonplace
emotions with Charles; they enabled him to carry on, or to beat the devil.
For all the critical analysis that has been directed at him, maybe the most
plausible thing I can say is that while he put up with deprivation and scorn
as a black man, he was clearly very privileged as an artist. Mingus understood how degrading the business of performing jazz often was, but he had
no doubts about how good he was and what he had accomplished. That
perceptual discord often made him angry: "If you're going to be a physician
or a finished artist in anything, like a surgeon, then you got to be able to
retrace your steps and do it anytime you want to go forward, be more
advanced. And if I'm a surgeon, am I going to cut you open 'by heart,' just
free-form it, you know?"

The avant-garde pretenders made him crazy because they posed as
"ready-born doctors." Their pretensions put the lie to everything Mingus
had worked and studied to do in music. A further dilemma was that he, by
most critical accounts, was labeled an avant-gardist. Another thing to make
you crazy. The audiences and critics sometimes made him crazy.

Mingus had other demons that pursued him. More than most jazz musicians, he was always critical of his output, always trying to discover how to
get away from jazz and create some kind of ideal, eclectic music that could
truly represent and fulfill him. His paranoia was legendary; his imaginary
ramblings and distortions, especially at this period in his life, tested both his
friends' and an outsider's credulity. Except for drugs (which he never got
into), his life, like Bird's, was in some way a testing of every limit of excess.
It was all part of a spiritual quest that he couldn't really identify.

I don't want to defend or excuse the outrageous and hurtful things he
did—and there were plenty of those. Jazz people have sometimes gotten off
the hook for behaviors that would put the rest of us in jail. Bud Powell's beating at the hands of Philadelphia cops is certainly the other side of that coin.
But Mingus—because he was verbal, very smart, and loved the limelight—

never hesitated to put forward that duality of race and art, outrage and joy, that made him such a unique voice in jazz.

As composer and bandleader, Mingus seemed to have two models—Duke Ellington, of course, as many have noted and, to a lesser extent, Jelly Roll Morton. He had Morton's swagger and some of Duke's charm, though surely not his urbanity. His music was often Ellingtonian in concept, if not in execution, and like Morton, he found a way to bring what he called "spontaneous composition" to jazz. As a performer, Mingus brought supreme execution and brilliance to, of all things, the bass. No one in jazz has ever played that instrument with his musicality and skill.

Like many people who met and spent time with Charles, I was at first bowled over by his insights and humor, his knowledge of jazz, the jazz business and its people, and the quickness of his mind.

Never mind that I had trouble translating the staccato yet slurred speech that issued forth. It was like listening to the Source, the Buddha, the Wizard of Jazz. Eventually I found I could not only participate and engage with Charles but that we could converse. That has to be one of the great kicks of my life, and I must presume others who have had that experience would agree. Mingus wanted such exchanges, though he sometimes frustrated them by acting like a Toscanini.

Village Vanguard founder Max Gordon noted that there wasn't a lot that was lovable about Mingus, but you could be his friend. In our talks, I sometimes got the sense that Mingus was performing, but it was the performance of a man who believed in everything he was saying—for the moment and maybe forever. Moody, he could clam up and offer the most laconic answers, or he could spout like a geyser, and you soaked it up and followed his rush of words to the end—or the next jump in subject. Yes, it was like his bass solos. And if you were lucky, you could say something that advanced the conversation.

I'm still not sure why I got on with him so well that he chose to reveal some very personal and painful hurts and feelings—not to mention his sometimes brilliant musico-socio-cultural aperçus. Part of our association, brief as it was, hinged on my attempt to be totally open with the guy. I was also willing to engage with him in writing a book, and that effort seemed to him a way to set the record straight, to talk about the realities of his life in music beyond the stylized attitudes and limits of *Beneath the Underdog*.

Mingus's health—mental and physical—came up frequently in the course of my talks with him and with those whom I interviewed in the course of doing this book. He was terribly concerned about it and mystified by the symptoms he experienced. Who can say how far he saw into the depth of his situation? In 1974, five years before he died from ALS, his physical appearance was far different from what it had been two years before.

In our lengthy 1974 interview with Sue (see commentaries in chapters 6 and 12), he sat on the floor while she and I did most of the talking, contributing little but listening to everything. He looked tired but there were flashes of the old Mingus, with talk about cigars and food. His music was still good but of a different quality than the music of two years earlier. This was the period of *Changes One* and *Changes Two*, with George Adams, Don Pullen, Jack Walrath, et al.

It was a time when Mingus and Sue seemed to have reached an equilibrium in their relationship, and perhaps he had resolved some of the tumultuous feelings of the past two years. But at best, it was Mingus in coasting mode. The second *Friends* concert on January 19, 1974, featured an exceptional reunion with Rahsaan Roland Kirk, and in May we had a book proposal in to Doubleday, the one already mentioned that ultimately fizzled. In July he undertook a long, too-strenuous tour to South America, Europe, and Japan.

I saw Mingus one more time performing at a club in New York in 1977, and it was not a good evening. For someone who was more alive than anyone I've ever known, he looked drawn, the music was dispiriting and our reunion perfunctory.

But the reality of Mingus playing, talking, bitching, and dissecting the world around him remains totally unforgettable to me. When the man was energized and the creative force was flowing, when the words rushed out and his thoughts tumbled over one another, it was indeed a window opening on the process that made such extraordinary music.

After so many years, I continue to miss him.

After the first *Mingus and Friends* concert in February 1972, I came back to New York in May for my first real exposure to the man. He was scheduled to appear with the band on Julius Lester's *Free Time* PBS-TV show. I drove in from Pennsylvania (where I then lived) to attend, wondering how Mingus would get on with the show's host, Julius Lester—musician, writer, outspoken civil rights iconoclast.

Lester had been tied in with SNCC (the Student Nonviolent Coordinating Committee), had gone to Cuba with Stokely Carmichael, and had written a book that some of us read for its great title, *Look Out Whitey! Black Power's Gon' Get Your Mama!* But word had it that he was changing his tune. At that point, I didn't know what Mingus's tune would be on such subjects.

Finally off the plane from Boston, Charles walked into the WNET studio in a long leather coat, carrying an enormous shopping bag of bagels, salmon, pickles, peppers, and cream cheese. Sue and I and the band were already there and, before anything else happened, the bag was opened and the contents set out for all to share. The rehearsal went well, as Mingus felt calm and in charge. He and Lester got on famously, and the show was mostly music (as I recall it) with a minimum of talk.

The band was his regular group at the time (May–June 1972): Charles McPherson, alto; Bobby Jones, tenor; Lonnie Hillyer, trumpet; John Foster, piano; Roy Brooks, drums; and the leader was starting to play like the Mingus of old. Joe Gardner might have substituted for Hillyer in the group playing on the recording I made in Philadelphia in June. I can't be sure.

The first extended interview we did was over a kitchen table (Mingus was never far from food) at Sue's place on East Tenth Street—as it happened, about a block from where I used to live (from 1965 to 1971), and it felt good to be back on that familiar turf.

A young man from some Italian publication had come to interview Mingus too, so he went first and I was happy to sit in and tape the proceedings, after which Charles and I would talk alone. Sue was also present and made an occasional comment.

What followed was about an hour of vintage Mingus, an interview which opened up many of the themes he and I would subsequently pursue over the next three years. It was also remarkable in showing the mixture of deference and disdain that Mingus could muster in the face of some remarkably stupid questions—even allowing for the language problem.

The interview covered many of the topics we would discuss later on:

- Watts, race, and politics;
- ethnic music for the people;
- phony African music, black intellectuals;
- Mingus music, as it comprehends all music;
- electronics in music;
- tradition and study;
- jazz audiences.

The session was typical of the way Mingus intertwined his thinking on race, politics, economics, and music and thus can set the scene for what follows in this book. I'll interrupt occasionally to add a gloss or two.

· · ·

FIGURE 1.   Mingus with cigar, on his rooftop, 1974. Photo by Sy Johnson.

INTERVIEWER: And how do you sympathize with the view that music, and most of all, jazz, reflects a state of mind or a human condition?

MINGUS: Man, will you rewind that statement again—rerun that?

INTERVIEWER: Yes. Jazz is a very old form of music that started a long time ago. I don't know exactly when it came to life, but anyhow, we are now in 1972, and many things have happened. Does 1972 jazz reflect what has happened during this last part of, uh . . .

MINGUS: No, of course not, 'cause nobody knows what happened. How's the music's gonna say what happened, when nobody knows what's happened [anywhere] in the last seven years?[2] There's been a camouflage by the government to make it look like there was some black race riots when there wasn't any at all. They probably hired people to do it; I can't figure it out for sure—I'm trying to look at it from the people I knew on the inside who were involved, who lived in Watts. It could be the Communist government or the Nazis or even the American government, or it could be the Southerners. I don't know who, but somebody set it up. The police department, maybe, I'm not sure.[3]

Do you know what I'm sayin'? I want to be sure you understand what I'm sayin'. I think they hired a few people . . . that camouflaged a revolution, the black revolution. But the real one is about to begin, ha ha.

INTERVIEWER: You see, our audience knows you very well. However, I wish you could give, you know, for our audience, a sort of little rundown on how you started, from the very beginning. It has to be brief, you know, but I really would like to start there.

MINGUS: I'll do that for you, only be sure I answer the question, the first question. You said, you know, does the music reflect what is happening or what did happen. And I say again, it can't because no one, no black man, knows what happened yet. Maybe me, maybe a couple of others, I'm talkin' about musicians that know. I'm not too sure of that—McPherson [Mingus's alto player] said he thought the riot was a fake, looked fake to him.

• • •

In typical Mingus fashion, he leads off by throwing a bomb at the interviewer. His point of view about such things was generally to take the inside track from his own experience, whether the subject was politics, music, or social concerns. It's no wonder that he and the poor Italian guy were often at cross purposes. This happened frequently in his other interviews too, and sometimes Mingus would deliberately exploit the disconnect. Later, Bobby

Jones would tell me that this was a trick to throw the interviewer off the track.

Watts and race (theme 1) would reappear shortly. Now he was getting into music as food for the spirit (theme 2), a favorite topic.

. . .

INTERVIEWER: Well, as a matter of fact, you know, I heard an awful lot of black Americans speaking in terms of, we are acquiring a new sense of awareness, or something. Do you feel that music, and in particular, jazz, can help, you know, these people to better understand themselves?

MINGUS: Well, if good music could get to the minds or the subconscious of people, it could help everybody, not just racists. Music has been used as therapy, you know, in mental wards. I was told about a program on NBC television about using poetry with schizophrenics. When I was a child, in 1942, they were using music as a shock treatment to patients. For example, I think music was used to uplift people in the first Russian revolution. So you don't even need me to answer that question.

If the people are separated from their music, they die. If the black people have a music, if jazz was their music—umm, although the masses of black people never went for jazz; they were segregated from it; they went for rhythm and blues. Not rock blues, rhythm and blues. That's probably why they're so confused and so separated, because they don't have a religious music like the Jews, who never changed their music; the Greeks, who never changed their music; the Armenians; the Italians never changed their music. But the black people don't have a music, actually, unless that is gonna be jazz. But I would say jazz is for a progressive black man; it's not for the masses.

I still think that the black people like the blues—the original blues, the T-Bone Walker blues. I don't think they're growing out of that or ever should grow out of it, until the blues is killed, you know, until the reason for the blues has died away. It shouldn't be a sudden change, it should be a gradual progress of society to rid itself of the things that causes the blues.

INTERVIEWER: You see, you as one of the most outstanding representatives of the jazz world, how do you view, how do you visualize, this new revamping of gospels and spirituals here in the States?

MINGUS: Revamping? It's Madison Avenue doing that. Gospel went away in a sense, but it never went away for the people who liked it. They still bought the records and listened to Mahalia Jackson, things like that. And we haven't lost any jazz fans, it just seemed that way [because jazz] wasn't publicized. The concert I just gave at Philharmonic Hall proved we never lost anybody. We had three thousand people. (I give Bill Cosby five hundred because he wasn't actually performing) and most people just came to hear the music. I'm saying that, uhh, I never lost any fans. I stopped recording, but the people never forgot, the ones who originally heard the music.

I'm not sure I could put it on a competitive basis because I don't know if an artistic music is supposed to appeal to masses of people. The black masses didn't go for our song; America went for it, but those were mainly white people. The black people still was for gospel music, and, uhh, blues, not rock. They used to call it race music, way back in the '30s and '40s. Then they called it rhythm and blues. And later, country and folk which was for the white people. [*To me:*] Do you remember those days—were you around then?—country folk music?

And then one day they kind of amalgamated all of it—Madison Avenue did—because the thing was to sell to both black and white, and jazz would not have sold if they had kept on pressing rhythm and blues records. But you can't beat the system. Right now if one company had enough guts to stay with the rhythm and blues and with the country and western—you got a lot of cowboys who still want country and western only. My mother used to listen to cowboy music, what they call country and western, and she wasn't white.

INTERVIEWER: What part of the country was that?

MINGUS: I was born in Arizona and lived in Watts. And that's why I know the Watts riot was a fake. Many of my friends were out there, and Peter Thompson and Dr. Ferguson—they don't even mind their names being called—when they saw the riot happening, one of these guys was a doctor and he went to his roof to get his gun to protect himself from the people who were starting to riot.

It was strangers, black people breaking down doors of groceries and stores, and they disappeared immediately on a truck. It was very organized, like a strategic plan. And as soon as they got on the truck, three, four, five minutes later, in come the police shooting at everybody that was black. So, as I was gonna say, it was a Madison Avenue race riot in Watts. A few people would say Newark [1967] was the same way. . . .

INTERVIEWER: An awful lot of black intellectuals say [musicians should] bring the African tunes, you know, from Africa. For example, I'm speaking in terms of a musician like Quincy Jones, like Ornette Coleman—they have gone to Africa and then they wrote some music stating their inspiration had been African, like *Mataculari* or something, it's the name

of one of the latest LPs [*Gula Matari*] by Quincy Jones. How credible is
that supposed to be for you?

MINGUS: [*Calmly, not provocatively*] I don't know what they're talking
about, but I've been exposed to African music for about forty years. I'm
trying to think—I know they've got music of the Bushmen on records, but
I was never there. But I found that they're making a lot of these records
right here in Harlem.

INTERVIEWER: Excuse me, where did you go to?

MINGUS: This was in California.

INTERVIEWER: No, no, I mean for the Bushmen music?

MINGUS: This was, I'm trying to think where it was, South Africa,
Bushland. A friend of mine in Mill Valley named Farwell Taylor always
used to play African music for many years.[4] He had this huge drum that
he used to sit on. It was kind of like a drum in the shape of a tree, and you
blow into it. I used to know the names of the tribes of music, but it's been
so many years ago, I've forgotten.

INTERVIEWER: Bushmen Negroes in Jamaica, and in Surinam—

MINGUS: It's nice that these guys are discovering the music, when it's
been there all the time. Hollywood has used it, you know, and Phil Moore
did the score for a movie, *The Road to Zanzibar*.[5] You can look it up in
[Joseph] Schillinger and find most of the theories of African music.[6] You
can't really learn how they send messages, and all that, from the music,
but you can get the nucleus. There's nothing new, there's always been
African music.

INTERVIEWER: Probably it is new for us, because we are not used to it.
Now, how about going back to my second question that I proposed to you
before. We would like to have a little bit of rundown on your past life.

MINGUS: Well, I don't see why I gotta do that, cause you can get a book
and read that. My whole life is in it.

INTERVIEWER: But if you say that to my audience, my audience may
even believe that I'm shitting around, whereas if you do say that, and
they hear that, from your very voice, then they probably, you know,
really . . . would lend their attention.

MINGUS: Well, take an average record['s liner notes]: they tell you some
history of a guy, when he's born, April 22, 1922, Nogales, Arizona . . .

INTERVIEWER: No, I don't want you to give me this kind of news. l would like, artistically speaking, you know—say, if you have changed from one style to the other style and how are you—

MINGUS: I don't change styles. I've always been a musician, whatever kind you want to call it. I studied music in school, and I always did things to get a job—if I could get a job playing any kind of music, I would do that, you know, but I had one music in mind, as a goal, and there's only one music. And that's all music, you know. It may encompass a lot of other musics, but in the meantime I'm working in jazz, and I play in that medium. But my goal is much higher than that. Not that I think black music or African music or any kind of music is inferior—it's just one kind of music, you know. I can't say to myself there's just one kind of music 'cause I like all kinds of music, if it's good. I like all kinds of music, particularly folk musics from different tribes of people.

· · ·

I think Mingus looked at all music as basically deriving from folk music, and he certainly heard the folk forms in concert music, particularly in Bartók and Stravinsky. Disguising them, "revamping" them, putting them in stylistic boxes for sale, was a way to dilute, if not kill, the folk spirit.

The black blues for him was a way to reunite black people musically and spiritually. Avant-garde free jazz was simply an arcane way to deny the spirit because you could play it without being a musician (theme 3). You had to study and know the blues-in-jazz tradition to be any kind of serious jazz musician and play for the people.

This idea came up frequently in the course of our later talks.

· · ·

MINGUS: As I'm sayin', the black people of America don't have a folk music, unless it be church, which is pretty corny, or the blues. Joe Turner is closer to it and T-Bone Walker's closer to it than some of the people they have today [that] they call blues singers. But the spirit of Billie Holiday, she has the blues spirit; so did, uhh, who else? Sorry, she's the only one I know that's got a jazz, a pure blues spirit, which is religiously involved without the Christian tones. [*Pause.*]

I don't know how to say it, man—[whatever] music the black people would adopt would have to give them a chance to hear all kinds of music and then find what they like. I find certain types of black people like, still dig, Charlie Parker. They took that as an awakening to them. There's a certain type or class of person who still digs Bird. They'll always dig Bird, or an extension of Bird. They like Charlie McPherson and the way he plays 'cause it reminds them of Charlie Parker.

Bird's music is a very hip thing, but, uhh, I find there's something lacking in it for me. It's not enough. There's not enough complex harmony, theoretically, for me. I enjoy more complex harmonies, or no harmonies. I don't particularly like chord changes all the time. I like many melodies at once, created without a chord in mind, that *may* form a harmonic chord, you know? I can tell, usually, if it comes from one man's mind, or if it's mechanically done, or if he heard all these melodies at once. I feel that if a man writes four melodies at once, he's got to play them at once, and he hears them at once. If he expects people to listen to those four melodies at once—or five, like a Bach fugue—then he must conceive these all at once. Not mechanically put them together because he has a theory that says it will work.

I've been working—rather than doing written compositions—to do spontaneous compositions where I'll do some string quartets, some of 'em by meditating and playing, some composing from the piano. "Adagio ma non troppo" from my latest album on Columbia, well, that was a spontaneous composition. It had about two or three melodies going at once. It's not that complex, it's a lot of feeling and emotion, but it's not meant to be intellectual, or anything like that. I don't know any intellectual niggers—what's an intellectual black? Is it that intellectual blacks are going back for African music?

INTERVIEWER: Yes, as a matter of fact, you know, an awful lot of them do. I'm not speaking only in terms of musicians, but even of playwrights, writers, artists, visual artists, or performing artists. There is a tendency now, you know, which strangely relates well to the first Harlem Renaissance, that politically was probably reflected by Julius Garvey and Booker T. Washington, this kind of back-to-Africa movement.

MINGUS: You mean Marcus Garvey?

INTERVIEWER: Marcus Garvey, that's right. So I was wondering whether you too were on to this, cognizant of that.

MINGUS: See, I don't know how to deal in terms, like you say, this guy's avant-garde, or this guy's intellectual. I don't know how to be any of those things. I'm just me, man. I don't see how you could possibly be in these 140 years a black intellectual. A black intellectual means you should be able to cope with Einstein, a guy goin' to the moon, plus cope and communicate with the guys in the Bowery. That's what a black intellectual means to me. But he don't exist—[someone who will] go down where the bums hang out—and so anybody who's been sittin' in front of a television set claiming to be a black intellectual to me is a phony. I haven't met one yet, 'cause he doesn't know the people.

I been tryin' to get to be—I didn't force myself, but by being kicked out of my position, my financial position and everything else, for the last six years—I got to become a bum, and live with people who were poor. And [to] even like them more than people who were successful, and not want to move away from them, because they were more for real than the rich people I've been around before, or the half-assed rich black people, you know, the ones who are satisfied with selling their own people out for a few more write-ups and a few more dollars.

[*Pause.*] What else?

. . .

End of solo. One of the reasons you have to love Mingus is for his capacity to demolish such concepts as "black intellectuals."

. . .

INTERVIEWER: Yeah, well, what else now? I just would like to go back to your music, you know, if you don't mind. You mentioned your latest record on Columbia—are you now working on a new album?

MINGUS: Well, it probably will be an album because George Wein's people always record at Newport [in New York], and some way I'll have a big band there, and a couple of weeks before that I'm going to be at a theater. If everybody comes from Italy, tell them to come to the Mercer Arts Theater.[7] I'll be working the band out there, plus I'll have a string quartet, not the usual—I'll have two cellos, a viola, and violin. And I'm going to write some music for that. It'll be at the foot of the program; we'll do Bach, Beethoven, and Brahms, too.

. . .

Enter new theme (4): electronics in music.

. . .

MINGUS: I think it's time that good musicians get rid of electric instru-ments, because a good musician can't play an electric instrument; it plays you. For instance, if you want to bend a note, you've got to push a button to bend it. You can't control the dynamics. You play soft-loud with the bow on a violin, but it all comes out the same volume on the electric machine. You've got to have another hand to turn it down soft and low. So it's not meant for real music, it's meant for someone who is not sincere about playing how he feels.

INTERVIEWER: You may probably clarify for me one idea I've been acquiring by being here, by interviewing other people. Is it really true that jazz is getting a little, uhh, shall I say, is getting into rock and rock is getting into jazz?

MINGUS: I don't know what musicians you're talking about—not me. All I know is if you guys are going for electric instruments, I've heard nothing better than a Steinway yet, all over the world. I've heard nothing better than a violin. Electric music is electric music. If a guy uses this music, then he's not a serious musician. I mean, they're not gonna make a better piano, man.

INTERVIEWER: Then wouldn't you agree with me that electric music today is probably 1972 stuff. I mean the equipment is sophisticated, the gadgets are kind of hard to grasp, you know, wow.

MINGUS: Well, I'm tryin' to say something! If you want, if a man was free enough, he could take an ordinary symphony with ordinary instruments and be more atonal and farther out or weird or avant-garde with everyday instruments, because of one thing—you can control the dynamics. There's nothing you can't write for a full orchestra that electronics are doing [any better].

Electronics are doing the same thing in music as elsewhere: they're replacing people. Push a button, it sounds like an oboe, but not a good oboe player; another button, sounds like a French horn. The guy who plays this stuff is a nigger because he can't afford to get a violin player or a French horn or oboe player. He might like to have the oboe—I would—but [he] will go to the commercial extreme because it's popular to use electric instruments.

And the great men like Charlie Parker and men who played legitimate instruments would laugh at these guys because they're not in it for the love of music but because they think they're going to make a lot of money—like Miles Davis did. Miles didn't even need to make any money; he was already rich, or his daddy was rich, so I'm not even sure if Miles made that much money, I just assume he did in music. But I know he's an electronic man, and eventually somebody like me is going to make him come back and start playing again, put that bullshit down and play his horn. He's gonna have to because [otherwise] he'll be laughed out. Because you can get a little kid to push a button, and with these machines they got now, it'll sound like they're right.

Look what happened for seven years in this country. Most of these kids couldn't read a note or sing in tune. But electronics can make 'em sound OK: they hit a wrong note and you push a button and it's in a vibrating machine plus an echo chamber, and it's [*sings*] wooo-wooo-wooo-wooo, so you don't know what note he's singing. But I want to hear a singer, man, I don't want to hear nobody bullshitting.

I want to be able to go to a hall with no mikes and hear the guy play his cello like János Starker. If he can't play it, send him home. Give him a rock-and-roll instrument and let him play. But don't tell me he's no musician, don't put a musician label on him. Say he's an electric player, find something else to call him.

The guitar players, they have a little bar on the neck of the guitar, so if you want the key of B-flat, they move it to B-flat position; for the key of A, they move it down to A. That way, they only have to learn one key, they can play in the key of C all the time. I was on a TV show with a guy like this and I say, "Do you move the bar on your guitar?"

He says, "Yes," and I say, "Why do you do it?"

He says, "It makes it easier."

I say, "Well, why doesn't Jascha Heifetz do it? Why shouldn't he play everything in the key of C?"

I mean, are you goin' to kill the fact that people can play in B-natural and A-natural? That's what Madison Avenue is trying to do, man. [*Pause*]

I don't believe in everything about classical music. I don't believe in stiff classical singers. I think there should be more folk voices in it. A lot of things could be changed, improved on, and people are doing that, like Henry Brant.[8] He did an opera, with classical singers, but he also had a hot-dog man—and other people who would just be singing what they felt, really. [*Sings:*] "Hot dogs!" you know? "Peanuts!" you know? [*Laughs.*] That's the way the old Italian operas were, and weren't they kind of for real? [*Imitates basso voice singing:*] "Would you buy my popcorn?"

·   ·   ·

They took a break after some talk about Northern Italians, blond Italians, Sicilians, and pizza men. But Mingus wanted to get to one of his favorite points, about jazz tradition, styles, and "progress." He understood that art moves by fits and starts, that there is rarely a straight line of influence or stylistic development. At the same time, if an artist couldn't understand and incorporate tradition, he'd never be a creator. And if he couldn't master the fundamentals of music, he'd end up being a fraud.

All the previous themes were coming to a recapitulation.

. . .

MINGUS: See, this thing you call jazz: if Lloyd Reese, Eric Dolphy's teacher, my teacher, had become famous, Dizzy Gillespie would have never made it—because Lloyd played like Dizzy back in 1928. So I'm trying to say that even though Louis Armstrong and King Oliver and those guys came along, here was another guy who knew a little more, had a different kind of education in music where he could have been playing atonal then: Lloyd knew Schoenberg, Beethoven, Bach, he'd studied that. He'd be playing those kinds of solos, and guys would say, "He's out of tune." Therefore people have to come in line, follow the next guy, step by step, "OK, that's progress."

Charlie Parker was the most modern thing, but actually I should have come before him because I had a whole new thing that had the weight and had to do with waltzes and religious music—a period of my music was like that. Then Bird should have come in, but instead they completely ignored me and I had to go play Bird's music. Which I'm glad I did— I learned a lot from that—but it's not honest because it makes kids come up and think [jazz has] gotta fit to this form right here.

Now it's gone to the other extreme: each guy's gotta be different, and now this is where they all full of shit. If you're a musician today, man, you shouldn't be playing like Louis Armstrong. If you're a trumpet player, you should be playing like Dizzy, Roy, Cat Anderson, Maynard Ferguson, all them guys or you ain't no trumpet player. If you play bass, you play like Mingus, Oscar Pettiford, Ray Brown, all them bass players or you ain't no bass player. You should be able to play like Art Tatum first or quit. I was a piano player and I quit cause I couldn't do Art Tatum. I knew I couldn't make it.

It's like when you go to Juilliard, they give you all the things composers have done, and they say "study it." After four-five years of you studying, one day they say, "Now, let me see you write something that's good." And you're going to *think*, because you know damn well that teacher knows when you're lying and stealing from over here or over there. You've got to throw all that out of your mind and compose something. And only the person himself knows, and most of the other guys quit if they know they can't cut the guys in the past.

But America gave us a new thing, it's called avant-garde, which nobody has ever explained, for Negroes. Some of these guys, you know [*does flutter-tongue trill and a squook-squawk*] as long as it sounds undescribable [they think it's music]. It's not music, because in the olden days a guy had to play his solo back. I met one of these guys and said, "Can you play this off the record?"

"Of course not, man, I don't want to."

I said, "What if I wrote it down, could you play it?"

He said, "You couldn't write it." That's bullshit. I can write it but he can't play it 'cause he doesn't know what he played.

And I'm tired of these people fooling our people. Because if you're going to be a physician or a finished artist in anything, like a surgeon, then you got to be able to retrace your steps and do it anytime you want to go forward, be more advanced. And if I'm a surgeon, am I going to cut you open "by heart," just free-form it, you know?

We're on an island and you say, "Look, man, use a book."

"No, I don't need no book, I'll just ad lib it."

"Well, look, Mingus, we're out here by ourselves, it's dangerous, and I don't want you to make no mistakes, so just look in the book."

"I can't read, man, I don't read no music, but I'm going to cut you open and take out your appendix 'cause it's bursting."

Well, you're gonna hope that, since I'm the only guy there, I will look in the book. Don't take me for no avant-garde, ready-born doctor. Don't let nobody fool me and tell me that they're avant-garde, don't need to study—and make the black kids think they don't need to learn how to read to play flute, oboe, French horn, and all the instruments.

Let these people know that there gonna be openings in all symphonies everywhere in the world for them and that jazz is just one little stupid language hanging out there as a sign of unfair employment. Jazz means "nigger": if you can't get a job in a symphony you can get a little job over here where you get a lot of write-ups and no money. But you'll never get in the symphony. Maybe in all America we'll hire one of you guys for the Philharmonic, one for the Jersey Symphony. We'll let these two be a sign that we found two good ones.

Now we know goddamn well that we got a cello player better than any you all got—what's his name? Kermit Moore—he's better than János Starker, man, warmer, plays more in tune, I couldn't believe him. You'll hear him in my string quartet.

Yet the white man can go on forever saying, "Well, we've got Jascha Heifetz . . ." Sure, but we may get one of them if you free the kids, I mean little babies, let them come up and think there's a place for them. Wouldn't you feel good to think that someday we'd have another Jascha Heifetz, regardless of what color he was? It don't have to be Isaac Stern or Yehudi Menhuin. They don't always have to be Jews, right? It's kind of weird they all Jews [*laughs*].

I'm trying to say let's find out what jazz is. Jazz is, or was, a very powerful force before seven years ago to a certain group of white people. They hid the sales of the records, they didn't let you know how many they were selling, they gave the guys a lot of write-ups, very little money. First place, second place in the polls—when you took third place, you didn't work no more. White or black, Red Norvo, all the guys, once you're voted out of first place, you're in trouble, from Lionel Hampton to all the rest of them.

SUE: He just sent all his medals back [from the polls he had won].

MINGUS: I don't want none of them damn polls. I know what kind of bass player I am. I auditioned with the San Francisco Philharmonic in 1939 and I was the best one except for one guy, his name was Phil Karp and he got the job. But they hired three bass players and I was better than the other two, and the conductor told me they just couldn't do it. So I know where I'm at.

And I've been waiting till the day when I get a chance to write classical, pure, serious music that came out of all the musics. For a guy to go study Africa—fuck Africa, man. Now here's the guy I'll study with: I want to know how those guys do this [*beats a complex rhythm*] and send a message in Haiti. You go to Western Union and you live in the mountains like Katherine Dunham, when you get a wire it don't come on no piece of paper. In the mountains it comes to you on the drums. And they bring it to you by mouth. Now, those guys, when you get to that, I'd like to study that. 'Cause some guys in America think they can do that—one is dead, Eric Dolphy.

. . .

Now the coda. After an hour of turning the interviewer's mostly general questions inside out, Mingus changed key again and offered up an analysis of the jazz audience, bending the question to his own purposes.

. . .

INTERVIEWER: One last question, what is the American audience like towards jazz . . . nowadays?

MINGUS: Well, each town is different. Let's put it like this: I'll try to tell you the best towns in America. For Charlie Parker's music, the bebop period, when we went to Philadelphia, I couldn't believe how people loved Bird. And they listened like you could hear a pin drop. Bird played there ten to twenty times a year when he was popular. I've always had the same following and I recognize the same faces in New York. At the Half Note Club, the Five Spot, and the Vanguard for the last thirty years, I recognize the faces, can call a lot of the names. Some get married, bring new husbands, new wives, but they still come back.

Now what are they like? My audience is very, very hip, and some of the young hippies are starting to dig me, I don't know why. Maybe because some singer called my name on a record—do you know that guy, Sue? Right, Donovan. I think it did me a lot of good. I was in San Francisco when it first came out and I used to walk by this college, and kids would say, "There goes Mingus," you know, and before the [Donovan] record came out nobody'd say anything.

American audiences are not like Europe. But I tell you what is better than Europe is Georgia, Tennessee, the South—they are just now waking up to jazz. They got jazz in by television. And the places where Martin Luther King picketed, they've changed, the integration is there. It's not overdone, the people sound like me, they're for real, they try to be serious about it, listen like it was classical music, same way I listened when I first went to Europe. It was a hell of a feeling to go to the South and have that happen, man. 'Cause when I went to the South [in the late 1940s] with Lionel Hampton, man, there was just noise, dancin', jumpin' around, and drunkards. I couldn't believe [the change], man.

So I haven't been to Europe in quite a little while, but the audiences there have always been the same as—what's the closest thing to classical? Sarah Vaughan when she was first making it? They used to give her a lot of respect, just like a classical singer. They'd treat her just like Marian Anderson or Duke Ellington in the '40s and '50s. When you went to his concerts some people wore tuxedos. They knew it was a pure music.

Bird never got that. Bird always got the balling crowd, people high on something, very hip, swinging, hustlers and pimps. Which is nothing wrong, just saying what he had. And from all races. In Philadelphia he mainly had the black hustlers and pimps. As far as people accepting—the last crowd I had in Philly was a pretty good crowd, pretty good audience, because I recently had a concert there with the big band. I guess there were some of Charlie Parker's people there too, because I've been there with him so much. I guess they remembered him and especially because I recorded with him too, 'cause there's a mixture of audience there, plus the hippies are starting to show too. The clean little kids with the Levis. I can tell you how they look, but how they feel—they don't feel together yet. I feel this is an assorted crowd, they're searching for something. It's not like it used to be.

Like when you went to see Count Basie you saw a Count Basie crowd. You go to see Duke, you saw a Duke crowd. The two didn't meet, man. The people who dug Basie did not dig Duke. If you had put jazz together like George Wein does now, you wouldn't have made it. You would have had one section booing the other. I can't prove this, but I'm pretty perceptive about feeling out audiences and things.

For instance, I've always had the knowledge about how to please an audience, which I don't do. Anytime I'm uptight, I got a thing I do with an audience which I guarantee will get applause for one of the guys in the band. Not what I do physically but do musically. But I don't like to do it. I call a solo and stop everything behind the soloist, leave him play by himself, and then when the rhythm section does come back in, the people always go crazy. What are the reasons, I don't know, but that's the way you do it.

To answer your question better, I'm glad there is a European audience. I'm trying to think where the best in Europe was for me—France, and Italy, and Germany—all very close. In Italy we were near Rome. Do you think in Europe it's always the same audience that goes to hear [someone]?

INTERVIEWER: No, I wouldn't say so. They actually are not so prone, like here, to be a one-man audience. Maybe probably a two- or three-man audience.

MINGUS: I haven't checked this, but there's a club in Boston, and after I closed there, I went back and didn't see anyone I saw when I was there earlier. It was a whole different kind of people that came to see that next group. Plus, that was a good sign because they were known there, and it was packed. So whatever you call jazz is coming back, evidently, in this country.

·   ·   ·

If you read the interviews and books in which jazz players talk candidly— like Arthur Taylor's great compendium *Notes and Tones* (Da Capo, 1993)— many if not most support views like Mingus's, in particular about the necessity of education and training in jazz. Other musicians have been willing to broach the phoniness of the New Thing, the false call of Africa, the need for black people and their culture to reunite. But few have come down as emphatically as Mingus did about these things. You know, there's a strong "don't criticize your brother" injunction among jazz people.

Despite that last remark about the club in Boston, I think he saw traditional jazz culture (and the audience) disappearing and wanted to save it.

NOTES

1. The first comment is from Ross Bennett, writing the Disk of the Day feature on the *Mojo* magazine website, at www.mojo4music.com/blog/2009/03/charles_mingus.html; the second, from "mikedurstewitz" in response to "Charles Mingus: The Black Saint and the Sinner Lady: Track A, Solo Dancer," YouTube video, 6:39, posted by "bassigia," Nov. 9, 2009, www.youtube.com/watch?v=17KTUqLyNcU. Other comments there are informative as well.

2. This is the first of several mentions of "seven years" or "six years" as the dark period in Mingus's life. This term seems to signify, variously: a period of social turmoil, a bleak time of withdrawal for him personally, a time of musical decay and decline for jazz—perhaps all lumped together, as in some gloomy and sustained minor ninth chord. For this period, see Brian Priestly, *Mingus: A Critical Biography* (New York: Da Capo, 1982), 159–71. As to causes, Priestly mentions: the impact of Eric Dolphy's death (June 1965), the growing displacement of jazz by the pop musical-industrial complex, the noisy rise of the jazz "avant-garde," the diminishing size of the Mingus bands, a reduced number of club and concert dates, and, finally, the public eviction from his loft and school in late 1966.

3. The Watts riot occurred in the summer of 1965 and shocked the country. A *Washington Post* piece thirty years later, nominally about Waco and the Oklahoma City bombing, may help explain Mingus's paranoid reaction. In it, author Virginia Postrel notes that those who burned Watts were never caught or tried. She affirms that "black inner-city communities are rife with conspiracy theories, with paranoia, some of it spread by talk radio: AIDS is a plot by white people in the government to wipe out blacks. So is crack. A few years ago it was widely repeated that an upstart soft drink made black men infertile." Because inner city blacks believe the government's message that "officially sanctioned violence is okay," their paranoia continues, Postrel says. Virginia Postrel, "Reawakening to Waco: Does the Federal Government Understand the Message It's Sending?" *Washington Post*, April 30, 1995.

4. Farwell Taylor was a painter and lifelong friend of Mingus, who introduced him to the culture and thought of India. Among other sources, see Todd S. Jenkins, *I Know What I Know: The Music of Charles Mingus* (Santa Barbara: Praeger, 2006), 7.

5. Phil Moore, was a pianist, arranger, band leader and accomplished studio musician prominent in the 1940s. See "Phil Moore," Space Age Pop Music, www.spaceagepop.com/moore.htm; and http://en.wikipedia.org/wiki/Phil_Moore_(jazz_musician).

6. Composer and music theorist Joseph Schillinger influenced many in the 1930s, including George Gershwin and Benny Goodman. See Daniel Leo Simpson, "My Introduction to the 'Schillinger System,'" *Joseph Schillinger: The Schillinger System of Musical Composition* (blog), Dec. 16, 2008, http://josephschillinger.wordpress.com/; and http://en.wikipedia.org/wiki/Joseph_Schillinger. Mingus mentions in chapter 5 that his second wife Celia studied Schillinger.

7. Once labeled "the downtown Lincoln Center," the Mercer Arts Center was an ambitious venture created by some off-Broadway heavy-hitters to provide venues for the performing arts. Management had booked Mingus and his Vanguard big

band (see chapter 7) for a couple of weeks in July, and at the time of this interview he was excited and had begun rehearsing the band. Unfortunately, a neighboring hundred-year-old hotel collapsed on August 9, 1973, and caused the Mercer to close. See Emory Lewis, "Hotel's Fall Was Also a Cultural Disaster," *The Sunday Record*, August 19, 1973.

8. Iconoclast and experimental composer Henry Brant died in 2008 at age ninety-four. He promoted acoustic spatial music which combined different styles—classical, Indian, Javanese, jazz, burlesque, and others—with the special placement of instruments of his own invention. See David A. Jaffe, "Henry Brant's Home Page," www.jaffe.com/brant.html; "Henry Brant, 94; Daring, Prize-Winning Composer," *Washington Post*, April 29, 2008, www.washingtonpost.com/wp-dyn/content/article/2008/04/29/AR2008042902918_2.html.

1 Avant-Garde and Tradition

*"Bach is how buildings got taller. It's how
we got to the moon."*

The history of the jazz avant-garde is interesting, even if the music frequently is not. Could a white person have any business writing that history? Or even understanding the music? That's the kind of question that was being asked in the late 1960s.

I didn't form my opinions on this music based on what Mingus had to say; I came to them after a long period of trying to be sympathetic to the widely advertised intentions, protests, and sounds of much so-called free jazz. One of the problems I had, as our conversations demonstrate, was trying to separate the apparatus of protest from the concerns of music.

Mingus always claimed to play "American music," and yet his idea of creating a music to appeal to the spiritual and cultural needs of black people, a revitalized ethnic blues, is an old one in jazz, though not widely recognized.[1] The free-jazzers wanted that too, and Cecil Taylor, for one, tried to bring music to the black masses. Still, it is hard to imagine a worse way to reach large numbers of people than through avant-garde free jazz. Mingus at least thought a broad-based blues might be the answer.

He also brought politics overtly into his music, which generally worked because the politics were subordinated to the musical concerns. Avant-garde jazz came alive in the '60s as part of so much other political protest, of course, and was a response to that political environment, the rise of rock and roll, the growing exclusion of jazz by the record industry, the diminishing jazz audience, the entrance of jazz into the academy, and more.

Amiri Baraka (LeRoi Jones) has been a great champion of the avant-garde, and his writings in *Blues People* (1963) and later in *Black Music* (1967), a mixed bag of essays, reviews, and notes, frequently get close to the essence of the New Thing and its people. Yes, there is a lot of "Crow Jim" in Baraka, but he knew the music, its players, their aims—and he was black.

Finally, a literate black jazz critic spoke out—going beyond Ralph Ellison, one might say.

It's difficult to read the old Baraka/Jones today, at least for me, because of the ethnic venom that took him over for a long time. It's also hard to make that jump back into a period when art was so deeply politicized, in every sense of that term. Politics and art have never merged easily and have frequently failed, as they did in the New Thing, to merge at all. The Africanism in much of that music was often just an overlay, and it was simply not cool to stress the importance of training and tradition: that was too Western, too white, too Brubeck.

Not everyone saw it that way, of course. *Time* magazine in a basically sympathetic 1962 piece entitled "Music: Crow Jim," begins by reporting Mingus's angry threat to leave the United States forever (for Majorca).[2] The article concludes by quoting Cecil Taylor on the destructive effects of this kind of prejudice: "Noting that modern jazz owes much to the European classical tradition, pianist Taylor points out: 'Crow Jim is a state of affairs which must be remedied; jazz can never again be music by Negroes strictly for Negroes any more than the Negroes themselves can return to the attitudes and emotional responses which prevailed when this was true.'"[3]

A 1958 piece by Kenneth Rexroth, one of jazz's best and least-acknowledged critics, predates this observation and presents "Some Thoughts on Jazz as Music, as Revolt, as Mystique" with references to Mingus (whom Rexroth knew well) throughout. I don't know of a more interesting, quirky, "I've been there" approach to these subjects.[4]

Regarding jazz as protest, Rexroth says, "The sources of jazz [as dance music] are influenced by racial and social conflict, but jazz itself appears first as part of the entertainment business, and the enraged proletariat do not frequent night clubs or cabarets."

Many members of the New Thing scorned the entertainment and business side of jazz. But trying to be "relevant" while making a living playing *any* kind of jazz in the 1970s was a serious and growing quandary. That's the context in which Mingus and I spoke.

· · ·

GOODMAN: The people most involved in this free jazz, like Archie Shepp—do you think they're trying to con the white folks or that they conned themselves in this thing?

MINGUS: I don't know about using their names, but I think what has happened is that they're trying to cut Bird, to say this is a new movement. But you don't take an inferior product and say that this is better than

Vaseline. Everybody knows it's not—everybody who's listened seriously to the other thing. "This isn't Vaseline; it's got water in it." They may be serious, but their seriousness hasn't gotten through to me yet.

Everybody's got ego, and everybody who lives in a human body thinks they're better than another guy. Even if a guy's considered to be a nigger in the South and the white man says *he's* better, if the guy's on his own and creating, he says, "Man, I'm better than that guy." I got a tenor player (I won't call his name), wanted to be in my band a long time, and he can't play. But when the people see him, he's moving like Sonny Rollins and John Coltrane at the same time, and man, they clap, and he ain't played shit. And so I know that he feels, "Hey look, Mingus, I moved the people, you saw that. Why don't you hire me?"

I try to explain, "Well, I don't move no people like that, man; that's not what I'm here to do. I guess I could kick my leg up too, spin my bass," and he don't believe me so I do it, do the Dixieland, spin the bass and they clap. I mean that's showmanship, but this is supposed to be art. I mean the only time they Uncle Tom in classical is when they bow, you know those classic bows, the way they had, man? Especially the women, opera singers, that crazy bow [curtsy] when they get down to their knees? They had some class.

You know, anybody can bullshit—excuse my expression—and most avant-garde people are bullshitting. But Charlie Parker didn't bullshit. He played beautiful music within those structured chords. He was a composer, man, that was a composer. It's like Bach. Bach is still the most difficult music written, fugues and all. Stravinsky is nice, but Bach is how buildings got taller. It's how we got to the moon, through Bach, through that kind of mind that made that music up. That's the most progressive mind. It didn't take primitive minds or religious minds to build buildings. They tend to go on luck and feeling and emotion and goof. (They also led us to sell goof.)

It's very difficult to play in structures and play in different keys. When a guy tells you all keys are alike, he's a liar. If so, give him a pedal point in B-natural or F-sharp or A-natural and see what he does. Even if he's playing another instrument like the alto saxophone (which if you're in the key of C it puts you in A-minor anyway), if you put him in A, he's in F-sharp; if you put him in B, he's in G-sharp. So he's hung while you look at him. Guys like McPherson who play bebop are the best; they can run right through the changes.

I don't do anything hard, just play the blues, and to see these guys turn . . . With Shafi Hadi we played five choruses; we modulated the second one to the key of F (in the "Song for Eric"), we then went to B-natural—and he stayed right in F all the way out. He never even heard the fact that we modulated. Then the trombone player finally came in, in the right key. That goes to show you how even musicians don't listen. Here's a guy paralyzed to realize something's wrong with the bass notes: he stayed right in the key of F. It was like going wrong down a one-way street and you don't even see the cars coming. It was pitiful.

And it wasn't only Shafi Hadi. Eddie Preston soloed and stayed in the same key. He finally caught himself after three or four choruses. You can tell when the piano player and I were doing it for fifteen-twenty minutes, changing keys all over the place, and finally the guy came in, in the key the tune was written in, a blues in F. But by then we had gone to B-natural and chromatics.

There are some famous avant-garde guys playing only in C-natural, man, and it's very sad that Bud Powell played in F all the time. I remember him playing in D-flat once and B-flat, but the key he always chose was F. If he played in bands, the tunes Bird played, he played 'em, but if he chose it was always in F.

GOODMAN: When I interviewed Teo Macero [Mingus's friend and producer of *Let My Children Hear Music*] a few days ago, he was moaning about Ornette Coleman, saying just what you did, that he couldn't play a straight chorus if he had to.

MINGUS: He couldn't, man. It would be pitiful if he was forced into a jam session and somebody called "Body and Soul." He couldn't make it, man. When we played the Protest Festival some years ago at Newport [1960], we played "All the Things You Are," and Ornette was lost after the first eight bars. It's OK to play avant-garde and say, "I meant to get lost," but Max Roach clearly said, "Let's do something simple like the blues or 'All the Things You Are.'" He couldn't even play the melody, man.[5]

But if a test comes by, man, to say, "I'm a jazz musician," you should be able to play the blues, or "All the Things You Are," or "Sweet Lorraine." I got a son named Eugene, and all over Europe, man, he said, "Boy, can I play the piano!" So people thought he was a piano player. And he could play a little bit, he's got talent enough to go where his ears tell him to go, but then he starts picking up other instruments, flutes and things. Now if someone tells me my son can play the flute, saxophone, bass—he's plucking the bass too—so if he got famous, man, I'd have to tell you something is wrong, somebody's fooling somebody.

I got in a fight with my piano player [Don Pullen] about Art Tatum. I said that Art Tatum was the world's greatest. I was going to say Bud Powell too, but I said he'd never be cut, man. He said, "Why do you want to tell me that? I never heard of Art Tatum." He's never heard of Art

Tatum? How could a guy play piano and never hear of Art Tatum? Look him up! Art Tatum can play with his left hand what most of the kids today do with their right *and* left. And don't mention Bud Powell—he's creatin' every moment.

And I heard a record where Ornette tried to play some [familiar] tunes. You hear that one? He played some melodies, but it was like a lot of kids who try to play Charlie Parker: he never made it. Once when I heard him play in California, I got to understand him better. See, when you play without a piano, you can sound avant-garde up front, 'cause a piano boxes you in. Unless you got a piano player who's gonna play like Monk does—everything in a minor key. Monk is smart; he doesn't block you in.

Ornette had a piano with him, and he sounded like a poor man's Charlie Parker. I couldn't believe it, that this is the same guy everybody was saying was so creative. Very strange. I think that he'd be a hell of a musician if he'd continue to study the alto. He may be a lucky composer. That may be his natural thing, 'cause I don't know anything bad about his writing.

GOODMAN: The first records he made—for Atlantic, I think—were kind of exciting to me.

MINGUS: For his own good he should try to learn from his own solos off the record, play them back. The other guy, Albert Ayler, [*does a flutter-tongue trill*] and those guys: let those guys try to play one of their solos back. They'll make up a new one every time. It's sick, man, it's sick shit. You can bullshit some people, but see, they came in and said, "Let's see how far out you are, we can make a living like this!" But they can't enjoy doing that, man. It's impossible to enjoy that.

You want to hear some of that music? Get me and Clark Terry and some guys who know music to play like that and put 'em on. Nesuhi Ertegun was talking to me about doing an avant-garde date with some guys who can really play.[6] I called Clark and he said, "Baby, let me get at it." That would upset those guys, because he can play to begin with, and if he decided not to play he would unplay playing [*laughter*]. I want to get with Clark and make an avant-garde record. And Teo Macero.

Take John Coltrane: he went back to Indian-type pedal point music, but he got in a streak [rut]. Why couldn't he do other things too? Why do guys have to stylize themselves? Don't they know that in the summertime you wear thin clothes and straw hats and in the wintertime, you know, you got a right to play a different tune? You don't have to be stylized. A preacher preaches a different sermon each Sunday. He don't preach the same one. They turn a different page, and I'm turning pages all the time because

I have a special page I want to get to and if I'd thrown that page open many years ago, I'd have never even got this far.

'Cause it's very way out, man: it'll make the weird guys sound like babies, make men sound like girls [*laughter*]—at least some men. No, baby, I been waiting to do this for a long time, man, it has to do with three-four keys at once, atonal, whatever you want to call it. But I couldn't just lay it on everybody at once, because the musicians have to read and improvise at the same time. I had to train the guys to improvise; I've got a few of 'em now. I'll be able to inject 'em into a reading band, and when I get that thing going, you'll see.

GOODMAN: You're going to start that in the Mercer [Arts Center] band, or what?

MINGUS: Well, you heard a little of it on this last date [*Children*], 'cause I used improvisation in all my writing on the record, like on "Shoes of the Fisherman's Wife," where I overdubbed the solo. Now on "The Clown," I couldn't have written that and had the guys do it right, so I had them overdub it. But I knew before recording that I was gonna do that.

I had two spots in there that definitely make fun of the avant-garde musicians. If you listen, you'll hear McPherson and [Lonnie] Hillyer playing Charlie Parker, and then at the end of the "Fisherman's Wife," you hear Ornette Coleman, played by Teo Macero, and then playing all over, this beautiful alto sax, just like Bird, but McPherson's tone cut everything they were doing. Teo got [the rest] so soft you gotta listen for it. But the idea is that with all this noise going on, here's this guy playing music and going to good notes behind or against this bass melody [*demonstrates*], and [McPherson], he's playing pure honesty, not saying, "Look at me, I'm a king" or "I'm better than you." Just doing his best he can, like Bird did through the changes, and it's beautiful, man. [*Pause.*] This tenor player I got yesterday [Bobby Brown] got a helluva sound too, man.

It's a drag to have to put down people. But I've always known there's something else to learn, and I really found out what it was just recently when I started saying: "Wait a minute, man, I used to play with Art Tatum, and he used to say, '"Body and Soul," Mingus.'" Or he wouldn't say nothing; he'd just start and I'd come in in the key of D-flat. And all of a sudden here's a guy starting on D minor and I'm used to playing E-flat minor. Or some night he'd come in and play in C minor. And I got all hung up on the chords and positions. He'd say, "I'm in the key of B, man, come on, let's go." Or, "I'm in the key of G. Can't you think like this?"

So I go to the piano and realize I can't do [my old style] no more. So for the rest of my life, I do what all these guys gotta do: study the keys they can't play in. Then as they study them, minors and majors, they'll be able to play in 'em. And that's the truth of music, and that goes for symphony guys too. They are still trying to play in the hard keys. It's simple to write in D-flat because we play in it all the time. And F, we done wore it out, and we wore out B-flat. But nobody wore out B-natural yet. They ain't wore out E-natural or D[-natural] or F-sharp.

GOODMAN: But why can't a musician catch the modulation in a tune? How can that pass them by?

MINGUS: Because we all want it to be easy! I would know something was wrong, but I'm talking about the guys who can't do it, who haven't got the fingering to do it, yet they call themselves musicians. You gotta know how to do the fingering. You play piano? You can't play the C scale the same way [crossing your thumb, etc.]. So you gotta know what you're doing. It's like starting over and admitting that even professionals gotta study and practice. Plus go to teachers. I'm sure all the guys I know do it, who are in the good positions. Buddy Collette talks about going to his composition teacher. Red Callender's going to a teacher; these guys are my age. Who else goes?

This little kid trumpet player, Lonnie Hillyer, said, "Man, I wish I had his chops." Wish he had his chops? He was talking about John Faddis, and I said, "He didn't have no chops, he studied to get that proper embouchure."

Lonnie said, "No, he was just born like that."

"No," I said, "he's got a teacher right now."

"No, he don't need no teacher right now"—and now Lonnie wants to study. But it took a long time to prove that to him . . . First of all, his parents should be shot. They sent him to Barry Harris, who's a piano teacher, to teach him to play the trumpet. Well, the proper start would be send him to Barry Harris for theory but Barry doesn't know anything about an embouchure, you know, how to blow through a straw and strengthen your chops and all that. It's Barry's fault too; he should have told the parents, "I can teach him theory but you need a trumpet teacher, a good one—one of them old men who can sit and blow B-flats all night long."

One thing I'd like to clear up a little more in case I haven't is the fact that all those eras in the history of jazz, like Dixieland, Chicago, Moten swing, all those styles, man, are the same and as important as classical music styles are. The movements—like you remember Moten swing? Count Basie swing is another swing. And Jimmy Lunceford had another swing. Remember Jimmy's band? The two-four rock [*demonstrates*].

Well, man, there should be a school set up where all those styles and movements are exposed to the students, and they find their medium, what is closest to them, and come out with that. I don't mean copy that, I mean they should be able to copy it and then find themselves, as most composers do in classical music. Find which one they like and that's where they are, through direction.

You think about it, man, even the guys in jungles, they weren't just born as a baby and picked up a drum. Their daddy taught them how to play drums, to send messages and all that. "Somebody's talking something." They heard it and loved it, went and fooled with it for a while, and daddy would say, "Well, here's how you do that, son."

They didn't just say, "I'm Jesus born here, hand me a drum, baby; lay a flute on me, run me a clarinet next; now I'm gonna play a little bass. Where's Jascha Heifetz's violin? I'll play that for you, better than him. When we get through, hand me Isaac Stern's."

Yeah, that's where the guys are today: "Give me a violin and I'll play it for you. Jascha played it, I'll play it too."

And intelligent people still listen to this crap, man. I don't want to be fooled anymore: I know when I'm out of tune, and I've done it intentionally and watch critics applaud. And that's when avant-garde has gone too far. "Let's see, here's a B-flat seventh. I'll change the chord from a B-flat major seventh, I've got an A-natural in B-flat; I'm gonna play a B-natural." And I'll get applause for it. Well, on the major seventh chord, that's the wrong note. Now if the chord was not a major seventh and was a B-flat cluster, and if the chord is a row, then I can play all the notes. But [not on] a major seventh. I can play wrong notes in a chord if I want to sound wrong and have a clown band like—what's that guy had a clown band? Shoots guns and all that?—Spike Jones. If you want to say Spike Jones is avant-garde, then we got some avant-garde guys playing, some Spike Joneses.

GOODMAN: Only he made music.

MINGUS: He could do everything, man. I don't want to be so junglish that I can't climb a stairway. I got to climb mountains all day long? We're going to the moon, right? Well, I'm with the guys that wrote music that got us to the moon. Not the guys who dreamed about it. Bach built the buildings, we didn't get there from primitive drums. In a sense we did, because primitive drums was the faith. Primitive music is the faith—like Indian music—of people who want to find out how to get there. Bach was the intellectual pencil that figured out mathematically "does this work?"

"Yes, this does, now put that aside."

And finally, "Does this work with this?" Bach put all these things together and called them chords. Well, we go with progress and call it scales, and these things have been broken down by Schillinger and a whole lot of other guys. Now if you work in that form and then go back and say, "Man, we don't need to know this theory," fine, then I accept that you're a primitive. But when you come on the bandstand with a guy who may not want to play primitive for a minute, can you play with him? That's what the question is.

Maybe I can play primitive too but for a minute I want just one chord, a C major seventh. Now how many guys can play that—and play something on it, improvise something on it clearly? That's what Bach could do, because that's the foundation, and then he could put the D-flat major seventh against that. Now then you got a building, black and white, concrete and stone, and it can grow taller. Now that's the way it is, man. Though I'm not saying that's as modern as you want to be.

But I can't hear for a moment when Bach was in the church. I can't hear for a moment when he left his *theory-ism*. He's the greatest theorist that ever was, man, the greatest mathematician ever lived, I know that. But he was never in church, he never realized he was in the church, man. Excuse me, he was never a minister in the church. He only wrote his self, his theory.

GOODMAN: You mean he wrote church music without being a believer?

MINGUS: Without being a member, without being a teacher. But he taught another way, man. It's too intricate for church, unless they played him too fast. There's this theory that they played Bach very fast.

GOODMAN: Yeah, Glenn Gould holds to that.

MINGUS: You play him slow, and it's another story. Well, who was there to know?

GOODMAN: Now let me ask you something . . .

MINGUS: We'll go back to Bach later.

GOODMAN: I wanted to go back to the wailing and the African thing.

MINGUS: You want to talk about John Coltrane.

GOODMAN: Well, yeah . . . because I wrote a piece once, I'll send it to you, with the idea that all the people who were making the biggest noise about African music—talking about it more than playing it—were misunderstanding what African music was really about. African music is really . . . tribal music.[7]

MINGUS: Tribal music?

GOODMAN: A man plays a drum to convey a specific message, and if he's playing for a dance he's playing to arouse very particular emotions. The African music I know is very specific. The New Thing, as they used to call it, was totally unspecific, like an expressionist painting.

It seemed to me that people who said they were trying to get back to Africa in their music were just putting a lot of con on everybody. Or they didn't know what they were talking about.[8]

MINGUS: See, I'm closer to America in a lot of ways than Africa, never been to Africa and I don't have any African friends, but I tell you I've done a little reading, and I used to go with an Indian girl whose grandfather was Sicilian born. I'm sure tribal people are all the same, African or Indian, like this girl. The high-degree order monks, they write music in the cloisters. Now we have guys in the police department, they have a police band, in parades, and a dance band. The Marines have a band, sailors have one. This girl showed me a funny thing—that even though we look at people as being primitive, that the guys who played the drums for the war dance weren't the guys who played the drums for the religious dances.

Now the people who were going to meditate and do these long five-day hikes in the mountains—what the kids now use LSD for instead of peyote—these were another set of Indian guys. What I'm trying to say is where was the governing of where the music was for all the people? When the chief was involved, elected by the tribe, that was someone who everybody respected—in primitive music—and they had dancing and celebrations. So that meant—

GOODMAN: A different music for each purpose.

MINGUS: I imagine the warriors brought their drums too, but they didn't all play at the same time. Now, what music they did respect as being Indian music is mainly the dance music or the folk music for people who were enjoying themselves. Now, religious music—John [Coltrane] was a preacher, and I accept that.

He was trying to tell the people, "Stop shooting up dope, stop getting high. Go on a vegetarian diet, get yourself together. Get your body and mind together and see what the society's done to the poor black man."

He was trying to get it together. The fact that the white kids liked it, some liked it as much as they did rock, right? Like at rock concerts, they were packed in, I saw 'em. It wasn't done exactly like the Indians did it, it was done with new religious tones. You say African, I heard more Indian in his music—Indian-Indian music.

GOODMAN: I think that's true, and I don't mean that John was playing African music, but a lot of the people who were talking all this pro-Africa stuff at the time used him as an example. And they're full of shit.

MINGUS: They are, and they never heard Indian music, man.

GOODMAN: And they never heard African music either.

MINGUS: I'm sure if John had wanted it to be, he'd have gone to Africa and studied it out. But presently there's not that much African music other than Olatunji, if you want to call that representative of African music.

It's just drums. African music I've heard—there's a tribe—I can call Farwell Taylor and ask him—but this tribe had this huge saxophone they'd sit on, and they'd all blow into it. Four, five men would play it, and it would sound *o-o-voo-voo, o-o-voo-voo,* like a drum played by a mouth.

GOODMAN: Like a bagpipe, sort of?

MINGUS: Man, this was like a rock, the picture I saw of it, like a rock they was blowing into and sitting on it, like a big mountain, and it was an instrument. It was from the Belgian Congo, I remember that. It was the first music I heard as a kid, seventeen years old. And this man [Farwell] loved African music, he had everything you could get.

But then one day he got some records and found out that some of them were made in Los Angeles in a studio with bamboo and shit on the floor and some local cats. And it broke his heart, 'cause he thought it was real. Here's how he found out.

I said, "Farwell, I can't imagine them going out to the jungle—'cause they found some very dangerous music, music from the Pygmies, who were going to shoot the warriors with darts, poison arrows. How did they get all the equipment out there? They had stereo and hi-fi. Where did they get the electrical stuff to record them?"

They didn't have these little things [*taps my recorder*] in them days. And they couldn't get those lows and highs the way they got 'em. Unless they got a powerful truck in there, and the scene was set up so Hollywood.

And wait a minute, man. What is African music? Don't bullshit me, man. Let me go there and then I'll know, [I'll] come back and report the truth to you. Don't tell me what they do. So now they send some people over, like Miriam Makeba and her brother who played trumpet, but they were black people, Africans, influenced by American jazz. What is *their* music? I'm still waiting for them to show me. Don't tell me that John Coltrane gonna show me, 'cause he ain't been there yet. Randy Weston ain't come up with nothing yet that says "this is Africa."

GOODMAN: There were some old African records on Folkways, remember? They used to do all those wonderful ethnic things from around the world.

MINGUS: Yeah, I don't doubt that. [On Farwell's records] they had a sacrificial suite, and I thought, "Wait a minute, man, they really killed somebody on this record?"

Farwell says, "Well, that's what it says."

Sorry, man. These nice American guys go in with cameras and sound equipment and watch 'em have a sacrifice? OK, and it sold a million copies. I mean this country's so full of bullshit it's ridiculous.

John was a very good man, very nice person, and the music he played told that. He was a very serious person and seriously in love with his music, a very religious man. He actually invented a new music in his so-called attempts to display African religious music. Which I haven't heard yet, I haven't heard him playing African.

GOODMAN: What burned me most was an article in *Jazz & Pop*, about five or six years ago, with some hip white asshole [Frank Kofsky] coming on about how Coltrane is the African messiah—and that's what made me write my piece.

MINGUS: Did he mean African or did he mean American black?

GOODMAN: He was talking about African, and so was A. B. Spellman or some black guy.

MINGUS: Well, that's why I don't read too much because how can you say someone's a Watts exponent unless he [the critic] lived in Watts? Let alone Africa, which is over the water. How's a guy gonna tell me how they play music in Watts when he's sitting in New York City? I'm not being biased, but saying he represents a new music for the black people? That'd be nice because they sure need one to bring 'em together again, man.

· · ·

MINGUS: Does history show that there has always been a battle between the avant-garde, the up-and-coming artists, and the established artists? In painting, in anything? When the king said, "I award this man, I want this man to paint my portrait"? Maybe Van Gogh was one of the great portrait painters, and was there a critic around to say, "He did a lousy job on the king"?

GOODMAN: Talking about the last two or three hundred years, yeah, critics were around. They're easy now, compared to then.

MINGUS: Yeah, because then they tore you up. Tore up everything about you, as a human being, where you came from, who's your father, your mother . . . Has there always been the avant-garde?

GOODMAN: In a sense, yeah.

MINGUS: I got the word from Barry Ulanov, who laid the word on me. He once called me avant-garde, and it's not so, man.

I'm not avant-garde, no. I don't throw rocks and stones, I don't throw my paint. How could he say something like that?

GOODMAN: Well, a lot of people think avant-garde means anything or anybody that is making a new sound, or a "new thing." And that's wrong; it means more than that.

MINGUS: Well, where did the word come from?

GOODMAN: It's a French word, and it means literally the advance guard, like in the army, troops advancing, the front rank—

MINGUS: The best—

GOODMAN: Yes, and everybody else follows along back here.

MINGUS: So this man was saying that Coleman Hawkins and Charlie Parker were all behind Teo Macero and John LaPorta and myself?

GOODMAN: That's why it's wrong.

MINGUS: He's an idiot. I'm just discovering this, man. I didn't really know it was a French word, it never really got into me. All I know is that he said these people were the avant-garde, and he named 'em—John LaPorta, Lennie Tristano, Charlie Mingus. This was Barry Ulanov. He's an idiot, man.

GOODMAN: Well, no, because he was using the word in a 1950s, labeling way. But in terms of the arts, it also means somebody doing really new things. See, this is what we were saying about Varèse the other night—

MINGUS: Varèse! That's the composer, that's the one I was telling you I was listening to, when I was listening to Red Norvo.[9]

GOODMAN: Varèse started all kinds of wild things, began to do electronic music before there was even tape!

MINGUS: Right, and he was avant-garde.

GOODMAN: He was called the most avant-garde composer around. And he knew better. He once told somebody who called him the leader of the avant-garde, "No, there's no avant-garde. There are only people who are a little bit late." And that's beautiful, because it really shouldn't be a question of people being either advanced or late.

The reason the critics use this is because it's a handle, a label, an easy kind of way to put people in categories. No musician, no artist likes that because they all say, "Oh, I just play music, I just do my thing, I paint." Well, OK, that's fine, but—

MINGUS: But when their system has shown up what they're doing—

GOODMAN: Yeah, you want to say, "All right, what do you relate to, man? What the hell *is* your thing? You do your music, your painting, your dance, but how do you relate to whatever has happened *before?*"

So a term like avant-garde comes into being, meaning in shorthand someone who is doing things that haven't been done before. So when Barry Ulanov said that about your music, he probably was saying it in a complimentary way, you know?

MINGUS: Yeah, but when you think about how painters go about doing their paintings—or some of the painters—I'm told they put blindfolds on, go over to the canvas with any color they want and smear it on. Or they stand back, take a big bucket of paint and splash it on the canvas, then they go to the canvas and clear it up.

GOODMAN: Or the thing about the baboon, a couple of years ago, remember that? They had a baboon throwing the paint. He had a good time. Everybody loved the painting, man [*laughter*].

MINGUS: Yeah, I remember the baboon. Now, I love children, man. I have some of my own, less than teenagers. But finger painting, it's beautiful for kids.

GOODMAN: Yeah, my kids are doing that.

MINGUS: But it's not beautiful for adults. They should grow up.

Let's say it like this, man. The guys who throw paint on the canvas with rocks and glue have won. They destroyed us, the guys who can play, the guys who can paint, man. They have won the game. I go to museums now, I see shit.

GOODMAN: Literally, on the canvas.

MINGUS: On the canvas, man, and they're winning now. I went to the Louvre, man, and I saw shit. They are catering to—you know whose fault it is, man, in this country? I don't know whose fault it is in Paris or in

Copenhagen, but the fault [here] lays on Nat Hentoff, Barry Ulanov, they're like all the guys who left the ship when Jesus stayed on. They're like all the guys who stayed under the canoe when Jesus Christ got out and walked the water. They left the boat when it was sinking, man. No, they didn't leave, they stayed on and it sunk. He had to come back and save 'em. It's sad, man, it's very sad.

GOODMAN: OK, I got a question for you about what the aesthetic people call form. I hear a piece of Ornette's music and, for the sake of argument, I hear the form there, I know what he's doing.

MINGUS: Wait a minute, are you saying that Ornette Coleman is avant-garde? Do the critics call him avant-garde?

GOODMAN: Let's take somebody else.

MINGUS: Do the critics call him avant-garde? *Down Beat* hasn't said anything in the last ten years.

GOODMAN: I wouldn't put that label on him because it means two things—a person's doing things that have never been heard or done before, and it also means that he's a creative genius, or at least that's the figurative meaning.

And both of those meanings are bullshit, so all you can really do is throw out the term. Like you wrote in that *Changes* piece ["Open Letter to the Avant-Garde"], where you said Duke Ellington told you about doing avant-garde music—"Let's not go back that far"—[meaning] we shouldn't even deal with that. He was right because it's a term that you want to avoid.

MINGUS: I like Duke's word better than the other guy's [Varèse]. No, they're both just as good.

But you know why it concerns me so much? Because it's keeping jazz musicians out of work. This classification, it's keeping jazz musicians out of work. All the fights that are going on in jazz, the rock-and-roll guys are still working—that's the enemy—and they can't even blow their nose yet.

GOODMAN: And they've got *their* avant-garde too. Shit, rock-and-roll's been going for twenty years, as bad as it is, you know. So they got an avant-garde too, John McLaughlin and people like that.

MINGUS: That's good to know. John McLaughlin's out of work?

GOODMAN: Far from it.

MINGUS: But [our] avant-garde is out of work, man. That's me, I'm out of work.

GOODMAN: You always said that they cut you out of work because they're fooling people, they're taking your market. Albert Ayler, God rest his soul, and Pharaoh Sanders and those people are involving folks in phony music who should be listening to *you*, to put it bluntly. I've heard Ayler's records, heard him play once at Slug's, and he turned me off so bad I had to leave.

MINGUS: God rest his soul. I never heard him. I read an article about him.

CHAPTER 1 COMMENTARY

John Goodman on Mingus and the Avant-Garde:
Reflections over Time

When we had our talk about the avant-garde, I was really rapping about a term I had obviously grown to detest. Mingus had been burned by it but wanted to know more, so it was a good discussion. On many occasions he had a lot to say about avant-garde jazz, so-called, but his major points are in two pieces: the original album notes to *Let My Children Hear Music*, and a 1973 blast, "An Open Letter to the Avant-Garde," that codified some of the opinions he expressed in this 1974 interview.[10]

By then the avant-garde concept had been debated up and down, in part because of confusions over where and how it applied. Some of this confusion was reflected in my comments. We talked about it in cultural, artistic (formal), critical (categories), and economic terms. A major point I didn't get to is that the avant-garde is nearly always in some sense oppositional— either in a political way (there is lots of that in Mingus's music) or in response to attempts to co-opt it by mass culture, as art critic Clement Greenberg discussed back in 1939.

When he and Harold Rosenberg did famous battle in the art world of the 1960s, jazz too was more than ever subjected to ratings, polls, sales figures, and bookings, and a few critics began to talk very negatively about these things. "Avant-garde" in their eyes was just a marketing label, though Barry Ulanov might not have agreed.

The term also means "cutting-edge" or innovative and in that sense has become so inclusive and commonplace as to be worthless. Rosenberg saw that the interaction of art and business and politics was crippling artists. As the champion of action painting and the abstract expressionists, he talked of painting as "an event" and seemingly stood with Mingus's enemies, the guys who throw paint at the canvas.

Rosenberg also loved to throw brickbats at the art establishment: "What better way to prove that you understand a subject than to make money out of it?" Being so dependent on commerce, jazz has always fought for its independence—not only from the record business but from many of the pressures of mass culture. Bebop's insistence on being regarded as art music—not entertainment or pop—is only one example, and Mingus was always and forever on the side of art. Our subsequent interviews go into the economics of the jazz business and how they frequently collided with the demands of his art.

So the avant-garde concept seems to contain two contradictory sub-meanings. One makes it an expanding, liberalizing, form-breaking, democratic, sui generis force à la Rosenberg; the other, as in the Greenberg view, makes avant-garde art a breakaway outgrowth of an outmoded but still valuable high-culture tradition.

Salim Washington, jazz musician, teacher, and critic, wrote an interesting piece proposing that Mingus represented the true avant-garde spirit in jazz (as opposed to some of the noisy revolutionaries of the '60s), that Mingus synthesized tradition and "self-expression" functionally and more musically than anyone else in jazz has done.[11] By that assessment, Mingus's music would subsume, to use my terms, the Greenberg-Rosenberg controversy.

Washington looks at Ornette Coleman's music and its influences on Mingus (a subject I haven't seen treated anywhere else—and the influence *is* there: listen to 1960's *Mingus Presents Mingus*, for instance). This musico-sociological approach to jazz history prompts one to look at Mingus through a new lens, though Washington tries to show (not always convincingly, I think) that the avant-garde aspect of jazz has deep historical and performing roots, going back even beyond Ellington and Bechet.

He wants jazz to contain the avant-garde, not segregate it as some weird 1960s offshoot: "The historical [European] avant-garde, in its seeking to shake up the foundations of the art world, strove to separate itself from the traditions upon which they were commenting. By contrast, jazz artists—of all stripes—have not tried to flaunt their prestige and artistic standing or mock the sacral aura of the art world, but rather have been preoccupied with attaining such prestige that European art music routinely enjoys."

From all the comments Mingus made on many occasions—not just in these interviews—I think he would agree with that. As he concluded here, it boils down to making a living. And further, he would maintain that there is no real avant-garde unless it's great musicians like Clark Terry who have learned their craft and mastered their art.

Alex Stewart, in his book *Making the Scene*, offers an interesting comment on Mingus and the avant-garde:[12] "Many of the techniques championed by Mingus—additive composition or layering, collective improvisation, lack of concern with playability, rich unisons—form the core of the experimental or avant-garde composer. Although Mingus often disparaged the avant-garde movement, many avant-garde musicians continue to cite Mingus as a prime influence." Yet Mingus's innovations always built on either following or fracturing tradition, and "avant-garde" seems a real misnomer for that kind of development. His music is, above all, eclectic. The only sense in which the term avant-garde really applies to Mingus may be in his political-cultural stance.

Perhaps his greatest breakthrough was to reconcile collective improvisation in a modern context with the formal demands of the music. Nobody has been able to do that with such gutsy power and joy since Jelly Roll Morton, another so-called avant-gardist, the first to make jazz into a compositional art. If Morton led the way to modernism in jazz, Mingus was its first true postmodernist.

Sy Johnson on Collaborating with Mingus

As one of the insiders participating in the creation of *Let My Children Hear Music* (he orchestrated and arranged much of it), Sy had exceptional stories to tell about how the album came together. Our talks also contributed a great deal to my understanding of Mingus and his music. As frequent arranger and sometime orchestrator for Mingus, Sy became (I will say it even if he won't) the man's musical right hand.

These comments also help explain how Mingus used traditional—even classical—procedures and methods to produce music that was anything but traditional. That is to say, how he both used the rules and broke them. Maybe all "avant-gardists" do this, but Mingus was very precise about which rules and how they were to be broken.

Sy refers in this 1972 conversation to a piece that was done in concert and *did* get recorded but was only issued later, "Taurus in the Arena of Life." How Mingus infused Art Tatum into that work gives insight into how he used musical materials of all kinds and how the band participated in that process. Yes, his approach sounds like the way Ellington did things—but Duke never stitched the quilt together quite the way Mingus did here. Sy's description of the process in "Don't Be Afraid, the Clown's Afraid Too," reminds me of how Mingus typically worked in the small-band context, the Jazz Workshop, and how he invariably got musicians to play things his way, though with their own voices.

. . .

GOODMAN: Two things I thought of that I wanted to ask you. One was precisely what kinds of innovations you hear in Mingus's music. The other is your idea of where his music comes from, what kinds of sources you hear him using, besides the obvious with Ellington and so forth.

JOHNSON: Right. Well, I think the fact that Mingus came on the scene when he was about eighteen or something like that, about 1938 or 1939, when he first began to come out in Los Angeles, he came out as a fully developed artist at that point. He was a bass virtuoso and he had his thing very fully developed at that point. He had influences. Everybody knows about the Duke Ellington influence. It is not as well known that Art Tatum was a very important influence on him. Mingus keeps referring to Tatum voicings. He played with Art Tatum briefly and there was also a teacher he had, Lloyd somebody—

GOODMAN: Lloyd Reese?

JOHNSON: Lloyd Reese, right, who was an important influence. But basically with Mingus, the music came out of experience. I mean, he is constantly transforming material that he picks up from [all kinds of sources]. There is, for example, a section that is very difficult for the trumpet to play in "Ecclesiastes" that Mingus told us one night was a French horn cadenza from a classical piece, inverted. He just turned it upside down, and the minute he explains that you say, "Ah yes, absolutely. That's where it came from."

He gets expansive every now and then and says, "Hear that? Well listen to that real carefully and you'll hear that it is really—" and it's some old obscure pop tune or something like that. He just transforms material, a lot of material that's around him. Composers have always been doing that; it is a perfectly legitimate thing. But he just takes in enormous amounts of music from every source that he can. And it all gurgles around in there and is finally spewed out as something that is quite uniquely humorous.

We are doing a piece that we did in the concert but [that] has not been recorded yet ["Taurus in the Arena of Life"]. Partly because I helped him make the orchestration for it, because he thought he might like to do it in the album but he hadn't finished writing the piece yet. There is a whole middle section that he has completed since then that we are going to have to deal with, I guess the next time we record, and I'll [orchestrate] the whole thing.[13]

But there is one section of that, at the end, and he just said, "There is an Art Tatum voicing and I've always wanted to use it someplace." And he played this Tatum voicing on the piano for me. He said, "I have always wanted to use that someplace. I think I'm going to use it right here." So he immediately took that fabric, and it was like a quilt and he stitched it into the piece and it immediately became part of the piece. It was not capricious at all.

GOODMAN: That also makes me remember your story about adding the 8/8 piece toward the end. Then he comes along and changes the whole thing.

JOHNSON: On "Clowns"—"Don't Be Afraid, the Clown's Afraid Too"— our original routine on it, the tune didn't seem to come to any conclusion. It was lacking a final section to it, at least I felt it was. So I called Mingus the next day and explained my feelings about it. I told him I thought he should write something to open it up. Maybe just something with one chord but something that would get away from the very strict structure that the whole piece had going for it.

He agreed, thought that would be good, and he says, "You write something. Just write something that you hear and if it doesn't work, you'll know." So I wrote an 8/8 section, a very funky 8/8 section. In a sense I was thinking, well, this will probably be the first time that Mingus has ever played anything in 8/8 on record. I thought it would be interesting to see whether he responds to that as an extension of himself or how he gets to it. It was like a vamp with solos running through it.

So we got to the date and started to rehearse that part (we were rehearsing in sections because it was such a long piece) and we finally got to that section, and the band seized on it as something familiar that they could get their teeth into. They began to get a good feeling right away. Dannie Richmond particularly began to really cook on it. We ran it a couple of times, and then suddenly Mingus stopped the band and said, "That's rock and roll." He says, "You're not going to find any rock and roll in my album."

And he just started walking around telling people what to play. He walked up to the tuba player, Bob Stewart, and said, "I want you to play in 3/4, I want you to play just *um-pah, um-pah*. Eddie Bert, I want you to play something like this . . ." He assigns specific roles to two or three different people and then he says, "Anybody else who feels like adding to that, we are going to play some clown music. Now I want you to make it sound like a clown." And so we went back and it worked immediately. It was obviously what the piece needed at that point. Then later on, in the overdubbing of that, he deliberately included references to the old bebop themes that are in there.

GOODMAN: Oh, that came after.

JOHNSON: Right, that came after, and he just wanted a subliminal reference to another kind of music. It is his own private little inside thing. It is not terribly audible. Teo was dying to play his alto. He loves to play and does not get many chances anymore. And Mingus likes his alto playing and talked him into bringing his alto around to one of the overdubbings. So he got Teo to play and Teo sounded, you know, he can play space music like a freak. And so Mingus kept saying, "Yeah, we are going to have the masked marvel on this album," and actually Teo didn't get credited in the notes with it, but he was delighted that he got Teo actively participating as a player. And Teo was having a ball. He was really elated.

GOODMAN: So after they were playing your 8/8 section, and then he stops it—you said the band was getting into it, it was going well. That reminded me of another story you told when you all got cooking and he was off the stage, not participating, and then had to jump back in there and destroy the tune. Of course, this time he did not.

JOHNSON: No. He just made a decision, which I couldn't get him to make before.

GOODMAN: And I don't know what to conclude from this except I guess he has to always have his hand in it.

JOHNSON: Oh, I think that's true, but in some ways he impresses me as not being egotistical about his music. Or about having to take charge constantly. And that he's willing to let it go.

One of the things he understands is that other people may be performing some service that he doesn't care to. Because he can orchestrate but he does it in a very deliberate, slow way. I mean, he just—it's laborious. He actually leans on the pencil. It's quite a process. And so under those circumstances it would take him forever to orchestrate something, orchestrate a body of pieces, and so he has used other people to orchestrate his music.

Bob Hammer was very successful at that. He's a piano player who was around here, in 1962 or something like that, when he did Mingus's masterpiece, as far as I'm concerned, a brilliant piece of orchestration and brilliant performances of *The Black Saint and the Sinner Lady*. That texture, as far as I'm concerned, is the definitive Mingus texture. It was the texture also, in doing the writing for this album and the [*Mingus and Friends*] concert, that I decided to deliberately not emulate.

I told Mingus, it isn't adding anything to simply find whatever secrets I need to know in order to make the band sound that way and then go ahead and write. There were some other qualities I could bring to the music, that I was hoping he would find acceptable, and he has. I know in particular—with "Shoes of the Fisherman's Wife," he's very moved by his own recording of that now. He always holds it up to me as an example of success, as far as my efforts were concerned.

So he constantly says now, "You really worked too hard on this, Sy." He says, "On 'Shoes of the Fisherman's Wife,' you were really working on that one."

But it's been . . . a fascinating experience. And he's quite content to give responsibility to other people when he prefers not to do it. He doesn't like to conduct, for example.

Oh, another interesting note about his compositional thing is that, in going over to talk with him about music that frequently only existed on a tape of some kind, or on an old record with no written notation or score—in talking about that, I found that he hears the music in a very emotional way.

I mean, he knows when it goes up and when it comes down. He has got the emotional peaks and valleys of the piece down, and frequently the specific pitches aren't terribly important. He could just as easily have written down other notes that would have satisfied his needs at the same time.

So when he talks about it, he'll say, "Oh that probably goes here," and he will take it to another place in the piece and move on right from there.

GOODMAN: Kind of like tape editing?

JOHNSON: No, it's just that what he hears is not as much specifics as far as pitch is concerned, as [it is] intensely emotional energies, flows of matter and volume and all that business. The pitches in a lot of his pieces are very specific. I mean, you can't fuck with "Clowns." When he gets into that kind of thing, it takes an enormous amount of discipline to sit down and just keep channeling those lines, one on top of the other. I mean, layering the thing.

But in a lot of cases the music is just much more expansive than that, so there is a big contrast between the tightly disciplined Mingus of "Clowns," which I think is one of his masterpieces, and some of the more expansive, impressive pieces.

GOODMAN: Like *The Black Saint?*

JOHNSON: Right, that kind of piece. He could have easily gone someplace else with that music. It isn't like a John Lewis composition, for example, which is inevitable. One thing inevitably follows everything else. John will never forget exactly the sequence of things happening. With Mingus, the options are open, they're open to change even after the piece is played, recorded. He's responding to another drummer or another source in his head. And some of the most volcanic music he has written has been written in that way.

GOODMAN: Then you're suggesting this is a kind of polarity in his music. I mean, the "Clowns" Mingus and then the *Black Saint* Mingus?

JOHNSON: Right. Or even with that piece for Roy Eldridge—the "Little Royal Suite"—which is that [second] kind of Mingus. It's the volcanic, volatile music that is very difficult to get people to play because they frequently have to make noises and he has written nonmusical instructions to them on the music, and they are expected to supply a wide palette of sounds. Again, it's helpful to enumerate: he's got the very disciplined Mingus that can write a piece like "Clowns" or like even "Shoes of the Fisherman's Wife," which is somber and very, uhh, controlled—although that could have gone other places too. "Shoes" is one of the pieces, once you see the structure of it, that he could have taken some other place. But "Clowns" is quite unique. He was very surprised to find out that that was not a sixteen-bar phrase.

And that's another thing. His music frequently comes out into odd numbers of bars. He sometimes has a tendency, if one thing comes out at fourteen bars, to make the next section eighteen bars long. So that in totality, it turns out to be a thirty-two-bar phrase. He thinks that it should be more regular than it is. He's a little suspicious of his own instincts in that regard. But if he breaks a three-bar phrase, then he will follow that with a five-bar phrase.

In "Taurus," he had written a brilliant series and built the whole piece on three-bar phrases. The recording of it was left off the album for space reasons and because Mingus actually finished the piece after the recording was done. But it was brilliantly written in three-bar phrases.

On the recording date, Mingus yelled something about "we need to settle down someplace." He inserted one four-bar phrase, just extending one of the three-bar phrases for an extra measure, which killed me. I hated that. It drove me right up the wall because it was such a perfect structure before. Mingus very obstinately decided that he needed to settle down somewhere in the middle and added one measure to it, which destroyed that beautifully conceived framework that seemed to have been entirely subconscious on his part. It wasn't planned: he was following his ear, and whatever his muse was telling him. Only after the fact of dealing with it, when trying to record it at an earlier time, did he want to "settle down" and make it more regular at one place. He just had to change it.

So it still galls me slightly that he would fuck with that perfect structure that he made. 'Cause it was perfect. He just had to lengthen one of them out to conventional length to satisfy some other requirement that had nothing to do with the act of writing the music. It was separate from the creative impulse of putting the music down.

But, his music is just full of earth and it's always got its feet in the dirt. I mean it's jazz, it has human cries in it, and it's full of humanity. Mingus's humor is [*unintelligible*].

GOODMAN: I suppose in his sense of form he's got to have something to grab onto.

JOHNSON: Right, I know that. He mistrusts though, sometimes, his own . . . So he will, after the fact, regularize something. He'll come across a chord sequence that seems to exist, it doesn't even have a melody sometimes, just a series of chords that seem designed to do nothing but finish a phrase. He doesn't have anything particular he wants to write there but he feels he should have a certain number of more bars. It will be just some chords that will finish it. Then he will have written sixteen bars and that will be the end of it. It's just an interesting thing.

NOTES

1. There is a good discussion of the subject in Eric Porter's *What Is This Thing Called Jazz? African American Musicians as Artists, Critics, and Activists* (Berkeley: University of California Press, 2002), with a full chapter on Mingus. See especially 22–23, 37, 192.

2. Mingus intended to move to Majorca to "work on his autobiography and composition," according to a *Jet* magazine notice: "Bassist Mingus Heads for Venice, May Quit U.S.," August 30, 1962.

3. The full *Time* article is here: www.time.com/time/magazine/article/ 0,9171,827882,00.html.

4. Kenneth Rexroth, "Some Thoughts on Jazz as Music, as Revolt, as Mystique," reprinted in *Bird in the Bush* (New York: New Directions, 1959); or see www .bopsecrets.org/rexroth/jazz.htm. As of 2010, the Mingus Orchestra continued the explorations into jazz-poetry performances that Mingus, Rexroth, and others began in the 1950s. See www.mingusmingusmingus.com/MingusBands/ ChamberMingusPR.pdf.

5. Ornette could read; that wasn't the problem. There's no "simple" answer as to why he couldn't or wouldn't play straight, despite what he said in talking with critic Whitney Balliett: "The other night, at a rehearsal for the concert I played in of Gunther Schuller's music, Schuller made me play a little four-measure thing he'd written six or seven times before I got it right. I could read it, see the notes on the paper. But I heard those notes in my head, heard their pitch, and what I heard was different from what Schuller heard. Then I got it right. I got it his way. It was as simple as that." Balliett, *Collected Works: A Journal of Jazz 1954–2000* (New York: St. Martin's Press, 2002), 116.

6. Nesuhi Ertegun partnered with his brother Ahmet to produce some of Atlantic Records' best-known jazz and pop musicians, including Mingus, Coltrane, Coleman, the Modern Jazz Quartet, and many others. He was also Mingus's friend.

7. It would probably be more politically correct today to use the term "ethnic," but this was 1974 and I meant "tribal" in the sense of totemic, a specific and integral part of the culture.

8. A good discussion of Coltrane's "Africanism" and related issues is found in Ben Ratliff, *Coltrane: The Story of a Sound* (New York: Farrar, Straus and Giroux, 2007). See especially 154–78.

9. Recently, the story (rumored for years) came out about Varèse's fascination and work in 1957 with New York jazz musicians, including Parker, Mingus, Teo Macero and others. The "improvisations" are diagrammed and recorded for playback by the International Contemporary Ensemble in "Varèse, Charlie Parker, and the New York Improv Sessions," *Edgar(d)* (blog), July 19, 2010, http://iceorg.org/varese/?p=200.

10. Sue Mingus has published the full *Children* liner notes online as "What Is a Jazz Composer?" See www.mingusmingusmingus.com/Mingus/what_is_a_jazz_composer.html. It is a brilliant, rambling, ranting piece in which Mingus declares his allegiance to tradition in jazz and classical music. "An Open Letter to the Avant-Garde" broaches the Clark Terry idea he followed up on here, of getting really accomplished jazz musicians to show up the pseudo-avant-garde players. Read it at www.parafono.gr/htmls/mingus_openletter.htm.

11. The piece is entitled "All the Things You Could Be by Now: Charles Mingus Presents Charles Mingus and the Limits of Avant-Garde Jazz." No longer available online, it has been collected in *Uptown Conversations: The New Jazz Studies*, ed. Robert G. O'Meally, Brent Hayes Edwards, and Farah Jasmine Griffin (New York: Columbia University Press, 2004), 27–49.

12. Alex Stewart, *Making the Scene: Contemporary New York City Big Band Jazz* (Berkeley: University of California Press, 2007), 224.

13. Sy added this note in a follow-up interview in 2011: "I was doing my usual thing of minimizing my role so as not to spoil his image. Actually, he only gave me an eight-bar fragment that he said had some Tatum voicings he knew from rehearsing with him, and he wanted it used 'the way Duke uses Harry Carney in the band.' The Spanish vamp, and the ending which I really liked, he wanted to [use to] flesh out the piece. I wrote the open harmonics and the counter-motifs to fill in the spaces and reflect Carney, I guess."

2 Studying, Teaching, and Earning a Living

"Lloyd Reese . . . was more than a genius."

I asked Mingus to talk about his first days in New York, when he was married to Celia. A good part of what he had said about that period in *Underdog* was fiction, and I wanted to hear the true version. He couldn't make a living by teaching, he said. He got into describing his work at the post office, which led him to the problems of writing music for a living—and how Bach and Beethoven handled that, with some asides about Beethoven's living style—and finally some musings on the high life and the low life for a musician.

Many of his thoughts on classical music and musicians concentrated on the conditions under which that music was composed and played, the economics of writing and performing it, if you will. There were lots of bons mots here—among them, "the best job [Bach] could get was to write for Christians." For Mingus, at least in these interviews, it was mostly about how to make a living in music.

. . .

MINGUS: When I first came to New York I was teaching—Percy Heath, then I had Jimmy Garrison, several white students—one of the guys became a big gambler, Italian kid, can't remember his name now. He went to the horse races and found he could make money that way and quit playing—and he was a very good player. Had them as private students, singly. But that wasn't enough money.

Anyway, Celia told me in these very words before I got started teaching: when she finds herself getting loose or wanting to go to bed with another man—she said she had been working at living with her [former] husband, John Nielsen, and every day the stairs just got higher and higher. So she came in one day, before I started teaching even. I was practicing, we were

48

living in New York, and I'm getting ready to go to work in the studios—because I didn't come here just to go to work with Charlie Parker.

She opens the door, and I say, "Hi, how you doin', baby?"

She says, "Whew, those stairs are getting higher and higher." And that's all she said, man.

I said, "Well, I'll tell you what's going to happen, baby. I'm going to get me a job, quit playing music."

She said, "You can't quit playing music," but she said it in such a sour way that I knew she wanted me to help her get some money.

I said, "I'm going to work, find a job." I wanted her to say no, but she didn't say no.

She said, "All right, if you feel you should do it. What can you do? You can't do nothing, you're a bass player."

GOODMAN: Sounds like my wife, man, about what I do.

MINGUS: "Yes, I can, baby. I can carry mail. 'Cause I'm a stone mail carrier; my father was a mailman."

So . . . I went to the post office, it was around Christmastime, man, and she was getting tired of the stairways, and I didn't want no woman cheatin' on me. So I went to the post office and got signed up for temporary service. I got to carry mail, I think. No, I didn't, in California I carried mail. In New York, they gave me the bundles and the chutes, that's all I got to do, the heavy work. I worked my ass off, and I remember the guys who were there permanently used to laugh at me 'cause I'd still be working when they were sitting down eating sandwiches. Not at lunch time: they had breaks, little breaks, coffee breaks.

They said, "Mingus, what are you gonna do? There's always another sack coming, you can't win."

But I stood there every day. I said, "Fuck 'em, man," and I kept throwing the mail, you know. When the chute packs up, the conveyor belt stops. And they all began to like me because I wanted a permanent job. I was doing their work in a way. But they laughed at me, man. Reason I know I was a winner for the post office, which is not much of a claim, but I would just as soon be in the post office as to be here where I am now. I would rather I had stayed there, and I could have stayed. After Christmas came, I stayed on, all the guys liked me, foreman and everybody. You know who got me to quit? Charlie Parker. [Usually] you only worked about two months and then you're through with it. I worked three and four months, going over the period. I'm bragging about this, man, 'cause not too many cats can work in the post office.

GOODMAN: I think it's in the Ross Russell book where he says Bird got Mingus out of the post office.[1]

MINGUS: Well, he didn't get me out of the post office, man. You know how I feel about it? I feel like this, man: I don't know what Bartók or Beethoven did for a living, but they didn't write music for a living. There's rumors around from the avant-garde and the collectors of history, like Phil Moore will tell you. But what I heard about Beethoven is that he used to go to a nightclub [*sounding a little drunk here*] or where musicians would go to hear their music, because in those days they didn't use their horns, they used their pencils. Said, "Let's write some counterpoint, let's write some fugues."

Bach could be sitting in the corner, you know, not being bothered with the jazz musicians, 'cause he knew he was Bach. But you know there had to be a scene like that. Finally, someone would come up and say, "Well, I wrote the baddest. This is the best." And they find a judge, and ask Bach to come over. And Bach walk over and say, "Well, I don't know, I can't compare, but I'll write you a fugue." So, what was he doing for a living? He was walking to church on Sundays to pay his rent, he played in church.

GOODMAN: He had his church position, and that's what paid his bills—

MINGUS: Well, put that in the book!

GOODMAN: Right, and a guy like Beethoven had his patrons, because the system was a little bit different then. He was writing a symphony for Count So-and-So, and he had to make his living that way. But Bach had a stipend, a regular thing.

MINGUS: He was [subsidized] to one position, put that down. Suppose he ever had a chance to write for some dancers, what would he have written?[2]

GOODMAN: He did, he wrote dances. They are transcribed and sometimes altered, but you're right, and it all had to be appropriate for his church position. He was the cantor of Leipzig, for Christ's sake.

MINGUS: Put that in, make me sound intelligent.

GOODMAN: I will [*laughs*], I'll try—I mean I'm not that intelligent!

MINGUS: Phil Moore made the classical guys relate to me the same as the jazz guys did. So, fuck it, if Bach was a guy who went to church, the best job he could get was to write for Christians [*laughter about this*]. . . .

FIGURE 2.   Mingus, Sue Graham, Alvin Ailey (at end of row), and dancers rehearsing "The Mingus Dances," 1971. Photo by Sy Johnson.

GOODMAN: Want to get out of here?

MINGUS: No, not done in here, I ordered a hamburger. My friends are bringing you and me some fine smoked Nova Scotia salmon and bagels. Well, that's like about nine-thirty or ten, so that'll be our little snack, you know. . . .

   Phil and Red [Callender], they knew the history of music, but they're musicians. But I never saw 'em, I never went to school, I went to a private school. They were more concerned with the fundamentals than with what Bach did. They would play Bach for you, the music, and write it for you. But listening to it was for guys like you and me.

   Beethoven used to shit in his house, in the corner. Did you know this? You can read that.

GOODMAN: Sure, I've read it, but I don't necessarily believe it.

MINGUS: But it's possible to read, right, that he lived like an animal? That's what I read.

GOODMAN: Yeah, he was a piggy guy, and we know that.

MINGUS: Well, so am I, man, you should see my apartment, that's why I'm gonna take you there. You ever see it?

GOODMAN: Sure, you took me there once. Fuck it, who cares?

MINGUS: I can't help it, man. If I were so organized to put things on shelves, I couldn't find nothing.

GOODMAN: I once wrote a column about a writer who criticized Beethoven for his "slovenly habits"—that he lived like a pig, you know, and was a terrible person. He insulted and was rotten to everybody. And all these books about Beethoven and how impossible a guy he was—that is the worst kind of music writing.

I mean, if he hadn't written the greatest music in the world, would anyone have cared one good fuck whether he lived like a pig or like a king?

MINGUS: Well, you know pigs are very important, you know, you eat pigs. So if you live like a pig, you don't bother me, man.

GOODMAN: It's irrelevant and dumb.

MINGUS: We should talk about it though, man, we should talk about it in a different way. I think that this showed that the man wasn't making any money. That's what I was talking about. The fact that he had to live the same way as I live.

Everybody in the band gets $450 a week; I'm making $2,500, and I pay the agent, the plane fare, expenses—I don't make nothing, man. It's like doing it for kicks. And I can't go on for kicks anymore. That's why I'm writing this book. That's why you're going to write a good book. That's why I can't fuck around. [*Pause.*] You got to go inside my head and take out all the cobwebs and take out all the real things and all the bad things. I think you can do it, man.

GOODMAN: I hope so.

MINGUS: Well with the *Playboy* thing, I thought we could do it.

GOODMAN: I'm glad you think that, and I'm happy because I think we can do it.

MINGUS: Why don't you talk about some things that bug you? You should talk about the fact that people write criticisms on Beethoven that talk about him living as a pig. We should talk about it, and the fact is that maybe he did, and maybe a pig's life ain't so bad, man. Maybe he was so busy with what he was doing—

GOODMAN: Obviously, right. You know, Sue said something to me the other night: "If only Charles had gotten that nice studio overlooking the river, he could have gotten rid of that lousy apartment he's got."

I said nothing but I thought, well, if he really wanted to get out of that apartment he'd get out of there, and why should he have to get out of there? It doesn't mean anything. I live in a very nice house, and I'm thinking of getting out of that.

MINGUS: This is good material, man. I've lived on Park Avenue, 1160, I lived in one of the best houses they have for white folks. I had to send a white man in to get the apartment for me. They wouldn't rent it to me. Sent in a guy who said his name was Mingus, introduced himself and got the apartment for me. And I've lived in Harlem, the best apartments in Harlem—which are just as good as the best apartments on Fifth Avenue. And I wrote the same kind of music, but I still haven't written the music I want to write. It's weird.

I'm still playing jazz, on the bandstand, in pigpens—'cause Max's Kansas City is a pigpen—still playing with people, one of these days, *ding-ding-ding-ding*, I'm gonna get a chance to write some music, *ding-ding-ding-ding*, 'cause you can't work in these clubs like this, *ding-ding-ding-ding*, with Dannie Richmond and these kids who don't even believe in what I believe in. You can't write a composition of what you are, you can't even improvise a composition of what you are and play it in these kind of places. And play this often. And travel in the airplane, travel on the train, travel on the bus. You can't do this, man. This is tougher than Beethoven had to do, man.

GOODMAN: Yes, it is. He could sit on his ass.

MINGUS: He had no travel problem. That's what I'm saying. If Beethoven had been a garbage man and wrote the way he wrote, if somebody could hear what he's doing and say, "Here's a guy who wrote beautiful music, more than beautiful music, he wrote real music, pertaining to his society completely, wrote music pertaining to the hereafter." [*Chuckles.*] He had a hell of a belief—he had more of a belief than Bach. I don't notice in any of Bach's writing any fact for a moment where he believes in Jesus. Yet in Beethoven's music, I hear where he might have believed in Jesus, and he never wrote for church.

GOODMAN: I'd argue with you on that, but it's another discussion.

MINGUS: Well, the way they play it, man, the counterpoint or fugues, on piano especially, I'm talking about piano music, Bach on piano, I can't hear no more where he believes.

GOODMAN: But Bach on piano is not the real thing, you know.

MINGUS: I'm glad you're here, man. . . .

. . .

In discussing classical influences and how Mingus used them, we rambled
and zigzagged as usual. His talk started with how he used music to seduce
women—writing string quartets for them—and, after some excursions,
finished again with that theme. Mingus's string quartets were known only
to a relative few, and I never got to hear them.

The most obvious example of classical influence in his music is "Adagio
ma non troppo" from *Children,* which, as Mingus says below, uses classical
forms and procedures to highlight jazz improvisation. It is the most obvious recorded bow to classical sources and forms he ever wrote, though "The
Chill of Death" from the same album clearly owes something to Richard
Strauss.

Symphonic suggestions are sometimes woven into his other work—
obbligato parts and voicings in the big band music particularly—yet the
result is nothing like Third Stream music. What he did learn from the clas-
sicists was how to use tone color. But I don't hear much in the way of "classical," neither concert analogues nor direct borrowings, in Mingus. When
he says he "always wanted to play classical music," I think he means music
with that depth, structure, and complexity. When he talked with the Italian
interviewer (see Introduction), he said he was waiting for the chance to
write, not Western concert music, but "classical, pure, serious music that
came out of all the musics." Mingus the composer was a synthesizer, a true
eclectic, one who totally integrated those multiple sources into his music.

As Alex Ross has pointed out, the compositions of Mingus, John
Coltrane, and Ornette Coleman expanded the tonalities of bebop, and as
composers they had "much in common" (well, something in common) with
Stravinsky, Debussy, and Messiaen.[3] Along with the music of Ravel, the
music of these composers was in the air, and many jazz musicians were
listening. They wanted to be taken as serious musicians.

Yet here's a guy who loves the "bitches" and is desperate to get laid,
while at the same time he's at the piano "improvising in symphonic form"!
I took that as some kind of epitome of Mingus.

. . .

MINGUS: It's funny, man, I know the name Mary Campbell [see chapter 11] means something to you now—Campbell's soup maybe, and

she told me about that later—but before she told me about it I was still in love. When I looked at her I just forgot all about the bitches I looked at at home base. I figured this broad had been in some kind of church and knew classical music. I had some classical repertoire. She asked was I trained in school and all that, and—Lloyd Reese never taught me this, I was born with this—I used to improvise in symphony [form]. I got proof of that, a composition on Columbia, an improvised thing in *Let My Children Hear Music,* one of the tunes in there, "Adagio ma non troppo."

GOODMAN: Are those tunes that early in your life?

MINGUS: That kind of playing was.

GOODMAN: "Half-Mast Inhibition," that wasn't an improvised piece?

MINGUS: No, that was partly jazz too. But the basis of my playing was always the desire to get over the music I was playing, to make enough money to play the music that I wanted to play. I always wanted to play classical music—not Beethoven or Bach or Brahms, but improvise and compose new string quartets. Like I had a string quartet to do—I hate to jump fifty years on you—for the Whitney Museum.

I didn't write [the quartet] out, I composed it on piano. But when people heard the composition, they thought I had spent months writing it. I played it on my piano. I reveal this in my book. And it was not for critics, because I played it at Newport. Most people picture me in there writing, taking time, because it takes six months to write a string quartet with all the bowings in it.

GOODMAN: I remember when I last saw you [in 1972] you were writing them. You had done two.

MINGUS: Well, I did one with the pencil and never finished it. I have sketches for about four more that [*unintelligible*]. I only have the copy of the one of 'em here, the one I did already, six-seven minutes.

GOODMAN: Did you perform the other? Kermit Moore was going to play it.

MINGUS: Yeah, Kermit Moore played it, and he also did it in Newport.

GOODMAN: Who else played? I wish I'd heard that, goddammit.

MINGUS: I wish you'd heard it too, man.

GOODMAN: Matter of fact, George Wein is the guy who said "[*Whistle*], Mingus's quartets—I never heard anything like them."

MINGUS: Yeah, well, don't tell him yet. Don't tell him till the book comes out. He doesn't know about my writing them on piano, he thinks it's a [composed,] written-out thing.

GOODMAN: You transcribed it, then?

MINGUS: Same as you and I are doing now. But the one I did with a pencil, I could see myself cutting the writing I did on the piano. Started one on the piano, it was one of the poems, poems for that guy, a whole concert was for him, at the Whitney Museum. Sue told you about it—the guy that got killed on the beach at Fire Island, a poet.[4] Funny I don't know the name.

That's one thing I did write down and memorize, though: the word part, the slurring, legato thing that went through the melody that the cello and violins and all were playing. I sang that, didn't play it, couldn't play it [*sings it*]—those kind of sighing things, like in Hindemith, Bartók— Bartók, the theory was Bartók.

As a kid I was always very gifted in hearing something done by a classical composer and then going to the piano in the middle of it and just playing it. I don't have perfect pitch either. This [would be] after the record [was] off, and I'd say, "I know what that is" [*sings a phrase*]. Red Norvo, I did it once for him, they were playing, umm, some difficult composer, a Spanish composer—know any?

GOODMAN: Albeniz, Villa-Lobos—

MINGUS: Villa-Lobos, they were playing Villa-Lobos at this house, and I was with Red Norvo then—this was many years later—and they said it was quarter tones, a quarter-tone piece. So I told Red, "This isn't quarter tones; I can show you it's not."

Well, his attitude was, "Go away, boy," you know.

And so when the concert was over with, I didn't say nothing. So fuck it, I just went to the piano and did [*sings melody phrase*] and I played every note that every instrument was playing—not too long, I couldn't play the whole piece.

They said, "How'd you do that? How'd you do that? You got perfect pitch?"

No, I haven't got perfect pitch, man, and that's not quarter tones. If it was quarter tones, I couldn't have played it on the piano. That shows how the public can be fooled. They put on [the album description] that it's a quarter-tone piece done by so-and-so, and the poor public buys it, and it ain't quarter tone.

GOODMAN: And if the public can be fooled, you know damn well that musicians can be fooled too. Red Norvo is a good musician, and he got fooled.

MINGUS: Sure, musicians can be fooled, sadly. Red got fooled. Tal Farlow's a guy who's got perfect pitch, and he got fooled.

GOODMAN: Chuck Wayne was the guy I was trying to think of the other night when we were talking—

MINGUS: Bad man!—the one who was playing with the other guitar player at Bradley's?

GOODMAN: Double session, yeah, he's awful good, goddammit . . . So let's talk about Stravinsky and Bartók and all those people—

MINGUS: That's where we are now.

GOODMAN: Very honestly, I don't hear a hell of a lot of that in your music, but I know that they are important to you and that you've been involved in a listening way.

MINGUS: It's funny. I was talking to a piano player, Tommy Flanagan, in Copenhagen—he's with Ella Fitzgerald—and we were talking about Coleman Hawkins, and so I was telling about how great his library, record collection, was; he had records all over the house. Flanagan said he didn't have no jazz. All he had was Beethoven, Bach, Brahms, Stravinsky, Bartók. He'd try and play Bartók in the middle of "Body and Soul"—and this cat knows.

We had a whole discussion about piano players, because I love piano players, good piano players. So I made him go to the piano and play the changes to "Body and Soul," and a couple of things that guys don't do any more. He says, "Hawk would take and play this against E-flat, Mingus. Wasn't he crazy? That's called 'Clair de Lune.'"

GOODMAN: Same intervals, you mean?

MINGUS: Same intervals but not in the same key. You'd think he'd play in the original key he'd get off the record.

GOODMAN: Well, that's the kind of thing Debussy did too, you know. So Tommy Flanagan heard that?

MINGUS: Well, he's a musicologist. I was so embarrassed, man, he knows so much music, listening music. We were sitting in a nightclub, and they played some music [on record] with Bird on tenor, and he knew who all the guys were—Sonny Rollins and Bird. He said, "Sonny Rollins didn't play good here, he played wrong."

And that's what a musicologist is, because Tommy Flanagan is something else. He said, "This cat *missed*. Bird fucked him up." That's on Prestige, I guess, eh?

GOODMAN: Yeah, I have it, it's a great record.[5]

. . .

MINGUS: The way I feel now is I should be having some students over at my place. But I've still got to work until that day comes when I can build a school and get some students to play some real music.

GOODMAN: And an audience that knows you. Like what classical music is doing, but they are in hard times too.

MINGUS: Kids should be educated to music, man; [classical is] not bad music. Our society should be listening to operas and everything else by now. It's just noise to them, they can't relax for a minute, it makes them sick. If a guy came in and played a beautiful violin for two-three minutes, they'd go crazy—over an ordinary microphone or no microphone.

Don't you think they could appreciate Pablo Casals if he was young today? Sure they could, man, if this damn country would push it. I don't know why they don't want the kids to hear good music. Is it because it would make them healthy? They might throw their pot away. They might, man. You going to print that? And the young Casalses, they're stopping them.

GOODMAN: The conservatories and the system for making it in classical music is hard, it's a hard apprenticeship. But they're still playing the same old Beethoven's Third Symphony for the same old ladies in fur coats.

MINGUS: What about classical modern composers? There are some good ones. We had a guy named David Broekman that to me was great as anybody who ever lived.[6] But they killed him. I heard his symphony, an unaccompanied cello concerto, no comparison, and he knew he was a master. He first played down in the East Village, Third Ave. and St. Mark's—what's that place? across from the Five Spot [Cooper Union].

David Broekman, I used to study with him. He used to come to all our concerts. Teo had a thing called Composers Workshop with Teddy Charles, John LaPorta, George Barrow, a blind bass player.[7] You know, they used to call us avant-garde, and if you listened to the stuff [we were doing then] it was more advanced than what they're doing today. Yeah, I hate to say it that way, but we were really experimenting and trying to do it right. We weren't bullshitting. And it's much more complex, more advanced. I did one back then—used Teo and John LaPorta—and that wasn't even modern, I wrote that one in the '40s. More complex as far as the bass is concerned.

David used to come to our concerts, and Henry Brant—someone else, a classical composer—they came a lot because Teo was there, but they were enjoying more than just Teo, because they came more than once. David was prematurely gray, and I went and talked with him. He said, "You're a composer. I can teach you how—instead of putting twenty notes down, you take seven and do the same thing with it."

I said, "That's what I'm looking for, I'll be over." And he would take a run of notes [*demonstrates*] and pick out the ones that were important. Find the melody that was really in your mind. The excitement could come from the percussion [*demonstrates*]. How to orchestrate for full orchestra, get more out of what you're doing. He didn't say "never do that," but the whole composition was [*demonstrates*]—no breaths, like right off the piano. I seen my piano player now [John Foster]—since the concert he told Sue he's gonna write four compositions every day! Yeah, but he hasn't got one rest in his tunes! Man, he needs sixteen rests. Something else he hasn't got is syncopation, and that's what jazz is.

People think jazz is just playing the melody. Charlie Parker cut everybody; Charlie Parker invented new rhythms, just like a tap dancer. All the time he was playing not only melody but rhythm patterns. That's what those [young] guys are not doin', man. They just copy his riffs, and when [Bird died], that was it—they just end up playing a few riffs. But the guys that know, a few of 'em could go on, and, uhh . . . well, see, I want McPherson to do more than play bebop. He learned a lot but still has to invent more than that.

If Bird were here today, he wouldn't be still playing bebop. You think he'd let Albert Ayler or somebody like that cut him? He'd do the *squeek-squawk* too but only a few bars of it. He wouldn't do every tune like that. He would be avant-garde at the end of the composition or in the middle as a laugh and then go back to playing the music.

You don't just eliminate the beat. Music is everything—the beat and the no-beat; jazz wants to beat, emphasize the beat, so you don't cancel it entirely. Especially if you call yourself black, because African people ain't gonna never stop dancing. Puerto Ricans, the gypsies, Hungarians, they all have a dance music. You know? But they also have mood music that don't have a beat to it sometimes; Indian [music] don't have a beat to it, but when they dance to it, they got a beat to it. I don't see why these cats are ashamed to have a beat to their music.

GOODMAN: Tell me about Lloyd Reese, Charles. You said Eric [Dolphy] studied with him?

MINGUS: Yeah, I studied with him, Buddy Collette studied with him, Harry Carney used to go to him for clarinet and bass clarinet. He's a well-learned man. If you say genius, well, everybody says genius, but he's a man who did 90 percent work and got the results. Or he might have done 100 percent because he was above the average genius, more than a genius. He played and taught piano, played all the woodwinds, all the reeds, and trumpet.

Lloyd was in a guy named Les Hite's band, and somebody in either the saxophone section or the trumpet section died. [Lloyd] was the first alto player, right? And they kept finding trumpet players to take the man's place who died, and they never liked them. So Lloyd told Les Hite, "Hire Marshall Royal to take my place, and I'll take off and learn the trumpet, because your trumpet's not right."

That's how he became a genius—went and studied the brass, came back, took his job back and was considered the greatest first-chair man going in that period—in the late '20s. Les Hite's band came after Fes Williams's famous band, but Les's band lasted even up to Duke Ellington and was one of the greatest jazz bands ever heard, man. Snooky Young played in that band, but later; plus some guys you know.

Lloyd was just an unbelievable player, man. He played so much trumpet at jam sessions that nobody thought he was playing anything. Crazy [*demonstrates with lots of notes, runs*]—like a flute or something. I don't know how to explain it to you, man. And the man knew what he was doing. I'll tell you how bad he was: at the musician's union they had some helluva musicians who everybody respected, and I forget what the question was, but somebody put a bet, a lot of money on it: "The book says so-and-so."

"But that's *that* book. *This* book says so-and-so."

"Well, I'll tell you what, man. Call Lloyd. Do you respect Lloyd Reese?"

All the students said, "Yeah, we respect him, man, let's call him on the phone."

So Lloyd came over and said, "I have no favorites here, guys, but this is the answer." And he said neither was right, and they all took their money back.

He did have a rehearsal band though, because we all read [music]. He gave us the inner thing, and he'd make us change instruments. Gave me trumpet or something. I don't know why he always gave me trumpet, but then he'd show you how to set harmony, how to make up tunes with a big band—without [written] music—by someone starting the melody in one of the sections and by the time the reeds set their five-part harmony to it—mainly the blues, you start with—then the brass would take the same melody and harmonize to it, then the 'bones would take the same melody. By the time each section's played the melody, then somebody else figured out a reed riff or an organ point to play behind 'em.

In fact, Lloyd said there was a day when he used to go to work with no [written] music at all. Just hear a tune, play it, the brass got it, and [they'd] open the chorus. I know a guy who played in a band like that, but he used to talk like it was a lot of fun. People had music stands sitting there, and nobody had any music—played the latest tune, everybody making the harmony up. Or [Lloyd would] bring blank paper, and he used to write down: "You're in B-flat"; "you got G"; "you got A," you know. [He'd assign parts] and we'd play it and it'd be unbelievable. But he wouldn't use no score.

Great trumpet player, great teacher. And some of his students, man. A guy like Harry Carney with Duke and playing as good as he plays now, as good as he was then, tells you something's going on.

GOODMAN: It reminds me of what I heard about the Duke—teaching without a fixed score.

MINGUS: Then writing stuff down on paper.

GOODMAN: But there are no more teachers like that—or do you know of any?

MINGUS: Well, there was gonna be some. Buddy Collette was gonna come down here and I was gonna build my school. Berklee and those places, they're teaching jazz, eh?

GOODMAN: Yeah, what do you think about that?

MINGUS: Ah, the white guys got enough things. Why don't they let me build my school, let some guys who have been into it do it, you know? I'm not saying guys like Boots Monselli [Mussulli?] shouldn't do it, 'cause he's a jazz player, or John LaPorta. But some of the teachers they've got can't even play, man.

GOODMAN: Is that so? I thought they had all jazz people on that faculty.

MINGUS: Oh yeah? Well, maybe it's the way they approached me. I never heard him blow, but a guy comes in and says to me, "Me, I never really dug your music, you know. Why don't you come up to school and show us what you're doing?"

I said, "Motherfucker, if you don't know what I'm doing by now, why don't you come to work in the Jazz Workshop, show me what *you* doin'? If you're so great, why don't you get yourself a job as a jazz musician?" Like, I got here the hard way. "Show him what I'm doin'!"

GOODMAN: That's marvelous. You should audition for them, right? . . .

NOTES

1. No, it wasn't in the Ross Russell book, which is all the same a fascinating, flawed biography of Parker: *Bird Lives! The High Life and Hard Times of Charlie (Yardbird) Parker* (New York: Charterhouse, 1973). Russell was a postwar jazz producer and founder of Dial Records. My source here was likely the remarks Mingus himself made in Robert George Reisner's *Bird: The Legend of Charlie Parker* (New York: Bonanza Books, 1962), 151: "One night I get a phone call from Parker: 'Mingus, what are you doing working in the post office? A man of your artistic stature? Come with me.' I told him I was making good money. He offered me $150 a week, and I accepted."

2. Mingus collaborated with the Joffrey Ballet to create music for "The Mingus Dances" in 1971, choreographed by Alvin Ailey and performed at New York's City Center (see figure 2). Mingus explored music for dance in many compositions—from "Ysabel's Table Dance" in *Tijuana Moods* (1957) to what he called "ethnic folk-dance music" in *The Black Saint and the Sinner Lady* (1963) and as late as *Cumbia & Jazz Fusion* (1976).

3. Alex Ross, *The Rest Is Noise: Listening to the Twentieth Century* (New York: Picador, 2008), 519.

4. The poet was Frank O'Hara, and the Whitney had commissioned a competition to commemorate him. See Gene Santoro, *Myself When I Am Real: The Life and Music of Charles Mingus* (New York: Oxford, 2000), 308.

5. Miles Davis, *Collectors' Items*, with Miles in two sessions (1953, 1956), the first of which includes Sonny Rollins, "Charlie Chan" (Bird's recording alias), Walter Bishop, Percy Heath, and Philly Joe Jones, Prestige LP 7044. Parker is not in the second session.

6. A noted Hollywood film composer, classically educated in The Hague, Broekman became prominent for his film scores in the 1930s and 1940s—among them, *All Quiet on the Western Front* and *The Phantom of the Opera*. Before his death in 1958, Broekman was quite involved with jazz and conducted Teddy Charles's "Word from Bird" in Holland in 1956, with the composer performing. See "David Broekman Revival," YouTube video, from a Nov. 6, 2008, performance, posted by "doeszicht," Nov. 7, 2008, www.youtube.com/watch?v=xCoJEbOMtmk.

7. Teddy Charles, one of Mingus's closest accomplices (see chapter 11) and fellow musicians died April 16, 2012, on Long Island, age 84. See Tim Kelly, "North Fork Jazz Great Teddy Charles Dead at 84," *Shelter Island Reporter*, April 18, 2012, http://shelterislandreporter.timesreview.com/2012/04/15388/north-fork-jazz-great-teddy-charles-dead-at-84/.

3 Recordings:
Children and *Friends*

"The music is very original. Nobody's heard a band like it."

Let My Children Hear Music was recorded on several dates, September through November 1971. A smaller band with many of the same people played the *Mingus and Friends* concert that followed in February 1972. In June of '72, when we did the following interview, Mingus was rehearsing a big band for the Mercer Arts Center gig (see Introduction), again with some of the same players, most of whom had formed his Village Vanguard band in March. You will hear mention of and discussion about all these morphing "big" bands throughout our conversation.

Children contains some of Mingus's most astonishing and powerful music. The fact that the album came off as well as it did is also astonishing, given the problems that occurred in its recording and the personalities involved. The commentaries that follow our interview describe some of what went on. Yet with all the difficulties I would make the case that *Children* is Mingus's masterpiece, and there is evidence that he thought so too.[1]

. . .

GOODMAN: I hope that Mercer gig goes well for you, that would be marvelous. Everybody I talked to thinks of you as fronting a big band, somehow. I don't know why that is. Are you happier with a big band, or small? Or do you need 'em both?

MINGUS: I always wanted both.

GOODMAN: Is the Mercer band gonna be pretty much like the one you had at the Vanguard?

MINGUS: I can't change the book. I made up a few new tunes, and I'll get a chance to write 'em as soon as Sue stops booking me.

It'll be a good band, probably one of the best. The music is very original. Nobody's heard a band like it.

GOODMAN: Any way you can get it on a more permanent basis? Is rehearsal time the main problem?

MINGUS: I don't know. Sue's trying. You have to find some guys who want to rehearse [for free], that's the main thing. Duke Ellington's band doesn't pay for rehearsals—[*unintelligible*]—but with no rehearsals, you don't get the job.

GOODMAN: I hear Teo [Macero] played on the *Children* album.

MINGUS: We had him playing alto like Ornette Coleman for a reason. I knew he could do it, he had done it before.

GOODMAN: Does he play much any more? Publicly?

MINGUS: Hadn't been playing in a long time, but he keeps up with his horn. He was a great tenor player, very underrated.

GOODMAN: It's a beautiful album, Charles.

MINGUS: It's old-timey, but then, you know, I like old-time instruments. If I decided to do an atonal piece, I would go to it gradually, I wouldn't just stop what I'm doing. Before I did that I would use the small combo, because I want to do some things that are modal, brooding music. You know [*hums bass figure*], those kind of things.

GOODMAN: The six basses you had—they didn't come through well on the record. I don't know whether it was Teo's recording, mixing, or editing, but the sound was muddy.

MINGUS: See, Teo could have done that better, man. It don't sound like six basses, does it? It sounded good on their equipment in the studio, but in the playback at home it's just not six basses.

GOODMAN: Didn't they mike them individually?

MINGUS: No, and they should have used individual mikes, up close plus some mike catching the room sound. You could hear those basses in the room but not on the record when he [Teo] recorded. He put the mikes far away on "Chill of Death," then decided to do it close the next time. I made that same record in '39 with Red Callender, Artie Shapiro, Artie Bernstein, Dick Kelly from the Philharmonic, Gil Hadnot, Dave Bryant. I didn't play then, I talked [the vocal]—and it sounded better than when Columbia did it, with one or two mikes only. Then [in '39] they put the mikes near the basses and got the bass section sound. They didn't block us off, they got the room sound. I still think that's the best way to record, man.

GOODMAN: Sure it is, particularly for jazz. I don't understand that sixteen-track stuff.

MINGUS: Those basses should be like the Chicago Symphony, on top. Did you tell Teo about the record?

GOODMAN: I told him I thought some of it didn't come through as clear as it ought to, and the basses were part of it. I wasn't going to get into a big discussion with him about it . . . since he spent a lot of time mixing and overdubbing.

· · ·

In other words, I didn't want to antagonize the guy. In a later 1974 session with Mingus, Sue, and myself, we got into discussing the recording and editing of *Children* and the first *Mingus and Friends* concert. Charles said he wasn't happy about the results on either album, but in fact he had permitted both to be issued and, according to Sy Johnson and Teo, definitely had his say in the editing room. I said some things about Teo that were pretty harsh—and should have realized that he and Mingus went way back, both as colleagues and as friends.

· · ·

GOODMAN: Well, have you talked to Teo? What does he have to say about all this?

MINGUS: I hadn't even left the company [Columbia] then. I was telling him about how bad he edited the record. He says, "Well, let's bring it in, Charles. Show me what you're talking about and let's do a new one. Remaster it all over again."

GOODMAN: Which one? *Children?* The first concert?

MINGUS: Yeah, the first concert.

SUE: *Mingus and Friends.*

MINGUS: Ain't no baritone sax on it.

SUE: What, no Mulligan?

MINGUS: I had two baritones; you can only hear one.

GOODMAN: Well, I'm glad you said it, because when I got that record in the mail I thought the recording was pretty bad, and I didn't know who did it.

MINGUS: Teo did it.

GOODMAN: And the editing is worse. I remember the concert; I was there. And nothing went together on the record. It was terrible.[2]

SUE: Teo was conducting, wasn't he, that night?

MINGUS: Yeah.

GOODMAN: Well, let me ask you: I spent some time talking with him, and I must say he really bugged me. Supposedly, the subject was you, we're talking about your music, what you were doing and all that and some of the history of you and him. And all he did was—

MINGUS: Talk about Miles?

GOODMAN: Right! I'll play you the tape if you want to hear it, it's embarrassing. He talked about Miles and he talked about himself.

MINGUS: Yeah.

GOODMAN: And he talked about how he had to be objective and cool and sit back and listen to these things and provide another set of ears for people, and how important his function as a producer was—

MINGUS: Yeah.

GOODMAN: Well, what a lot of crap that is. And in fact, a guy came into the studio while I was there and kissed his ass all over the place, bowing and scraping: "I just hope I can someday learn the business as well as you've learned it, Teo," which he loved, you know. And I must say I came away from that interview thinking the guy's a pompous ass. [*Long pause.*]

CHAPTER 3 COMMENTARY

Sy Johnson on Let My Children Hear Music *and* Mingus and Friends

When he came to New York from Los Angeles in 1960, Sy played piano with Mingus for two hectic weeks. (He talks about that experience in chapter 4.) Later, in 1971, he arranged and conducted most of *Children*. In our conversation, Sy offered valuable insights into what went on in those sessions. While *Children* was very much a unique album for Mingus, the processes of making such complex music come alive also demonstrate how Mingus often functioned in the studio.

. . .

JOHNSON: After playing with him at the Showplace [in 1960], basically Mingus was out of my life for about eleven years. Then one day he came into the office that I have, an arranger's and copying office in [Emile] Charlap's office on Forty-eighth Street. He walked in one day last September [1971], and said that Max Roach had sent him up there, so he could find an arranger.

And we chatted awhile and he asked me if I was an arranger. I said I was. He said, "Well then, I want to talk to you about something." So then he promptly opened his briefcase and pulled out all these scraps of music and different things he had, and we went into the back room and began to talk about writing the album.

It was a stunning situation. I was not prepared for that kind of thing. And it has been marvelous. It's been frustrating, confusing, everything. You know, you can't deal with Mingus without running the gauntlet of emotions. But, in general, I have been very excited about the whole project. To begin with, it was exciting to work on a bona fide jazz album again. I mean, my association with jazz has been writing jazz-oriented arrangements for the Mort Lindsay Orchestra or the Doc Severenson band or something like that, and writing arrangements of "Mack the Knife" for singers. I mean, it has been a peripheral kind of work. So to really get both feet firmly planted on such a totally jazz experience was really refreshing. I mean it revived my whole spirits.

GOODMAN: How many records like that come out every year, or even every five years? I mean, *Children,* that's a major statement.

JOHNSON: No question about it. In a sense I've had a sort of historical wonder. A little part of myself is looking at this whole experience in its historical perspective, you know.

GOODMAN: Teo thinks of it that way. I interviewed him yesterday and he's impressed with the fact that they've done some kind of milestone.

JOHNSON: Oh, yeah, I am sure he does. And there isn't any question about Mingus's historical significance. He is such an important figure. He just is such a catalyst for music. For example, 6/8: there wasn't any jazz 6/8 being played until "Better Get Hit in Your Soul."

GOODMAN: Really?

JOHNSON: No, that was the first, the beginning of the whole 6/8 feeling. Now it's just a common part of our jazz and also rock and pop experiences. But that was the first time anybody did that. I mean, it was a gospelly kind of device before. But to make a jazz composition based on that in such a compelling way as "Better Get Hit in Your Soul" just transformed everything overnight. All of a sudden everybody was into 6/8. And that record did it, single-handedly.

And that's not the first time Mingus has had that kind of effect. I mean he was writing polytonality, he was writing pedal tones, and using so many devices long before they were current, like writing in modes. . . .

GOODMAN: On the *Children* album, how much of that did you actually arrange?

JOHNSON: All but three [pieces]. "Hobo Ho" is Mingus's own arrangement, which was dictated to Bobby Jones, who actually wrote it out. But Mingus, in effect, sat down and did the whole thing.

GOODMAN: The album got kind of botched up with the editing and so forth, as I understand.

JOHNSON: Well, I am not thrilled about the editing. I just think it was capricious. The music was also terribly difficult to record. We spent about a day and a half on "Hobo Ho." Well, a day and a quarter, maybe four hours altogether, four and a half hours on that one piece. And it goes on in layers.

Mingus is suspicious of the devices that arrangers use to make music play easily. He thinks people are trying to charge him for more pages of orchestration. When he writes himself, he will have a thing repeat eight times and, with directions written out, there is more English to read than there are notes: "Second line, play this," "Third time, lay out," and "Fourth time, ad lib on the beat." And everybody's part is covered with dialogue. It's just an amazingly confusing document.

People just lose it: "How many times do you repeat that?" and "How many times have we gone through that?" There are entrances in there in which somebody will come in with a figure on the down beat and somebody else will come in on the second beat with the same figure, and somebody else will come in on the third beat with the same figure. It is just layers of music. And people were just losing track.

So, as conductor I was up there and, I mean, it is not a thing that you conduct like Leonard Bernstein. My main function was keeping track of everybody, letting them know where they were at any given time. So I was counting frantically, you know. If somebody played a particularly energetic entrance off the beat some place, the tendency was to go with that, you know. It was a pain. It was a difficult thing to do.

It is a brilliant piece, but it needs editing. Not the same kind of editing that Teo did, which is done after the fact, and Teo was trying to make as exciting a piece out of it as he could, considering the difficulty we had in writing it down. But Eddie Bert, for example, who is a very enthusiastic player, just loves to play—

GOODMAN: Is he playing on it?

JOHNSON: Yeah, he's on the date.

GOODMAN: Why in the hell they didn't put the personnel on the liner notes? That just bums me out. All the great people they had playing, James Moody and—

JOHNSON: I know, but the one who decided not to put all that information in—he will kill me for saying it—was Mingus. I was there when he decided not to put it in. Apparently, he did not want it known how many people were in the band at different times and on different dates, you know. He was the one who approved the notes and all that business, and he decided to just credit soloists. And he left some of them out. He fired off a telegram to Columbia accusing them of being prejudiced about musicians for not putting all the people in there, but he's the one who decided not to do it. As I say, I was there when he made the decision. It would have taken up half the insert on the album to list everybody who was on there. There was an enormous number of people.

GOODMAN: Well, I missed that, I really did. With that caliber of band.

JOHNSON: Oh, I did too. As I say, there were great players in those bands and they worked very hard to make the music happen. They should have gotten some credit for it.

Anyway, two of the pieces had no music available—none, not even a lead sheet. They were on a very poorly recorded album that somebody had made at UCLA after the great [1964] Monterey concert that Mingus had done. That was one of his really creative periods and as great as that [Monterey] album was, there was a lot of music that never got recorded. His output was enormous at that point in his life.[3]

And so there was a lot of music in that [UCLA] album that had never been released by anybody, and Mingus . . . just felt the music should be played. So we considered several things in doing that. [One was] the instrumentation that we needed to play "The Chill of Death"—which

Mingus had written years and years before, in the late '30s, like 1939. I think Ted Nash had something to do with helping Mingus then. They were friends at that time and Mingus told me once that Ted Nash helped him orchestrate it, gave him some advice and looked his score over, something like that. It is a very ambitious orchestration, but it was done years and years ago and he never had gotten the opportunity to record it. But I think that they did play it: Ted Nash assembled an orchestra in Los Angeles back before 1940, I think, and they played it once.

So "The Chill of Death" had been dormant since that time. He wanted to record it and it called for six basses plus Mingus. [On the *Children* date] we actually had three jazz bass players and three classical bass players. The jazz bass players were Richard Davis, Ron Carter, and Milt Hinton. And then there were three legit bass players also, and they were all playing arco. It is interesting in that company that the concertmaster for the bass section was—there was no question among the basses [about] who was the concertmaster—it was Richard Davis. Whenever something had to be decided they turned to Richard, and he let them know what was happening.

So, there were a lot of woodwinds, ten woodwinds. Just four brass: two trumpets, a trombone, and bass trombone. Two percussion and rhythm. The most fascinating instrument in the orchestra for me was the contrabass clarinet, and having a contrabass clarinet to write for was so luxurious. Danny Bank played it so fantastically that I went apeshit with it. You can hear that contrabass clarinet all the way through "Shoes of the Fisherman's Wife."

GOODMAN: I always thought it was a bass clarinet.

JOHNSON: No, it is a contrabass clarinet, and it has that low G-flat on it. So the piece has a G-flat tonality at the very outset and you can use the lowest note on the contrabass clarinet at the beginning and end of that opening section. And the basses are bowing along with that, and there's a chance to really exploit the low sonorities. It is a very light orchestra as far as brass is concerned. There are only four brass. So a lot of climaxes that I might have liked to have gotten were limited by the number of brass players I had to deal with.

But still, there was a very interesting orchestration problem. And then I had to [get] the music off the tape or off this old record, which had been edited somewhere along the line, just to take out mistakes, I guess, and sometimes it was just capricious. There were little things left out—you [knew] there had to be something in between and you had to figure out what in heaven's name was going on. So I had to fill in a lot of holes, which [are] very difficult to hear. [The original record of] "Clowns" was particularly difficult to hear because of all the lines going on. It was just a question of writing down the first two lines that came in and then turning them off and concentrating on the next line, and then concentrating on the lines after that. I am sure I could not possibly have heard it all right but, as it turns out, I did. It was a perfect transcription.

GOODMAN: Tell me again about how you lightened up the texture—or whatever you did—and then how Mingus would cloud it up again in the overdubbing.

JOHNSON: Well, I obviously was not Charles Mingus, and [not] operating at the density that he deals at, but as a goal—considering you had almost legit instrumentation for that piece ["Clowns"], and that all these were very linear pieces—my goal was to *clarify*. I used a lot of legitimate scoring devices; it's scored more like a legitimate piece than a jazz piece in order to make everything sing, all the lines sing, make it as transparent as I possibly could.

I think it's successful. I think it worked very well from that point of view. But then in the overdubbing process and the process of editing, Mingus frequently clouded it up, increased the density deliberately. He went in and began to mix his huge cauldron of sounds together. And by adding things like double solos, for example, and sound effects and all kinds of other things, he put a lot of that back in again. He thrives on that kind of texture.

GOODMAN: And I thought that's where the album could be criticized, in fact. It's a little heavy.

JOHNSON: I am surprised, considering how volatile the dates were at times—not volatile in the sense that Mingus was volatile, but that there was a lot of tension in the air because the players recognized that a great deal was expected of them in a three-hour recording date. A piece like "Shoes of the Fisherman's Wife" should easily—I mean it is a long piece, and it should have easily been allotted a three-hour date by itself. We recorded that and "The Chill of Death" in the same date. I mean, I think we went a half hour overtime.

GOODMAN: That's a lot to ask.

JOHNSON: That's a lot to ask. The album had also grown. The initial premise was that Mingus was going to have about a twelve-piece band, and he kept coming up to Teo, talking to him and coaxing him—first of all, to do "The Chill of Death" and then coaxing him that we needed another piece to fit that instrumentation. Eventually there was a third piece too. So Teo felt he had to cut down and left one clarinet out of the instrumentation of "The Chill of Death" when he had it copied. Mingus had the old score he'd written way back when, but Teo decided not to double the clarinet in it, you know, to save a man.

And Mingus was offended by that. He could hear the absence of the one clarinet player. He was running around during the recording session: "I am not hearing something, there is something missing." He finally found out it was one of the clarinets that was supposed to be in there. There were ten woodwinds, and there were supposed to be eleven of them. For that one clarinet, he made Teo do it all over again. They took the piano piece of Mingus's that somebody had transcribed for him, and Alan Raph did a brilliant job of orchestrating. But that was a legitimate problem, a legitimate type of orchestration. He really did a nice job on expanding and opening up that piano piece and making it work.

. . . At the [*Children*] date, Columbia fucked up a little in not giving more thought to making the musicians comfortable in dealing with this very complex music. And they were so concerned about getting separation and a fantastic sound, and then they *still* fucked up. I mean, can you imagine in a studio with all those instruments and a big orchestra, and they use overhead boom mikes to record the six basses? Overhead fucking boom mikes! We got so much bleed into those microphones that you couldn't turn the basses up without getting everything else in the orchestra blinding you in the face. So the only time the basses really sing is when nothing else is going on.

There is one voicing, in "Shoes of the Fisherman's Wife," that I wrote—the six basses in *divisi* [the section plays more than one note]—which I never heard anybody do before. I decided it would certainly sound warm and Richard could certainly play up high enough in the cello register, so I could get a very warm sonority out of the six basses. Once the others got over the confusion of never having seen it before, and how to divide their parts up—Richard and I finally just said, "All right, you play this, and I'll play the top note, and you play the next ones." They just divided the music up, made the *divisi* up. We had to turn that way the hell up, all the way to the top of the gain—and we could do that only because nothing else was going on except the alto playing a little cadenza—so it was an open place.

But most of the time the basses are lost, as far as really being an important sonority in the orchestra. And imagine having a section of six fucking boss bass players in that studio and to hear what they were doing in the studio, just to hear the sound that the six basses got in the studio. And it's just lost on the record. I mean, that sonority was so warm and rich.

GOODMAN: Jesus, Columbia is usually very careful.

JOHNSON: Well, but they are not used to these demands. Also, one of the bass players, I heard, afterwards objected to having his bass miked on the instrument. That's how they should have done it. They should have had separate bass mikes on the instruments for every one of those basses. There is no reason why they couldn't have done that. Somebody objected, apparently, and so the engineers—I don't know if they just didn't care or what—for some reason, they had mixing problems in recording that music.

[In] "Hobo Ho," for example, the separation, particularly in the rhythm section—having Dannie sitting in an isolation booth way the fuck in back and not being comfortable with earphones on. When he put his 'phones on, trying to record with the headphones, he got claustrophobia practically. His eyes started rolling around in his head. Just having that noise coming at him in his ears, he just couldn't contend with that. So consequently he was very, very uncomfortable. He still sounds marvelous on the record. I mean, the rhythm feels good very frequently. But the recording process was made much more uncomfortable by the discomfort caused by the layout that we were forced to contend with.

GOODMAN: Well, that's a whole other subject, but I think that isolation thing is just incredible—for most jazz. Sixteen-track recording for a small jazz group is just crazy.

JOHNSON: I know it. Well, people are willing to sacrifice some of the feeling to get an aural sound that will pop your ears out, if they can grab you by a so-fantastic presence, they feel that they have gained more than they have lost.[4]

GOODMAN: I don't even think it works out that way.

JOHNSON: It doesn't work out that way. Well, I think the sound in the album is not nearly as stunning as it should be, considering the resources we had to deal with. I think the problems in mixing were enormous. We were constantly at the top of the gain. It was a question of, "What do we take down in order to make this heard?" So we're constantly subtracting gain from the sound just in order to move something enough to make it audible. It was a compromise all the way through the problem.

GOODMAN: That's terrible. Who played in the bass section again?

JOHNSON: Richard Davis, Ron Carter, and Milt Hinton, and then there were three legit bass players. I mean, it was just a delight to see those guys sitting in the section.

GOODMAN: Did they enjoy it? The Philharmonic people?

JOHNSON: Oh, yeah. Everyone really got their kicks. There was some interesting music to play, and it was an unfamiliar role for most of them, and they really enjoyed the novelty of it. It was a very exciting thing. Recording "Shoes" was a joy in every way, almost every way. The recording process for that—the initial problem of getting people to understand what was called for, you know. I mean, what the music required. But that piece just played beautifully, played beautifully. There was a sense of like being in church, a feeling in the recording studio when that was going down was very, very awesome. That is one of the few things that worked that well.

GOODMAN: And didn't have to be tampered with so much?

JOHNSON: Well, yeah. But that's just the whole take. I think Teo miked one section where it goes into swing time and just laid it in again, so there were repeats where we didn't repeat it in the original score. But it's one basic track, one take from one end to the other. Whatever tampering was done with it later was to make it more complex—I mean this process of muddying the music up somewhat—well, Mingus's need for layering the music took over after that. But basically it was lovely.

GOODMAN: What's the story of the title?

JOHNSON: "Shoes of the Fisherman's Wife"? Actually, the title refers to the pope. 'Cause he thinks the pope is a faggot. I don't know where he got the fisherman reference but I hear it has to do with . . . *Shoes of the Fisherman* was a novel. And so there is a homosexual reference to the pope in that. Among other things.

GOODMAN: I've got to ask him about that.

JOHNSON: Yeah, well, that's only one part of it.

GOODMAN: There has got to be a whole cluster of meanings.

JOHNSON: Oh, no title has a simple meaning. The clowns—"Don't Be Afraid, the Clown's Afraid Too," for example—on a superficial level you listen to that and it's not circusy music. It goes into a 3/4 part, *do-ba-daba-da, do-ba-daba-da,* and until it goes into that section it's not circusy music at all. It's a very sophisticated music. The clown reference is a comedic point, the humor in it. There is a second meaning to that. But Mingus has always referred to himself as a clown. I mean, he has done a number of clown pieces. Mingus has always referred to himself as a number of things, as the Baron Mingus and any number of things. When he had a big band back in the late 1930s he called himself Baron Mingus. So one of his other roles is a clown. In a sense he's reassuring everybody not to be afraid of him, that he's as afraid of them as they are of him, with all the bluster.

"Us Is Too" sounds like a grammatical error. It really is a very complex title. I asked him about how to spell *Too,* whether it's "two" or "too," and he wouldn't tell me. I decided arbitrarily to spell it "too" on the part. But it could be something referring to his relationship with Sue, which a number of pieces refer to. "Hurricane Sue" was initially a [Mingus] reference to her temperament to some extent. Then "The Eye of Hurricane Sue"—he decided he wanted to add *The Eye Of* and then he was going to have it spelled "Eye." Then he got into the ego thing, the "I" of Hurricane Sue—meaning her id. So there are layers in those titles. *Us Is Too,* for example, has to do with "we are a couple"—also an affirmation of his status as a man in a society that has denied him.

GOODMAN: That's what I was thinking about when you said "Too."

JOHNSON: And then there was also reference to "U.S." too. Like the U.S. is two armed camps, two something? So many layers in just that simple three-word title. Bill Cosby [as MC for the *Friends* concert] made some reference that Mingus should have consulted with his English teacher before writing that title, which just missed all the implications except for the most superficial ones. It sounded like a grammatical error to him.

GOODMAN: I remember, he did say that.

JOHNSON: And so just the layering of the titles alone. Also, the "Shoes of the Fisherman's Wife," for example, has a folk origin too. Apparently, there is some sort of source for that which comes out of folklore. In other words, there is some saying Mingus can remember which has to do with sandals; but the title was initially slippers.

GOODMAN: Isn't that what it is?

JOHNSON: Isn't it sandals? Is it jive-ass slippers?

GOODMAN: Slippers. Yeah.

JOHNSON: Then even I'm confused, because it was originally called the "Shoes of the Fisherman's Wife Ain't No Jive-Ass Sandals." So that was one of the changes that went down in coming up with the title. I remember debating about that when we were mixing the tune. Yeah, so slippers finally turned out to be the thing. But it refers to the working man's wife who can't afford slippers.

GOODMAN: Oh, this is beyond the pope thing.

JOHNSON: Right. As I say, it's an insight into the man.

Well the funny part of it was the "Shoes of the Fisherman's Wife" had another title on that UCLA concert. It wasn't called that at all. [It was "Once upon a Time There Was a Holding Corporation Called Old America."] He makes an announcement on the UCLA concert to the effect that the title might get him in trouble in some way with the authorities. That there was something subversive about it.

But whatever meaning Mingus read into that as being subversive in some way existed only in his own dark imagination someplace. There was nothing that anybody could find offensive in the title. But he found some dark meaning somewhere in there that was obscure to everybody. And he made some remark that he was going to call it that even though it got him in trouble with the FBI.[5]

· · ·

Sy and I also talked about the *Mingus and Friends* concert, which came after the *Children* recording, building on much of that music with some of the same players. The concert—to promote *Children* and *Beneath the Underdog*—was part chaos, part genuinely fine music.

· · ·

GOODMAN: At the concert, why was Mingus conducting half the time?

JOHNSON: No, he wasn't really conducting. Teo was conducting but Mingus was cajoling and directing vocally. He gets into the process. He just gets turned on and will just as easily yell at Teo or tell Teo what he wants as anybody else. The conductor isn't sacred, as far as Mingus is concerned. He's just another tool that Mingus is using to get his directions across. So it's not uncharacteristic for him to react that way.

Also, it's another way of making the density greater. In concerts they were supposed to be using guest players in the band—and the orchestra was supposed to be a lot smaller for the concert than it turned out. But he hired Roy Eldridge, and then Roy couldn't make it so he got John Faddis to play his part. Also, there were supposed to be two trumpets in the band.

[Mingus] ran across another trumpet player that he had used once and invited him down to play some solos, and the next thing we know we had four trumpets. Once they showed up he wanted them to play all the time.

The saxophone section really got out of hand. The book was supposed to be written for two altos, two tenors, and a baritone. And so Teo invited Gerry Mulligan to come down and play a solo—two solos with the band. They were going to have Lee Konitz featured as a guest star. And [Mingus] wanted Charlie McPherson to be featured in a small-band setting outside of the regular orchestra. But once everybody got there, he had them all sit down and play.

There were eight saxophones suddenly playing five parts. And two baritones in particular can just overblow a whole band. So, the whole thing got out of balance; it was a terrible task to try to get the thing back in perspective again. Because we had all these extra people, and he hired an extra bass player, who was really the biggest problem of all. Milt Hinton's a great bass player but they were on opposite—I mean, Mingus was out in front and Milt Hinton was in back by the drums—and they just couldn't even hear each other in the concert.[6]

GOODMAN: I couldn't hear Milt Hinton. I mean, I had a moderately bad seat, but I couldn't hear him.

JOHNSON: There was a lot of confusion, muddying up even the rhythm section. Once they were all there, Mingus wanted to use them all. All the time. He gloried in all those extra players. And finally I started to write the music and realized I had to contend with all those extra people, so I began to write parts for them.

But one thing I really wanted to tell you is a lovely illustration of Mingus's thinking. There is a whole section at the end of "Little Royal Suite" [the piece written for Roy Eldridge] which, at the rate he orchestrates, he would simply not be able to get down on paper. So he called me up two days before the concert, something like that, and I had to rush over there, and he gave me an idea of what he wanted for that section. There were three different sections that he didn't have time to finish. But he knew what he wanted and it was a question of his giving me a few melodic ideas here and there, and a textural idea here and there.

Finally, for the closing section of that, the blues, that slow blues, he had the saxophone vamp all figured out. The rhythm and the saxophones were playing this augmented ninth chord, a D-flat augmented ninth chord. Every conceivable cluster of—just a dense structure with Gerry playing an extra bass figure which was kind of improvised. But this texture of those seven saxophones was just *bluuaaa,* this thick texture.

And he sent me home to write that and he told me he would think of something for the brass to play. He had an idea in mind for the brass. Finally, we were at the point where Paul Jeffrey was over there copying parts. As fast as I was finishing, Paul would take the pages from me and start copying them because we were in an emergency. We just had to get the music done. Like Duke Ellington, Duke works the same way.

And then the phone rang suddenly and Mingus said, "Listen to this." And he played—first of all, we had a vamp with that D-flat augmented ninth chord—and then he played this *wa-wa,* he was singing one of the lines and he played this on the piano to me. It was just, *wa—wa—wa— wa,* everything going against that. And it was so beautiful, it was so right for it, that I was standing there and tears started to run down my cheeks. I just started to cry. It just struck some place in me.

There were tears running down my face and everybody was saying, "What's the matter?" They thought I was going to die or something. I was so struck by that I just stood there with the tears going down my face, and it was so beautiful. And so I climbed on my bicycle and pedaled like hell over to Mingus's house so I could get all this down.

GOODMAN: What was the humming bit? The brass part that he was doing?

JOHNSON: Yeah, he was going *wa—wa—wa—wa,* singing one of the lines and playing the other that he had written. And so when I got over to his house—on the phone he only had two parts there; he was singing one of them and playing like a third thing on the piano. By the time I got over there, twenty minutes later in the middle of the night, around two A.M., he had filled it out. He made a whole voicing out of it, with the trombone going in contrary motion to the trumpets who were coming down.

The chord had very few tones in common with a D-flat. It had, for example, instead of the dominant seventh note in it, he had a major seventh note in it. So he had a C-flat in the saxophones and a C-natural in the trumpets. And also in the trombone as a matter of fact. And he had an E-flat in against that, and he had the ninth and the flat ninth in it. And then at the very top he had a D-natural, and *none of those things have any business being in there,* but he does it one note at a time. He's following the thing that he sang to me first on the phone. He heard that and he found it on the piano and then, one note at a time, he would find another line.

He doesn't care, the rules didn't mean a goddamn thing to him. He's depending on his instincts. In a fit of creativity, he was, like, playing me the next note. And if he was one of those guys who sat down and said, "Well this is what it's supposed to be," and went from there, he would never have found it. But he just did it instinctually and wasn't at all offended by the fact that it had no right to work. There was no reason for it to work. And some people who were at the concert told me that section stood the hackles on the back of their necks when it happened. It was just such a right thing to happen, but it broke every rule that I had ever heard of. Why did it work? I don't know.

GOODMAN: Bobby Jones said that he breaks every goddamn rule of composition he's ever heard, and it works.

JOHNSON: I want to show you something while you're here. This is a score, a series of ballads he wrote all at one time. That's "Weird Nightmare," which he once recorded—but have you ever seen anything as dense as that? I mean that's really—you can't write any denser than that. That's typical of Mingus's orchestration. The complexity of it is awesome. And two of the ballads that we did in the concert were exactly like this. And understanding the general orchestrating of that music at the very outset was staggering. "Eclipse" was one, and what was the other one?

GOODMAN: That's a great piece.

JOHNSON: Yeah, it works beautifully. I mean once I understood him and knew how to distribute that music and filled it in—in other words, like where the texture needed broadening, reinforcing, and all that business. But it took me longer to understand those ballads and to make an arrangement out of that stuff than . . .

GOODMAN: That score is awesome. I've never seen anything like that.

JOHNSON: I'm in the process of making an orchestration of that now for the Mercer band.

Teo Macero on Producing Mingus

Teo had a lot to say, and not just about Mingus. I heard details of how he recorded the *Children* album and the *Mingus and Friends* (Philharmonic Hall) album, which was in the works when we spoke, in June 1972. He also pontificated at some length about his role as a producer, the need to

FIGURE 3.   Mingus and Teo Macero in the editing room at Columbia's Thirtieth Street studios, 1971. Photo by Sy Johnson.

guide musicians, and the negativity of know-nothing jazz critics (see chapter 8).

The interview wasn't all self-promotion by any means. Mingus and Teo went way back, and in fact if it weren't for Teo, there might not have been either a *Children* album or the *Mingus and Friends* concert. His comments on Miles Davis and the other "strong men" of jazz were really part of the man's persona. I thought he had absorbed their strengths into his view of himself, in a way. Teo produced most of Miles's middle and later albums— some done well, some not, as with Mingus.

We talked in the control room and offices of Columbia's Thirtieth Street studio in New York, one of the great recording venues in the history of the music. Rusty Payne, Teo's engineer and right hand, was present, fielding phone calls and adding an occasional comment.

. . .

MACERO: Well, our association goes back to, I think, 1950 or 1951 when I first got a call from him to do a date. He had heard that I played saxophone, and he wanted a saxophone player so he called me up. I went down to see him, and we've been associated ever since—at different levels and at different times. During the '50s, when he was done heading up Debut Records, and I made an album for Debut and he performed on it, we then made a lot of albums for various companies: Savoy, Jubilee, and some other labels. Then we did some things for Atlantic.

Mingus did a thing called *Pithecanthropus Erectus,* you remember that? When it was ready to come out, he needed somebody to overdub the squeaky notes on top that we had been associated with for a couple of years. So I went back and did that, overdubbed a lot of things for him. Then I came to Columbia and he did two albums for us here, *Mingus Dynasty* and *Mingus Ah Um.*

GOODMAN: Which you just reissued?

MACERO: We reissued them, right. All through that period I was still working with him as a musician. We played many concerts and record dates together. He finally came back about a year ago, at which time I did his new album called *Let My Children Hear Music.*

We were friends but didn't associate for a number of years because he went his own way and I went mine. But all during the '50s, early and late '50s, we were pretty close. We practically lived together. Wrote music together, performed it, did concerts together. We started the Jazz Composers Workshop, which he later took over. We started with Teddy Charles and the other guys. They became a nucleus for a lot of serious jazz concerts here in New York City.

Well, after the workshop he just sort of went his own way and then he was off the circuit. We did Newport, after that he did the Protest Festival in 1960 [see chapter 6], and I wasn't with him then.

GOODMAN: And then the Monterey Jazz Festival in '64?

MACERO: Yes, Monterey in '64. After that, he just sort of laid low until about two years ago, when he did his own records, his own thing, because nobody would record him. I don't know whether it was his own choosing or not, but then all of a sudden he showed up at Columbia one day and asked if I would produce him again. I said, "Why not, it was fun before."

GOODMAN: This is the *Children* album.

MACERO: Yeah. Some of it was chaotic and [we had] a lot of problems but, making a great album, one has a lot of problems. There are no short cuts for something like that.

GOODMAN: Were you happy with the results?

MACERO: I think the results are terrific. I don't think they could have done any better if we had stayed there for a month. The band got together and it made an impact. The people who pick up on the record dig it and they all think it's a great record, probably the best record Mingus has ever made. We shoved some things around here in the editing room a great deal with Charles.

GOODMAN: Yeah. Was he in on that, or did you do most of the editing and mixing?

MACERO: Well, he was here, but we did the mixing. You know, he contributed some things and we had some ideas and we just kicked them back and forth with Rusty, the engineer, and we all sort of worked on the same project together. It was a cooperative thing, and the end result is a terrific album.

Then we did the *Mingus [and Friends]* at Philharmonic Hall.

GOODMAN: Yeah, when is that going to come out?

MACERO: Well, we are working on it; it will probably be out for August [1972], released in August.[7] We have half of it finished but it's a gigantic project. Again, you know, you just can't go in and mix it and put it right out because it takes a lot of time and a lot of editing. A lot of thought goes into it. At least the records we make here, that Rusty and I make, a lot of thought goes into it. We just don't put them together helter-skelter. When you listen to them ten years from now they sound just as good ten years from now as they do now. We did *Sketches of Spain*—

GOODMAN: You did *Sketches of Spain?*

MACERO: Sure. You listen to the Brubeck albums. They say the quality of those records [is] fantastic, the editing and balance and performances are first rate. If you compare the records we made in the last ten to fifteen years here at Columbia with other companies, so to speak, with other jazz artists, the difference is night and day. The Columbia collection of jazz records will outlive all the others. I think they are superb records because we spend a lot of time on them.

GOODMAN: No, it shows, definitely.

MACERO: We just don't take the first take and put it out. It's just not that way. We fight with [the artists], we argue with them, we have all kinds of battles here, which is part of the function of a producer.

GOODMAN: How long did the *Children* album take to do?

MACERO: Eight or ten sessions, I don't know. I could go back and check it; eight or nine sessions. A lot of sessions, a lot of money, a lot of hours, and a lot of editing. Mostly the money was spent in the editing room because to mix and to cut sixteen tracks and to get them in shape, we took things from different sessions to different studios. From Thirtieth Street to Studio B, [we] had to cut them and intercut them and everything else. Some of the things we didn't think would work. But working it all out, we changed speeds, we did everything here. We created new sounds for *Let My Children Hear Music.* We created a whole montage of jungle sounds and hurricane sounds for "Hurricane Sue." That took us quite a bit of time.

GOODMAN: It's very difficult music, hard to play those pieces.

MACERO: Yeah. And it's a funny thing, when you listen to it, it comes off and it sounds good.

GOODMAN: How is it selling?

MACERO: Not great. You know, I don't know whether the music is too far ahead of the consumer or what, but it's just like when *Mingus Ah Um* came out, it was the same way. Now "Fables of Faubus" is very famous and "Porkpie Hat" and the other things that he did are all things he does now; fifteen or sixteen years later he's starting to do them in concert. Which goes to show you that the effort and the initial impact is one of gigantic importance and it lasts. It's not like a pop record, on the market today and gone off the market tomorrow. I just don't have it in my heart to make those kind of records because it takes us a long time. Pop records are pop records. These to me are not pop records, they're not jazz records, they're not classical records. They're collectors' records of great performances.

GOODMAN: Mingus would never probably be party to [a pop record] anyhow, would he?

MACERO: No. It was the same thing with Brubeck. In Brubeck's records are a lot of the things he never played in concert. A lot of the things, the studio things, were so difficult and were so well done that to play them [in a concert] was almost an impossibility.

GOODMAN: The Miles stuff is that way?

MACERO: Well, Miles is different than the other people. He plays in concert what he records. He gets it together either in the concert first and then comes in and records it, or records it first and then takes it on the road and plays with it. So the stuff you hear him do he has on records. His concerts he has on records, and vice versa. That's the difference with Miles, because his band is a smaller unit and he can do that.

But Mingus is of great musical importance on the whole musical scene. His contribution—whether you like it or don't like it is immaterial. He's contributed a great deal of difficult music and good music and music that will live forever. Why do people, all of a sudden after so many years, come to Philharmonic Hall to hear him? You couldn't buy a seat for that concert.

GOODMAN: I was there. Wasn't that incredible?

MACERO: Yeah. We don't even know yet whether the performance was great or not. Only the proof is in the tapes and we haven't finished with them. Once we get it all organized, then we will let the critics and the people decide. But I think it will be of gigantic musical importance. Because a lot of things happened that night that never happened before and never will again. He's contributed great music, and he's a great musician, a little difficult at times. All creative people are very difficult this way.

GOODMAN: Do you think he is headed for any kind of breakthrough in his career at this point? Do you think he's really going to achieve some sort of greater popularity, I should say, than he has?

MACERO: Well, I think with proper guidance—I don't mean from a studio point of view, but I think from a business point of view and everything else—I think he could have it all over again. It could happen big, because the kids dig him, they dig what he's doing in terms of music, and they get excited about watching him and they get excited about hearing his music.

GOODMAN: You should have seen that audience last night in the studio [the WNET taping; see Introduction].

MACERO: I know, I have seen it. I have seen the reaction that the kids have to him, and I think it's just a question of time. With careful guidance and careful preparation—like, you just don't go in and do a concert without one rehearsal; you go in and to do a concert, you got to have ten or fifteen rehearsals to make it.

GOODMAN: Well, that's what struck me about that concert. To be frank, it's awful tough music to play.

MACERO: Yeah, well, we had a lot of rehearsals. But guidance, in terms of limiting oneself to a few pieces as opposed to a lot of pieces, may be doing a few great performances rather than doing lousy performances of a lot of pieces—not to say this happened in the concert, but I think Mingus and all our tendency is to do so much.

I know myself when I'm going to try to write a movie score—Jesus Christ, I write so goddamn much music that it's never-ending. I think, "How can I possibly record all this music for a five-minute film? I have written enough to last an hour." Then after that, you record it all and whatever you don't like, you throw away. You keep just the cream. But you can't do this in concert.

GOODMAN: I thought it was too ambitious, I really did. He tried to give a retrospective of his whole career. That bothered me because I thought, you know, these guys are playing their hearts out.

MACERO: It was a retrospective concert, but maybe it covered too much ground for the limited amount of time we had up there.

I think concerts should be small in terms of time, less time. Instead of a three-hour concert, have an hour-and-a-half concert, but a real tight concert. I think this is what's going to happen with Charles. I think it happens with Miles. Funny thing about Miles: when he gets tired, he stops. When he doesn't think he's making it, he just cuts out. Or if somebody is not making it and is playing a solo he will jump in, and Mingus will do the same thing too.

But when you get an organization of fifteen-sixteen guys and you've got charts—brother, you got problems, and you got a conductor, like me. The dialogue that he and I had that night was quite something. Either he's going to be the leader, or I am going to be the leader. Somebody's got to take charge and get everybody together. I thought the feeling of the concert was great. From standing where I was, with all the pitfalls and all the things that went wrong, the impact was tremendous. . . . But I kept saying to Charles, "You've got to be kidding. I never can get through even this piece because it's too long. Rehearsal doesn't give us enough time to make this piece really happen."

So he cut one piece down; we cut some other pieces off. With all of those problems, it's still that we'd like to show the best we have available. But, as I said earlier, with guidance and proper direction, we all could do a better job.

You know, in our relationship with Mingus and anybody else, Miles and Brubeck, there is a lot of trust. They know that you are not going to throw them a curve. You're going to help them because your job is to help people, not to hinder people. My ego doesn't come into play at all. I can't

afford to have an ego. As soon as I get into the studio and start working
with these people, my ego is subservient to theirs.

It becomes a mutual trust. I know Mingus and when he gets on his
high horse, like everybody does, I say, "Gee, come on Mingus, for Christ
sakes. Relax, we're going to make this thing. We're doing this together.
This is a together project. I don't have to conduct the band. I don't need it.
I don't need $130. I don't need ten years of aggravation. I am here just to
help, and if I can help and make it better, I'll be glad to do it."

You see, that day [at Philharmonic Hall] I should have been in the sound
truck instead of conducting the orchestra. A couple of days before the
concert, I tried to put it in shape. I went to the rehearsal and saw what was
happening, and finally Mingus said, "Well, I want you to help me out."

I said, "OK, good, what do I have to do?" I just jumped in there and
started rehearsing the band. I got my crew all organized and my engineers,
had many discussions with them so they knew exactly what they were
doing. I had them all down in the hall and checked everything out before
the concert. I didn't have time to check every little detail, because they all
arrived late to rehearse, to balance up the band for the concert. But I was
there only to help them. And he [Mingus] almost didn't go on that night.

GOODMAN: Really?

MACERO: Oh yeah, he threatened not to go on because somebody had lost
the music and that upset him because it was an emotional experience he was
going through. See, I realized what he was going through because when a
man gives a concert, and he has all his people there—Bill Cosby is there [as
MC], and all his friends are coming to hear him—and I didn't want to upset
him any more. But he was upset when I went on to do the concert.

So I said, "Look, Mingus we're here together, let's make it together.
Goddamn it, you get out there and just play. That's all you gotta do. You
do your thing and I will certainly as hell try to do mine." And we hugged
each other upstairs in the dressing room. We came downstairs and then
we had another go-round because of the excitement of all of this. You
know, when somebody is excited, the least little thing will throw him off.

GOODMAN: Set him off.

MACERO: Set him off. And so I was the majordomo. Finally he just wasn't
going to go on. After we got downstairs—this is interesting—some cat
had upset him backstage and I was running through the music, I had a
dress rehearsal backstage just before we went on. We ran through every
number in the first half of the program, bar by bar, letter A, letter B,

letter C, the solos, and we marked everything and everybody was checking their parts. And some cat just turned him right off and got him all excited.

So then he left and went outside, and the band went on the stage. I say, "Mingus, you are going out there now, with me, and this is it." I remember the guy trying to tell us, "Hey you two guys, you can't get on the stage, the band is on it." I don't know if they thought we were a couple of janitors or something but we had a go-round with the guard just before we went on. I am standing there and I push Mingus outside and I said, "You are on, baby, go."

GOODMAN: And this other guy is trying to tell you to—

MACERO: Yeah, telling us to get off the stage, and we couldn't look out and see what was happening out there! In the meantime our musicians were going out. I was saying, "Well, he's the artist and I am the conductor and you want to throw us out? Good." It was a tense moment. The music came off fairly well. The intensity was there.

And little mistakes, little balance problems, they never bother me. It's the excitement that's created by the audience, the enthusiasm and the charisma of the whole thing that is actually taking place at the moment.

GOODMAN: Oh, that audience was so—I mean you couldn't maybe know this—but that audience was so primed. Jesus, they were just perfect.

MACERO: Oh, yeah. And Cosby was great and everybody was right on it. They all wanted to be part of it, which was really a great tribute to Mingus.

Paul Jeffrey on Working with Mingus

Paul had a long association with Mingus throughout the '70s as copyist, arranger, and occasional performer. He also played tenor, off and on, with Monk through the same period. Later, as a teacher, he became director of Duke University's jazz studies program, and now, as I hear, is retired.[8]

We sat in a noisy raw bar on Seventh Avenue where we talked for well over an hour in June 1972. Paul had recently come off a stint playing with Monk, and I wanted to hear about that. His basic theme about Mingus was his honesty and sense of ethics.

· · ·

JEFFREY: I didn't know Mingus personally, so I called him up and told him I was supposed to get him help [with copying the scores for *Mingus and Friends*, January 1972], but I couldn't get any help and so I would do my best alone. By next rehearsal, which was the next day, I finally got it to him—I guess about twelve o'clock that night—but I would stay up all night and copy all the parts up to a certain point so he would be able to rehearse the whole band. And he did, it worked out. In fact, I finished Friday, and the concert was Friday evening.

GOODMAN: And you were probably ready to die, eh?

JEFFREY: Yeah, I stayed up three whole solid nights. And from there, he asked me to do some other work for him. Then I went out to California for a month, where I worked with Thelonious Monk, and Mingus sent me some music out there to copy. We talked on the phone a number of times, and he told me about the big band for the Vanguard, asked me would I work. I said I could be cajoled to join, and that's how it started.

GOODMAN: I wish I'd heard that Vanguard band.

JEFFREY: It was a very good band, unbelievable. I was talking to Gil Evans last night; he heard it, said it was great.

GOODMAN: What did you think about the *Let My Children Hear Music* album?

JEFFREY: I think it was a very good album, I think it could have been much more successful if Mingus had done all the editing.

GOODMAN: But he willingly gave it over to Teo to do.

JEFFREY: Willingly?

GOODMAN: That's the feeling I get from talking to both of them.

JEFFREY: There is some fantastic music on that album.

GOODMAN: Yes, and it should have been better. Yet he was in on it all the way along, and he approved, I guess, what Teo was doing.

JEFFREY: He had a lot of problems on that album, because some of the tunes were written for specific musicians who didn't do the album. And then, if you do a piece of music with Mingus, I've found that you really have to stay with him, tell him, "OK, you got the score"; or "Gimme the score"; or "Is this what you want? I'll go home and do it." You've got to work with him; this is where a lot of musicians make their mistake. A lot of times he'll tell you something, and you might not get a clear picture, or he might change his mind next day—and this is where a lot of musicians make a mistake.

GOODMAN: You've got to be in constant touch with him.

JEFFREY: You've got to be in constant touch with him. And then when the music comes out, if it's not exactly what he wanted, he gets very bugged.

As with all artists who are doing something and are pressed for time, he might not be the easiest person to work with—because he's agitated and he realizes he has less time than he needs.

GOODMAN: The thing about the album that seemed strange to me was that, for a man who is pretty damn definite about what he wants, he seemed willing to compromise.

JEFFREY: Well, sometimes you have to compromise. There are lots of things going on behind the scenes that an artist—like, he makes a concession here to get this across; it shouldn't happen, but it's business. In order to be a successful businessman, you have to be able to compromise and know when to compromise and when it's advantageous. And I would say that this was an advantageous compromise.

GOODMAN: And there had to be awful problems putting all that together.

JEFFREY: Right. It was a momentous project, with little time, and Teo understands his music as well as any A&R man has understood it, I think. I don't know the man that well. He is an excellent musician and he has been associated with Mingus for many years, and that's what it takes.

They've been associated much longer than I have. But the main thing is to understand exactly where his music is and understand him—that's the main thing, understand him. The errors that have been done were done in interpreting his music. In other words, if he gives you a sketch, a lot of people say, "Well, this sketch is something I can take and add in what I want." Oh, no. His sketches are usually so complete that if you take it and do exactly that, you've got it. See, that's hard enough.

This is something I learned with Thelonious's music—those two persons, *their music is a finished product* [*bangs on table*]. That's it. Because their compositional facility and talent is so great that it's a final thing. It's like if he writes a melody, it might look simple, but that's final, no embellishment on that needed. Anybody who orchestrates for him had better learn this. He might just write a little melody, and you might say, "I think I should add this"—or maybe there's a voicing that is so strong at that particular time. Well, you better not mess with it.

GOODMAN: That must be very hard for a lot of jazz people to get.

JEFFREY: Yeah, to comprehend. Or he might tell you, "Well, do what you feel? I'll leave it open." But you have to think about it: it's open to what? It's open to development but development of that basic theme, not an embellishment. Mingus can play two notes, [or something] like Beethoven's *dah-dah-dah-daah*—simple, but that was the basis on which he developed that [Fifth Symphony]. By itself it's nothing, but it's what's done with it. And that is something that has also sometimes fettered Mingus's music.

GOODMAN: That's why he gets bugged from time to time with what he calls the avant-garde jazz.

JEFFREY: Right. In the beginning of "Taurus in the Arena of Life," he had a simple bullfight call that a chick who was a flamenco dancer sang over the phone to him. [*Sings it.*] Mingus says, "I want that to begin the number." And there's a whole lot of things you can do with that: you can voice it, you can jam up the voicing. But he wanted it to be pure. He said, "Well, the flamenco trumpet players don't play up that high, so I want it in this register." Then as far as voicing, he said, "I want it pure, like an innocent kiss, no harmony, and the reason I want it this way is because if I overload it here, [it will affect] the development further on." He had a call further on, but it was a different call. And he did that first one very simply, and we orchestrated it.

Now somebody who would have gotten this, like played over the phone, might have said, "Maybe I can add something. I can make it sound very big, like a Roman call," and it would have messed up the whole feeling.

Just different things like that. Take one note, and maybe he'll voice a chord and it will be all jammed up. One note is very important. He told one guy in the band, "Look, my main melodies are in my baritone." That's the thing that Duke has, melodies all over the place. So if you add something, you never know where the important part of the music is.

GOODMAN: He wants the control of it, and that's the way it should be.

JEFFREY: Sure. He should have complete control. I think if someone else wants to write what they want to write, they should do it on their own time. One of the most successful alliances was in the things Hall Overton did for Monk. He did the job of orchestrating exactly what Thelonious dictated. You see?

GOODMAN: That was good, yeah. Fine orchestration.

JEFFREY: And Hall Overton is a wonderful writer, but he was able to discipline himself to keep it functional. Actually, it's all mostly laid out for these guys. They just had to make definite in their minds what they want to do. Mingus has a very definite thing in mind of what he wants to do.

GOODMAN: Yeah, the problem is to get that out of him.

FIGURE 4.   Mingus and Bobby Jones during the big band's booking at the Village Vanguard, 1972. Photo by Sy Johnson.

JEFFREY: Well, he'll tell you if you ask him. The main thing is for a guy to submerge his own personality enough to get into the music. And this is something a lot of people don't do or haven't done. And he'll say, "Well, that's not what I wrote."

Bobby Jones on Working with Mingus

Bobby (who died in 1980) was a warm, perceptive tenor player and a fine musician who gave me not only helpful hints on dealing with Mingus but great insights into the man's character and behavior (see his comments in chapter 4). Here he talked, in New York in 1972, about how cuts were made in a piece that was to be played at the *Mingus and Friends* concert, and charged that Teo had done some editing that made the piece unplayable. Since Bobby mentioned that this cut was left off the *Children* album, it must have been "Taurus in the Arena of Life," which was finally included on the 1992 CD version.

.   .   .

JONES: I guess the first twenty, I'd say between twenty and thirty measures, maybe more, were taken out of this thing, and it almost seemed like at random, they had just cut a little piece out and put it over here—

GOODMAN: Oh, really? Rearranged it!

JONES: Oh, it was just terrible, man. Now the reason they're calling me was the Lincoln Center [the first *Friends*] concert was coming up. Now, they had screwed with this thing so much that the beginning of the record sounded nothing like the arrangement. So, they wanted me to listen to the tape and fix the score, adjust the score and the parts, all the parts, so that they would fit all this editing that had been done. Well, it took me fifteen hours to get that straightened out.

When I finally got it straightened out, it was such a Rand-McNally affair that I started to explain it in the rehearsal, and the explanation, even though it was the simplest one I could possibly find, was still so involved that they finally said, "Well, we won't do that one." And we didn't. We haven't played it since. And one reason we haven't played it, is because of that editing that took place. They really screwed it up.

GOODMAN: Well, Charles had a hand in that, obviously. Didn't he?

JONES: Yeah, but Teo is a very persuasive person, he's slick. Plus the fact that if he doesn't like what Charles is doing, all he's got to do is wait until Charles leaves and then do it the way he wants to anyway, which probably happened in some cases. And all that boils down to the fact that—and I'm sure this happens a lot in the recording business—producers who are dealing with someone as creative as Mingus don't really have much to do. Not really. But, they're on the payroll of this company and they've got people peering over their shoulders.

GOODMAN: And their egos are on the line, you know, how to get their hand in.

JONES: And in the meantime, the boss is looking like, "Oh, what's this guy doing to earn his buck?" So they got to do something. Even if it's wrong, they got to do something. [*Chuckle.*] It's terrible. They mess up so many recordings, man. How many times have you heard a jazz recording and the star, the guy whose name is on the cover, you can't even hear him?

GOODMAN: I still don't understand. If Teo is screwing around with Charles's music to the extent that you say, like on that album, even though he may be persuasive as hell, I don't quite see how he—

JONES: How he can get away with it?

GOODMAN: Yeah, how he can get away with it—or, if he really has interfered musically to that extent, how Mingus puts up with it. It can't just be because they're old friends.

JONES: No, it's not, and Mingus has swung on him too though. Well, for one thing Teo didn't do it all that much, and another thing was the manner in which he did it. See, first of all, Mingus didn't write most of that music. He did and he didn't. He sketched it out, then he either gave it to me, Sy Johnson, or Alan Raph, and we did all the work.

GOODMAN: Did Teo do any of the arranging on the album?

JONES: No. Not that I know of.

GOODMAN: Shit, I put that in the ["Acts and Entertainments," *Playboy*] piece because Charles told me that he did.

JONES: Well, it's possible he did. If Charles said he did, then he did. It's quite possible that he did because he's capable of that. But, Teo's been a producer and involved with recording for so long that he can outslick Charles.

For instance, like on "Hobo Ho," there's maybe five or six guys soloing at one time. OK, now Teo, as long as he doesn't fuck with the important voice in Mingus's mind—like if Charles McPherson was soloing, and maybe I was supposed to be heard and James Moody was supposed to be heard and Julius Watkins was supposed to be heard and Snooky Young's supposed to be heard—any one of the rest of us that Teo wants to fuck around with, he can do it, as long as he doesn't—because Charles is zeroed in on one man, you know? You get it?

GOODMAN: OK, I get you. How many tracks did they record on that, do you know?

JONES: I don't know. It's hard to say. Damn near everybody in a twenty-six-piece band had a microphone. Yeah, almost everybody had their own mike. Never saw so many microphones in my life. Looked like a spaghetti factory in that studio.

GOODMAN: When the man in charge, who is really Mingus, loses control—

JONES: That's right, of course he does. No, I may never know to what extent, but I am sure they fleeced Charles quite a bit. The whole setup. Like I say, it's possible. If you are slick with the editing and mixing it's possible to change it around so it would not be noticeable even to a guy like Mingus. Because, when we got into this studio, many times Mingus was hearing the music for the first time. He had no idea what actually was down there on the paper. Sy Johnson knew what was on the paper; I knew what was on the paper. For instance in my score, and it probably worked the same with Sy, I would go to Charles and say, "Charles, you better check this."

"Ah, that's all right."

Then we would get in the studio and he would start screaming at me. I said, "Charles, I told you to check it." [*Laughs.*]

"I can't hear the French horn."

I said, "I told ya, man, you got too much shit going on here." Twelve guys soloing in one pack!

GOODMAN: Yeah, it got too heavy.

JONES: Yeah, it really did.

Dan Morgenstern on Mingus, Children, *and Bobby Jones*

I met Dan Morgenstern before he became director of the Institute of Jazz Studies in Newark in 1976, from which position he recently retired—after serving thirty-five years. The Institute has the largest and most significant collection of jazz materials in the world. Over the years, Morgenstern has written more about jazz than almost anyone, edited *Down Beat* and other jazz journals, and served on countless panels and boards. He's been a producer, writer, lifelong booster of the music, and friend to Mingus.

Here we talked a bit about how Mingus works with his people.

• • •

MORGENSTERN: Bobby Jones, who I assume you talked to, was on the verge of leaving him several times because [Mingus] wasn't working enough. He was working enough for himself but not enough for the men in the band. Bobby said there were all kinds of jobs that he [Mingus] could have had but did not feel like taking. Now I understand he just came back from Boston and he is doing something in New York, and it looks like he's ready to work.

I think with any musicians—jazz musicians especially—if they aren't working it's bad for them. It's very encouraging also that Columbia signed him and, of course, they had problems with the album [*Children*]. He is a perfectionist. Mingus is a peculiar combination of a perfectionist and—I don't know how to put it—someone who always wants to experiment. In other words, he wants it to come out right when he wants it without considering the other elements that are involved. They worked very hard on that album and had a lot of overdubbing sessions.

I think there are some very good things in the album, overall. I mean the album is not a complete success, in my opinion. Considering the problems, it came out well. I could do without the monologue, that sort of thing. You listen to it once and then it loses its effect. But there are some beautiful things there. The concert, which some people did not care for, I enjoyed very much. . . .

When Bobby was working with him, had been working with him for awhile, he found out that Bobby was a good copyist and could write music very well. Once he found that out, he wanted to use him. And he wanted to use him for impossible things, like he would call him up during the night and say, "Come over, I want you to write down some music." He would sit down at the piano and play something and say, "This is the trombone, this is the saxophone, this . . ."

So Bobby tried but then he said, "Look, I can't do this. If you put it on a tape for me and then tell me, then maybe we can do it." But then he [Mingus] gets furious. As good a musician as he is, there are certain things that he just feels anybody should be able to do, just like that, and they can be terribly difficult problems. He's like a child in that way. I don't mean that he is childish, but when he wants something, he wants it to be there right away. The same thing goes for rehearsal of his music. He can be very patient but he can also be terribly impatient with something that doesn't come out the way he wants it to.

GOODMAN: He showed that a little bit last night, although I thought it went pretty well—the rehearsals for his TV show [see Introduction]. Bobby told me that he changed the "Faubus" piece in rehearsal and they had never played it that way before. It was quite different.

MORGENSTERN: Well, he would do that, and that's one thing that makes him the great creator that he is. He can take a piece of music that he has done a hundred times and still make a little change in it and make it come out differently. It keeps his players on their toes. It never becomes a routine thing to work with Mingus.

NOTES

1. One reviewer noted some of the problems discussed below, yet said: "Mingus thanked producer Teo Macero for 'his untiring efforts in producing the best album I have ever made.' From his deathbed in Mexico in 1979 he sent a message to Sy Johnson (who was responsible for many of the arrangements on the album), saying that *Let My Children Hear Music* was the record he liked most from his career." See Brian Olewnick, "Let My Children Hear Music: Review," www.allmusic.com /album/let-my-children-hear-music-mw0000074687.

2. Sy Johnson said in a follow-up interview (2011) that when the entire concert was reissued, "we found the whole thing was recorded in a bad setting and we were first to finally fix it."

3. *Mingus at Monterey* is indeed one of his great recordings, originally issued by mail order on Mingus's own Jazz Workshop label. A subsequent 1968 release, by Saul Zaentz and Fantasy Records, appeared as a double-LP set (JWS 001 and 002) with a separate note by Mingus appealing for funds to "alter [his] deplorable financial condition," which resulted from his 1966 New York eviction (see chapter 10). This set has been issued on CD.

The second Monterey concert, in September 1965, turned out to be a disaster. Sy explained what happened in a comment to me in 2012: "Mingus went back with all this new music and was upstaged by John Handy's group. John had starred with Mingus a year before and Mingus felt betrayed: Handy had a triumphal set that ran over and when Mingus's group was announced, people were already leaving. Charles came out, hurt and offended with nobody paying attention, and he angrily pulled the band off the stage."

But Mingus felt the music intended for that abortive concert needed to be heard, so the following week he brought the same octet into Royce Hall for a concert at UCLA and subsequently released it in 1966 under his own private label. Sy notes, "Maybe three people bought it. . . . The UCLA concert was difficult, as you can hear on the record, but some important music was recorded and it led to *Let My Children Hear Music.*"

In 2006, Sue Mingus released the UCLA concert as *Charles Mingus: Music Written for Monterey, 1965. Not heard . . . played in its entirety, at UCLA* as a two-CD set. This reproduces the two-LP set of the same name that Mingus Enterprises issued (in a pressing of two hundred copies) in 1996. This album was a clear ancestor of *Children,* as it included "Don't Be Afraid, the Clown's Afraid Too" and "Once Upon a Time, There Was a Holding Corporation Called Old America," to be later enhanced as "The Shoes of the Fisherman's Wife Are Some Jive-Ass Slippers." For more information, see Sue's notes to the UCLA set.

4. There's no excuse for the way most studio jazz albums are recorded, and the isolation practice has continued. For example, in a Kenny Barron session done in 1994 by System Two in Brooklyn, with Roy Haynes and Charlie Haden (*Wanton Spirit*, Verve/Gitanes), Kenny's piano was under a blanket and Charlie Haden was relegated to the isolation booth. Nor was the result worth the effort. I have a very good playback system, and the bass is far too heavy, as is typical of System Two efforts of this era. Recording technique makes a big difference, and Columbia should have been held to account for botching the *Children* session, not to mention *Mingus and Friends.*

5. On the UCLA album, Mingus disclaims any political intent—after making a few slyly suggestive remarks.

6. Sy Johnson notes in 2011: "On remix, it was a wonder to hear Milt step up when Mingus floundered, as he sometimes did, and step back when Mingus was up."

7. The two-disc set was not released until 1973.

8. The (rather out-of-date) website for the Duke Jazz Program, plus a bio for Paul, can be found at www.duke.edu/~pjeffrey/.

4 Authenticity: Whose Tribe Are You In?

"I know what music is; it's medicine, man."

Mingus had gotten word that Kenny Dorham was very sick and in the hospital. This was the cue that somehow led him to Dylan, the Beatles and their "borrowings" from American music, phony nicknames and "titles" for musicians, Madison Avenue (one of his favorite targets) and the royalty system, and finally some ideas on what might be an authentic ethnic music for black people.

Then we had talk about attempts of the young to take over the old jazz language, and finally he punned his way into talking about the Cocoanut Grove fire of 1942.

All of this had to do with authenticity and earning your right to be part of a tribe. As the commentaries to this chapter illustrate, Mingus was always testing people, particularly his musicians. Prepared properly, music was the medicine to heal the wounds of the people—and it could not be just any music.

. . .

MINGUS: We should have had a benefit for [Kenny] right then and there and took all that money and given it to him. Should have had the benefit seven months before he got sick, given a benefit for him, all of us showed up, and asked the Beatles to announce this. Or John Lennon—he's got so much money, off of using our music. He could have announced it, got the other little guy to sing, do some bird solos, what's his name? the little guy—[*descending bird-call phrase: dee-dee-bob-o-boo-boo*], them long melodies. He ain't no Beatle; the other one, all by hisself. Johnny something—no, not Johnny, sound like a little girl, he built that kid a race car, he's a folk singer. Wandering melodies, soft, gentle, pussy voice . . . Bob Dylan!

Get a guy like him who's borrowed from certain compositions that he knows he's borrowed from—unless he went to school to study and had someone teach it to him, like the Beatles did. The Beatles should announce our jazz concert—because they copped from us, man, they copped from a lot of other composers. They will introduce it and put that bread into a foundation, man, no taxes.

Because music has made this fucking country survive, man. They can't make us all dogs. When a country starts looking for "titles" for its music, people looking for titles to make it sell, there's something sick. Like right now the latest thing is called "free," next we'll call it "wow," next we call it "panic," then finally "jungle wow," then "cold chaos." Well, you keep naming the thing and you run out of names.

But who's playing? Can that guy play a pretty single-note melody? That is what is important. Then can he play ugly? Then can he play sad? Then can he play happy? But first, can he play in tune? Then, if he can do that, can he play out of tune again if you need him to play out of tune? Can he play quarter tones, or 132nd tones? Not just, can he play weird or free. If he's a musician, all musicians can do *that*. Jascha Heifetz can play free, Yehudi Menhuin.

I tell you what: get Clark Terry, Jascha Heifetz, Duke Ellington, uhh, Pablo Casals, Max Roach, Buddy Collette, and Dizzy Gillespie—and we'll make you an atonal, avant-garde record that will cut everybody. And get one of these Indian guys or one of them Japanese guys with us, one of them cats, they be doing their thing—

GOODMAN: Ravi Shankar—

MINGUS: —and a Japanese girl to play her thing too, and we'll play avant-garde and free. Clark and I were just talking about it with Dizzy last Monday. But see, when you start in with titles to make a living, the title is making it, not your music. I knew a long time ago, and so did Teddy Charles—in fact, it's in the book [the long, original version of *Underdog*], talking about guys and calling them names, like we called a guy "Blockbuster." He said, "Yeah, I'm Blockbuster."

You say James Cedric Allen plays alto saxophone, and people say, "Who is James Cedric Allen?!"

But you say, "Blockbuster," or "Stripper," or "The Ripper" or "Mack the Knife," you know: "Oh yeah? He's *bad*, ain't he?"
[*Laughter.*]

But don't tell me that Cedric Tillery Jones McPherson Mingus plays any music! [*More laughter, including Mingus.*]

Look at your history, man. The Animals, Gorillas, the Monkees—and the Monkees? Ask one of those kids to hum a melody: "Well, how does the tune go, honey?"

GOODMAN: They took 'em out of a TV studio and taught them how to play; the Monkees couldn't play a note.

MINGUS: You know something? The Beatles were trained the same way, and they actually learned to play after five, six years. By the time they learned to play, they made enough money to quit. But our guys, our country's so greedy they stick it out and stick it out.

It's bullshit. I should retire and let my kid into it. I mean the agents over there are better. Maybe I'll go over there and get me an agent, find one of them to book me. In fact, the Beatles' manager was going to take my band, the last time I went to Europe. Yeah, he followed our whole tour with Eric Dolphy. But he died.

GOODMAN: Who, Brian Epstein?

MINGUS: Yeah, that's the one who died, he followed us all over Europe, he and his partner. They were going to book us on a tour and he passed away before he did it. He said that the kids liked us, those kids liked us.

GOODMAN: Here, they never get to hear that music.

MINGUS: Yeah, it's society. Madison Avenue, radio and television. I played a high school and packed it. Little kids, I couldn't believe it.

GOODMAN: I dig what you were saying [to the Italian interviewer] about the kids needing to use the bar [the capo] on the guitar, sliding it around.

MINGUS: Plus now, they don't even stop and tune the guitar different. For a minor key, they'll tune it to a minor, you know, and just play minor chords all the way through the tune.

GOODMAN: At the rock concerts they spend a half-hour tuning up.

MINGUS: But they'll stop in the middle of one tune and retune for a different tune. Make you think they're not using the bar—because they just tune up sharp.

GOODMAN: Is rock music bugging you, or do you just sort of ignore it?

MINGUS: Rock doesn't bug me, I never listen to it. What bugs me is what it's done to the public, how Madison Avenue pushed it. They didn't have to push jazz out, off the radio, off television. . . . They do it because kids will work cheaper than adults. Let's face it, man, a kid will do anything to get on record. They record cheaper, then when their price goes up, the company guys find new ones. So they keep discovering new ones. As soon as they get a little famous they ask for more money.

But you can't tell me the public is so stupid that for seven years they'll just listen to a bunch of words, all those words.

See, I learned this a long time ago when a guy walked up with a nice cellophane package, ribbon around it, and he sold me a dog turd. I bought a dog turd watch. So that's what they're doing: if you wrap the package up and publicize it enough, you can sell a person shit. Madison Avenue knows that, so why sell them Charlie Mingus? I don't even want to be sold now.

But you can bet when it's happening, from what I saw last night [when the band played at Gino's Foxhole, in Philadelphia], it's gonna be the blues, the black blues.[1] That's what says, "Boss man's still got the company store and the package store, and everybody wants to buy a high, so let's go fellas; [*singing*] goodbye baby, gonna get drunk tonight." Yeah that's all it is, man.

GOODMAN: Package Store Blues.

MINGUS: Put that in too, man, not that I'm against communism, but I've seen it in the communist states, and, man, the restaurants look just like a package store. Like how they paint the ceilings, how they paint the place. It's like taking an old barn—which is nice, I'd like to get a barn and fix it up and live in it—but they don't do anything with it, they just put these ugly colors up, and it's cold and in fact I don't see how the whiskey can retain its alcohol percent. There has to be atmosphere to anything. It would kill my eye to walk in a place and buy some juice like that.

GOODMAN: Well, that's what bugged me about that fucking Horn and Hardart where we did the first interview.

MINGUS: Same way, that's what you pointed out to me. Instead of putting up walls with paintings.

Well, let's face it, man, I hate to say it, but jazz itself will never disappear, because it will eventually go into the churches of black people. If this society practices equality, black people will be employed in all music, I mean progressive music and try to develop it as a science, whether the kids know it or not, to become more modernized with the times. That is where the fun is, where the pleasure is, to deal with that kind of music, even if it's alone in your house. That's where the pleasure of life comes, to know you're dealing with that even if you don't get it recorded.

But when that day comes, when people are that free, there'll be jobs in the studio, jobs in the symphony, jobs in jazz or so-called dance bands, and people who get together to remember old-times' sake will probably have something like a blues or jazz music improvisation—that's what jazz is, improvisation—and later, as some guys do, they capture it, like Quincy Jones, they'll take something, somebody's improvisation, and put it together, arrange it. I'm not saying he [Quincy] can't create but he doesn't deal in it right now—at least I haven't heard him.

And it will end up where it came from—for the people by itself without selling—like nobody tries to sell Jewish records or religious music except to themselves. They don't try to take it and force it on nobody. "If you all buy this, well, this shows how we feel." Then the black people alone will support it, the same way they did the Christian music of Mahalia Jackson, that kind of thing. They will buy it to support that direction, for the people's survival.

Like "Eli Eli" [Jewish folk tune] or some of their music—if you take that away from the Jewish people, they'll kill you. And the Armenians and the Greeks, the music they dance by, if you take their dances from them, they'll kill you, man. And that's what you done to the black man, you've taken his dance music from him and you substituted a music to make them buy it, a music that has part of the blues in it, so they say "OK, we'll go for it," but they're getting the inferior product.

If you go back to 1939–40, when they sold what they called rhythm and blues records, [real blues lovers would] run them cats out of business, [the ones] selling that bullshit to the black people. They remember the real music, man. I saw 'em do it last night [at Gino's]. I said, these people are the same age I am, when Bird was living [that was his audience]—plus T-Bone Walker and Jimmy Witherspoon, one of the best blues singers.

And that's what's been taken away, and that's where jazz really belongs. Anybody else wants to come to those churches, like Doris Duke does, they can go and listen to the music. Minimum fee, probably, because the guys who wrote music in the old churches, they got paid for writing, the choir got paid. This is where the music really belongs, it's not meant to be pop like the Beatles, who stole from classical, from jazz, from Bach, Brahms, everybody. And the lyrics ain't said nothing yet, man. Eleanor Fuckin' Rigby . . . I mean, draw me a picture, here's a broad stands in the window, she looks out, [*sings*] "all those lonely people." So what? It's really a hypnosis thing. You know what I think?

There was a movie I saw called *Andys*. These Mayans made some mechanical people that looked just like real people. And everybody expected them to look like the white people that had survived. There were no black people's pictures to go from because they killed off all the black people. And the white man had to have some things to play with 'cause there were no niggers around. And no Puerto Ricans and no Jews and no Italians! No dark hair, no black-haired people at all, not even the pubics!

Now they made a thing looked just like one, but they didn't know they made one that cut themselves 'cause this cat fell in love with one of their broads, you dig?, and as a machine he was supposed to blow the broad, to dump her. They're called andys [androids].

GOODMAN: Like the mountains?

MINGUS: Amos and Andy, that's the way I got it. The girl said, "Look, you're just an Andy." But he said, "You forgot one thing. They goofed the mechanism when they made me. They were short of one thing, love, or they wouldn't have had to make me, 'cause I fell in love with you and there's nothing you can do about that."

She says, "What is love?"

He says, "You look in one of your books"—and that's what she's been doing, reading the books 'cause this is a science fiction movie—"look in your books and you'll find what love is. And you'll find that that's what I got that I can't do anything about and that's why I'm not supposed to destroy you."

And he got her [*laughs*]. He took her from the guy who he was set to kill, he took the whole thing over, 'cause they computed all the facts in his mind and he didn't kill them, he took it with love, man. He got all the broads together—yeah, it was a beautiful film. Television movie, that was what was so weird about it, I thought everyone saw that.

The andys, they took the country back and cleaned it up, and he even learned to make love, and he was supposed to be void of that. But for some reason they built the dick on him evidently—they didn't show it in the film—but they must have built a penis on him 'cause the broad went for him. Or he must have given good head, but he got her. And she said, "You mean this man was supposed to kill me?"

He said, "You open my box and you'll find where I'm supposed to kill you." She opened the box up and found he was really supposed to do her in.

He said, "Put my box, my heart, back in me 'cause the one thing I got, you ain't got." Finally it ends, and something like this happened: I think they killed him and he bled, and he wasn't supposed to bleed. It was a sad thing, man. Now that's a great book, isn't it? I didn't make that up.

But I got a feeling that England is the mother country of a planet where the people came and spread their English-speaking language, and they spread it all about, and even the Americans are their andys, black and white. First the whites. Queen of Virginia—you follow me?

GOODMAN: No.

MINGUS: I think that America, for as much as they think they're free, for the Beatles to be able to come here and take all the millions of dollars away from this country by copying our own music and composers, selling it back to 'em and nobody even suing 'em yet! Plus other groups, the Animals, from England. They came and took our own music and sold it to this country and took the money out and laughed. And retired—and *retired*, man! No musician—Peggy Lee ain't retired yet. The Beatles made millions.

So somebody with a great mind, or who understood the Andys of America, made this [Beatles] machine and said, "They think like this, so every now and then we back up our trucks and take some gold out." These people said, "Look here, man, we'll take four bars of 'Stardust,' turn the first two bars around backwards."

I got proof, man. Hoagy Carmichael'd be rich if he sued the Beatles. George Gershwin's dead but his brother and family wrote some of those tunes. Vernon Duke'd be rich, and the "Nature Boy" guy [Eden Ahbez]. [*Sings that phrase and then a phrase from "Eleanor Rigby," very close.*]

All tunes they stole from here, 'cause English music was completely different, man. I know the forms; you know 'em too. But it was not what they were doing. They stole what we call rock, studied it—not the Beatles did it but some great classical minds from England. "Americans come and take money from France with their jazz stuff. Let's take some money from them for a change."

They sit down and analyze, "How do you take money from these stupid people? With their music or something they'll like or hit on." And they built the Beatles and the Beatles was a machine, and they promised these kids so much money, and they trained them. They were not musicians when they came. They even became musicians in four-five years, they learned.

And they weren't money lovers, like Americans are. They made enough and said, "We quit." You dig? And Peggy Lee and Sinatra, all them cats, work right to the end. They don't take no vacation. Sinatra has retired, but I say that's what they did, man. Working to the grave. And they don't make no room for no young kids. Now some of the young ones like them have run the old ones out. Everybody wants the young faces all the time.

And America runs it different: they take the young kids and as long as they work cheap, for 1½ percent in the contract instead of asking for 5 percent or 10 percent when they're famous, like they should get, like the older people got, the big companies pay what's called child labor salaries.

They so glad to be famous: "Mommy, look, we famous," you know. And they'll work cheap to be famous. Then they wake up and see they ain't makin' it, ask for a raise and don't get it, or maybe get a little raise. Finally the companies say, "Wait a minute, they're getting out of hand." So they get somebody else and build 'em up over night 'cause that's the system.

But if somebody'd blow the system like I'm doing now, it would be a little tougher. The kids in the United States are supposed to be getting at least 7 percent to begin with. I mean I knew that Sarah Vaughan was getting 35 percent, and these kids will work for nothing. It's ridiculous, man. Suppose a kid walked into your town and said, "I'll work for half your salary." Of course they'll take him—if they can make him bullshit your job. But, see, your job takes a little bit more, so they ain't ready to do that yet. Or we'd have a president that's seventeen years old. How'd you like that? Well, that's what they're really doin', man.

Now God has taken it into his hands, or the Unknown has taken it into his hands to say, "You kids wake up." 'Cause they didn't grow up, they smokin' pot, gettin' high, ain't learnin' nothing, laying around listening to some loud music, so loud they can't even hear each other talk, can't even feel each other's titties 'cause it's so loud it vibrates the titty more than your hand. So they wake up and get married and say, "Wait a minute, man, I heard a guy named Charlie Mingus mentioned on a record by Donovan." So maybe they'll come out to hear us. And I can be Max Roach. But I don't want to be like that: Louis Armstrong and all that.

I think it should become a sacred music for our people, or our folk music, meant for us and y'all let it alone. Don't tell us how to play it, 'cause we don't tell you how to play "Eli Eli." Give us an "Eli Eli" that we can have for our people, which might be something like the blues, I don't know, maybe it's John Coltrane too. Whatever it is, allow that to be exposed to our people; they'll find it, it may be several different musics. But don't tell a guy like, "Look, Miles Davis, get in that studio and play with electric instruments." I mean let the guy play what he wants to play, you know.

GOODMAN: Well, what about that? He did it, he wasn't pushed into playing that shit.

MINGUS: I'm sure he was, financially. See, I never played music for money. Maybe some guys do. Bird never played music for money, and I fell in love with Bird so I can't play for money. 'Cause I know Bird's message, which is not to sell out, to keep on the pulpit and keep saying the same thing to the people that's listening. And if you go down, get up again and keep sayin' the same thing. Till it's right. When it's right, then you can pull out your classical scores—I got five string quartets over here, and I wrote a symphony in 1939, let's do that. And now and then somebody will say, "Wait a minute, this guy's really a musician. He's not just a blues player."

See, it's unfortunate for me and Phil Moore (I hate to call his name, but there's a genius who was too hip to ever get into jazz). I won't say I know as much as Phil but I got to know as much 'cause he told me as much as him, 'cause he loved me and wanted me to be a musician. He said, "Mingus, come on, leave that damn bandstand." He knows the suffering up there, but I know the necessity of getting the message to the people, man.

I've seen Gene Ammons as a preacher, man. When he was gone, they missed him. They tried to replace him with, uhh, Tommy Turrentine's brother [Stanley], and he's very good. Some people loved him but they all were glad to see Gene back, man. I can't explain to you what it is, but they hear Gene and say, "Amen," just like it's church. When I was in California, I couldn't believe it, man, I thought I was in church.

See, when Bird came to Philadelphia, he did the same thing. He didn't walk up there and let 'em know he was avant-garde. He said hello to the wino in the corner, "Hey, babe, wake up there." [*Sings:*] "Got the blues this morning, got a suit on clean as yours but I'm sufferin' inside just like you." I heard Bird wake up people, man, I've seen Bird walk in a main street bar in Los Angeles, California, we got bums comin' in with twenty-five, thirty cents and say, "Hey, man, play a tune." They go out and beg, and instead of buyin' wine they ask for a tune.

I've seen Bird make them feel good. I know what music is; it's medicine, man. And for my children's sake I wish I could have been a Phil Moore. I wish I could have been cool enough to turn and say, "Man, fuck it. I'm going to get some money to support my family. You all got it [you can have it]." But I was born to be . . . I can't change who I am.

GOODMAN: What did he want you to do? Write, or what?

MINGUS: I [finally] quit the studios in California. Oh, man, I made more money in the studios! Red Callender turned me on to that. And Lee Young, Lester's brother. I was in the studios. Ed Safranski was out there, we don't know why he left. In fact, he got smart and went back. But, I remember in the '30s it was $500–600 a week. I never made that on the road with nobody. Every week.

My first job with Red Norvo was $125 a week, and a $135 raise on the road. And Red didn't know I was making that much in a day in the studios, man. I remember then I thought, is it my ego, man? But I enjoyed [playing the clubs] more, I enjoyed life playing like that. I didn't enjoy going into the studio and just playing some . . . maybe four bars is good but the rest is so sickly commercial it's a drag.

GOODMAN: Well, alright, but I don't understand one thing. If you think that jazz ought to be a kind of spiritual music for black people and an ethnic music for them, you said before in order to get there you need to get people decent jobs—in studio bands, in symphony orchestras, and so forth.

MINGUS: [*Excited*] Well, let me say something before I forget it—you won't forget what you gonna say. I'm talking about to get the thing together, to get the black people to realize that if they raise their kids right, they can be musicians. But if they had a healthy music, they could also let their kids know they could be doctors and attorneys.

The point is that since this is called America, you're missing the fact that I'm saying the word "black" will be dropped. We'll all be called—I hate the word—but it's "American," man. It's our country. Maybe we'll vote a new name in or something. France sounds nice, "I'm French," you know. But "I'm American"? It sounds like . . . I can't say . . . maybe somebody should invent a new word.

GOODMAN: We're all embarrassed to say it.

MINGUS: Yeah, maybe somebody will invent a word that means American, or maybe the president will vote for a new name. "United States of America": maybe we'll pronounce it different, or something, 'cause it's really a Spanish word, isn't it?

GOODMAN: From the Italian, I guess [Amerigo Vespucci].

MINGUS: Italian? There's the Mafia again. See, what I'm trying to say is this new music—since society has integrated, even in the South—it would involve more than just the blacks. But first of all the black people have got to get back together again. They been separated from hearing their own music. Once they get it so they can hear it, then it'll be an honest music for them. No more bullshit: a guy can't [proclaim] "I'm avant-garde for the soul of the people." He can go be avant-garde someplace else. And that's fine. I've got some things I want to do that are avant-garde too. But the first thing to do is to doctor the people, get them to find the music they love.

They cannot live without having folk songs, man, without having a folk music. But it's never happened because there is no unity among the black people now. And until they find some way of finding meaning. . . . For some reason music has always got the subconscious. [Black people] always found something in painting. [They say,] "I like that painting," but they never used painting—or have they? Yes, they do, they use symbols. They say, this is our sign, so they use painting too as their symbols. And they wear certain kind of uniforms.

And they should find the music too to go with it. Since they're all split up, maybe they'll find some ancient Arabic chants and use those. But I always thought Americans were together with the blues. I always have thought when they heard something [*sings blues phrase, pounds the table*]—you know, the slavery days, the hammer kind of blues.

GOODMAN: The work song.

MINGUS: There's a little of that in it, plus it has, the first six bars seem to have—funny, it's a twelve-bar phrase, not thirteen—it has the first six bars [that] usually are one phrase [*hums*], then the last four [*hums*], then repeats that one again. But in the olden days the guys got so advanced they could set two phrases, two different melodies, on the bandstand at the same time with the first six bars one way and the second four different. And keep changing every chorus.

But they've forgotten the blues: I tell my guys to play the blues, and they try to find a riff to go through the whole thing. Because a riff does go through the whole thing, but that's not the blues. I've got to teach these kids that, these guys in my band.

Man, you know a man who knows the blues hates to hear 'em played wrong. And in fact don't get up in front of no blues audience and say you're going to sing the blues and don't sing 'em right. You get shot, man. You get cut. You get cut both ways! Cut singing, and cut with a knife.

I've seen guys have blues contests in California—T-Bone be running 'em—and they would ask kids to come up and sing the blues [*sings*], but if you come on with a corny feeling, "BOO," right away, man, not even two notes out. Just the way he stood, the guy couldn't sing the blues and grabbed the mike wrong—he grabbed the mike wrong, getting ready to open his mouth—"BOO, get off the stand, man." The real blues singer, he'd walk up like, "Hey, everybody here, how y'all doin' this morning?" and you know it's blues, man.

I tell you, Joe Turner, that's why Duke probably used him in that play *Jump for Joy*, 'cause Joe had the presence. When he came in the room, [*big hearty voice:*] "How's everybody here this morning?" And he took the whole joint over, man, yeah.

GOODMAN: So I was trying to ask you how you could get the kind of ethnic music you're talking about while you still had people who couldn't even play in studio bands. And I think you answered it, because you're talking about a future time, a hopeful—

MINGUS: Yeah, a hopeful day. Because kids today see Charlie Parker, Charlie Mingus, and they see just drums, bass, saxophone—they don't see it all. If they do, they see other kids playing bullshit on instruments they can't really play yet. And they should have teachers, man. You know, I want my kids to have teachers.

The older guys can go get a violin, hold it on their chin, or their navel if they want to, and fool the public. But I want my kids to learn it properly because they find you can finger it better up there. If you could hold it on your navel and play it, they would hold it on their navel, but it's been proven over so many years that to hold the violin on the chin [lets it] rest on the shoulder, so you don't hold it on your chest. And you don't play it with your left hand, you play it with your right. If you're left-handed you can switch over. But usually a teacher will tell you if you're left-handed, you're even better 'cause the speed is more important in the left hand. So you stay left-handed but bow with this one. Don't tell me you're gonna switch hands because you're left-handed. I had a student like that and I finally taught him the way he wanted to learn. He wanted to change his fingers around. Played with Billy Taylor, can't think of his name [Earl May].[2] I said, well, try to learn it this way, and I taught him bass backwards.

GOODMAN: And it worked.

MINGUS: Yeah, it worked, using the same fingering, but we changed things around and I had to change my mind around too. I wouldn't want to do it. It might have been good for me, now that I think about it. At that time I didn't want to do it 'cause it made me forget my coordination. If I started to think the other way, I'd be going backwards [*laughs*].

• • •

Since we had gotten a bit more comfortable with each other, I suggested we sample a little Pernod while we talked. I knew Mingus liked the stuff; so did I; and so we did. And things picked up as the Pernod went down.

• • •

MINGUS: "Waitress, waitress?" [*To me:*] Put the bottle away. We need a little ice. Soda and ice. "Hey, baby, can we buy a bottle of soda and some ice?"
    . . . She gave us a whole pitcher, didn't she? [*Sounds of pouring, etc.*]

GOODMAN: That tastes very good.

MINGUS: The Pernod?

GOODMAN: Goddamn right.

MINGUS: Oh, yeah. "Boss," as the hippies say.

GOODMAN: What about all the language they've "adopted" from the jazz people? Does that kind of bug you? It does me.

MINGUS: Yeah, first of all, they slipped me in Slim Gaillard's book, look up one word, "groovy" and other words that said "hip" and "down" and "dig."[3]

And they call themselves "hippies." A person who's hip, the first thing he would never say was "I'm hip." Unless, the word *hip* meaning "I'm into that, I understand that one thing." But you don't say, "I'm the total." Hip, hip, "I'm hip" means "I know it all."

Hip really meant: "Say, man, do you know so-and-so?"

"No, I didn't know that."

"Well, man, so-and-so went this way."

"Oh, it did? Oh, I'm hip to that, yeah, I dig now."

But these guys, when they start saying *only* . . . "This ice cream is nice, man. It's groovy, Mingus, isn't it groovy?" Wait a minute! He went to a movie, and "Oh, that was groovy, wasn't it?" [*Much laughter.*] Nobody's telling me to say one fucking word all the time, man. I know it was groovy, but I said that last year. Now it's down, it's up, it's right, it's tight, it's nice. And finally I'm gonna say, "Gee, it's beautiful."

You know we were saying all that shit, and in fact we ain't said groovy since 1939. Groovy was really out. Groovy, man, groovy. That went out with the Cocoanut Grove. That's where it came from. When the Cocoanut Grove burnt down they stopped saying groovy, 'cause everybody was saying we used to groove at the Cocoanut Grove. 'Member that?

GOODMAN: No, I don't but I'm laughing because I wrote about this once, man. I'm tickled to hear you say this because of all that bullshit lingo they talk. It just got to me at one point.

MINGUS: It got to me, man. It put me in bed, thought I was going to die. The only way to get away from it, just laying out ready to die. But my heart refused to stop. The Milkman's Matinee, *ooozee*, the first real disk jockey in California—how could I forget him?[4] He's bigger than Symphony Sid. Milkman's Matinee [*singing*], he's the one that started "groove," man. Well, he didn't start it, he heard the niggers talking about being grooved by a broad. And he used to advertise the Cocoanut Grove and said "Everybody's groovy at the Cocoanut Grove." I remember that, man, way back.

I also remember the fact that Benny Goodman came to the Grove with Lionel Hampton and Charlie Christian and Teddy Wilson—came to the front door and they wouldn't let 'em in. We were all working Hollywood and going in the back doors at the time. I was with Zutty Singleton one time, the drummer in the band I was in. Everybody looked around, "You mean Benny Goodman walked off the bandstand, eh? He said, 'You mean they can't come in the front door, right? Fellows, pack up.'"

"But can we go out the front door?" And they walked out the front door, man, and that message hit all the clubs at once. Zutty walked in the front door, and nobody said nothing. Black cats used to come in back by the kitchen and go up to the bandstand.

"You mean Benny walked off?"

"Yeah, with Lionel—they wouldn't let him on the bandstand."

So Martin Luther King was just a sample, man. Benny Goodman and Lionel Hampton—that's what started integration, but they did it with music, they did it another way. Benny Goodman wouldn't take no Jim Crow jobs.

GOODMAN: And that was good, and a lot of people have knocked him because they thought he was condescending or some bullshit like that . . .

MINGUS: Bullshit. He walked off a job that must have paid him twenty thousand that week. . . . And it's so weird about the Mafia again, man. I'm not saying they had anything to do with it, but they pulled some shit about paying Benny his money . . . Well, let's not talk about that. I don't like to talk about fires because burning is wrong.

GOODMAN: Tell the story, I won't put it in.

MINGUS: Well, that was in my original book—it's funny that [the Cocoanut Grove] burnt down two weeks later.[5] It actually burnt down. But it's very sad that a bass player—he was the only one in the band who escaped. He made a hole through a brick wall. Very good bass player, in fact, though his hands are all burnt off now, one of the first of two guys who can bow, sorry I don't know his name, all the musicians know him though.

This cat got *out* that place, man. I asked him, he said, "Everyone was going to the doors. I looked at the crowd around me, took my bass, said 'Here it comes,' and *boom*, right through the wall." Said he couldn't believe it. He got some people out through the wall. He made a door, and he got his bass out. Got his bass out, baby. Now, I think about it, I saw it happen again in San Diego.

GOODMAN: You can do it because mortar can sometimes be soft.

MINGUS: Building just collapsed the other day over in the East Village.

I saw a woman chase a guy out of a club in San Diego, same way, I was in Illinois Jacquet's band. And this cat pulled a knife on her, man, and she picked this cat up like a monkey. Great big broad, man, me and Jacquet couldn't believe it. When he got up, his knife all scattered around, she says, "Pick your knife up again now." She started coming towards him and this cat ran into the crowd, he turned around and prayed, and went through the wall [*laughter*].

GOODMAN: That's desperation, I'll tell you.

MINGUS: I have never messed with no woman, I never hit no woman since then, man. I used to be a little tough with broads. But when I saw that broad, I said, "Wait a minute. No good." Not only that, man, she was jabbin', she had her dukes up, *pop!*, like Joe Louis, *boop!*, she didn't just only pick him up. And she goes, "Come on, motherfucker, *pow!*, raise your hand, baby." What gym did she go to? She's Cassius Clay's trainer. *Whooee.*

Next time you see him, ask Illinois Jacquet, 'cause you into this thing now, you might as well get the whole thing. We'll never forget that day in San Diego, because he happened to be talking, "Mingus, don't think you're so bad, man, 'cause I know some chicks as bad as you are!" He said, "You'll see." And we started to go down South on the road, and we hit this club and stayed a week. Kind of clubs Jacquet worked in anyway, man, always somebody getting cut and stuff, you know.

CHAPTER 4 COMMENTARY

Sy Johnson on the Mingus Temperament

When Mingus was on a roll, as he clearly was in this chapter's interview, you had to be pretty quick to keep up. Sometimes, as Sy Johnson relates here, you didn't know how to read him—or how to react. Everything was a test.

• • •

JOHNSON: I had come to town in 1960 from Los Angeles and was trying to find a friend of mine, Paul Bley, who I knew was playing with Mingus. He was playing at the Showplace on West Fourth Street, and I went down one night during the week to talk to Paul, to see Paul. And there wasn't any piano player in Mingus's band. I got there during intermission and the band got up and started to play a blues. I always felt a real affinity for Mingus's music anyway, and the blues was just calling me home. So I got up after a few minutes of playing and asked Mingus—I thought the piano

FIGURE 5.　Mingus at the 1974 recording of *Changes One* and *Changes Two* at Atlantic Records. Photo by Sy Johnson.

player was late—if I could play until he came. So Mingus said, "You better be able to play because if you can't play, it's your ass."

I said, "Well, I think I can play."

"OK."

I squeezed onto the bandstand and was a little intimidated by my own audacity to start with. I just played the first chord of the blues after a few seconds of reflection, an F-seventh chord, and Mingus looked up at me and said, "You can play, you're a jazz player, I can tell."

And I thought that was very unusual until Ted Curson told me that he once called up a piano player to play with his band one night, and the guy showed up and played one chord and then was fired. And so apparently he makes these very fast decisions as to whether people can play or not. It was a very exciting band because he was breaking in Eric Dolphy; Booker Ervin was still in the band but was leaving, and so there were two saxophone players. Teddy Curson was very young, and he was playing trumpet and Dannie Richmond, who knew Mingus's music inside and out, was playing drums. Dannie would give me a great deal of help. He would sing everything that I had to play practically. Any figure, for example, what's the name of that piece? [*Sings a few bars—*]

GOODMAN: "Better Get It in Your Soul."

JOHNSON: "Better Get It in Your Soul." He knew all the vamps that the piano player had to play in that and he would sing them all to me so I would just use my ears and pick up on them. After a couple of nights—nothing was written out—I learned the book.

GOODMAN: Is Teddy the guy he ran off the bandstand?

JOHNSON: Oh, Teddy Curson was very young then, kind of mouthy, and this was one of his first big jobs. Mingus was really pissed off at him and so he would suddenly throw the bass down and Teddy, who was very young and agile at that time—still is pretty agile—would just scramble off the bandstand, go running out the front door of the club. Mingus would lumber after him and come back and stop on the front steps someplace, and Teddy would stay away for fifteen to twenty minutes and come back to the bandstand. And Mingus would act as though nothing happened.

He was always cajoling people on the bandstand, telling Eric Dolphy, "Play with taste! Play with taste, man! No, I don't want to hear all them notes. Play some of the melody, man; I don't know what melody you are playing, man."

It was a very exciting and nerve-racking situation to be in. My stomach would be in a knot every time I came to work. Baby Lawrence, the great tap dancer, was dancing there. Mingus had hired him with the piano player's salary, and so he kept telling me, "I got to pay Baby Lawrence this week, but if you wait until next week Baby Lawrence is going to leave, and then I will hire you as a piano player."

So I would come in the following week and Baby Lawrence would still be there and he said, "I couldn't, man, Baby Lawrence needs the bread, man, I can't really. Wait until next week." Then Baby Lawrence would be there again. Finally, about two weeks later, Baby was about to leave and the next week I was supposed to be on salary with the band, and so I came in the following week and Yusef Lateef was on the bandstand. There were three saxophones and Yusef was available and Mingus, in a very typical way, asked him to come on the band and was paying him the piano player's salary.[6]

GOODMAN: That was quite a saxophone section, Jesus Christ.

JOHNSON: Yeah, it was a fantastic sax section. Like I said, it was a very exciting time for me, as he was writing a lot of marvelous music. For example, one night he decided to listen to the band. We were playing "I'll Remember April," and Mingus frequently made it very difficult for people in the band to play. I mean if things got grooving in a conventional rhythm section, if things just started to cook, he would go into 6/8, start playing 6 against 4 or use all other kinds of devices, and this would unsettle everybody. So he got off the bandstand and sat down at the front table. He was sitting like Buddha, listening to the band.

Without Mingus, the band really started to cook. It was like a big weight was taken off the band. Everybody really started to cook, and Mingus was getting more and more furious. We were having just a marvelous time. The band just sounded great. All of a sudden he came back on the bandstand and destroyed the tune. It was like [*crunching noises*] somebody threw sand in your engine. It just ground to a halt. Then he just put the bass down and walked out the door.

But then the two most vivid things I remember were playing this piece based on "All the Things You Are" called "All the Things You Could Be by if Now Sigmund Freud's Mother Was Your Father," or something like that ["All the Things You Could Be by Now if Sigmund Freud's Wife Was Your Mother"]. He had constructed a real obstacle course to go through and had chromatic changes, with every bridge different from whatever section was going on. It would be in 3/4 or rubato. All kinds of substitute chords, Latin rhythms, and you had to wade through about four choruses of this, I mean just plow through it. Finally, if you got through to the other side of that, then he would let you just cook for one chorus.

Again, he had no music for this, and learning particularly all the chromatic things was rather taxing. I was very nervous about that tune for the first week. I finally got to the point where I was confident about it and felt good about it. One night we were playing that tune and Mingus started to yell at me, "Pedal tones, play pedal tones!" I didn't know what he was talking about because the tune changes keys every few measures. That's one of the reasons jazz players like it. It's got shifting tonality all the time, it's a marvelous thing to play on. But pedal tones just seemed, to me, I couldn't imagine what he wanted. I started playing the dominant of any of the keys that we were in as a pedal, and that didn't seem to work. He was getting furious and he was yelling, "Pedal tones, pedal tones!"

I mean, he threw the bass down, ran back to the piano and shoved his elbow in my chest and shoved me back from the keyboard, and he had his face flat against my nose, his nose right up against mine, and he was glaring at me and he made double fists and swung it down on the key-board and hit the bass end of the keyboard. The piano was like an atomic explosion. It's surprising it didn't just fall apart. He hit it about three or four times with this devastating impact, and I was sure he was going to turn those sledgehammers on me and that would be the end of everything and my life flashed before my eyes. I was sure it was over. And suddenly he ran back and picked the bass up and started playing furiously.

So, after my heart started beating again, I began to get angry. I thought, "How dare he? The bastard isn't paying me anything, and he's humiliating me in front of all these people." And I went through this whole trip. I thought he was a fucking—if I could have left the bandstand I would have but I couldn't get past him. So I was just not going to play anymore. I had my arms folded across my chest, I was sulking, getting angrier and angrier, and Dannie Richmond finally turned around and said, "Play, man, he didn't mean nothing, he always does that, man. Play."

I was like, "Fuck him, I ain't going to play again."

So finally I got so angry I just glared at him and I hit the bass end of the piano with both fists. I just slammed down on it, and Mingus turned to me and said, "That's it! That's it!" He said, "That boy can play."

The only other real sign of approval that I got during that time was one night when the piano was in the back of the bandstand. Right directly behind the chair was an open pit where there was a hole in the risers. Dannie would store his drums, the bass case and a whole lot of other things were stuffed down in there. In order to play you had to sit with your navel just about up against the keyboard.

One night I was a little bit stoned and decided I needed more room to stretch out. I pushed the chair back a little too far and toppled backwards into this pit full of cases. I was scrambling around trying to get my feet on the floor among all these cases and it was dark down there, really spooky. I was trying to pull myself back out onto the riser again.

And Mingus smiled at me: "Can you do that every night?" As far as he was concerned, it was a legitimate happening in the music and he would have been really pleased if I could have found a way to do it every night without killing myself. It really made him very happy.

Yeah, that was the situation we started with. Well, I guess when I came in and found Yusef Lateef on the bandstand, I left. After that I would see Mingus on the street periodically when he was walking around in his Bermuda shorts, Hawaiian shirt, and sandals. Smoking his pipe on Third Avenue when he was starting a school.

Bobby Jones on Mingus's Tactics and Theatrics

Bobby was a very open guy who shared some good Mingus lore with me. Coming out of the Ray McKinley and Woody Herman bands, by 1972 he had been with Mingus for about two years. In Mingus's band, Bobby found himself as a tenor player able not only to cope with but actually to grow with the Mingus approach. Since I knew he had had periodic, shall we say, disagreements with Charles, I hoped he would talk about him as a person. And he did.

. . .

JONES: You know, he hates to be interviewed and he's hard to get answers out of. You haven't actually interviewed him yet, huh?

GOODMAN: No, not yet.

JONES: Well, I can give you some hints. For one thing, one of his pet peeves with interviewers is the racial thing. And, I've seen him do this a thousand times. If he gets the impression that someone is digging up that pile of sand and, he being a black man, they want him to say pro-black things, he will, as soon as he senses it, go the opposite direction. And he does that with a whole flock of things. When he senses where an interviewer is going, he takes entirely the opposite side that they expect him to take.

GOODMAN: Just to be ornery?

JONES: Well, he likes to play games with them.

GOODMAN: I've thought that I didn't want to ask those standard god-damn questions [on the race issue] that people ask him.

JONES: Yeah, I know. Well in his case, it's pretty obvious how he feels. He doesn't particularly love white people, especially as a group, or in their entirety, you know. But by the same token, color doesn't really make that much difference to him. He's never had a whole flock of white people around him, but he's always had a few.

GOODMAN: So the racial thing doesn't particularly come up, then?

JONES: Not very often, no. The only time it comes up is—and I've learned to live with this—is that he knows who he can use and who he can't abuse. For instance, in this particular group that we have right now, he knows he can scream at most everybody in the group except Charles McPherson, so he does. For a long time, he was under the impression that the only guy he could scream at was me. So he did.

GOODMAN: Was there a racial thing in that?

JONES: Yeah. Like, quite often, quite often. Many times it's gotten to be the, you know, "white boy" type thing, until finally I just had to tell him, "Look, man, I'm only me. I'm not representing the whole white race to you." He's the kind of man you have to take a stand with. He has no respect for people who won't stand up. You have to do that, even at the risk of your job sometimes. Take your stand.

For one thing, you never know when he's playing with you. You never know when he's really serious. Most of the time you can tell, but he's so adept, he's such an actor, that he can fool you. You can swear he's dead serious and he's not serious at all.

GOODMAN: What an education to be around him. Well, what else about interviewing?

JONES: Let me think. Well, he's the type of guy that you don't say, "I'm going to turn the tape on." You just turn it on. Preferably without him knowing about it. Put it so he can't he even see it. That's even better, so that he don't know when it's happening. Very simple reason. In the first place, he's got this thing about being interviewed. He doesn't like it. So if you can interview him without him knowing he's being interviewed, that's the best way to do it. You'll get a lot straighter answers. Keep it conversational. In other words, you have to act. The interviewer has to act.

GOODMAN: Well, that's kind of the way I thought about it. Just sort of toss out things and let him take the ball—which, if he will do, great.

JONES: It's probably fairly obvious just from watching the man that he's very stage-conscious. He's theatrical, which is part of the experience.

GOODMAN: He really put it on last night.

JONES: I learned a lot about how to get attention from being around this man [*laughter*]. He's a master, and he'll jump onstage at a moment's notice.

GOODMAN: Whenever he thinks there's one to jump on.

JONES: That's right. Whenever he thinks there's one to jump on, boy, he's onstage, and he's acting. I've seen him go to fantastic lengths to get attention.

GOODMAN: Like what?

JONES: Well, for instance, clothes.

GOODMAN: Yeah. The hats?

JONES: Hats. For a while, it was African dress. And then, well, for instance, he'll take a situation that means absolutely nothing and make a big thing out of it to create—not only to get attention, but to create attention for a long time. In other words, the kind of thing people will go away talking about.

For instance, we were working in a place in England. We had to take two nights off from Ronnie Scott's because Ronnie had Buddy Rich's band booked for the weekend. So on those two nights, Ronnie booked us one night in Liverpool and the next night in Leicester—[*spells it*], you know, we call it "Lester." So, when we got to Leicester, we find a university, a small college, a very small auditorium, a narrow, small stage, not too many seats. We had only the sextet, maybe a quintet by that time. And, there were people sitting behind us on the stage.

So we're performing, we finish the tune and, mind you, we've got people in back of us and people in front of us and a very small stage that was raised about so high off the floor. So we finish the tune and a guy comes up out of the audience, a college student, throws his arm around Charles, and I can't hear what they're saying because there's a trumpet player between us. From the looks on the guy's face, I assume this is an old-time friend of Mingus's. Until finally I hear Mingus say, "Get off the bandstand."

So the guy jumps down off the stage and goes back into the audience. Mingus reaches down into the body of the bass where he had a mike in the tailpiece, the thing that holds the strings on. Now he could have said this without doing the microphone thing, but he reaches down, grabs his mike, turns to me and says, "Hey Bobby, who was that motherfucker?" [*Laughs.*] All that could have been done without the use of a microphone and nobody would have known it but me, but he wanted everybody to hear that.

GOODMAN: That's theater, man.

JONES: Plus, he knew I'd never seen the guy before. I'm in England for the first time.

GOODMAN: That was a gesture for the crowd.

JONES: Mmm-hmm. And he does that all the time. One night at the Vanguard recently, some woman was bugging him and he insulted her a couple of times, bad enough that if her boyfriend had any manliness about him, he would have jumped up and hit Mingus. And the guy made no move. Finally Mingus says to the woman, "Your breath stinks. Get away from me." And loud. Boy, everybody in the joint heard it [*laughs*]. It's a wonder the man doesn't get punched out a lot. But he uses the element of surprise.

It's great. I really learned a lot about show business hanging around him. He really taught me a lot. And it's especially helpful when I'm a leader, you know.

GOODMAN: Don't the crowds, like the hip Vanguard crowds, don't they kind of know how to deal with Mingus, and what he's all about?

JONES: No, you have to be around him awhile to find all that out. If you're seeing him for the first time onstage and you're in the audience, if you haven't had a chance to get to know him a little bit, he has the advantage. He can really shock you. He can do it even when you know him [*laughs*].

One of the ways I have learned most about him is from the people who have been around him a long time. People like Charlie McPherson, Dannie Richmond, Jaki Byard. In particular, Dannie and Charles, because they've been around him more than Jaki has.

GOODMAN: He hasn't played with Jaki for a long time?

JONES: Right, he [Jaki]'s come and gone, quick little moments. Piece of a tour here and piece of a tour there. So I haven't gotten to know Jaki all that well, not enough to observe the same thing that I do with these other guys. But they have a way of . . . "IGNORE-ance," I guess. They have a way of just ignoring anything that he does or says. They'll be talking to him and they act like he's not even in the room.

GOODMAN: Does this bug him?

JONES: Doesn't seem to bug him when they do it. Bugs him if I do it [*laughs*]. Of course, I don't do it that much because it's not a natural thing for me to do. For them, I guess it's a defense mechanism.

GOODMAN: When he's spouting off to them.

JONES: Yeah, when he's into one of his tirades and they don't want to hear it.

GOODMAN: But they all have a good feeling about him, right?

JONES: Yeah, well . . . he's the easiest person in the world to love. Easy.

Paul Jeffrey on Mingus's Behavior

JEFFREY: You know, Mingus is really contrary to all that stuff that you read about him, the sensational image that they want to project.

GOODMAN: They talk about his fights and throwing knives and all.

JEFFREY: That's not him. Sonny Rollins did a documentary about three or four years ago, and it was a beautiful documentary, supposed to be shown like a film in the theater.[7] You know what the complaint against it was? It wasn't controversial enough. Isn't that ridiculous? I mean do you have to

be screaming or jumping off a roof to get any kind of response? And
Mingus is someone they seem to think is commercially sellable. Well,
everybody gets mad. Some people keep it in; he doesn't. Every time he
gets mad, "Charlie Mingus has done it again."

GOODMAN: That's a bad image for him because he is a volatile guy, and
nobody like that needs to be poked and goaded.

JEFFREY: Right. I think a lot of times he feels very sensitive about that.
He says, "I'm not that way." And he isn't—from what I can see. Actually
if somebody does something wrong to a person, they're gonna get mad.
And a guy as big as him, he has no other recourse, right? Whereas a
smaller guy, smaller in stature, if something happens, OK, they'll expect
him not to do anything. They don't expect Charlie Mingus not to do
anything. That's one of the—shall we say—disadvantages of being a large
person. Everyone expects you to live up that.

GOODMAN: You ever seen him get wild?

JEFFREY: Umm, no, not really. I've seen a couple of instances, but I wouldn't
call them wild. But he is capable of getting—you know, everybody is.
But that's not basically his personality. I've never seen him do anything
unprovoked. So that's why I would discount all this so-called propensity to
be basically a destroyer, a violent person.

A lot of guys told me, "I wouldn't be bothering with him. You know,
he's crazy." Which is very unfair. It's a false accusation. And you can listen
to the music that he writes and composes: it's not violent music. It covers
a whole spectrum—powerful, emotional, tender—I mean how can a
person be a sort of maniac personality and write tender music? I think
he's a person that, if he's pushed, a lot of times he will react, which is
justifiable. He has to express his emotions.

Knowing what you can do and not getting the opportunity to do it is
another thing that will make a person, you know, sort of bitter. But I've
seen instances where he really goes out of his way to be nice when you'd
ordinarily get provoked. There have been instances when I myself have
been provoked for him, but he's just laughed.

GOODMAN: I think a lot of the frustration he must feel is because he
knows his capabilities and what he's got in him, and he hasn't had the
chance to display them.

JEFFREY: That's an awful feeling. He's got the music, he's done it, he's got
scores laying around, and different individuals will, you know, mess with
his music. And he's had his problems with different musicians—

GOODMAN: And record companies.

JEFFREY: Record companies. They try to make a commercially saleable product. I think every musician, and especially a musician of his stature, if they even set foot into a recording studio and make an album, they should have the right to edit every piece of that tape. They should do the mixing and the editing—something that at this point is not really permissible. Nobody understands his music better than he does, so he should have the complete say-so as to which take is used, how it is mixed, etc. That's the only way he can really get to the core of the sound he wants.

... Usually in his associations with musicians, he's primarily warm and open, and then when his confidence is betrayed, the result is the incidents that always get publicized. He takes on the aspect of a wounded bull, I would say. I've never had any problem whatsoever with him; it's been a beautiful relationship.

GOODMAN: What are some of the good things?

JEFFREY: Well, he's a man of his word. And that's important. He gives you all the help he can musically, and in the business aspect of music. A lot of people have never taken time, musicians particularly, to understand him. And one of the most important things in doing Mingus's music is to understand exactly what he wants. Even if you become repetitious in asking him about it, he never objects to that. The one thing that really gets him mad is if he says something about what he wants in his music, and you don't understand it and do it—

GOODMAN: You mean try to fake it or something?

JEFFREY: Well, he has a certain idea of things he's trying to get across in his music, and a lot of musicians, instead of actually finding out exactly what he wants, they will not want to appear ignorant so they'll go and assume something, and this is where the conflict comes. This is a real problem, when somebody is that meticulous.

GOODMAN: Is Monk like that?

JEFFREY: Monk is very meticulous, but they are two different per-sonalities. Monk is demanding but it's not so much what he says but the implications. Whereas Mingus will say, "Stop. No, this is so-and-so," Monk might let it go on for a little while and say, "Hey, about that such-and-such: it goes like this." Sometimes that works more effectively with a musician with high integrity because he can feel very shamed. A lot of musicians, if you tell them right away, "No, this is not what I want," their egos get bruised, and then they may start building all kinds of rationalizations about how they're right.

GOODMAN: So Monk's approach is a little easier in a sense, at least in the short run.

JEFFREY: Right. Monk might not say anything for a period of time, and all of a sudden, at the opportune moment, he'll say it.

GOODMAN: Charles is incredible the way he talks to his people. The band was on Channel 13 the other night, and they were rehearsing from about seven o'clock on, and it was interesting to see how his moods would change. The way the music was going would determine that, but so did a lot of other stuff, obviously. I guess he and Bobby Jones had had a fight in Boston the weekend before—

JEFFREY: That's ironic because I think Bobby Jones understands his music.

GOODMAN: He's got a feel for it. Oh, I guess they have fights all the time.

JEFFREY: Yeah, I believe that.

GOODMAN: But as the music was progressing, he'd get extremely pissed off for maybe thirty seconds, and then he'd smile and shift gears, and that's hard for a lot of people to take.

JEFFREY: Yeah, but that's his personality. In anybody who is highly creative, change is a very evident part of their personal makeup because in order to get a high-quality product you have to go through many checks and balances and changes. So Mingus might be highly satisfied with something one minute, and the next minute he might hate it. That's the genius he has for composition. Because he's very meticulous, and a lot of musicians aren't able to adjust. So at the time I don't think it's a personal thing with him; it's actually more or less getting the musical nuance that he wants.

That's why he does workshops, and he's very staunch in that because he says: "My music is constantly changing, and I don't want people to judge it on some one thing that might happen in the course of the music. It has to be loose, it has to be open. When you say, 'one, two, three, four, *bang*,' you [unstack] the product in a sense."

GOODMAN: Yeah, he's got all that density and change in his writing too, it's a wild mixture.

JEFFREY: It's challenging. It's a mixture, that's right. It's a hard mixture.

GOODMAN: How do other people you know feel about Charles in terms of working with him, and his stature in the music?

JEFFREY: Well, his stature cannot be denied. Musicians have a very peculiar type of thing, which is "I'm not going to commit myself or make any comment about anybody else." And if you say something good about somebody else, the press always tries to misconstrue it—that you're saying their product is more valid than yours. It's like a saxophone player won't say anything nice about another saxophone player because it's always misconstrued to say, "If I say he's good, that's saying he's superior to me."

And it's often a matter of dollars and cents. When you have a poll, and you say you're number one, two, three, four, this means earning power and recognition. Mingus said something which was very hilarious and very true. He said, "We ought to run a poll on the symphonic musicians. They don't run a poll on them."

GOODMAN: Damn right. He sent his medals back. Did you know that? Medals for his awards, the *Down Beat* and *Playboy* things.

JEFFREY: He did? Knowing him, he will get things off the ground now. He'll get it. I think so. I have as much faith in that as in the sun rising. He's done a lot of things that people said couldn't be done. When nobody was doing independent recording, he did it and made a record that is a classic, the Massey Hall thing with Max Roach, Bud Powell, Charlie Parker, Dizzy Gillespie, and Mingus [*Jazz at Massey Hall*]. You'll never get that again. And he wrote a book, a successful book. Just a many-faceted guy.

Dan Morgenstern on Mingus's Moods

MORGENSTERN: Well, I have known Mingus for quite some time. I like him very much, although he is a difficult person. Not only to get to know but also, once you do know him, you still never can be quite sure what kind of mood he is going to be in. That bothered me for a while in the earlier years but it doesn't bother me any more. If he is in a bad mood, you know, I just ignore it, and the next time I see him he might be very friendly. He is extremely emotional and he just wears his emotions on his sleeve, I guess.

Mingus doesn't restrain himself when [he's angry]. At the same time he is a very warm and good-hearted man. He's had a lot of problems, some he created for himself. Right now I think he is in a very, sort of, a peak of his career because things have been going well quite consistently.

I don't know many people who dislike Mingus in spite of the kind of experiences they might have had with him. But there are a few who don't have the patience to deal with him. If you are going to work with him, you have to be very patient. But there are rewards. Basically, for a musician, the rewards are that you get to play some music that really is out of the ordinary. People like McPherson who have been with him for years and years—I have seen him sort of slightly mad at Charles from time to time but never really angry. He likes him.

GOODMAN: Bobby told me that he is the one person Charles doesn't mess with too much.

MORGENSTERN: It must be very difficult to work with Mingus because he is so unpredictable. On the other hand, I think once you show him—he wants you to prove to him one way or the other that you are a bad guy or a good guy. And once you have proven to him that you are one or the other, then that's where it's at. He tests people, he likes to test people.

GOODMAN: Everybody I have talked to said that. He loves to test you.

MORGENSTERN: I don't think there is anybody in the music field whom he has dealt with in one way or another who he has not threatened to kill at one time or another, including his best friends. You just learn to live with that, not take it seriously.

GOODMAN: Bobby Jones told me he threw a hunting knife at him a couple of weeks ago.

MORGENSTERN: Yeah, but he missed.

Of course there are people who he has—Jackie McLean, many years ago, he hit Jackie in the mouth, which was a very bad thing to do to a musician who happens to be a horn player. He did the same thing to Jimmy Knepper, but I don't know how he stands with Jackie. They did not do much together after that, but Jimmy is back with him. I think Jimmy was more hurt than anything else, his feelings. Mingus demands a lot of people.

Jaki Byard, who is very temperamental himself, I thought when they finally split up there was supposedly—I don't know if this is true—but I was told that Mingus tried to slam the piano cover on his hands. I thought for a while that Jaki said he would never forgive him. But, about three-four years after that, he [did]. There are people who have taken advantage of him [Mingus] and he has not let it destroy the relationship. There are musicians who've worked for him who have almost blackmailed him, like when he was about to go on a tour, and they tell him at the last minute when they're coming to the airport that they want more money. Which leaves the man helpless.

GOODMAN: Jesus.

MORGENSTERN: And he stood for it. The one time that I have really been angry with him was once at the Village Vanguard there was a special [event] put together mainly for recording purposes, which had Roy Eldridge and Coleman Hawkins and Earl Hines, opposite Mingus, who was working there. It was done on a Sunday, starting in the afternoon and going into the evening. I think this was around 1965, and nothing much was really happening with Mingus's group. And the other band was really beautiful: even though these guys hadn't worked together in a long time, they were really enjoying each other, and most of the audience was there for them. They got big standing ovations, and then Mingus went on and people would start talking.

So during Mingus's last set—the other group was supposed to go on after—and Coleman Hawkins was sitting at a table, people were talking to him and Hawk, without realizing, had a very booming voice. His voice had as much volume as his playing, and when he would laugh you could hear him clear across the room. He didn't really want to spend that much time with these people, but they were buying him drinks and he was being nice to them.

But he was making a bit of noise, and Mingus stopped the music and said, "Hey, Coleman Hawkins. I don't talk when you're playing. Why should you talk when I play?" So Hawk moved closer into the table, very firmly as a matter of fact, and more or less ignored him.

Then after the set break, I was in the kitchen with Hawk and Roy and Earl Hines and George Tucker, just talking, and Mingus came in and was furious. "They were talking and carrying on during my set . . ." Everybody more or less ignored him, Hines especially because he hates scenes.

Finally, more out of frustration than anything else, Mingus says, "You're nothing but a bunch of old niggers anyway."

So everybody was stunned for a moment, and then Roy was the first one to break up, he broke up laughing. A little later Mingus came back and sort of apologized, as much as Mingus ever would, I mean sort of obliquely indicated that—

GOODMAN: —he was a little out of line.

MORGENSTERN: Yeah. The only one who really got mad was Hines. And of course at the same time Mingus had tremendous admiration for all those people. If there's anybody he really admires, it's Ellington, Tatum, and all the giants from that era because they were his mentors. They have always been his idols and I think his real ambition is, in a sense, to be like Duke. He got his start in Duke's band in the 1950s. Of course, he seems temperamentally really the exact opposite [of Duke]. Ellington very, very rarely flies off at his men.

Max Gordon on Mingus's Anger and Integrity

I had met Max Gordon (1903–1989), the Village Vanguard owner and proprietor since 1935, a few times in the course of reviewing jazz.[8] He was always genial and generally happy to talk. Max ran the Vanguard not as the jazz institution it was but as a casual, homelike space for musicians and fans to gather. The kitchen, now defunct, was the place where musicians and sometimes journalists gathered to tell lies to each other between sets.

Max's wife, Lorraine Gordon, now runs the joint in the same fashion her husband did.

· · ·

GOODMAN: Tell me something about your associations over the years with Mingus.

GORDON: Well we have a long association. I think he worked here for the first time sometime in the middle or late '50s. Something like that. We have had, I would say, an interesting, sometimes a stormy association. But we are friends now. And we have been friends more or less over the years, even with moments of tension. Frankly I don't remember what they were, all of them. I remember only one time we had something—I mean, he does things he doesn't mean.

He once held a knife in front of me, but he did not mean it. And I knew it, and he knew it, and that's Mingus. And he tore off our front door and threw it down the stairs one time in a fit of rage. And broke a bottle of booze on the floor, a full bottle of booze. Also he smashed one of our seating lights, a recessed light in the ceiling, with his fist. Which he did in a fit of rage not so much at me but over something that happened—maybe at his own men or some customer. In any case, that light is still there askew, slightly askew, and we have kept it that way. We like to point it out to people sometimes.

GOODMAN: The Mingus memorial light?

GORDON: As I say, I have a great respect, and I really have a love for the man because I know what he is and I know what he is made out of. And I understand some of his rages too. Today as I say, we're good friends. He likes to work this room, he told me.

GOODMAN: He has been here more than any place in New York?

GORDON: Probably been here more than any place in New York. He works here all the time. Although he took two years off at one time. I think he sort of retired from performing.

GOODMAN: This was his bad time, apparently?

GORDON: Yeah, he did not work anywhere, but when he decided to work again he came to me and asked me if I wanted to use him in the room, which I did, of course. I remember that time and I remember how many people came in to see him because there had been a great sort of buildup of people eager to hear him over those two years, and they were all pouring into the Vanguard when he opened up. We did tremendous business, and I remember that very well. It was his homecoming. That was about three years ago.

GOODMAN: You say you sort of understand his rages? What do you mean? Do you mean how they can develop out of problems with the band or problems with things in his life?

GORDON: Well, I've watched him, you know, I hear him, and I know it's mostly as a result of his frustration, musical frustration. And there's interference and the problems of working in a club where there is sometimes a lack of discipline on the part of the audience, or on the part of the men making the music.

And here's a man who has a kind of integrity and, true enough, he has a temper. He has a manner of not confining himself when he has something to say. He doesn't mind letting loose his feelings on people. So I can understand what it is sometimes, although I must say it tests me too, naturally, because I am running a club, so that's a problem, keeping it together without falling apart, you know, without incidents that would upset people, cause trouble and things like that.

GOODMAN: Yeah. But a lot of it is theatrical too, isn't it? I mean, in the sense that he loves to get a rise out of people.

GORDON: Well, I don't know. I am not prepared to say that, no. I think he is certain kind of a person, a temperamental person. He is a talented person and he has a way of sounding off without thinking and without disciplining himself. He is that way and has been that way for a long time. I don't think, I don't know—I don't think he would do anything for show or to make impressions on people.

GOODMAN: Certainly not in a planned way?

GORDON: No. Or in any way. I mean I have seen him, you know, do things and all that—but I never felt he was doing them in order to impress a person or an audience in any way.

GOODMAN: How do musicians feel about him, as far as you can observe?

GORDON: Oh, I think a lot of musicians I talk to, or who've talked to me about it, there is a matter of fear. They fear him a little bit. They also almost feel that they want to stay away from him. It's mostly fear, I think, that he generates in people who work for him. And a kind of respect.

GOODMAN: I was going to say, there must be some of that.

GORDON: Yes. There is that respect. Because they know him, they respect his musicianship, they know it and appreciate it. Nonetheless, they do fear him. I have seen some things that happen to musicians, so I can understand why they feel that way.

GOODMAN: Like what, fights?

GORDON: Yes, fights. Threats of fights mostly. It is mostly words. The words. He can be very caustic and he can be very funny too.

GOODMAN: Yes. He has a sharp tongue.

GORDON: He has, and he has got an original kind of style. He's an unusual man, an unusual character.

GOODMAN: What are the good qualities about Mingus that you think about?

GORDON: Well, as I have said, I think he's a generous man. I think he's a man who at one time can be headlong, and he's also built in a kind of big style. He eats big. He drinks big. Maybe not so much today, but I have seen him eat a half-gallon of ice cream before going on. I have seen him bring in red meat, chopped red meat, and eat it raw here. Maybe a pound a sitting, if not more. I have seen him that way. And he is sort of gargantuan in his habits. This is the way I feel about him.

GOODMAN: His whole style is that way.

GORDON: Yeah, his style of living, his style of talking and feeling is that way. I think the word to describe him is gargantuan. That may be a little bit heavy a word for him.

GOODMAN: Well, people constantly suggest he is that. This is not just tied up in his music, but some of his personal qualities are still very endearing, I guess I could say. Even with all the other shit that goes on.

GORDON: Well, I don't know about that. I don't know how endearing he is. I am sure he has had good relationships with certain people over the years. I can't say he is endearing to me, especially. But I think we are good friends. I do like the guy and I respect him for what he is.

GOODMAN: Well, thank you, Max. Anything else you can think of? Anecdotes or funny stories?

GORDON: Yeah, he tore off the front door and threw it downstairs. He hit a man, he hit one of his men on the bandstand once in the stomach. I don't know why. And I know this man, I know he is a good man, but something happened. Maybe words passed, or he hit the wrong note or something. I felt the man would never play with him again, but the man came back for the next set and played.

And he struck him right on the bandstand. This is a kid by the name of Jimmy Knepper. You know Jimmy Knepper, the trombone player? He hit him right in the stomach and I saw it happen.

GOODMAN: Yeah, and he's played with him again. I have heard that about several people who Mingus has had, you know, physical contact with.

GORDON: But he was hit one time too, you know, John. That's a famous story about somebody hitting *him*. I think it was a great bass player. They are tough men. They are tough physical characters too. I never saw it happen but I remember it was kind of a legend and it was talked about. This bass player died in Europe some years ago. What was his name?

GOODMAN: Oscar Pettiford.

GORDON: Oscar Pettiford, yes—Pettiford knocked him down one time. Everybody was quite happy to have seen it happen. Because people are always on the receiving side of Mingus. This was one time he got it. A lot of grateful people.

You heard about that story?

GOODMAN: Yeah, well I had heard that some musician supposedly flattened him, but at first I didn't know who it was.

GORDON: I don't know the circumstances, and I don't know where it happened. I don't think it happened here. It may have happened here, but I don't know.

GOODMAN: He is a lot of man to put on the floor.

NOTES

1. For an extended, rambling, interesting interview with Web Christman, who started Gino's in the basement of a church, see "The Foxhole: Reflections of Web Christman," March 20, 2005, www.sas.upenn.edu/music/westphillymusic/jazz /student_sites/WebChristman/interview.html. The club is long gone.

2. Earl May (1927–2008) studied with Mingus until 1951, then played with Billy Taylor through 1959. Earl was indeed left-handed and played with many jazz greats. See his bio at www.allmusic.com/artist/earl-may-mn0000128778.

3. Slim Gaillard's *Vout-O-Reenee Dictionary* listed all kinds of weird jazz and bop argot. Cory Doctorow calls it "a promotional leaflet" and dates it from the 1930s. See Cory Doctorow, "Slim Gaillard's Vout Dictionary: Jazz Hipster Argot from the 30s," http://boingboing.net/2008/08/22/slim-gaillards-vout.html.

Gaillard was one of my favorites when I was growing up and learning the jazz language—a great musician with a zany sense of humor. I saw him play piano with the backs of his fingers one time in New York, and it was good music! Mike Zwerin did a nice profile ("Slim Gaillard: With a Floy-Floy," *International Herald Tribune*, January 3, 1984, www.pocreations.com/slimarticle.html).

4. An all-request DJ program on WNEW-AM, New York, the Milkman's Matinee started out in 1935, running from two to seven in the morning. Apparently people sent DJ Stan Shaw requests by telegram. I think this is the program Mingus is talking about, which he may have heard in California. See "Radio: Milkman Stan," *Time*, Aug. 14, 1939, www.time.com/time/magazine/article/0,9171,761856,00.html.

5. The Cocoanut Grove nightclub in Boston was destroyed in a disastrous fire on November 1942, killing 492 people. For an eyewitness account by a busboy who worked there, see Steve Wilson, "An Ex-Busboy Recalls Part in Tragedy of Coconut [sic] Grove," *Providence Journal*, Nov. 30, 1980. The bass player who escaped was Jack Lesberg.

6. Sy tells this story, with less detail than he does here, in the foreword to Todd S. Jenkins, *I Know What I Know: The Music of Charles Mingus* (Santa Barbara: Praeger, 2006), xi–xii. As Sy tells it there, when Mingus hired Yusef Lateef and Sy got angry about it, Mingus replied, "If you was me, and you had the chance to hire Yusef Lateef or you, who would *you* hire?"

7. *Who Is Sonny Rollins?*, a 1968 film by director Dick Fontaine.

8. A good history of the Vanguard is here: http://en.wikipedia.org/wiki /Village_Vanguard. See more in chapter 7.

5 Musicians: Reminiscing in Tempo

"Jazz is over. . . . It's impossible to see how the music goes on."

The great beboppers always fascinated me, and it was not just their music. They had a mission, which Mingus defined as being messengers or ministers to the people, but they made themselves into a sect. They were immensely creative, yet self-destructive; they dismissed blues and old-time jazz even as their music consciously grew out of it. Charlie Parker was, as Mingus said, a blues player.

A woman came to my house recently and, when asked what music she wanted to hear, said, "Anything, as long as it's not bebop." The reaction is still there, even now. But bebop helped define the postwar black identity. The extraordinary musicians who made that music took jazz private, as it were, and it's been trying to go public in many forms ever since. It probably should stay private.

• • •

GOODMAN: Charles, I always thought of Bud Powell as such an important figure from that time [the '40s and '50s]. I once wanted to write a book about him, but nobody even talks about the man anymore.

MINGUS: He's a hard one to talk about, man. I'm sure he could do more than play in the key of F, because he was classically trained. His brother was too, Richie Powell. On the back of some of Bud's scores there would be other writing, and it would be Richie Powell's, because Bud had given me some music he [Richie] had written out. I still got some of it—if I could find what they threw away when they evicted me.

Well, Bud, Fats [Navarro], and Bird—they're like saints to me. There won't be many more of those guys, I don't think. Like sacred musicians, they gave everything. I think they really thought they were telling the people—being like ministers in a way, to give the people the message, the spirit to live, whatever it is. They weren't egotistical, or [thinking] they were the greatest either. Bird was never like that. Bud was never like that. Fats was never like it. But he [Fats] knew if he was cutting a trumpet player, if a guy couldn't play, and he'd love to walk in and blow him off the bandstand.

Now, Fats Navarro's a strange guy. I'll get to Bud if I can, but I know more about Fats. Fats Navarro used to walk around to those Cuban joints—you know, those Cuban bands like Perez Prado's, he knew them all over the country when we traveled with Hamp [Lionel Hampton]. He would say, "Let's go to a jam session."

I'd say "fine," and go in with him, to listen. I couldn't [always] understand 'em, but he'd go up and play all the tunes with 'em. Run 'em off the bandstand playing their own tunes! They all thought he was Cuban, that's why he knew all the tunes.

But Fats always said that I played with hate. For instance, the first time he came with the band—Lionel Hampton invited him on the stage, with myself and a little group, we had a jam session on the stage. Hamp wanted us to rise to a great guy like Fats. So nobody had ever heard a bass solo in that band onstage. Well, I got one on "How High the Moon," and I played my ass off, I thought. I played more notes, I played fast as horns. And I could play bass fast when I was young, can still play pretty fast [*vocal demo*].

[*Imitates Fats's high-pitched voice:*] "Goddamn, Mingus, you cut even the trumpets! You cut everybody! But you didn't play shit." Damn, I thought I played well, but you know I respected a guy from New York City—big fat guy, and I wasn't even that fat then.

"You played all the right changes, Mingus, didn't you?"

"Yeah, I played 'em."

"G, G minor, but you didn't say nothing, Mingus, you just played the theory. You didn't tell me how you felt. You didn't say, 'Hello, Fats, I love you.' You didn't play nothing beautiful."

So he woke me up and that's how he did it. And I realized there was something wrong—going out and playing theory, that's what Lloyd [Reese] didn't tell us. Lloyd gave us the theory, and that was Lloyd's hang-up. Maybe in the jam sessions Lloyd was just playing theory. I think it's still great to have that, but when I think of Eric Dolphy coming out the way he did, maybe I missed it and got it late.

GOODMAN: But Fats picked that right up.

MINGUS: And told me about it. You know he wouldn't take nothing from nobody if they were insulting music. Lionel Hampton used to do a lot of dancing onstage, had the saxophone players dancing. Well, Fats could play tenor saxophone too. So he got somebody's tenor one time and when the guys were dancing—you ever see a dog when he's on the grass wiping his ass? Well, Fats came onstage blowing his horn and dragging his butt on the floor, crawling out. He broke the house up. [*In Fats's voice:*] "See, anybody can be a monkey," and he bows to the audience. Fats was always against guys who clown. But he sure could play, man.

GOODMAN: Jesus, he did make some great records. You know, I started to listen to bebop in a serious way about that time, and I didn't know what the message was, exactly, but I got it too. Bud, Fats, and particularly Parker—I don't know why that bunch seemed to have it in that special way.

MINGUS: They had it, man, they had a religious thing. They had a communication with a quiet life, even though they used drugs, some of 'em, they had an insight into . . . they weren't afraid of life, they weren't afraid of living and dying, that's one thing I know.

Now, I can tell you a Bud story—you may not like it, but it's true to fact and Billy Taylor will tell you the exact same way. Art Tatum and Bud Powell and Billy Taylor and someone else were playing Birdland the same time. Billy says, "You know my respect for Art and you know my respect for Bud, but there's no comparison as far as technique is concerned." And there isn't: Art had the technique. So Bud got drunk one night and came up to Art and said, "Art Tatum, you don't play shit, you just play fast." Same as Fats told me.

Art says, "I know that, Bud, but you're drunk tonight. You come in tomorrow night sober, and everything you play in your right and left hands, I'll play with my left." 'Cause you know Art's an old battler, and he don't take no shit from nobody. And he said it just like that, plus he said, "I'll kick your ass."

Now, this ran Bud nuts. A lot of people think it was Fats Navarro playing fast on the trumpet, and that's one thing that started it off. It was the police stick at first to his head, then Fats's trumpet, and then Art Tatum's final plunge. Billy Taylor had been rehearsing, been coming in every day, rehearsing, practicing. Billy is a studious type, specially when guys like Art and Bud are appearing on the same bill. I think he even told me he felt he didn't belong there. So he heard a piano, sounded very sloppy in the left hand. He thought it might have been Art—drunk. Walks in the bar, and it was Bud Powell, going crazy, banging his left hand on the piano, trying to get a left hand going.

He got it going because, three or four months later—well, six months later, I was in Florida with Art Tatum, finally got with the Art Tatum trio, and we were playing Birdland in Florida, Miami Beach proper. We were leaving the club and I'm leading him out 'cause Art was blind and couldn't see. Art stopped me in the doorway—I wasn't even listening—and said, "Who's that? Who's that? We better go back and find out who's on that record."

I don't know who the hell he's listening to—someone playing a record. He said, "That's Bud Powell." It was Bud's first attempt to do the left hand, not "Sure Thing" but another record he made, a solo album where he used the left hand, moving open tenths, everything. He showed Art he could do it, and Art heard it, and he smiled. He wasn't unhappy, a big smile came on his face, cause he knew he woke him up. Bud at that time was just hitting chords and running the right hand. The right hand was a bitch, but as Art said, he could do all that with one hand. He said, "I may not have all the soul you're talking about, but what you're doing, the tune, is child's play."

I thought at Massey Hall [the famous 1953 Mingus, Powell, Parker, Gillespie, and Roach concert on Debut] that Bud Powell played more creatively than Charlie Parker did. I thought Bud was unbelievable on that session, particularly on "All the Things You Are" and "Sure Thing," his solos. Although he made it impossible for anyone to play on "All the Things You Are." He threw the chord on every beat. But no one else can do that shit. On "All the Things," he used to play 4/4 chords on every beat [*taps it out*]—listen to it again. And he got thrown for a minute, and Dizzy had to go out and play the melody and put him in time. But what he was doing was almost impossible to do.

See that's what's so sad about society . . . That's part of the thing that's missing now, the competition. Everybody's got their own schools; it's all academic. Now it's all mouth-to-mouth competition.

GOODMAN: How might that change?

MINGUS: I think it's over, man. Jazz is over. Jazz was born out of guys with big bands, traveling over the world, over the world, meeting in places like California, at Minton's, in Kansas City, any place they can find a piano or where a club owner'll let 'em play. In California the most popular was Billy Berg's. Jazz was born out of guys who were tired of the job they were on, because being in a big band traveling the road is no different from being in a studio—doing the same tunes show after show, one night a dance concert, the other night a jazz concert, no solos (only a few guys get to solo), just reading it off the paper.

And guys got together to play solos, man, to improvise, and improvisation is gone now, just a few old fellas left around still doing it and they're dying out. The avant-garde, I wouldn't even call that soloing. The wish is still there that guys would get together and see who's the best. That's what I tried to do at Carnegie Hall, have a battle to see who's the best: maybe Roland Kirk's not the best, maybe John Handy is—the records will tell.

What's that critic's name from the *Times?* John S. Wilson, John Ass Wilson. He's so sick, man, not to see what I was trying to do. I was trying to save jazz, because [it was] like a Norman Granz concert. They should have more battles on the bandstand, that's what jazz is. Jazz is not me getting up an organized, rehearsed group and playing—anybody can do that. Jazz is jammin', man. When the guys got off the bandstand at work and came on to jam, [it was] to see who was the best—because Charlie Christian cut many a horn-player's ass at Minton's—I wasn't there but I heard the records.

I remember at Massey Hall, the first thing Lennie Tristano said was that Bud Powell cut Bird. Lennie is blind, so that when Dizzy was clowning while Bird was playing and people were applauding, Lennie didn't know what was going on. So he asked me, "Why is the audience so excited? He didn't play anything already."

I say, "They're laughing at Dizzy yelling 'Salt Peanuts' and clowning and dancing."

It's like training for a bullfight; [you don't get that in] schools like Sam Rivers has, or by playing with Ornette.

GOODMAN: All the schools make for leveling.

MINGUS: This is so sad because it's just like the black race is. They're all separated out with a whole lot of different movements, and the people who really count, who make a dollar and could put some money into the movement, the working people, they go to work, go home to fuck, watch television, have a couple of drinks, and that's all. Other people want it this way because they're not capable of making the competition.

. . . When I was a kid, I was real snobbish about anybody who didn't study with Lloyd Reese or go to a conservatory or couldn't answer some of the questions that we learned, like what's the supertonic chord of E-flat? What's the relative minor of A? I remember I would feel that I was a real musician, and I was stirred on to this by Buddy Collette, my best friend, my runnin' buddy, we went everywhere together.

Well, we had a gig at Jefferson High School, a job to play with Roy Eldridge and a couple of guys older than us, and I remember I didn't used to like Roy Eldridge's cocky attitude. And this message is to the avant-garde, it's what's wrong with 'em, which was the same thing that was wrong with me. They're younger, the younger tribe, and I was younger than Roy Eldridge.

I walked in to him and said, "What's the relative minor of B-flat?"

He said, "I'm gonna tell you something, nigger. You young punks out here, I'm running into you every time I turn around. You don't know nothing about me, you don't know about your own people, you don't know about your own people's music. I bet you never heard of Coleman Hawkins, I bet you never listened to him, I bet you can't sing one of his solos. You come in and ask me if I know what the relative minor of B-flat is. How do you know I don't know what the supertonic chord is?"

I said, "What?" I wasn't that far yet.

He says, "I might know what that is." So that was a jazz musician, man, and I was born into that and the competition on the bandstand as to who could outtalk the other guy. But that's all these guys do today—they can talk their asses off. The average avant-garde musician, man, read his articles, they don't make much sense. They don't tie together, they skip all over the place—

GOODMAN: Like the music.

MINGUS: Yeah, they skip all over the fuckin' place, and they make up new terms, don't stick to the musical language we're used to, and I'd just like to say that Roy Eldridge's statement still lives today with me. "You young punks, you don't even listen to your own people, do you? You better get out and learn something about your own people."

Our people today are so separated, man. I heard a young kid who could play when I was in Chicago, and I don't understand how he could learn to play that good because the odds are against him, with rock and roll, rhythm and blues.

GOODMAN: Like John Faddis.

MINGUS: Yeah, where'd he come from? But there should be something or some way to support a guy like that, because he's a freak, a freak of nature. It's almost impossible to raise one of these. It's impossible to see how the music goes on. I hope it doesn't die, man, because that music is very important.

Yeah. I know that on the other hand the battle thing can be carried too far, the contest thing. Because in New Orleans not every musician of caliber could play. You go into the gas station with your car, ask the guy to put some gas into your tank, and he's got a little flute in his hand. Everybody's so musical. And Dannie Richmond taught us something else last night—about why he was dying to go to Brazil, because he heard the street musicians were better than the guys inside the bar. Some of the guys who work can't play as good as the guys in the street, somebody undiscovered. And it would teach some of the guys who got big heads, who overestimate their playing—

Yeah, when the people are into it and they come in on top, then you know you're doing something. Jaki Byard told me the gas station story. A guy says, "You're Jaki Byard, man," and he's playing his flute. Said, "I'll be hearing you tonight." He knows Jaki's gonna play good.

GOODMAN: Where is he now?

MINGUS: Jaki? He's working at Bradley's on Sunday nights but he still teaches in Boston, I think it's the Boston [i.e., New England] Conservatory. Comes down at least once a week, I think. Had his family up there for a while. That was a fingered piano player, man, along with Garland Finney, someone [most people] never heard of. Jaki Byard was as good as Garland Finney, good as Art Tatum and all those cats. Jaki Byard's very underrated, man, knows the history of music, can play that history on piano—old timers, young timers, avant-garde.

GOODMAN: Sy Johnson told me you were the first person to get him to play stride? Is that true?

MINGUS: Probably so, at the Showplace. Could be . . .

Ernie Henry should have made it on alto. Fats Navarro talked about him, and I think he was right: [called him] a Charlie Parker out of work. You heard Ernie Henry?

GOODMAN: Sure, yeah. What happened to him?

MINGUS: He's gone, he's dead too. Big sound.

. . .

We then talked about Dannie Richmond and Eric Dolphy. The subject of Eric led him once again into more thoughts on Ornette Coleman. Ornette's success had to be hard for Mingus to swallow, though here he tried to be, shall we say, accommodating.

Eric and Dannie probably meant more to Mingus personally than just about any other musicians—in or out of his bands.

. . .

MINGUS: You know, with Dannie I could think something in music: and *bing,* here it is. We'd do it together. But we didn't start like that. You know why he could do that? He came to me and said, "Look, man, I'm a saxophone player. I don't know why you want me to learn drums."

FIGURE 6.   Mingus and Dannie Richmond, recording *Changes One* and *Changes Two* at Atlantic Records, 1974. Photo by Sy Johnson.

Jackie McLean's drummer didn't show up one night in Richmond, Virginia, Dannie's home, and Dannie was a rock-and-roll tenor player, so Dannie said, "I can play a little drums, I'll keep time for you." Lotta guys do that—Wilbur Ware—I keep a little time, you know. So Jackie said, "That motherfucker could be the best drummer I ever heard. So what you want, Charlie, is a Max Roach. Well, this cat is not a drummer yet but you can make him a drummer."

So I believed Jackie and I got Dannie and said, "Dannie, first you got to understand what I'm doing."

He said, "Man, I'm not a drummer so I'm not going to understand anything you say."

I say, "Well, you start like this: four in this foot [*foot tapping: boom-boom-boom-boom*], four in this foot and three in this one [*boom-boom-boom*]: I'm playing 4/4 and waltz at the same time.

GOODMAN: Right, like 6/8 time.

MINGUS: So get that in your feet, and he did it. "Now get syncopated eighth rests, dotted quarter in your left hand [*tom-boom, tom-boom, tom*], now eighth notes on the cymbal—[*ding ding a-ding a-ding*]."

He says, "You're crazy."

I say, "Well, that's your first lesson."

So he went home, came back, and we got all our shit together and we're playing in one tempo, and I look at him in a certain way and that meant double tempo, and another [signal] meant one-half slower, another, go back to where you were, and another meant go into three [*etc., with sounds*]. We had all that shit down, and people thought we were doing it like magic, and pretty soon we didn't even have to do this [*facial gesture*]. I'd just think it and he'd be right there.

GOODMAN: Why? How?

MINGUS: I don't know, man, it made me start to believe in God.

GOODMAN: Everybody says that about the way he played with you and how you communicated. Was it the way the tunes were laid out?[1]

MINGUS: Well, man, we would even turn our backs to each other—later—and say we'll hit one note together. [*Shouting:*] "CLAP!" Just like that, man. Now he wasn't watching and trying to peek back and see if I was looking. And no way he could do it because my fingers were like this [hidden]. But I'd be thinking and waiting for the pulse to hit, and we hit together, man, so I said, "Wait a minute, man, let's quit." In fact, man, when I am really sincere about a prayer, man, I think of Dannie, 'cause he has a hell of a faith—he's a very religious man.

GOODMAN: Want to talk about Eric a little bit?

MINGUS: I'll try. When I lived in California, there was a jazz workshop band that Lloyd Reese used to run: Dexter Gordon, Ernie Royal—and some very famous guys of the day in it, Buddy Collette and others, Oliver Nelson.[2] Anyway, there was always a kid [Eric Dolphy] sitting on the steps when we'd come down from rehearsal. He never came in, he had a lump on his head. Good, full of very nervous energy, very enthusiastic about how we all were studying, and saying that some day he'd be with us. Then one day I saw this same guy cutting Lloyd Reese's hedges and cutting the grass; I realized he was working his way through school by taking care of the place.

Well, I never got to play with him in California, never heard him in California. I heard some records of his on which he sounded like Charlie Parker. He was on a Charlie Parker kick but went to a style of his own later on. In the '60s Chico Hamilton got very popular and Buddy Collette had been doing a lot of recording with him, but Chico came to town, came to Birdland, with Eric Dolphy. Anyway, Eric sounded about the same, he didn't play "out." So I hired him, and he left Chico's band and we went to work in the Showplace.

All of a sudden, I never heard nothing like that, I thought he was crazy, man, because he wasn't playing anything like I heard him play before. One thing I never do is tell a guy how to solo, I never tell him a solo is wrong, because I don't get blamed for solos. If a guy plays bad as hell, if he fools the public, it doesn't hurt my band, even if I don't like it.

So, Eric was always at my house, always somewhere, looking at my old music—otherwise we would have had just an ordinary quartet—and he found some music I'd written in California, one of the things was called "What Love" and "All the Things You Could Be by Now if Sigmund Freud's Wife Was Your Mother."

He said, "Why don't we play things like this, Mingus?"

I say, "That's written for Buddy Collette, you guys can't play it."

He says, "I can't play it as good as Buddy, but I'll take it home and study it and I'll play it."

So he took the music out of the book and began to practice on it. Out of those two tunes a whole style came. That was probably the greatest band I ever had. I never did like Ted Curson's playing, he could read good, his ensemble playing was good, but his soloing was always stiff—like he couldn't quite make it. (Say that in the book, I don't care.) And Eric to me was just . . . out. And something else—I had stopped soloing, and Eric turned around to me one night and said, "Why don't you play solos, you can play."

"Well, I want the kids to play."

"Man, you ought to play, this is your band."

So I started playing solos again, and got pretty good again. Got so very famous-good that—what's that name, the white bass player?—Scott LaFaro—used to come by every night, lay back in a chair and listen. Couldn't tell his playing from my playing sometimes.

You know, a person never knows his own temperament, but I don't remember ever doing anything to hurt Eric because Eric never cursed or used loud boisterous language, never got angry. This is in my band, I don't know what happened in Chico [Hamilton]'s band. All he did was blow his horn, he took it all out on his horn, a very quiet person. Got the release on his horn and shut up otherwise. The change in his music was this: if Ornette Coleman can make it, as less of a player, then I guess Eric said, "I might as well do some of the things I want to do and stop playing Charlie Parker." That's a simple way to put it.

Although I don't want to appear to put down Ornette Coleman because Ornette Coleman has fooled a lot of people, I mean he's convinced a lot of people, and to do that you have to have something. He may have something I'm not capable of hearing, something beyond music, something to do with a spiritual thing that nobody catches on to right away, because I like some of his compositions.

That's what people always do, especially critics. Soon as a new guy comes around they start asking musicians what they think about this guy. It shouldn't matter a damn what I think about him, because I don't have that much time to listen to him, I'm busy writing. I'm busy doing something about my own private life. If he's got a following, then he must be doing something.

Ornette Coleman says he likes me. But I'll tell you the truth, man, he can't like me, because I keep time. I started keeping time the last four or five years, while the rhythm-and-blues bass players started playing like I play. They all started playing patterns, and I used to play patterns with Teddy Charles, nineteen years ago.

He can't like my kind of playing because I play rhythm. Sometimes I play broken rhythms, sometimes I play like you say the modern thing is. But they're liars, they are either liars or they're reaching over their heads. I know what they've done.

Did you ever see Sam Rivers play piano at the Newport Festival? Wasn't nobody there, at the afternoon festival, and I'm glad. He just bangs the keys, he's not a piano player. Just hits any notes in the high register and tells the bass player to solo. It's percussion, but don't nobody think he's a piano player. Very fast, [*trill*]—playing very fast things, but he's no Cecil Taylor—we assume *he* knows what he's doing.

Sue keeps telling me I should go to Sam Rivers for sidemen, but there's no sidemen there for me, and there's no place I can go to find them, except to the old ones I know like McPherson. If we had jam sessions like I had at Carnegie Hall where the guys are honest and called tunes that everybody knew—or even improvised on a theme or improvised on nothing or just made some noise—let's see who can make the most noise—if they invited everybody in, instead of just their clan, I'd say they were doing something good.

Funny thing happened when I was in Copenhagen the first time. Dexter [Gordon] doesn't really listen to Ornette Coleman, the things happening in America, but he buys the records and plays them. He takes his horn out one day and says, "Mingus, avant-garde," and if they could play as good as he did for the five minutes he played, I could go for it. He was saying, "Lester Young, Mingus," and he'd play a little Lester Young. "Ben Webster, Mingus," "Coleman Hawkins, Mingus."

GOODMAN: He's a professional, man.

MINGUS: Yeah, you don't fuck with Dexter. And Gene Ammons either. If Gene Ammons wanted to play avant-garde, what could you do with him? I wouldn't want to hear that, man! I've heard McPherson do it, he did it for me one time. Man, it makes Ornette sound sick, like Ornette played backwards, especially because he misses on his horn—just like Ornette— *eeek*—and he won't cover it, he'll let it stay right where it is.

· · ·

We talked a little about the record he and Duke and Max Roach had made in 1962—*Money Jungle*. Mingus had been taken to task by some critics for walking out of the session (though Duke cajoled him back in). Max Roach later accused Mingus of being drunk and of leaving because he couldn't stand Duke's left-hand stride piano obscuring the bass.[3]

· · ·

MINGUS: If Duke Ellington's book [*Music Is My Mistress*] is as bad as his excerpt on me, the book doesn't make it, because he's lying to begin with —I didn't walk out because of, as he said, mikes or anything. I walked out because Max Roach wasn't playing good drums. Max was putting him on, playing old time, like an old man, like—I'll get his name, old time drummer, name some—

GOODMAN: Zutty Singleton.

MINGUS: That's who it was! Zutty Singleton. So I asked Max to stop puttin' Duke on, but he wouldn't pay attention during the session. "Why don't you play your way? Duke didn't hire us to come here and play what we think he's playing. He hired us to come in and be ourselves." And Max got worse.

GOODMAN: That's exactly why he got you together—to be yourselves. A beautiful idea.

MINGUS: Yeah, and Max didn't do it, man. I knew it all the way. He was trying to show he knew the history of jazz. I don't put him down for it, Max is a young man compared to me. So I can understand now why he did it. He figured, "Here's an old cat like Duke, I'm gonna play old-fashioned drums."
      But if he'd wanted Zutty Singleton, he'd have got Zutty Singleton. He wanted Max to play like he played with Charlie Parker. That's what Duke wanted because he didn't put me down in the book by my standards, 'cause he didn't even recognize why I'd walk off the bandstand or out of the studio.

GOODMAN: Now wait a minute, he didn't put you down in the book or anybody.

MINGUS: Yes, he did, he put me down, man. He didn't say why I walked off.

GOODMAN: No, bullshit. He just mentioned in the recent book—

MINGUS: I saw the book, man—

GOODMAN: He just said, "We made a record with Charlie Mingus and Max Roach." Period. That's all he said.

MINGUS: No, he said a lot of things—a whole long thing, I read it, man. He said, "I went and spoke to Charlie Mingus and told him that Impulse records . . ."

GOODMAN: Well, maybe I haven't got to that yet.

MINGUS: No, you haven't got to that. See, you wasting a lot of time with that bullshit, man. If I tell you something's so, it's so.

GOODMAN: I'll tell you what was nice in Ellington's book, the talk about James P. Johnson and Willy the Lion Smith, man. Have you gotten to that yet?

MINGUS: No. James P. Johnson? I never heard James P. play, but I have heard Willy the Lion.

GOODMAN: I heard Willy the Lion once when I was in college.

MINGUS: I heard him all the time at the Newport Festival, jam sessions, and at the parties. The rich people gave parties and he'd be playing there with his derby and cigar.

GOODMAN: Was he as good at the end of his life as in his early days?

MINGUS: Well, I don't know about his early days, I first heard him in the early '50s at Newport.

GOODMAN: Well, Ellington thinks he's the best.

MINGUS: No, I would have a different choice than that.

GOODMAN: Then there was a second generation, which was Fats Waller, and he [Ellington] didn't include himself but he's of that time anyway, and who else? Tatum he puts in a different category—says he's the master. Best part of the book so far.

MINGUS: Sure is funny, man. If I hadn't heard Teddy Wilson in the last five years, I would have called his name a lot, but he's playing so society, man, so prissy.

GOODMAN: He always had that in his music, though, at least I heard it. Too bad.

MINGUS: I guess Lionel Hampton and Benny Goodman brought him to play a little different, you know, because he sure sounded different than that. Yeah, piano players. Garland Finney, and so did Nat Cole—you never heard of Nat Cole?—they had both hands goin'.

GOODMAN: Yeah, sure, he was one of the first people I heard when I began to really listen to jazz music. The King Cole Trio.

MINGUS: Yeah, but they never recorded Nat as a soloist.

We used to go to jam sessions with Norman Granz, Art Tatum, Nat Cole, Calvin Jackson. We'd have the battle. I'd come late cause I'd been working. And I remember one night Art Tatum sat down and played "Body and Soul" and "Tea for Two" at the same time. With the chord changes still goin'. And Calvin's turn was next, and he did the same thing but he did "Tea for Two," "Body and Soul," and something else—"Perdido," I think, he got a "Perdido" thing going. That's another piano player, Calvin Jackson. He wasn't no heavy swinger like Art.

GOODMAN: I dig what you're saying about Nat Cole, just a fine, light touch, just some beautiful records.

MINGUS: He has a left hand too, man.

GOODMAN: Do you remember those records he did with Hampton? Like "Central Avenue Breakdown"? I think Hampton played drums on a couple.

MINGUS: Lionel Hampton's first band had—or was that Les Hite?—had Oscar Bradley on drums, Oscar Moore guitar, Nat King Cole on piano, and Johnny Miller on bass. Or was it Wesley Prince? I think he changed: Wesley Prince on bass.

It's just too bad then that guys like Finney stayed in California, because there's one good thing about New York in the early days of jazz: when the big companies were recording certain artists like Coleman Hawkins, there were small companies recording the other artists who weren't as famous but were playing in the same clubs. It's too bad we didn't hear Nat Cole and Garland Finney in those days when I was a kid, before 1939, when I was in high school, in 1937–38 when I was working with a piano player named Herman Grimes—

GOODMAN: Is he in the original *Underdog* book?

MINGUS: Naw, I didn't mention him. Anyhow, Herman Grimes, and he had a guy playing bones called Bones, played meat bones and spoons between his fingers, man, like kids used to play the bones, but it was a hambone. That was the rhythm section. And the thing about this piano player [Grimes], he could only play in F-sharp, B-natural, A-flat, D-flat—that's why I took the job: he played in hard keys, keys we weren't familiar with unless we were reading. And the kinds of jobs he used to get was big hotels—like this one [where we are taping] ain't nothing. The best hotels, and the dining rooms—I don't know how he got those kind of jobs.

GOODMAN: Did he have a group, or what?

MINGUS: The group was me [and the bones player] and him on the piano—bones, piano, and bass. That kind of music, hambone music, was—they sang, both of 'em sang, played all the tunes you hear on the radio, the blues, and things that were current. They played requests, anything someone asked for, they knew it, but the key they knew it in was unbelievable.

GOODMAN: Did they do that for their own enjoyment? 'Cause it would be lost on the public, they wouldn't give a shit.

MINGUS: I never found out. I just know he never played in B-flat, never played in C, in F, in G, in D. Well, D's a little rough, he might have played in D. They call it black-keyboard playing; the reason why B-natural came in there is that there are so many sharps you've got black keys anyway. But he was mainly a black-keyboard piano player—A-flat, G-flat, he skipped B-flat, man, don't know why, he only had a few keys. My job was to keep time . . . and live a Jim Crow life—you come in the back door, put on a waiter's jacket, then you would drink coffee all night long, 'cause they didn't allow you to drink.

They wouldn't sell us no booze or give us no booze. These guys didn't drink anyway, and I didn't drink myself—I was a kid—but I didn't see them drinking. And, see, those were the tortures of it.

•   •   •

Mingus also loved to talk about musicians both great and unknown, as if he wanted the latter to have their share of fame. Many were from California.

•   •   •

GOODMAN: In Ross Russell's book, *Bird Lives!*, he was describing the competition in Kansas City, which was incredible—

MINGUS: Yeah.

GOODMAN: —and it reminded me of what you said about the competition with the blues singers on the West Coast, I think it was.

MINGUS: Yeah, yeah. Wynonie Harris, Joe Turner, T-Bone Walker.

Well, you know Eddie Lockjaw Davis used to be the one to audition the guys who wanted to sit in at Minton's during the time of Charlie Christian, Ben Webster, Coleman Hawkins, Monk was playing. And he told me that you had to pass certain qualifications to show you could do some of the changes to the tunes they'd be playing.

And there was a guy called "The Demon" used to come in, just dying to play. He didn't know anything about music—he was like a shipyard worker or somebody on an airplane crew—but said he was transcending all the proper changes. Yeah, "The Demon." [*Laughs.*] And he would say, "If the Demon get up there and play, man, you're in trouble." Somehow he got to play; he must have walked up some time when Eddie wasn't there.[4]

Get a chance to make an audition and go on. Well, they didn't let him play, but that's why jazz survived for so many years—because they wouldn't let [people like] the Demon play.

In my original book I said that anybody that calls himself "Cannonball" or "Blockbuster"—those kind of names appeal to the public, and if you notice, those are the kind of names the rock-and-roll kids use.

GOODMAN: Yeah, really far-out names, goofy names. They're right, it's a good sales gimmick.

MINGUS: Blockbuster's a good one. Ain't nobody used it yet.

GOODMAN: Blockbuster Mingus and his Quintet. What else can you tell me about Minton's, Monroe's, and all that?

MINGUS: Well, I wasn't there, I got to New York after it was all over. I worked [one time] at Minton's in the proper lounge.

But I'd like to talk about some musicians that have not been heard. I was in Copenhagen, talking with Dexter. He said, "You remember a guy named Finney?"

I said, "Garland Finney, yeah."

And he was talking about Garland Finney, Art Tatum, Nat Cole. He didn't mention Teddy Wilson, but he was talking about top piano players, guys who had really made it and Garland Finney never made it. So then we got on to Lawrence Lees on trumpet, Red Back on trumpet, uhh, Eddie Taylor on tenor saxophone, Bumps Meyers on tenor saxophone—he's got one of those names—uhh, Jack Kelson, Buddy Collette got a little fame—a lot of good musicians came out of California.

GOODMAN: Dexter was playing with them in the early days?

MINGUS: Dexter knew them, he's from California. Jerry Wiggins—we had a trio with Dexter Gordon at a pimp's club, pimp owner. Dexter knows all the names, even remembers the name of the pimp, name of the club.

GOODMAN: "The Pimp's Club": that'd be a great name for a club right now.

MINGUS: Yeah, "The Pimp's Club" or "The After Hours Club."

GOODMAN: What time are you talking about now?

MINGUS: This is '39 or '40.

GOODMAN: Was that before the Alvino Rey time or after?

MINGUS: That's just about the same time.

GOODMAN: And you went on the road with him?

MINGUS: He never went very far when I was with him. He worked around Hollywood all the time—one-nighters.

I liked his book 'cause he had compositions written in A-natural, B-natural, different keys; it was good reading. And I was on a real studying kick then, I was studying bass then. And anything like that was very interesting.

GOODMAN: Well, that goes back to what you told me Lloyd Reese taught you, about playing in different keys.

MINGUS: Yeah, Lloyd taught me by ear, by systematic playing, but this was reading—with a big band. Uhh, Simano [Franz Simandl] covers it; it's just good to do it in person. Simano's a bass book.[5]

GOODMAN: When did you get into Schillinger?

MINGUS: My wife took it up, I didn't get into it, but I looked at it. No, I'm not a Schillinger man. She told me that I was doing the same things he was talking about already. She went through the book so fast, she knew more than I did about music. This is Celia, my second wife. Celia Germanis, Celia Neilson after that.

GOODMAN: Then after Alvino Rey, you went with Hampton on the road for a while.

MINGUS: Yeah, I don't know when, man, but it was after Alvino. And then I was rehearsing to go to the Art Tatum trio. I was supposed to go to the Nat King Cole trio, but I think my reputation stopped him. I think somebody must have told him I was a bad character or something. I went as far as to go to the tailor and get my suits cut down.

Johnny Miller was on bass before I came in. And, uhh, Oscar Moore, guitar. Yeah, "Sweet Lorraine," hard tunes like that. Kids don't play tunes like that anymore. The changes are hard to get through. That was Garland Finney's audition tune. He died, long time ago, died in the '50s.

GOODMAN: Does Dexter make a living over in Denmark?

MINGUS: He doesn't just play in Copenhagen; a girl told me last night she's got this club in Italy, in Rome, where Dexter goes, and Johnny Griffin, yeah, he's over there. She was saying that Dexter plays Sweden— he was in Sweden when I first got into Copenhagen, goes to Paris.

GOODMAN: So he makes the tour on the continent.

MINGUS: Yeah. He plays by himself, doesn't have his own band; he'll get a pick-up rhythm section.

GOODMAN: Is Don Byas alive? I know he came back here for a while.

MINGUS: No, he passed here . . . No, he didn't die here, he died in Amsterdam.

GOODMAN: So what happened on the Hampton tour? What was the band like, the whole experience like?

MINGUS: Lionel always had good musicians in his band. He had a guy named Bobby Plater who played first alto, probably still with him. One of the greatest soloists you ever heard on alto, but he never took a solo. I wrote some arrangements which gave him a solo, that's why I know he can play. He swings on his first parts, plays first alto.

GOODMAN: That was the first time you toured, right?

MINGUS: My first time. Cleve Dell was in the band, Fats Navarro. Fats took Kenny Dorham's place. . . . That's not in the old book, is it?

GOODMAN: In the *Underdog?* No, but there's a lot of stuff about Fats.

MINGUS: It was good to be with a guy like Milt Buckner who writes so well. The band was gradually breaking up, but still Lionel managed to get guys that could play. Morris Lane was in the band, tenor player. Morris, when I heard him in California with a quartet, had a style that he never changed from, but when Bird came out, he changed styles and started sounding like Teddy Edwards. Morris changed his style, and it hurt my feelings. He had such a beautiful sound, the way he played. He's dead too.

GOODMAN: He never made any records under his own name, did he?

MINGUS: No, the closest you can get to that was what we called a bebop session, with myself, Morris Lane, Dodo Marmarosa, someone else on drums. We lined up doing my tunes on that session, the small-band session [for Debut].

GOODMAN: . . . OK, in 1951 you came to New York. Who did you play with in your first time in New York?

MINGUS: First time in New York, I had to get a job because I was about to lose my wife. She [didn't] come along, I came first with Red Norvo, and Red had a television show—I'm backing up on you so I can get in a long story, you got time?—and Red Norvo became very Jim Crow, man, because he went along with the television company which was Jim Crow.

GOODMAN: You put that in *Beneath the Underdog*, and people jumped on you—

MINGUS: Well, let me tell the story, man. The television company was prejudiced, they didn't want any negroes, any dark skins on the first color TV show because it would be shown in private houses—I don't know what that meant—with Mel Torme, Red Norvo, Tal Farlow, and myself, and some other dancers and other things that went on. The guy who ran the show looked like the big impresario of New York, with the elephants on his show . . .

GOODMAN: Ed Sullivan?

MINGUS: No, the other one, before him. Tall slender fellow with the eyeglasses. Everyone's forgotten him, but he had the biggest TV show, biggest following of all, man.

GOODMAN: Jack Paar.

MINGUS: Go ahead, man, you'll get him. Plays piano—

GOODMAN: Steve Allen.

MINGUS: Yeah. So they couldn't get Steve, they got a guy that looked like Steve, a duplicate. It was that kind of a show that we appeared on. But we were also playing in the background for anyone else who went on. They didn't have no band, we were the only music they had. And I heard their guy say, "There's too much color on that set, too colored, have to do something about that."

Next thing I got a phone call from Red not to come. We had done about two-three days shooting. I didn't need no makeup, that's one thing that bugged 'em. So Red Norvo went on, and he began to not show up on his night job, which was at a nightclub on the East Side, so it was just me and Tal [playing]. And I quit, because I knew what he was doing. If he did show up, he was so drunk you couldn't say anything to him. He never paid me my back money. I used to go by his hotel in the morning and wait, I wanted to kill him, because I was more concerned about the race problem where he should have stood up as a man and said, "All of us go," that's all he had to do—

GOODMAN: Right, like Benny Goodman.

MINGUS: Because they had been shooting for so long, that to shoot the whole thing over again, they couldn't afford that. So if Red had been a man—well, fuck him, man—they would have just went on to do it with a black man in the show. But they fired me and got someone else to take the close shots, they reshot the close-up shots. If we were playing in the background, it was all right. They let that go, but when the close-ups for the trio came, they wanted another face. That was Clyde Lombardi. He's a bald-headed cat, man, [*unintelligible*] and I know I was playing the music, man, there wasn't nothing wrong with the music. That's a little about Red. Tal was from up in the mountains, with his moonshine, what do you call that? Moonshine territory, what do you call that?

GOODMAN: Kentucky, Tennessee.

MINGUS: Kentucky, he's from Kentucky. No, Carolina, he's Carolina Slim, they call him that.

And they had a piano player who was MC for one show, but his biggest downfall was that he looked like Steve Allen 'cause Steve Allen was getting big then, and he wasn't. He was also a disk jockey too. Steve was never a disk jockey.

GOODMAN: He was great, goddammit. I think Steve Allen did some great shows.

MINGUS: He had a hell of an imagination. I remember when he had Monk on his show. Monk doesn't talk to anybody—or didn't in those days, maybe he talks now—and Steve was coming to ask me, "What am I supposed to do? I got to relate to this man to put the show on." I was on with Monk, went to my manager Sue—uhh—Sue—Judy—uhh—Celia [*laughter*]—Celia got the show, she went to Steve Allen and asked him why he wasn't booking any jazz.

GOODMAN: Which he supposedly loves—

MINGUS: That's right. She was traveling with my band. He always talked about it and played the records. So she tried to get my band on, and he said "Mingus is not heard of enough. Can you get somebody like Miles Davis or Monk?"

She said, "I can get Monk." And Monk was in jail. That's why she knew she could get him.

GOODMAN: About the card?—

MINGUS: Yeah, the cabaret card. It's funny how people think—no one ever thought about getting Monk out before the TV show, but the TV show comes up, and they call Monk's name, and they say, "Well, we'll get Monk out of jail. Pay his bail. Must be able to get that for him, just a few dollars."

So I first went to this little house where he lived, he's such a beautiful man. I'm glad he doesn't talk, man, he says more with his silence and his music.

GOODMAN: When did you first meet him?

MINGUS: That was the first time I met him, early '50s, when I was with Teo Macero, Teddy Charles, the Composers Workshop. We always played with Monk. Monk sure led that thing though, man. He didn't care whether he got out of jail or not, he was gonna play his tunes. We played "Round 'Bout Midnight" and [*sings phrase from "Well You Needn't"*].

So, went to pick him up for rehearsal. I think I had a car; I used to drive all the time. In those days it wasn't as difficult parking as it is now, man. I got a lot of tickets five years later, man, never got tickets before that. (We got to get back to Red Norvo pretty soon.) But Monk was saying, "What we gonna play?" He was checking it out because he knew I had my own band [on the show].

And Steve Allen wanted to play piano with Monk, at the same time, and they worked it out, and he knew his tunes too, man. He sat down, played, Monk played. He asked questions like this: "Tell me, Thelonious Monk, what is it about your playing that makes you so different from the rest of the piano players in jazz?" On camera, man.

And Monk would say, "Mmm-hmm" [*laughs*] and Steve would say a million words, and Monk would come up, "Hmmmmm."

And, "How about you and I doing a tune together?"

Monk say, "Round 'Bout Midnight."

Steve would say, "No, I don't know that one, Monk. How about [*sings phrase from "Well You Needn't"*], and Monk loved it. Yeah. That was a good show. We didn't get much money but we got some publicity and I got another contract, helped us to get nightclub jobs. The same as when the Beatles came to America and did TV shows. They weren't heard of before the Ed Sullivan show—they got work out of that. Paid advertisement.

GOODMAN: Fantastic publicity.

MINGUS: You know, we need another Ed Sullivan. Put me on it.

GOODMAN: You haven't seen Monk lately?

MINGUS: He's been sick. Very sick, man. He don't play or nothing. He started playing about last week. The tenor player, what's his name? My copyist—

GOODMAN: Paul Jeffrey. He started his own group, an octet or something.

MINGUS: Yeah, Paul did, I don't blame him. Paul said he was talking to Monk and he's practicing piano now.

GOODMAN: It was bad, eh?

MINGUS: They don't know what it is, but he beats it with his mind. He couldn't lay down and die like the rest of 'em. He's got that shit, man, he's got that voodoo, he's a voodoo artist.

Put it down, man, he's a voodoo artist. He's a [*sounds like*] romo-juvenahl.

GOODMAN: Has he still got his lady, Nellie?

MINGUS: Yeah, he still with Nellie. And Nica's his friend [Baroness Nica de Koenigswarter]. Nica won't let anything go wrong with him: when he gets sick, he goes to Nica's house. Big grand piano, ping-pong table. Somebody went to visit Monk and beat him on ping-pong. Was it Paul? 'Cause Monk can play some ping-pong. It's just like he plays piano, man. You don't know when the paddle's coming. He throws you off. His rhythm throws you off, 'cause he waits till the ball's too late. There's a rhythm to it, when you watch a guy—*ping-pong-pada-bong, boom-boom*. No *boom-boom* with Monk, Monk goes "BAPP!" He waits for you.

'Cause I can play pretty good ping-pong, and Milt Jackson can play pretty good ping-pong, but he can't beat Monk. I know one guy can beat him—Britt Woodman. And Nesuhi Ertegun, I think Nesuhi Ertegun can beat him. They were both in the finals at the Los Angeles ceremonies. Britt and Nesuhi Ertegun played professional. I can play better, sometimes, but I've played Ertegun and I've played Bags, Milt Jackson. Bags played about one-tenth the game of Britt and Ertegun. Ask him if he ever played Ertegun. I gave him a pretty good game, but I played so much worse than Milt that I'm gonna beat him—because I got off-rhythms.

GOODMAN: You're doing Monk style.

MINGUS: Yeah, but this was about ten years later I played Monk. This was in the Berkshires, concerts up there. Ertegun came up, said, "You can't beat me, Mingus. You play good bass but you can't beat me. I used to be the champ."

GOODMAN: Well, man, it's the competition, right?

MINGUS: Yeah, that's the way music should be, man. Put the gloves on, let's see who's the baddest. I'm tired of all these critics trying—that's why *Down Beat*'s going out of business, man. *Down Beat*'s going out of business because everyone is afraid to say who they believe in. They're afraid that someone will knock 'em. OK, man, like Ornette Coleman's the greatest because of this. And the next day, I say, Ornette, Charlie McPherson, and three other alto players I know should go on the bandstand and have a jam session and find out. What are they gonna do?

GOODMAN: Or do the same thing in the magazine, have a little exchange.

MINGUS: That would be good, helpful, that would help the magazine a lot. But if there was someplace they could go and listen with their own ears and the critics could hear for themselves. And what are they gonna say? "Sit down and play a tune together." This is how deep this is, man, it's so simple it's deep.

Ornette's gonna say, "Hold, my man. I gotta bring my arrangements in. What do you mean, get on the bandstand and play together?"

Buddy Collette's gonna say, "Oh, man, let's play your music, Ornette, bring your music."

Benny Carter's gonna say, "Well, OK, Ornette, we'll play your music."

McPherson's gonna say, "Man, jazz is not reading music. Jazz is blowing together. Let's blow together. Let's play something that Ornette can play, and that Benny Carter can play, let's please find a tune that everybody can play."

So they start with [*laughing*] "All the Things You Are," "Body and Soul," they start naming tunes off, and if the guy doesn't know the tune, what are you gonna do? 'Specially if you tell him to take the first chorus. The first chorus is generally the melody. It's very sad, man. It's very sad that we will never know.

I think the world's coming to an end. I think that Jesus is coming now. And he's gonna arrive in a chariot and he's gonna take the sinners and put them in one corner, sitting by the devil, and he goes in with the angels and says, "Let's have a jam session."

And Ben Webster's gonna get up and bring his horn out, Coleman Hawkins gonna get up, Bird'll get up and get on the bandstand with Buddy Collette, Ornette Coleman, and Benny Carter, and say "What you want to play?" And it will be very funny 'cause the guys who can play don't care what tune you call. They either have perfect pitch and can hear the changes, or they know all the tunes, their minds are alert. I mean it's ridiculous that a guy can't play on another man's tune. I can play anybody's tune once I hear it. It's very sad, man.

CHAPTER 5 COMMENTARY

Dan Morgenstern on Eric Dolphy and Mingus

MORGENSTERN: I think one thing that can still make Mingus cry is thinking about Eric.

GOODMAN: Were they very close?

MORGENSTERN: They were. Musically and personally, and in a sense Mingus has had a lot of great musicians going through his groups, but Eric was perhaps the most gifted of all of them. Also, he was very young and his death came very suddenly. It was a big shock.

GOODMAN: How did he die? I've forgotten.

MORGENSTERN: Well, he died in Europe, and apparently he was diabetic without having known it. It's never been completely clarified, but I don't think they did an autopsy. I think it was natural causes. I always felt that there was something wrong with Eric because he had these strange bumps on his head. Like so many musicians, he never had a thorough physical. He must have had one when he was in the Army for a while; I guess they checked him out then. There were probably things he shouldn't have done, maybe; he wasn't a heavy drinker but he drank. It may have been a combination or something.[6]

GOODMAN: That time with Eric seemed to be an exceptional period in his life. I mean his music was sounding awfully good.

Paul Jeffrey on Mingus and Monk

GOODMAN: How do Mingus and Monk get along? Do they see each other at all?

JEFFREY: Yeah, they seem to get along very well, as far as I can ascertain. Mingus always speaks very well of Monk, and vice versa.

For me it was a rare opportunity. I consider myself very fortunate to have worked with both of them. I find that their approaches are different but the standards are equally high. In fact, they're both geniuses, with very different personalities. And that's all I can really say about that subject. Different personalities they certainly are.

GOODMAN: It's hard to live with geniuses too, isn't it?

JEFFREY: Well, I never really seemed to have too much trouble, you know. Like a lot of people say they have trouble relating [to Monk or Mingus], and I always believe that if you are sincere, a person knows when you're really sincere, and that's all I can offer and contribute. That's my philosophy and it's always worked out.

Music is such a vast thing, there's no corner on music. Myself I feel that the more I'm involved in its particular facets, the more I grow. I've learned a lot of music, you know, being associated with Mingus. He's taken time, sometimes just sitting down and playing the piano and showing me a lot of things he was doing, the way he thought about music, which is very rare. That's an opportunity very few people have ever had. Something I always remember.

GOODMAN: When did you start with Monk?

JEFFREY: I started in 1970 in the spring. I had a call from him to make a job in North Carolina, and I'd never rehearsed or seen the music. I was scared to death. Wilbur Ware called me for the job, he was in the band at the time. And I went down. Monk didn't say a word to me, just "hello" at the airport, that's it. I checked into the hotel and didn't see him until we went on the bandstand and started to play. I figured to myself, if I can get through this first number, you know—and I did.

GOODMAN: What did he call? Something you knew?

JEFFREY: I think he started out with "Blue Monk," and afterwards he played "Hackensack," then "Bright Mississippi." When we got done with that, he didn't say anything, nothing. I kept my ears open and had some of the music, and [the silence] went on until about the second day when I got enough nerve to say something to him. I didn't really know what to say, and actually there really wasn't too much to say. And he seemed ready to talk to me, though I still was afraid to ask him about the music. So the third night, I think finally I asked him, "If there's something I'm doing that's wrong or something, I wish you would tell me."

All he said was, "It's cool."

Then later he asked me to go to Japan. I worked with Basie for a month after that, and when I got back to town I called him, and he said, "We want to go to Japan. Get your passport." And Monk is a wonderful person. He never bothers you, says anything—you know what I mean? He's got to understand each individual. Mingus is a person who might say something to you, and if you've got an ego you might get real mad, or he might do something you figure is not fair. But in music you can't look at it that way. You have to look at the music.

GOODMAN: And keep the personal stuff out of it, as far as you can.

JEFFREY: Right. Anything a person does that benefits his music you have to accept. A lot of people take things personally, but there's no personality in music. The only personality is the music.

GOODMAN: Right, that's hard to remember, I guess.

JEFFREY: Very hard, and a lot of musicians feel in order to make money they have to—have to have a personal star image, see, and that gets in the way of the music.

GOODMAN: When you first played with Charles, did you get a response?

JEFFREY: I don't know. Actually my association with him was first not in playing, it was the scoring. So I didn't have to create any type of impression playing-wise. You know, I came in the big band to read the charts, and I read the charts. I didn't go in the band to be a soloist because he had a soloist. He had Bobby Jones, so then afterwards he asked me to play in the band, but mainly—you know, that's another thing that musicians tend to—at the time, he has Charles [McPherson] and Bobby and Lonnie [Hillyer], they know the music.

Everybody wants to jump up and take solos, but you know a big band is not just soloists, the band is the soloist. The ego gets involved. So playing with Thelonious really prepared me for a lot of standards in different types of music and for playing with Mingus.

GOODMAN: That's great, Paul. I compliment you. You've got a nice thing going there.

JEFFREY: It is a nice thing.

NOTES

1. Dannie Richmond talked about his communication with Mingus in a 1978 interview with Bret Primack ("The Gospel According to Mingus: Disciples Carry the Tune," *Down Beat,* December 7, 1978, 40–41): "It was all eye contact. It wasn't anything that he said, like, right here we're going to do this, or now we're going to change the tempo. Of course when we played a gig, all of this was known from the rehearsals. Long rehearsals and if possible, every day."

2. Mingus must have meant James Nelson, a then-contemporary Los Angeles tenor player. See Buddy Collette's 1989–90 interviews with Steven Louis at "Central Avenue Sounds: Oral History Transcript," Dept. of Special Collections/UCLA Library, available online at http://content.cdlib.org/view?docId=hb6g5010zj&chunk .id=div00021&&doc.view=entire_text, sections 75–76, and particularly his comments on Lloyd Reese (79–89) and the Watts music scene in general. Also very worthwhile is a two-CD set (*Buddy Collette: A Jazz Audio Biography*, 1994, Issues Records) of Collette talking at length about Mingus, Bird, Eric Dolphy, and the Town Hall Concert. An online interview series between Collette and Marc Myers of the Jazz Wax site is also available at "Interview: Buddy Collette," Jazz Wax, May 17, 2010, www.jazzwax.com/2010/05/interview-buddy-collette-part-1.html.

3. Max Roach tells his side of the story on NPR's *Jazz Profiles* series (Sept. 30, 2010). Listen to the audio file (with interesting comments by Nat Hentoff, Tom Hubbard, Jackie McLean, et al.) at www.npr.org/player/v2/mediaPlayer.html?action =1&t=1&islist=false&id=89852381&m=89837214. Max's remarks begin at 36:40. Mingus, he says, left because he couldn't stand the stride sound from Duke's left hand. Duke went after him and got him to return. In the book *Music Is My Mistress* (New York: Doubleday, 1973, 242–44), Duke says only that Mingus packed up and said, "Man, I can't play with that drummer." Duke shrewdly commented that the personalities of Charles and Max "were as far apart as the North and South poles."

Our interview compounds some mutual errors: (1) Duke didn't put anybody down; (2) Duke did in fact say "a lot of things" about the date, mostly complimentary; (3) the date was not for Impulse but for United Artists.

I just relistened to *Money Jungle;* Max does *not* sound like Zutty Singleton.

4. Horace Silver's autobiography *Let's Get to the Nitty Gritty* (Berkeley: University of California Press, 2006), 75–76, tells how musicians would cringe when the Demon came into Minton's.

5. He means one of the classic bass textbooks by Franz Simandl, probably *New Method for the Double Bass: Book I*, ed. F. Zimmerman and L. Drew (New York: Carl Fischer, rev. ed., 1984).

6. Eric died in Berlin, June 29, 1964, from a mistreated "diabetic coma." See "Eric Dolphy," musicians.allaboutjazz.com/musician.php?id=6340#.UGhycJiHJ8E.

6 Debut Records, George Wein, and the Music Business

"It's money and women, or it's music—
and you can't fool yourself. You don't
want music to lose."

On different occasions we talked about how the music business works, and Mingus of course had strong opinions on that subject. In 1972, he said on more than one occasion that the record companies had promoted rock and R&B music to such an extent that they drove jazz out. In 1974, he seemed to be changing his tune, saying that the problem really lay with the radio outlets, the media in general, finally "society."

What Mingus really wanted in music, as in economics, was fair competition—like those battles on the bandstand he talked about (see chapter 5). There had to be competition for the public's ear, meaning that they needed exposure to all kinds of music. Playing and promoting black pop music exclusively did in fact help drive out jazz. But there was more to it than that.

We talked about the power of fads. But neither of us factored in how jazz had changed and grown away from its wider audience. Mingus used Ella Fitzgerald as an example of someone who cuts across categories, but Ella was old-school. In attempting to stay current, jazz had taken on aspects of "soul music," electronics, and fusion—all of which proved to be subsequent artistic dead ends and failed, finally, to bring back a broader audience.

There have been many stories about how Mingus and Max Roach started Debut Records in the 1950s. Our 1974 interview clarifies some of the details. Max later said that the simple reason they started the company was that they couldn't get record dates.[1]

1972 INTERVIEW

GOODMAN: So why have jazz people always had such a tough time with the record industry? Every time you turn around you hear another story about a hassle with the record people.

MINGUS: Well, at one time jazz was a very big seller, and [the companies] never admitted it, they always underpaid—'cause most of the people were black and they took advantage of 'em. I used to find out how my records were selling this way: I'd go into town and say, "How many of you heard this Louis Armstrong record, raise your hand . . . How many heard Thelonious Monk, raise your hand . . . How many heard Mingus?"

Wouldn't all go up but quite a few did go up. When I was in New York I used to buy my own records, one thousand dollars' worth of 'em, and it never even showed on my sales, Columbia Records, even.

GOODMAN: When the so-called "race records" were big, did the companies deliberately keep the jazz separate from that? I can remember when I was a kid, they put R&B out on different labels and even different color discs.

MINGUS: No, jazz wasn't separate from that. Rhythm and blues was for the people's music, then rock came in. See, the big companies found that those things were selling. Same as the gangsters found the numbers were selling. "You niggers have a lot of money, you're buying a lot of records." There was a company called Black Label, one called Rhythm and Blues—big companies in California—Four-Star Records, Esoteric Records. These were all black men who owned their own companies, man, I'm telling you, except for Four Star, Esoteric, and a couple of others. Two brothers owned a place, and the René brothers, both songwriters—[owned] two other companies.

But they didn't let you make it no kind of way. If a company in Chicago, Detroit, started making it, the gangsters scooped 'em up; and most cats were afraid to battle them cats. I wouldn't be afraid 'cause most of the gangsters are famous, they all well known. If you want to play the game of "get," you just get them quicker.

But I don't dig somebody telling me, if I earn some money, they get it. They're not going to take it from me, man—unless they kill me, and I don't care about that. In a big company, man, they line the guys up against the wall. They sold out.

Take this, man, here's what happened. They got a system going, like whenever a black man makes it in a style—take the alto. They always remember Benny Carter, and one time it was Willie Smith, he was the king of the poll. Well the king, as long as he's the king, is making it. When they uncrown the king, he ain't making it no more, so that means the whole style [changes] and all the colored guys say, "*That* guy's the champ now, so we got to copy him."

They don't know any better or how to go out and be free individuals. The same for Louis Armstrong: Louis never stayed king to the kids because they knew it was bullshit. When Dizzy came along, they said, "Wait a minute, man, Louis ain't the king no more; Dizzy's playing more complicated than that." So they left Louis being the king of old time and Dizzy the king of progress.

Well, Dizzy got enough name for the guys to copy, try to copy. A few who couldn't play would copy Miles; the guys with technique would try to copy Dizzy. Miles played very simple; I don't know if he does now; I don't know what he's doing now.

. . . But be sure and put in the article about the *Playboy* deal—thirty cents a record, fifty cents a record. I didn't know they was going to give me a lot of money. I'm just too dumb to know it. I'm just too dumb to know it. Here's a guy who can't sell out; he doesn't even want three million dollars.

GOODMAN: How did that go again? They approached you and said they wanted to tie your record to a subscription, was that the idea?

MINGUS: They said they'd like to buy my record outright. Later I found out it was cash. They said, "Figure we'll pay you thirty, thirty-five cents."

I said, "Man, that don't make sense. And earlier you said fifty cents."

"Well, then we'll say fifty cents."

I said, "But that's no money, man, I'm gonna sell the record for ten dollars apiece."

And they look at me and they keep talking . . . and the girl keeps saying, "I see his point. Ten dollars is more than fifty cents."

I say, "Why don't you guys come and buy up the company?"

"Well, that's another business." But they never made it clear, man. Then they come back with a whole table full of guys and with girls— pretty girls too. They say, "Girls, we want you to meet the guy who turned down three million dollars." I just thought you have to set that up [in the *Playboy* article], man, make me look like a fool [*laughter*].

GOODMAN: Was that the Monterey record?

MINGUS: Yeah, *Mingus at Monterey*, two-record set. I just couldn't picture two records going for twenty-five cents apiece. But if he had explained to me what he meant: "Well, we have six million in distribution, and the minimum we expect to sell is . . ." I was just joking when I said, "Why not one dollar a record?" and I was laughing at them.

If he'd said, "Look, Mingus, we're going to package the thing, sell it to the public for two-three dollars or something. You get fifty cents, we get three dollars." But they didn't say it like that, man.

Did I tell you about the water pick I invented? I had a pocket in my gum the dentist told me about, told me I had to clean it out with dental floss. This is, oh, twenty-five years ago. But the dental floss would cut my teeth. So in the shower I'd take the shower hose and try to clean 'em. I got the idea to take a doctor's stethoscope, put a little fine faucet in it of my own making and put the other end of the shower hose onto it, to do my teeth. So I went to a dentist and told him about it. He don't say nothing but "good idea."

So I make my plans up, have an architect draw up plans to send in my copyright. Meantime several people heard about my book [*Underdog*]— my underground copy, the original, 'cause McGraw Hill had it then. He said, "Lemme see your book." I mentioned [in it] that I had invented the pick and why, how necessity is the mother of invention.

So a few years later, I go back with the doctor and say "I want to put this thing on the market."

"Well, Charlie, I think a guy did something like that. It's called 'Waterpik' and has been out for a few years."

I said, "What do you mean, a few years? I told you about it" . . . and we had a big fight. I mean I know he got a piece of the company, man, I just know he did. So now they got a new one on the market *exactly* like mine. His came out with a motor on it. The one they got now is just like mine: you don't need no motor on it to reduce the speed of the water.

GOODMAN: My wife's got one at home, yeah it's got a motor, a little pump in there.

MINGUS: Yeah, but that's the kind they put out, man. Besides, it came out five years after mine. But now they got the one like mine, another company's put it out. Just put it on the faucet, it shakes and does its whole thing. But I know that's mine. I don't care what they say. I know I invented it. I don't care about the money.

1974 INTERVIEW

GOODMAN: You know, you used to tell me that the record companies tuned in exclusively to rhythm and blues, the old black pop music, exploited it and just fed it to 'em and fed it to 'em, you know. More sophisticated music like jazz has no chance. The public is not exposed to it, except for certain people who have always been there and known about it.

MINGUS: Man, it's not the public's fault, it's the [promoters], the music they push on radio. There are one hundred stations to one that you can find some jazz on, especially on AM. Not only jazz, but how about Ella Fitzgerald, man? And Ella Fitzgerald can sing some rock and roll. Saw her in Copenhagen doing a show and she's got a little parody she does—she does all the styles in jazz, all the styles in 4/4, then she does a rock number for a few minutes, and she cuts the kids. Yeah. The range she's got—so high and so low—she's unbelievable, man. But the fault lies in the radio companies.

GOODMAN: You're saying that the radio stations have the power, which the record companies cater to. Because they're the outlet.

MINGUS: Yeah, they are the power. In television, they have guys that steal from jazz, for all the plays, the background music; they have modern music on TV, so the public could stand it, they've been broken in with television music.

GOODMAN: Right, it's not a matter of offending their ears.

MINGUS: No. They listen subconsciously, probably, to the music. [*A loud prizefight is playing on TV in the background.*]
   [The outlets] don't push the taste in that direction, it's just all they play, that's all people know exists. Because jazz isn't publicized that much. And record buyers are not aware that subconsciously they're educated by the television music. In old films they got symphony music playing.

GOODMAN: You used to tell me the record business was the big villain, but I don't think you're saying that now.

MINGUS: No, society is. The record business lays back and studies what goes on in radio and television, and they make music accordingly. You don't hear any Sarah Vaughan, any Billy Eckstine. Those were good singers.

GOODMAN: . . . Let's talk about your different experiences with the record business. I mean in terms of the labels you went with and how you started Debut, some of that history and the connection with Fantasy.
   You did a number of small-group sessions on the early Debuts, right? I wonder if those records will come back again, be reissued. Hampton did a lot of things like that, some of those Esquire records, you know.

MINGUS: I doubt they'll come back, 'cause they're on Decca. Lionel might release some of those he did when he had his own company, Hamptone.

GOODMAN: So he beat you out with the Debut thing, right? He was before you.

MINGUS: Yeah. His wife, Gladys, owned it, she ran it. He was gonna make it a rhythm-and-blues company but he did some jazz.

GOODMAN: Then why does everybody say you were the first then, with Debut?

MINGUS: I don't know. Lennie Tristano had a company the same time I had one.

GOODMAN: You were supposed to be the first black musician to have his own record company.

MINGUS: Is that so?

GOODMAN: Well, I didn't think it was so either. But I've read it a dozen times.

MINGUS: The René brothers had a company in California, Otis René and Don René, I think.[2]

GOODMAN: And all the different race labels that were going on, in the '20s even. Were any of those labels owned by black people?

MINGUS: I don't know. I doubt it very much. What's that woman's name, Big something . . .

GOODMAN: Big Mama?

MINGUS: Big Mama Thornton, yeah, May Thornton. She wouldn't have been robbed so much if she had her own company.

Well, let me tell you about Debut first, that'll be easy. I used to record with a company named Prestige Records, and I'd ask for a record date. In those days, lotta guys was using drugs, and so they recorded very cheap for some drugs. And I was offered this kind of money, thirty dollars to record my trio, I didn't know if it was per man or what, thirty dollars apiece I think. In the '50s. So I didn't try to make no records. Had a claim in against Sonny Burke, you know Sonny Burke?

[He] used to be [a] studio musician, trying to get a band in California, and I wrote some arrangements for him. I won a claim for five hundred dollars against him with the union, and I told my wife, Celia, I was going to start a record company; she said you can't start a record company with five hundred dollars. So I thought I'd start by recording two pieces, one a bass solo album with Spaulding Givens, and that's what I did.

And, after I got it out, some fans used to come into a place called the Downbeat Club—on Fifty-second Street West—they were young kids, and I told them what I was trying to do. One of the kids' dad was a cigar salesman, and he talked to his father about helping us get some money to do another session. I told him I could get Max Roach. And I was working

at the Bohemia Club with a five-piece band: George Barrow, tenor
saxophone; Dave Amram, French horn; Mal Waldron piano; and I forget
the drummer. I had so many drummers before I found Dannie.

Anyway, I convinced this guy and he put up as much money as I put
up to do this session at the Bohemia Club featuring Max Roach. That's the
album that Max and I played a duet together on—avant-garde, though I
hate the word.

Well, the company began to grow but it was very slow. We always got our
money back. I knew I had enough people come out to the clubs, so I knew I'd
sell that many records. Always got my money back. So a couple of years
passed by and I get this letter from a guy in Canada, Toronto, who asked
could I get Bud Powell, Dizzy Gillespie, Max Roach, Charlie Parker together.
I don't know why he asked me. But Celia did it, she did all the groundwork.
The hardest one to get was Bud Powell because he was in the hospital, and
Oscar Goodstein, Bud's manager, one of the owners of Birdland, said he'd be
out in time and would be glad to do it [the *Massey Hall* album].

That's what put Debut on its feet, even though the percentages went to
the musicians. Debut only got 10 percent but we still made money on that
10 percent. I didn't take anything, Max didn't take anything, so the royalty
went back to the company. Each musician got [equal shares], minus the 10
percent. The record got a lot of publicity and sold a lot, but what happened
was that my wife and I broke up, and the recording just stopped. I couldn't
run the company by myself. I'm not capable, maybe some other kind of
guy could have done it, but I couldn't leave my music long enough.

GOODMAN: So that was *Massey Hall.* 1953, was it?

MINGUS: Yeah.

GOODMAN: —I used to buy your records and you were making them
before that—a few.

MINGUS: Paul Bley, Art Blakey, J.J. Johnson, Kai Winding, John Lewis on
piano, Art Taylor on drums, and myself, Woody Dennis, and I'm missing
one—Benny Green. This was at a place Max Roach started in Brooklyn
called Stuyvesant Casino, which later became our record shop; we used to
keep our records over there when Celia left.

GOODMAN: Wait a minute. Stuyvesant Casino was in Manhattan.

MINGUS: No, [I meant] the Putnam Central Club, which was in Brooklyn.[3] Max used to do weekend things there, every week. He had Charlie
Parker there when he was livin', Sonny Rollins, he had everybody.

When Max left it in my hands, I tried to do record dates there and tried to get name people that would make it together.

GOODMAN: You did live things there?

MINGUS: Yeah. With Max we didn't make no money. Later on he thought we'd cheated him, but I didn't take any money either. Celia took the money and did other sessions with it—like with Honey Gordon, she's the little girl singing with my big band.

Yeah, she's singing Monday night in New York, a club that can do her some good, a sort of audition club. Celia's having a dinner Monday night to welcome her. That's about all about Debut Records; it was a hell of a lot of work. I used to do the labor work, pack records.

GOODMAN: What you're telling me is that Celia really kept it going, she did it.

MINGUS: She was the brains, but it was my ideas, and her carrying them out.

GOODMAN: What happened then after you got out of it? How is Fantasy involved?

MINGUS: Well, she left me, I couldn't afford to take care of the kid, so I just gave her my shares, and she bought Max's shares, but that didn't do any good because one share was holding the whole thing up, owned by an attorney—Miles Davis's manager, Harold Lovette—he had the deciding vote for everything.[4] Finally she was able to buy him out. She married Saul Zaentz who at that time was a partner in Fantasy. Now he owns it, they own it, and they're millionaires. She's a millionaire now, so she insults me. She says, "I didn't cheat you when I was poor; I wouldn't cheat you when I'm rich." But it's the company cheating.

GOODMAN: So therefore Fantasy has the rights to all the Debut stuff.

MINGUS: All the older stuff, not the newer stuff I made with Eric Dolphy and all that—which was on Prestige, which was more of a drag yet, to me.

GOODMAN: Saul Zaentz has got the whole ball of wax now, but before he owned Prestige, you made some sides that were under the Prestige label?

MINGUS: Celia axed Debut, and I went with the Prestige name, thought it was a bigger name.

GOODMAN: You know, Sue is right. We have to run down a discography some day, but I'd like to have a catalog of what went on under Debut if anybody has it.[5]

MINGUS: Yeah, I can get Celia to send it to you.

GOODMAN: Spaulding Givens was the first one that you remember?

MINGUS: Yeah, the first session. I think Teo Macero was the third, put his own money up, he wanted to record some things.

GOODMAN: I have a Bud Powell record at home, a ten-inch Debut LP which sounds like it was done in Massey Hall but it's all Bud Powell. Is that possible?

MINGUS: It was a live Bud Powell concert—we only did four tunes: "Embraceable You," "Sure Thing"—

GOODMAN: That's right, and "Lullaby of Birdland."

MINGUS: Right, and some fast tune. And that ain't me on bass. Probably George Duvivier. 'Cause I remember he did an album with Bud before we played together.

. . .

Starting Debut and making records had been a way to stay off the road, and Mingus hated the road, though he did a lot of traveling even at this period of his life when his health wasn't that good. He was back and forth to Europe several times during the summer of 1972 and in 1974, through bookings with George Wein. We got into discussing the ins and outs of their complicated relationship.

. . .

GOODMAN: I know you don't like the road.

MINGUS: No, I don't like to travel. But I have to.

GOODMAN: What do you prefer? The concert dates? Are you playing any of those now, like colleges?

MINGUS: A few, but it's a little late for 'em 'cause we have to book them a year ahead of time.

GOODMAN: Would you rather play those or the clubs?

MINGUS: [*Eating.*] I'd rather do the college dates. It's less restricting. We do two shows—unless they got somebody else on the bill. Yeah, colleges are a regular audience, man. They're quiet. I don't know how they go for rock and roll, 'cause [we've gotten] standing ovations and everything. For instance, the club where we're playing now, the Bijou [in Philadelphia], the house ain't even full but we have standing ovations. That's strange. Usually, when there's hysteria like that, there's a lot of people. A few jump up, and then they all jump up.

GOODMAN: You'll get a good crowd tonight, I bet. A lot of people know about it. Have they advertised it well?

MINGUS: I don't know, man. We're in the papers . . . I haven't seen any posters. In Chicago, they got posters out.

GOODMAN: Yeah, how was your Chicago thing?

MINGUS: Packed every night.

GOODMAN: That's a pretty good place [the Plugged Nickel], isn't it? I thought you'd like that.

MINGUS: Owner's very nice too.

GOODMAN: How'd the bass work out? You borrowed somebody's bass? [He hadn't been able to take his on the plane.] Was it alright?

MINGUS: Yeah, it actually made me change my own bass around: he had gut strings on his bass, and I was trained on gut strings and changed to steel just because it became popular. But it cuts your hands all up. So when I played on his, I was able to do things I couldn't do with the steel strings. So when I came back here, I put gut strings on mine.

GOODMAN: I always thought Chicago was a very good place for jazz.

MINGUS: This is New Town, they call it, where this club is. I've never been good in Chicago, to tell you the truth. Except for the Keyboard Lounge. I did good enough for him, because maybe he's got his own following. But those other clubs, I played a couple of other clubs there, and I didn't draw, man, so I was afraid to go to Chicago.

GOODMAN: They've got a hip audience there, I really think they do now, though it's changed a lot. In the '50s it was a great place too but different. I mean, places on Fifty-third and Sixty-third Street on the South Side, marvelous jazz.[6] So if you've got to tour, do you have any preference about towns?

MINGUS: Where I'd like to play? Well, New York, Chicago now, California—San Francisco, Los Angeles. We do very good in the South too—Texas.

GOODMAN: Is that right? Where? Dallas? Houston?

MINGUS: Dallas. No, it was Houston. We were there the same time the Maharajah was there. You know, the little kid who's a preacher, gonna be the messiah. You never heard about him? Well, you lucky. He packed 'em into the Astrodome in Houston, gonna be the second coming of the Lord.

GOODMAN: . . . What happened in Japan? I never heard you talk about that.

MINGUS: Well, we took a bad band over. McPherson was afraid to go by airplane. Jaki Byard didn't say why but he didn't go.

GOODMAN: Is that the story about him quitting at the last minute?

MINGUS: Yeah. And Dannie Richmond couldn't go because he didn't have his cabaret card.
    You have to have a straight record [to play in Japan]. If you've been busted for narcotics you can't go. So, we took a drummer that wasn't good, and we had just left Paris—Europe, rather—had Bobby Jones and Eddie Preston, and they're not enough to carry the show.

GOODMAN: Right, and you had no piano?

MINGUS: We had no piano. We were supposed to get one, but I guess the guy didn't like our playing.

GOODMAN: Jesus. That was about three years ago? Sue said you had a great following in Japan, loyal fans.

MINGUS: Yeah, a lot of people came out. [But the reaction] was very disappointing to me. It was no good, 'cause they knew it wasn't a good band.

GOODMAN: So you've got to have another tour back there.

MINGUS: Some kind of way.

GOODMAN: What about this summer? Are you gonna do a Europe thing again after Newport in New York, or don't you know yet?

MINGUS: If George Wein doesn't kick me out . . . because Sue's already talked to this Italian promoter, Alberto Alberti [see Sue's commentary later in the chapter], and he asked her, called her. Then when she got into it deeper, he asked some others. She saw George Wein in the meantime and he said he didn't want me to go over, because he wanted me to go next year with him.

GOODMAN: A year from now. Well, what do you think about that? I don't know, it's hard to understand him.

MINGUS: He's got too much power if he can do that.

GOODMAN: Why doesn't he tell the people who are booking with him what the schedule is, you know, so that it's all up front?

MINGUS: I mean, he's gonna keep you out of Europe because you get so much work in America?

But he has a tour that goes out once a year. I was on it last year.

GOODMAN: All around the country? Is that generally a successful thing, good draw?

MINGUS: Some places he didn't draw. I think he lost this time. We played the Houston Astrodome, and it was just a handful.

GOODMAN: But that's an enormous place, one hundred thousand people or something?

MINGUS: Yeah. . . . George's promises. He [once] worked through Bill Coss, from Metronome, and he kept telling us to work for very little money because he was going to have the big stars. They charged a lot of money, but as soon as Newport made it and drew a good audience, he'd give us more money, he said. They were tearing the gates down, and he still didn't give us any more money.

GOODMAN: This is around the late '50s, you're talking about?

MINGUS: Yeah. So then we had the Protest Festival [1960].[7] Max Roach, myself, we got guys like Randy Weston, Roy Eldridge, Coleman Hawkins, Ornette Coleman. We got this place called Cliff Walk Manor, and they originally had talked about giving concerts there, but it was too small. But the owner let us have his property. Put up tents to sleep in, it was like army camp. We rented the stuff from—what do you call that?—an Army-Navy store. . . .

Our concert was going very well, but he [George] had too many people at his. We drew, not 'cause we had any advertisement, just put up a sign. Tried to parade down the street in a truck but a cop stopped us.

GOODMAN: It was a word of mouth thing too, right?

MINGUS: Yeah.

GOODMAN: When I spoke to him he said, "Well, you know Charles got the Protest Festival together, with Max and these people, and I didn't make any move to stop it."

MINGUS: Yes, he did [try to stop it].

GOODMAN: "I let it continue, because it was their movement, their thing."

MINGUS: He tried to stop us, man, but I went to his hotel and was going to kill him. I had a gun, whatchacallem's gun. He and [Lorraine] Lorillard tried to stop us. Sent over different messages from the police department, why we couldn't go on.

GOODMAN: His story is just the opposite. "I told the police, let's be cool and let it go on."

MINGUS: No, he didn't, man. Nick Canarossa [Cannarozzi] was the hotel owner's name, and they wanted him running a concert license. Finally he realized he had an outdoor license for himself, a club license, so he told me he'd go run it [the Protest Festival] on his club license, and that's what he did.
    Finally, they stopped us because the riot stopped the other concert.

GOODMAN: I wonder if those things are dead now, if there will be any more big rock concerts, like the one where those people got killed in Altamont.

MINGUS: Rock concerts have riots because the music is so loud. People can't hear what they're saying to each other. Probably a lot of misunderstandings. And it stirs 'em up too, it's nerve-wracking because the [headliner] band won't play enough.

GOODMAN: Too much of the band that goes on first?

MINGUS: Yeah, it's called the butts band, the ass band.

GOODMAN: . . . Wasn't there a record, Charles, of the Protest Festival?

MINGUS: Yeah, Candid recorded it, but Ornette didn't want his things on it or he would have been on it too. So the whole thing wasn't recorded.

GOODMAN: I think I heard some of that; part of it was good.

MINGUS: "All the Things You Are"—which we did with Ornette and some other bands—they didn't put that out. We just called a tune we wanted to jump on, "All the Things You Are," and as soon as we were into it, he just got lost. We played a free thing first, and a kid there asked me, "Where are we, what's the chord changes?" Max Roach and I had been doing [free jazz] all along; we made one tune with just bass and drum one time, called "Percussion Discussion." Might as well put the name in, sell some records.

GOODMAN: Did you ever do that [duet] with Dannie?

MINGUS: No, Dannie does it by himself.

GOODMAN: I was thinking about that driving in here today. Not that tune, but wondering if you and Dannie ever did any duets of that kind anymore.

MINGUS: Nah, I just let Dannie do it by himself, "Percussion Discussion."

GOODMAN: Well, I was up at the Newport thing twice, I think, in Rhode Island.

MINGUS: Oh, yeah?

GOODMAN: And it was nice—

MINGUS: Oh, when it first started, it was beautiful. Wasn't hardly anybody there, though.

GOODMAN: I was up there in '68, something like that, and it was a good time, crowded but everybody was cool. I actually went to a party with Roland Kirk at George Wein's house.

MINGUS: It was like a family, everybody sat down and talked, Bill Coss, Barry Ulanov, you see all the critics walking around, Leonard Feather and his wife.
   . . . You know what was so sad, man? I saw Max Roach, and they say he was sick, but he wasn't sick, he was a little drunk or something. Well, Max is alcoholic and can't drink, but he was saying, "Mingus, you know what I did today? I took all my publicity—way back, *Down Beat*, first place—took all my publicity and went down to the bank and told 'em to give me a loan. And they wouldn't give me a nickel, man. And I was in first place too."
   It sounds sad, man.

GOODMAN: It is sad.

MINGUS: I know how he feels because Max is a genius, man. Harry Belafonte used to be called the poor man's Max Roach. In his younger days Max was a very handsome man. Sort of resembled Belafonte.

GOODMAN: When I was at Newport, he was backstage while we were waiting for Roland Kirk. He came by and, man, he had a robe on and he looked beautiful.

MINGUS: Max?

GOODMAN: Yes, had an African robe on, a dashiki. And my wife looked at him and she went, "Wow. That is a man."

MINGUS: Women have always done that. But he never enjoyed it. I understand that—you can't have that double life going. You can, at least some guys can, but you really don't want the money and the women. It's money and women, or it's music—and you can't fool yourself. You don't want music to lose. Only way you can survive is be free to be in love and

FIGURE 7.   Mingus intent on a score, recording *Changes One* and *Changes Two* at Atlantic Records, 1974. Photo by Sy Johnson.

get your heart broken, like Max fell in love with Abbey [Lincoln]. Play it for real, then you can retain your music. But if you're out there jiving, man, you'll lose your soul. [*Pause.*]

Maybe that's superstition, but it's worked that way with me. I would like to be fickle and polygamous, everybody would like to play that game, but it never worked for me. In my mind, I can't create. I feel a divine connection with eternal life when I write. I feel that someone better than me is coming out of me. And if I can't turn that on, there ain't nothing I can say with no pencil, man. I can't lie, it's like I'm talking now, I can't lie to myself and put it down there.

CHAPTER 6 COMMENTARY

George Wein on the Protest/Rebel/Rump Festival and Assessing Mingus

I spent perhaps forty minutes with jazz impresario George Wein, during which time the phone rang—I am not exaggerating—at least twelve times. The interruptions were irksome, but he got back on point (most of the time) and said some accurate and revealing things. Here is part of what we talked about, and it conveys Wein's real attachment to Mingus, despite their disagreements, and his multiple views of the man and musician. He always has referred to Mingus as "Charlie," despite the latter's preference for "Charles," but Mingus too slipped into the familiar form occasionally.

Mingus and Wein had developed a kind of financial codependency for years, which I don't think either ever sorted out. You can read some of that doubt and mistrust in Sue's comments, which follow. But Wein's positive remarks here about Mingus as an organizer and presenter of talent are singular and subtle perceptions of the man's ability.

. . .

WEIN: I guess I first met Mingus, though we didn't have any association, when he was with the Red Norvo Trio. But then his first work that involved me was at Storyville, my club in Boston. He came in there with a band, I guess a couple of times back in the '50s. Then of course he started the Rebel Festival in 1960, Mingus started that.

GOODMAN: I wanted to ask you about that.

WEIN: That was the year of the riot. The end of the first epoch of the Newport Jazz Festival; the second epoch ended in 1971; and the third epoch is beginning this year.

GOODMAN: That was the Rump, or Protest, Festival, as they called it?

WEIN: Well, you see, we've always had a problem that—not just Charlie but all jazz musicians—if you can't do exactly for them what they want you to do, it creates some sort of feeling that you don't like them, or whatever the case may be. Now the Rebel Festival was controlled by people I wasn't using on the Newport Jazz Festival that year, not because I didn't like them or anything. Most of the musicians on the Rebel Festival had appeared at Newport one time or another. Max Roach was at the first Newport Jazz Festival.

And we actually helped the Rump Festival because the town wanted to stop it, you know, and we made the town—a lot of people don't know that—we said the worst injury you could do to us would be to stop that festival. You must let that festival continue. And of course we were stopped, because we had the riot, but the Rump Festival continued.

Charlie Mingus to me is one of the geniuses in music. The only reason he might not have gone further than he has is his own personal problems, of which he's had many. You've probably heard a lot about them. His life has been so hectic and so involved in so many areas, that it would become a psychoanalytical job, you know, to find out why he would do certain things, why did he have to leave the music scene, why was he violent at different times, you know. I think he's made a remarkable recovery. I still think he's erratic, you know what I mean, but all of us are erratic.

The thing about Charlie is he basically has more love than hate. He may spew hate, but hate is bullshit with him. Charlie is not antiwhite. If he comes on in a very black way, chances are he's doing it for a very particular purpose. He makes good copy or it's very effective—but he is not a hateful person, and that I know for sure. In fact, the beauty about Charlie is that he responds to love, and that's a very important thing in the man.

Before his comeback, instead of people trying to keep him cool, they were always goading him, you see. And now, thank heavens, he's surrounded by people who understand that. I mean, Sue is his manager and his friend, and she's very good with him; she's a very, very smart person. And she understands him. It's a remarkable thing, because I truthfully thought that he was finished.

When we go on the road to Europe, you know—he was going back to Europe just last month—and we do have a good time. We pick out the best restaurants. Mingus likes good food. But I've got to educate him to pay the check once in a while. Last time I took him to lunch he ordered two orders of beluga caviar. I said, "Next time, Charlie, you take me to lunch." He said, "Well, I'm not eating anything else." [*Big laughs.*]

. . . Mingus's basic musical talent to me is an organizer of music. He can *present*. I like his work with small bands better than big bands.

GOODMAN: Do you?

WEIN: I do, very much so. I feel that with a small group he knows how to bring out the individuality of the people playing with him. That's why so many wonderful musicians stayed with him even under very chaotic experiences when Charlie was undergoing serious mental problems, you know, when he broke down a couple of years ago. They still stayed with him because when he presented them, when he wrapped them up in his presentation, they got a chance to shine better than they did under any other circumstances.

He had that great ability to write around the musician, to bring out his talents to the greatest. That's a very rare thing. Duke Ellington has it, with Johnny Hodges and all those great people he has as soloists. But he knew how to make them perhaps greater than they were. I won't say that for Hodges, but a lot of other players in the band might not have been as great if it hadn't been for Ellington and the music he surrounded them with. Mingus has that talent.

The only reason he's never been able to have a big band quite as successful as he'd like it to be is that he's never had the strength, the emotional strength that, say, a Duke or a Woody Herman or a [Stan] Kenton has,
to keep a band together come hell or high water, whether there's money or
no money, just to go straight ahead and go on the job. He's just not
constituted that way, and that's a very rare thing. Basically, if he could ever
do that, he might have the greatest big band in the world, you see.

But a big band is not something [where] you just wait till you get a job
and then hire guys. I mean you have to dedicate your whole life to the big
band. That's why most big-band people always are broke, you know,
because it's very difficult to keep a big band together. Kenton and Woody
after all these years have nothing to show for it, basically.

Duke—I don't know where Duke's at, and I don't know where Basie's
at. I don't imagine that they're very rich, either of them. Duke's fine
because of his composer's royalties, his ASCAP ratings. But if he had to
rely on his income from the band over the years, I don't think he'd be
very rich. A band is a very expensive plaything. You just don't take jobs
when they come; you have to rule a band three hundred days a year just
to keep it alive, and that is difficult.

GOODMAN: It takes a tremendous kind of organization, I suppose, and
Mingus can't do that, or he'd have to have someone help him with it.

WEIN: He could use an alter ego very well, and he's never really found one.
. . . I'd like to see him play more bass now. He seems to have some
[*unintelligible*] but there's a little mental thing there about not tearing
after that bass the way he used to. I think he can still do it, because up in
Boston this year he came up for the benefit we had for the Newport Jazz
Festival. He didn't have a band, but he and Brubeck did a duet, completely
improvised, the two of them just went out there, neither knew what they
were going to play or do, they just kept leading each other. Brubeck would
start to play something, and Mingus would get more powerful, then Brubeck would follow him, et cetera. And it was the high point of the evening,
and he *played bass*, you know what I mean?

There has never been a bass player like Charlie Mingus. He is to the
bass what Art Tatum was to the piano, as far as I'm concerned.

GOODMAN: And he has a lot of Tatum in his bass playing too.

WEIN: Yeah. But I mean in reference to his technique and his musical
content. His musical ability is so deep that the average person will never
fully understand it. Because it does relate to his leadership ability, which

isn't quite obvious in the music he plays sometimes. Because sometimes with the lack of organization in the big band, sometimes the big band gets very boring—you know, when he stops to rehearse in the middle of a concert, that sort of thing. And he's never got over the habit of doing it; and he shouldn't do it. He should, when he's in front of the public, go straight ahead. You know what I mean?

GOODMAN: Yeah, that bothered me in the Philharmonic Hall concert.

WEIN: He has such a sensitivity about it, that if it isn't going exactly right, he wants to stop and make it go right. But when he does that, I feel that, as a musician myself, the musicians can't get back in the groove. They might correct those mistakes themselves. But that's with the big band. With the small band, I don't think that happens.

With the small band, the thing just takes off. The guys really get into it. I love the small band. His big-band things would need much more rehearsal than he has money for, or time for. But he played for me the other day—and we're going to do it on the festival—a classical string quartet that he wrote.

GOODMAN: He's writing that stuff right now?

WEIN: Yes, well, this one is written, and it's a kind of concerto, and I just heard a little on the telephone, but the guy that played it, Kermit Moore, who's one of the great cellists in the world—he happens to live in this building . . . he gave a concert a couple of weeks ago at Alice Tully Hall, and he's an incredible artist.

He brought the group to play Mingus's work, an incredible work. I mean he wrote this thing, and it's an incredible work. So, after all the years I've known him [Mingus], here was a completely new facet of his musical ability that I knew nothing about.

GOODMAN: His writing abilities seem to have grown, if possible, in the last two years.

WEIN: He is in a very wonderful mood for writing right now. I think he feels slightly more secure now than he ever has. But I think he needs money, like a lot of people need money, and that always tends to affect your insecurity and your relationship to your art and everything else. A lot of problems have occurred because of that.

GOODMAN: He doesn't have to scuffle quite so much today, though, does he?

WEIN: Well, I don't know. I mean I'm not aware of his inner financial thing, I don't know where he earns a lot of money. I know he doesn't make that much money that he can afford to relax, you know what I mean? He's got to keep going.

GOODMAN: When he played at Storyville, what time period was that? 1950 to 1952?

WEIN: Oh, no, it was a little later. He played with the Red Norvo Trio until '53 or '54. I mean I don't have these dates in my head, but I remember when I went to New York and saw him playing at the Embers. That was just as he was emerging as a leader, right after he started in his own group.

GOODMAN: What was his playing like in those days?

WEIN: Well, he always was—once he left Red Norvo, once he became a leader on his own—he always was interested in very advanced music. But, the thing that makes Mingus's music great, of course, is the fact that he is basically a traditional musician, and that everything he does, no matter how far out he goes, is based upon tradition. That's why it has grabbed so many people, and that's why it grabs you, because you hear the things—you hear his love for Ellington, you hear his love for the great stride piano players. He's the one that made Jaki Byard play stride piano. Now when everybody thought that was corny, Mingus knew it wasn't corny, and Mingus fully understands the true history of jazz. That's why he can play like he plays.

A lot of people are great players but they don't have the great musical knowledge within their system. Not only don't they have it, but when they've been exposed to it, they've rejected it. Mingus never rejected it; he accepted it and he absorbed it, because his musical mind is so intense and so fantastic that if he hears anything that has real musical quality, whether it's one thousand years old or whether it's tomorrow, he will absorb it. And that comes out somewhere in his playing.

GOODMAN: Nobody else does that today, transforms music like that.

WEIN: Mingus is unique in that respect.

Sue, Mingus, and Me on George Wein, the Road, and Mingus's Appeal

SUE: Well, it's hard to know whether George Wein is an ogre or an angel, because he's done a terrific amount to promote and to back and to help jazz on the one hand, more than anybody else has done, certainly, in this country and Europe. On the other hand, one has the feeling that he is certainly in a position to manipulate the kind of jazz that's heard in Europe, at least. And we often have the feeling that he does this.

For example, once when someone told me that there were agents in Australia that wanted Charles to play there, and I'd gotten in touch with one of them by letter, I received a reply saying that he had spoken to George Wein a year or two years before that and George had said that Mingus wasn't interested in playing in Australia.

GOODMAN: Just like that?

SUE: Which of course is not true at all; he had never consulted with Charles about it, and I think we did confront George with that, didn't we, Charles? And I don't remember what he said about it, except that he thought it wasn't the right thing for you at that time—I forget what it was.

Then two years ago, I had set up a tour in Europe for Charles which depended on three or four concerts, which I had already gotten, and which were at the last moment cancelled—and we had the feeling at the time that George Wein wanted to be in charge of Charles's tours in Europe. Though that may not have been true.

MINGUS: I'm not so sure. I haven't been there [to Europe] in the last few months. Just make it clear what you mean.

SUE: A year later, I started out with my three or four connections, and then Columbia Records helped me down the line all over Europe. And Charles went over again about two or three months later with George Wein, but he went to different places, primarily, isn't that right, Charles? You went to Iron Curtain countries—

MINGUS: Yeah.

SUE: —and to Scandinavia, so they weren't competitive, evidently, the two European tours that summer.

Now, what happened recently is that one of the agents in Italy, Alberto Alberti, called me up about a month and a half ago when he was in New York. We met for lunch, and he said that he had two possible concerts in Africa and two or three possible concerts in Italy. And we discussed prices and so forth, and I said that [schedule] alone wouldn't be enough but if he could possibly get other concerts—and I would see myself what I could do. After that, I happened to talk to George Wein about it—did we run into him in the airport, Charles, in Paris, or was it before that?

MINGUS: Yeah, it was before that.

SUE: And it came up in the discussion, and I said I talked to Alberto Alberti, figuring that it was all out in the open, and [George just] hadn't known about it. He said immediately, "Well, of course, Alberto Alberti represents me."

I had said to him, "George, is there anything in Europe this summer for Charles?"

And he said, "No."

And I said, "I did see Alberto Alberti, and I know there are four or five things. I thought maybe you could supplement them." You know, just being very open about it.

Then I wondered if I should have said anything. . . . See the thing is this: I can understand maybe in George's position, he has everything mapped out, I would like to think, for the benefit of jazz as a whole. Maybe he feels, no, he can't send Mingus this summer, he wants to send Art Blakey or so-and-so. "On my schedule I see Mingus being there in 1976," or something like that. See, he's in a position to pretty much, I think, direct most of the activity in Europe. But there are times when he seems very much like an obstacle—

MINGUS: An ogre.

SUE: —to what we're trying to do. And on the other hand, certainly in this country he's been terrific. And I admire him because he's making money off of jazz, but also his heart is in it. He plays the piano himself, he has his own band, he loves the music, loves the musicians, and you can't dislike him.

GOODMAN: Well, what you're saying, as I get it, is that he wants to sew up the whole European end of it for himself.

SUE: Well, it tends to seem that way from our small vantage point, and I don't have an overall view. But it tends to feel that way when you suddenly can't get through to people who might help you, and you know that they do at times work with George.

Again, in Japan, I've been trying to get Charles back there. He was there three years ago with really a pickup band. He has a huge following in Japan, probably sells more records there than anywhere in the world. In fact, when we were there, people came backstage with records, half of which I'd never even seen before—

GOODMAN: Japanese pressings?

SUE: Yeah, there's a lot of under-the-counter stuff. But anyway, I have written many, many people in Japan to ask them why they don't have Charles back there with his regular band, with Dannie Richmond—who at the time wasn't able to go because they'd clamped down on drugs terrifically and he'd had some [drug] problem years before, which apparently now is no longer a problem. Charlie McPherson at that point in his life was afraid to fly, so he was gonna take a slow boat to Japan, which would have taken about two weeks, so that was out. And Jaki Byard at the last minute couldn't go. So instead of his seven pieces he went with four, with a substitute drummer, and it was awful.

And he *should* go back, and I've talked to George about it, and I've gotten the names of top booking agents there, and nothing's happened. Again, one wonders why. Is it all organized from the top, or is it just something else? Is it right now that they don't want Mingus, or—? You don't know. But I think in the old days—I don't remember what your original thing was with George, Charles, when you were so angry at him for a few years. What was that about?

MINGUS: All because [of] how he booked us at Newport. He was cheap. The next year and the next year after that he was going to give us more money. And he never did, so we did the Protest Festival. I just stayed mad at him, that's all.

GOODMAN: I've heard few people in jazz say good things about him, yet there's a sort of grudging respect, maybe, for the guy. And you wonder if it's because he's the only game in town, or because he's actively doing good things for people. I don't know the answer.

SUE: I think musicians always tend to feel, rightly and sometimes wrongly, exploited, and people are making a lot of money off of them— and he has certainly made money off of jazz, and at the same time he has also done more to promote jazz in this country, I think, than any single person.

Certainly, his Newport in New York [Festival] has opened up jazz to a lot of people who didn't know about it. A lot of the kids, I think, heard jazz maybe for the first time and liked it and I think a new following has been created. There are a lot of young kids in the clubs now. Before, it was sort of, you know, the jazz audience would be now in their late thirties or forties, maybe in their fifties, and Charles played Max's Kansas City a week ago, which was an experiment.

GOODMAN: Yeah, I wanted to come in and be there. How did it go?

SUE: It was sort of a breakthrough. They'd never had a major jazz musician there before. And it was packed. I'm sure they felt it was very successful. I know they were turning people away on weekends. Certainly this happens very often with rock people too, but we didn't know with jazz. Sy Johnson said in a piece that he wrote for us this issue [of *Changes*, her magazine] that it wasn't all that strange because Mingus has always appealed to a certain outside group, whether it was ghetto or glitter, as he put it.

He wrote a review of the band at Max's. And Atlantic Records of course is very interested in this because if he can bridge this, go beyond the jazz audience—I mean Miles Davis has become a pop star now. I mean, Miles can play anywhere. But there aren't that many jazz musicians that have gone outside the direct jazz audience. I mean, Herbie Hancock now, I understand, sold three hundred thousand copies of his last record, which is a tremendous amount. I mean, seventy-five thousand is a lot for a jazz artist.

GOODMAN: I know it. That recent one he [Hancock] did is better than [*laughs*] some other things he has done.

SUE: He has simplified his music, and I don't know, it depends on what you think of Herbie Hancock, whether you think he's sold out or whether there was nothing to sell out from in the beginning [*laughs*].

GOODMAN: Teo Macero brought up this same point—about Miles being some kind of messiah or something.

SUE: Of course, he produces Miles.

GOODMAN: And he implied that Mingus was going along that road, or could be made to go along that road. And I thought to myself, there's no way they are going to touch the same audiences. They are so totally different musically—

SUE: Yeah.

GOODMAN: —emotionally, personally, whatever. Except for the fact that a young audience was somehow involved and that a young audience was obviously coming to Charles, I don't see any connection.

SUE: No, I think that can happen and I think Charles can reach that audience too—not the same way that Miles does, 'cause I don't think many people are going to reach the huge audiences Miles reaches. And again, it goes beyond his music, certainly. His music now is not what it was anyway ten years ago, and it almost doesn't matter whether or not people are satisfied or dissatisfied with the music. He's become a certain kind of personality.

GOODMAN: Yeah, he's a public figure.

Sue Graham on Pitching Mingus

SUE: I started running a mail-order record company that he had for about a year. He put out four records on his own label, Charles Mingus Enterprises, after the success of the Monterey concert. He had a lot of tapes, but he put out just four albums on that label from these tapes. One was *Mingus at Monterey*, which he talked to you about, that *Playboy* was interested in marketing for awhile. One was a Town Hall concert, an album called *Town Hall* with the band—with Eric Dolphy—that went to Europe.

GOODMAN: There are two Town Hall concerts, then.

SUE: Yeah. One was made several years ago. And this one was made in 1964, the same year as the Monterey concert but it was made, I think, in February or March. The band then went to Europe and had that incredible tour, at the end of which Eric Dolphy died. He stayed on in Germany for a few months and died over there. That was the band that Ted Curson and Eric—

GOODMAN: Oh, that's right. The three-disc album?

SUE: That's right. Well, the *Town Hall* concert [album] has essentially the same music. In other words, it was what the band was playing before they went to Europe and that album had never come out here, while the three-record set came out in France last year. And he did two others: one, a concert that he played at the Tyrone Guthrie Theater in Minneapolis; and then another album when he went back to Monterey in 1965. It [that performance] was a shambles, he did not get to play all his music. He was on the program last and the concert had dragged out. So what happened is he played all the music he was supposed to play at Monterey at UCLA a week later, and that was the title of the album, *Music Written from Monterey Played at UCLA* or something like that.[8]

He'd had a lot of offers for these albums but he wanted to try it on his own. He felt that the record companies were ripping him off, record stores were ripping him off, people were pirating his records, and so he decided the only way to beat the system was to sell records mail order. It's what a lot of magazines, publications are doing now. Instead of dealing with newspaper distributors, they work on subscriptions. It makes sense, but it didn't really make sense for Mingus because you have to have a big advertising budget.

Well, [Ralph] Gleason was very nice, he was syndicated in a lot of papers, and he wrote about the albums.

GOODMAN: Yeah, I remember him writing about Mingus's efforts.

SUE: You know, he said write to Mingus, he has a mail-order record company. He gave the address, and he did this several times in a lot of newspapers. And a lot of orders came in because of that. And we tried sporadically a few ads but it was expensive. We just didn't want to put money into it.

GOODMAN: Right. How did you get in on it? Did you know Charles before that?

SUE: Yeah. I had met him . . . I don't remember when it was. I had been in an underground movie that Ornette Coleman was supposed to write the music for. He didn't get the kind of money that he wanted so we didn't use his music. But it was in that era when I was listening to jazz a lot and I met Mingus at that time.

. . . And after his eviction, that was just about the time Mingus stopped playing. Right after that, I think. Everything was going badly anyway. He was not getting the kind of money he deserved, and jazz was losing ground generally.

He was going through a lot of emotional problems, and he became ill and went to the hospital for about three or four months. And he simply stopped playing. At that time, he wanted to play only concerts. He was fed up with jazz clubs and with people who didn't listen and with the whole jazz club scene.

He was just very debilitated and very emotionally upset and he had gone on a crash diet at one point and received a lot of shots, a lot of medication, a lot of pills, and then he became addicted to some of the pills and he had to take other pills to offset those pills. In fact, there are pictures of him on that European tour where he has boxes that cover a table, he had a satchel that was this big [*gesturing*], full of all kinds of pills. It was really funny. Photographers took pictures of him walking with this thing.

GOODMAN: So now you are talking about the period around 1966?

SUE: Monterey was '64, so around '66, I think, is when he stopped playing until about 1969. And then I was working for a paper called the *New York Free Press* and we had a benefit at the Fillmore East. Norman Mailer spoke; and the Fugs; Peter Weir; Peter, Paul, and Mary; and a lot of people played; and Mingus played for us. That was the first time he had played in a long time.

And then what really started him playing again is there was a program for Duke Ellington, some sort of tribute to Duke, I think at UCLA. And he was asked to perform there, to speak and to perform. That got him excited again because, as you know, Duke Ellington has been a very important figure for him. So he decided he would do that. So to make it worthwhile to go all the way out to California—I had never booked anything in my life but I started finding out about it and I booked him in a few places out there, and that made the trip possible.

I knew nothing. I called someone who had been a booking agent for years who didn't know me, and I said naively, "How do you find out about booking people? Where do you go?" And he said, "Twenty years of hard work" and hung up. I have since gotten to know him and he is really nice, but at the time he didn't know who I was and people aren't about to encourage you. Art d'Lugoff [owner of the Village Gate] gave me some suggestions, and then gradually it just worked out. You know, it wasn't like selling . . .

His heart was certainly not in playing for the first year or two, I think. But he's in it full force now. He's excited and composing, and everything that happened in the last year or so—Alvin Ailey asking him to do music for a ballet was a turning point, I think. And then recording for Columbia and being able to write for a big band. That's what he's wanted to do for a long time and it's been economically impossible up until now. Mingus should be writing for a big band.

GOODMAN: Yeah, that's what everybody says. I must say I think that's right.

SUE: Now, I applied for a Guggenheim for him, which he got, I guess it was a year or two ago. And then he was also offered the Slee Chair at New York State University-Buffalo. He taught a musical seminar up there during the spring semester. Everything began to come together, between the Guggenheim and Buffalo and then going to Japan, and he went to Europe.

I am trying to apply for a grant now, whether it's the New York State Council of the Arts, or Ford Foundation or somewhere, to try to get a sustaining wage so he can perform with the big band. Sometimes they have matching funds—you know, for symphony orchestras they do this. And it would be an opportunity, I think, at this point for one of these foundations to show that they have an interest in—certainly jazz is one of the most important musical forms in America and it's never been really given the importance or the support that it should have.

That would be the only way to really make it possible. Thad Jones has played for seven years on Monday nights at the Vanguard with the big band. And just now I think things are really beginning to roll and he gets bookings for the big band. But it's not easy to do that.

GOODMAN: You know, I talked to Thad about that a couple of years ago, and he didn't know exactly what he wanted to do with the band. I'm glad he is going ahead with it.

SUE: Well, we'll see what happens at the Mercer Arts Center. That will be some kind of test to see if, in fact, it will pay off, if people will come.

GOODMAN: Yeah, but if people don't respond, that doesn't mean it's not a good idea or that you couldn't get support elsewhere.

SUE: Oh, no, absolutely, I would try to get support. Oh, yeah, I just mean—

GOODMAN: Morgenstern said to me that he was going to talk to you, or did talk to you, about getting some grants to make that band somewhat self-sustaining.

SUE: No, I don't think I have spoken to Dan about it. Yeah. See, I called New York State Council of the Arts, and spoke to somebody there who I think is in charge of everything. He was immediately very excited about it, and he said this would be an opportunity for them, and I had a feeling something was going to happen right away. It didn't, but I am sure eventually it will happen.

They do it for symphony orchestras, they have these matching funds. So, in other words, if I were able, or a booking agent were able, to book him steadily at a certain price, they would meet that price, you see. What they might pay for a six-piece band we could double.

What I mean about the Mercer Arts Center is that to pay twenty-two musicians a living wage is a lot of money. See, there are two major problems to this. Number one is rehearsal time. The musicians' union has these requirements that are almost prohibitive. So, either the musicians all have to agree to rehearse for free—and it's not easy to get twenty-two musicians who can do that because they have other gigs.

See, if the record companies would do it, if they would support it—it's just that it's terrifically expensive and they don't want to put money into jazz. They will do incredible things for rock groups because it's a matter of economics. That's why, when I spoke to the vice president at ABC Records the other day and he told me they have sent Alice Coltrane, Pharaoh Sanders, and some other jazz musicians on tours, and I don't think they made any money, but they did it and it certainly helped the record sales, no matter how it all came out.

I spoke to Columbia about it and they weren't interested. Steven Davis of *Rolling Stone* was with Clive Davis [of Columbia Records, no relation] and he said, "Why don't you send Mingus and the big band to fifteen cities? Fly it around?" They wouldn't do that.

NOTES

1. See NPR's *Jazz Profiles* series, "Charles Mingus: Fables of Bass," part 1, April 23, 2008, and the podcast at www.npr.org/player/v2/mediaPlayer.html?action=1&t =1&islist=false&id=89852381&m=89837214. Max's remarks begin at 36:40.

2. Their names were Otis and Leon René, New Orleans Creoles who settled in Los Angeles in 1922 and wrote and recorded some famous songs. See Ralph Eastman, "Pitchin' up a Boogie," in *California Soul: Music of African Americans in the West*, ed. Jacqueline Codgell DjeDje and Eddie S. Meadows (Berkeley: University of California Press, 1998), 66.

3. The beginnings of the Jazz Composers Workshop were at the Putnam Central Club. See Eric Porter, *What Is This Thing Called Jazz?* (Berkeley: University of California Press, 2002), 116: "In the summer of 1953, Mingus and Max Roach began a series of concerts and rehearsals at the Putnam Central Club in Brooklyn, whose participants included Thelonious Monk, Art Blakey, Kenny Clarke, John Lewis, Teo Macero, and John LaPorta. Out of the Putnam Central group emerged the Jazz Composers Workshop, a loosely organized group of musicians interested in collaborative jazz composition and cooperative economics.... Mingus recorded with various members of this group for Debut, Savoy, and other labels in 1954 and 1955."

4. Gene Santoro says it was Diane Dorr-Dorynek who bought Lovette out after problems with Celia: Santoro, *Myself When I Am Real: The Life and Music of Charles Mingus* (New York: Oxford, 2000), 150.

5. The Jazz Disco site has both a catalog (by album issued and performer) and a discography for Debut, though I can't vouch for its completeness: www.jazzdisco .org/debut-records/catalog-lp-ep-series/album-index/. For more info on Weinstock, Prestige and Fantasy, see http://en.wikipedia.org/wiki/Prestige_Records.

6. I heard Bud Powell one night in a joint called the Bee Hive on Fifty-third Street, in 1956 or '57 as I remember; and the Miles Davis band with Coltrane et al. at the Crown Propeller Lounge on Sixty-third Street. Ahmad Jamal was usually playing at the Pershing Hotel or the DuSable. And there were the fancier North Side clubs like the London House.

7. Marc Myers has a good short history of the so-called Rebel Festival, including recent comments by George Wein, posted July 2, 2010, in his Jazz Wax column: "George Wein on the Rebel Festival," www.jazzwax.com/2010/07 /george-wein-on-the-rebel-jazz-festival.html. Wein says the conflict with Mingus was basically over money. Mingus's organizing of the Rebel Festival was "a masterpiece of public relations," according to Wein.

8. See chapter 3, note 3 for more information about this recording, *Charles Mingus: Music Written for Monterey, 1965. Not heard ... played in its entirety, at UCLA.*

7 The Clubs and the Mafia

*"I might go back to the mob because
I want a big band."*

We had a great 1972 session talking about Mingus's experiences in the clubs and with the less savory elements of the jazz business. Some of his comments on the clubs and club owners were confusing, and I've attempted to straighten them out with a few notes in passing.

The important subject of New York's nightclubs—its jazz joints, that is—had not been much discussed or researched at the time of this conversation, though it has gotten more attention since.[1] Max Gordon wrote the story of the club he founded in *Live at the Village Vanguard*, with chapters on Mingus and on Joe Glaser, the agent. One of the great books about jazz, it's also an unvarnished look at the nightclub business that conveys the author's strong love for jazz and its people.

At one point in Gordon's story, Miles Davis is bitching about the nightclub audience ("I can't stand the whole fuckin' scene"), and Max acknowledges the scene: "I knew what he was talking about: the unemployed musicians and exmusicians; the pundits; the reviewers, columnists, and salesmen promoting fly-by-night jazz mags; the writers of liner notes and album covers; the record collectors; the heavyweights from Harlem; college kids bearing cassette recorders; the gossips, punks, and freeloaders who hang out in rooms where jazz is played."[2] People like Mingus and Miles had a great affection for Max (even if Mingus once pulled a knife on him, as Max recounts in chapter 4).

In my college years, in the mid-1950s, and later when I lived in New York, I was lucky enough to make the rounds of these clubs, including the three most famous ones—the Vanguard, Five Spot, and Half Note—that Mingus talks about. Despite the people and distractions Max notes (plus the audience noise that Mingus abominated), these places were *the* creative centers of the music. You heard jazz conceived, generated, received, and reciprocated loud and close-up. Musicians and audience took boozy communion in these meetinghouses (and of course still do); it's no accident that the best recordings are usually made live in nightclubs.

For Mingus, the club scene was something to be endured, but it was also the proving ground for his Jazz Workshops, the scene for some of his theatrics, and a venue for composing, for teaching his people and testing out the results. The clubs were also where he made much of his bread. The abortive Mercer Arts Center band was, in part, an attempt to escape from the strictures of the club environment.

· · ·

GOODMAN: What do you want to do about your teaching? Are you gonna be able to get that going sometime?

MINGUS: When I'm seventy-five or eighty I'll do it. Yeah, I've got a whole new crop of hair, man, it's very weird. I can't show you, but I'm going to shave it all off, down to one strand, and it will all grow back black. A whole different grade of hair, so I can get another chance on life to start over again—because I blew about seven years. . . . But I've got no pains, till my legs get hurting, so I know if I lose weight I'll be feeling pretty good. Been born again.

'Cause I got to straighten some things out, man. I don't care about money too much. But I gotta straighten my people's minds out about music. And I'm not the only one to do it. Gene Ammons has got a lot to do with it. He's not gonna pass the lies around to 'em. I went to visit some clubs when we were playing in California, and he said, "Hey, man, yeah, brother," like he's a preacher—and it's true, he is, man.

All the bullshit in the newspaper about what Eldridge Cleaver's doing [in Algeria]—they know that's bullshit. That was all set up, man. They probably even hired him: "Look, man, we'll give you a place out of this country to live the way you want to live instead of you going around protesting and saying these things." That's what happened. Not one change has happened since that bullshit race riot [Watts] happened. Not one better job or anything. One thing happened: the banks did open up and put some [black] tellers in; that's the only change I've seen.

GOODMAN: But they haven't given any more money to black business-people.

MINGUS: Right, no more money, and I remember they were having a picketing thing, they were building a hospital in Harlem. They haven't built the hospital yet because they still refuse to hire black men to build the building. They say there are none. Well, that ain't changed. A minister laid down to pray and a truck rolled over him. And the building went up, and they ain't solved that yet. So it was a bullshit race riot.

I'm sure it was planned by U.S. Marines and the Pentagon. See, a lot of black people are going communist, and I'm sure they had people besides me who reported it. But in my original book [*Underdog*] I went there because I was a Boy Scout. I said, "Fuck these motherfuckers, I'm not going to let them take my country from me." My fathers and mothers were slaves for the country, my father fought for it, and there's still more white people running it. I don't want that bullshit, man. I want capitalism, the same thing everybody else has got. I want to pile up some money, man. I seen the countries like that, man, and they got it. You want communism? That's some sick shit, man.

It gets out of hand because the people who've got money are going to get rid of their money regardless because they are very well guarded, they've got the gates of Rome surrounding them. They own the Mafia, that's the rich man's army, Rockefeller's army. The only time they did get out of hand against them [the Attica prison riot], then he [Rockefeller] calls in the Marines and the hand grenades.

And *they* couldn't win over the Mafia. Believe me, man. The Mafia's got extrasensory perception. I've been involved with them, and these cats are something else, man. I ain't talking about just Italians only. They can hear you think. [*Laughter.*]

GOODMAN: The Chase Manhattan Bank and the Mafia, man—that's a combination.

MINGUS: Joe Glaser used to own a bank my money was in, and I didn't even know it.

GOODMAN: Sue told me you were affiliated with him, or something, for awhile?

MINGUS: Joe and I were very good friends. There's one story I'll tell you. I was in California, just got out of music school, and Lionel Hampton came to town. His bass player used to be a teacher of mine and tricked me into going into a studio and playing. I jammed [with the bass player] and I didn't know he was leaving Lionel's band. So Lionel asked me if I would join the band, and I said no but I'd play the theater with him "if you play my music." So I wrote some music: "Mingus Fingus" and a bunch of things. He played all my music in town, man. It went over all right, so Joe Glaser came in and said, "Kid, I want you to join Hamp. Then when you come to New York, if you want to leave, leave him, 'cause I never heard music like this since Duke Ellington. You're a classic. Take my word, I'll back you all the way when you come to New York."

It took Lionel almost two years to get to New York, and I knew Joe meant I should stay with Lionel for a while. "Even if you don't join the band, you come to New York, and I'm with you." Now, why I had to come to New York, I don't even know. So when I did come with Red Norvo, we were having a bad time. Red Norvo had a TV show that wouldn't let any black people on—it was the first [jazz] color TV show. Red was on a regular job, and I quit, just walked off that night job 'cause Red didn't show up. He didn't send anybody in his place, just me and Tal [Farlow] was there. He should have walked off the TV show.[3]

So when he didn't show up on the night job, I went to his house trying to get my money. He wouldn't [pay], and Joe Glaser said, "Come up to my office and Red will meet you there." 'Cause Red was afraid of me. I got there, and Joe and I talked. He said, "Well, you can put a claim in with the union, but it will take weeks."

I said, "I just want what I'm owed. I'm more insulted than anything else. And I want you to book my trio."

He said, "All right, that's an agreement."

So I got a trio together and he booked it for awhile. He kept his word. But then I wanted to get a bigger band, and he booked that some too. That was good, but there wasn't enough to go on the road with and I didn't have no name. So I'm talking to Oscar Pettiford, and he said, "Ask these club owners for jobs." Man, I can't name the clubs [forgot the names], but one was Café Bohemia, we started there, and they didn't have no jazz there. Well, Charlie Parker had played there for their opening.

One night before that, Bird walked in drunk and ordered drinks on the house for everybody. Told the man he didn't have any money, and the man, a gangster, was going to beat him up, and Bird said, "Look, man, you don't beat Charlie Parker up. I'll come in and play one night and set you up in business." And he did just that. He brought some guys in and packed the joint.

So I did the same thing [at Bohemia]: "Well, I'll bring a band in."

"Who in the hell are you?"

I said, "Well, we'll see. Just pay the musicians, don't even worry about paying me if you can't pay me. If you don't make it, don't pay me, just pay the guys."

So we always made it, and I found I made more money by staying in New York than by traveling the road. In those days I'd work for $1,100,

$1,200, $1,500, so finally I realized it and got Art Blakey in the same club, Café Bohemia. He got big after that. We outdrew Lionel Hampton, who was booked right across the street from where Christine Jorgensen [performed].[4] This was in the [*Underdog*] book but they took it out.

GOODMAN: What time was this, Charles?

MINGUS: Middle fifties, probably 1954. Lionel was on his way down then, either that or he didn't advertise, I don't know what it was, man, but there was nobody in the club, ten people. Intermission, I'd go over there. And he's so proud, I don't even think he knew I was appearing on the street. "Charlie Mingus is here, ladies and gentlemen, he's down the street with a house full of people." Art Blakey drew good there, Horace Silver had a good band in those days. That's very funny, I was with Horace the other day. So finally, I realized I could build clubs.

Then I went into the Five Spot. They said, "You should have come last week. We made a group with Monk, he comes in in a couple of months."

I said, "That's not now; I'll come in now." So I opened the place up, and it was packed. You couldn't get in the place, and they didn't even want me to leave at first 'cause it was a gamble to get Monk because he hadn't even played in New York at that time.

Then I went to a club in Brooklyn.[5] Joe Termini from the Five Spot told 'em to call me, and the guy said he wanted a trio, but I said I didn't want a trio any more. He said, "I lost money, brought Randy Weston in, and I'd like to have a big band"—[Aside:] I didn't know you recording this! I thought we was just talking—Anyway, I said, "If you do like I tell you, I'll bring the combo in and the club will be packed in one week, but you got to do just like I tell you. You gotta have a press party, and you'll do even better than Joe Termini. One week, I guarantee you."

So they went with me. I got my wife, Celia, who knew all about it [meaning public relations], she got a mailing list, invited all the press and we had a big press party, Greek dinner and everything. They didn't do that in those days. I don't know where I got the idea from. Nobody was doing that in no nightclubs. But I knew that if I had opening night and wasn't in the *New Yorker*, then I'm not going in. No club owners used to advertise, but I noticed that every time I was in the *New Yorker*, people came. So I said, "If I'm not in there, the contract is cancelled." And everything I said to do, they did.

Now here's the proof I ain't lying, man. After I'd been there for a while and they packed the joint in, do you know that they asked me to sign a lifetime contract, which called for a minimum of twelve weeks a year? So by then Joe Glaser is with me again. He said, "Well, Charlie, your band's doing fine, let's go out on the road."

So, we go on the road and the first place I play is Washington, DC. And the club owner didn't tell me he was going broke, and he didn't advertise or nothing and, as usual, I never drew my money out of the kitty all at once, plus I'd take checks—I'd trust club owners, but the guy didn't pay me. And I'd paid everybody in the band. He didn't pay anybody. He recently robbed a bank, this guy, name is Tony.

So I come back to New York, wait, a month, another month, and here's the sad story about this [other] guy—I hate to tell you the name—"Who do you recommend we should get in, who could draw as good as you did?"

I said Lennie Tristano. "I'm looking at the whole picture, it has nothing to do with race. The most popular people in the music now to me is Lennie Tristano and Lee Konitz and Warne Marsh."

He said, "No, we don't like [that kind of] jazz."

"I'm not asking what you like; you're in business, and you ask me who's going to draw."

"We're thinking about getting in"—don't call his name—"Lou Donaldson."

I say, "He won't make it. He's got a following in certain neighborhoods at this time—he might make it now—but call somebody else."

"Mingus, we're going to get Lou."

"Well, you'll be out of business."

And it just went right back down: nobody was coming. I mean the people were looking for avant-garde then. We were playing semi-avant-garde. I've never tried to play weird. On record I've made some very way-out things: "Thrice Upon a Theme," a couple others with Teo. But when I played in public I was playing what Cannonball later did, I was playing "This Here," "Better Get Hit in Your Soul," "Wednesday Night Prayer Meeting," a new form people hadn't heard in jazz. I wasn't playing bebop—I played some bebop—and Jimmy Knepper was my biggest asset because anything I played he played right the first time, and the guys could follow him.

So I came back again to the guy who never hired me.[6] Lennie was doing well, and I went by and asked, "When can I come in?"

"Oh, pretty soon, we'll call you."

Some more months go by, so I finally go to the union and say, "This guy's got me in a lifetime contract and won't hire me." So they call down there, and in other words he's planning to keep [Lennie] living there forever, and he says, "Well, Mingus would not draw," and to him it's just money, you know. So, finally the union guy says, "Look, man, Mingus didn't hold a gun on you [when you signed him]," 'cause they [the Cantarinos] were talking about killing me.

One of them named Sonny said, "You're a coward anyway, 'cause I saw you fight one night." They did see me fight—I'd lost about a hundred pounds, I was little, man—and this guy did something, I hit him, and I bounced back. So I walked away [*laughter*]. I hit a guy big as I *used* to be. I hit him hard too. He looked at me, man, and he didn't get mad.

So Sonny—he's about my size—he says, "Besides, anybody who says you're tough, I saw you run away from a guy one night."

"I didn't run, I walked away."

"I know you're a coward, man, and I'm going to kill you because you talked to this other business."

Right then in the room Max Aaron [a Local 802 official] says to me, "What are you going to do, man?"

"Well, I'm going to bring a new group in—because I've paid the guys all their money, and they refuse to give it back even though I just paid them. So I'll bring another band in."

[One of the Cantarinos said:] "You're not going to bring the same band in?"

"No, I got a new idea: I'll bring in three cellos, alto saxophone, bass, and Elvin Jones."

"No, we want Dannie."

I say, "Look, man, Elvin Jones is a better drummer than Dannie." And they didn't even know that. I forgot who was on piano. So I wrote this music and, man, it was beautiful, in fact a woman came in and recorded it. You know what [the club owners] were doing? They were walking around, and instead of trying to help the thing, they had the waiters banging trays on tables, making noise.

And ten years later when Chico Hamilton comes in, they say, "Jesus Christ, man, you had a thing going like Chico Hamilton."

It was very weird about those brothers. Max Aaron, he made them keep their word—not to give up the contract but to give me one or two more weeks in there. Instead of their helping the thing, they hurt the club and killed the club again. The next thing I know is they had Lennie back in there, but Lennie got wind of, heard about the contract with me and he wouldn't stay. He said, "These guys play that way with Mingus? The hell with them then." So he left, and then they got stuck with Zoot Sims. Who is good, it lasted 'em, but the business we had, man—people were standing outdoors every night and even on Monday nights. They would ask me how to draw Mondays, and I said bring poetry in.

So Kenneth Patchen and some guys read poetry, and I'd come in and play Monday nights. It was very artistic, man, and this was before Joe Termini [of the Five Spot] had poets. We had poetry contests and gave prizes away. Well, they said they didn't like the crowd—dirty, wearing Levis, you know, they didn't like the poets—didn't spend money. I said, "Well, the people who come to see 'em will spend money." And they bought *something*, man. You can't make a million dollars every night. And they don't pay no money out. Print that, man.

For those days, the contract they signed with me for twelve weeks was quite a bit of money. I remember we got in Lee Kraft to negotiate it.[7] He said, "Mingus, these guys will sign for anything now. Why don't you let me handle it for you? You got a packed house on a Tuesday night, and they're begging you to sign. Let me handle it for you."

I said OK, and then they got mad at that. "You're our brother, why you getting someone else to sign?"

"Because I'm not business." And Lee got double what I'd asked for—or what they'd asked me to sign for. [Mike's] father called me "son," and I said, "If you do it the way I suggest to you, you'll knock that wall (they had a wall) down in one week, not six months."

GOODMAN: Yeah, the wall, and that terrible arrangement with the bandstand they had.

MINGUS: Well, they had to make it bigger, 'cause they couldn't hold the people. They could have put the bandstand somewhere else. I told 'em to put it in the corner. They said no, and put the bandstand right in the middle of the bar.

GOODMAN: What's that guy's name, the owner now?

MINGUS: Mike [Cantarino]: Mike, Sonny, and his father . . . and sister and mother.

GOODMAN: I met him once through a woman friend of mine who used to hang out with Elvin Jones, in fact.

MINGUS: You know what he [Mike] said, man? "It wasn't you that packed the people in and made the wall come down." I mean, how could he say that? We had Cadillac limousines out front, couldn't believe it, man. We had little Vassar broads that would bring their chauffeurs and things. I don't know where they came from. I still today don't know why

Monk and I drew them kind of people. We always drew people with a little bread. Each band drew a different kind of crowd. But we always had the so-called . . . I think I had them a little more than Monk if I remember. The kids would be sitting out front in the snow waiting to get in.

GOODMAN: I was going to college then, and I'd come down and hear you once in a while, and at the Five Spot later, just before it closed.

MINGUS: We packed the Five Spot, did very good, but it wasn't nothing like the Half Note. The kids standing in line, you'd think it was something going on like a circus. Like you see the hippies line up around the theaters. But I gotta say they [the Cantarinos] did believe in me, the guys gave an unbelievable party. They brought food out, I couldn't believe it, make people want to come in thinking they had food like that.

GOODMAN: I was there a couple of years ago; the food wasn't so great.

MINGUS: It used to be mainly a restaurant, you know, and it was good when they cooked for the workmen around there.

GOODMAN: It's too bad, that club should be better than it is.

MINGUS: Well, they're moving now. Another person's gonna buy it.

GOODMAN: Didn't I see you once, when I was a college kid, in the Downbeat Club in New York?

MINGUS: Yeah, Downbeat, Fifty-second Street, Billy Taylor. Yeah, that's when I picked up with all the gangsters. I didn't know who gangsters were; I thought they were things in the movies. And they were going to jump on Max Roach one night.

GOODMAN: You and Max and Billy had the trio?

MINGUS: No, Max wasn't in the trio. No, I was with Billy's trio and came by the Downbeat when Max had his band there. And there was a pimp, and the gangsters came out to protect the guy and grabbed Max from behind. I was knocking people all over the street. I thought, God gotta be with a guy like me, man. Ask Max, he'll tell you. I hit one, it was like a forest falling. Jesus Christ, I sure looked good that night [*laughs*]. That's where I got the reputation.

Man says, "This is Johnny Roberts, you don't know me? I'll kill you."

I said, "Well, go ahead, it's all right, you still got to get your gun out, don't just tell me how bad a gangster you are. Here are my hands. You go in your pocket to get your gun and then you're in trouble."

"Don't you know who I am?"

"Yeah, man, you been here all the time, Johnny Roberts, you're the doorman, bouncer. I know who you are." I saw him kick a cop, got him down, put his shoe heel on him and rip his face up. I saw him do that twice to people, man. I knew he was bad, but he was wrong this night, I know that.

And you know Max can fight better than I can fight, he's a boxer, he and Miles Davis is good boxers. He hadn't done anything, and Max is such a gentleman. So this guy hit him in the mouth and Max says, "How *dare* you?" and he's looking around (this guy's such a star) saying, "Mingus, this guy *hit* me while I'm taking my coat off. How *dare* you hit me while I'm taking my coat off?"

He started to box the guy and make him look like a fool. Then Johnny Roberts grabs Max so the other guy can hit him. I said, "You can't even whip Max, how you gonna hit me, man?" You know, this same guy is probably a killer—but he's dead now, the big bad Brooklyn gangster.

GOODMAN: We can talk about him in print now?

MINGUS: Oh, yeah, and here's a guy did all this bad talk, and what I want to tell you is very important about this night. . . . Something happened that night. Oh, later on he [Johnny Roberts] gets involved with Brunswick Records in some kind of way (don't say "Brunswick," say "records"), and I had just signed with some little guys—I didn't know who they were—two accountants, their names don't matter.

They said, "Look, Charlie, anybody who comes to you now, just let me know because you can't do any dates. You're with us permanently."

I said, "Well there's a guy named Johnny Roberts asked me about a record date for Brunswick."

He said, "You can't call anybody. You're exclusive."

Well, they thought I was stupid, but I knew that. I said, "No, this guy insists I do one."

"Look Mingus, how much you want to do a record date for Brunswick? You're ignorant, man. How much you want? We'll pay you a good price."

"I'd like to get four or five thousand."

"I'll pay you that." So I said to the accountant, "I made a commitment to this Roberts guy, I made a commitment that I'd make it for that much."

So he says, "What's his name? We'll talk to him."

So here's the big bad gangster one day and I meet him one day with my wife: "Mingus, what did you do to me? I just asked you to do a record date. You didn't have to send the gorillas after me."

I say, "You're the gorilla, man, you walk around making me [unintelligible] to you."

He said, "Look, you got the Gallo brothers after me, man. What are you trying to do to me? These guys'll kill you. They'll kill you and me too."

I said, "I don't know about this, I'm from California, Watts. I don't know about these killing things."

He says, "Look Mingus, tell the guys I'm OK, that I only asked you to do a record date and I offered you a good price. They're saying I'm trying to force you to do a record date."

I never saw such a nice gangster, and for five years he was nice. So nice he even quit and started studying law. Quit the whole thing, "I'm out, I'm gonna be an attorney." [*Laughter.*]

GOODMAN: So the accountants sent the Gallos after him.

MINGUS: Well, now here's how I got away from them. I don't care if you print it without calling the gangsters' names, because I respect the Gallos. It was the accountants, Al Ternoff and Max Kaufman, they're the killers. So I called Al one day. We were working in a place called Copa City, run by a drummer whose wife was—[he was] married to a daughter of Proficcio.[8] Nobody knows her father owns the club. They just think she's a little hustler who got a little money together.

So we had a bad week, and I just happened to mention to Al that I didn't get paid. "You didn't get paid?!" he says, and something else about he wanted his percentage.

"What do you mean, man, I booked this job, it's my job."

"Did you read your contract? It says that if you book a job when you're with us, any contract you take we get a percentage."

"Any contract?"

"Yep."

"Suppose I quit and dig ditches; you don't get none of that."

"Yes, we do. We're protecting you, we don't want you to dig ditches . . ."

"Well, I'm gonna get out of that contract, Al."

He says I can't; I say the union approved it [the contract]. He says, "Well there's one way you can get out, and that's to die."

So I'll tell you how I did it; here's the most important thing. This girl, the club owner's daughter, calls me: "Mingus, what did you do to me? You told me you didn't want to be with the gangsters, about Johnny Roberts bothering you and all that, so I put you in the club, told you my father is Proficcio—and you sent out some little punks who say they're going to make a garage of my place in three days. This is the Gallo brothers you with, Mingus, these guys are killers. They're not playing. They say if I don't pay you, my place will be a garage in three days. They're not that big, Mingus, they just think they're that big. And it'll take a long time to prove it, but they ain't that big."

So I said, "Elaine, I told these guys that you didn't pay me, and in this agreement they said very clearly, 'You must get paid even if the business doesn't make it.' I told them, 'That's not so, we have an agreement because the club was just getting built.'"

So she had a publicity party the next week and it was big. She asked me, "I'm getting started and what can I do to make it?"

"Well, nobody knows I'm here, that's obvious. They'll come from New York or wherever."

I had a hell of a lot of ego and said she had to have a publicity party. She had one and they started making it, but this was before the party.

So I called the accountants and said, "Why did you do that, man, this woman's a friend of mine. You gonna make a garage out of a woman's place?"

He said, "*Anybody's* place, man. Anybody where my acts is. Look, Charlie, you got three movies a year, read your contract."

"Yeah, three movies a year."

"Big band, anything you want, you got that, right? Your dream is answered. You got all the money in the world behind you, you're on five thousand jukeboxes all over the United States. Now look at what we're doing with Stan Getz and he's only been with us a year."

I say, "That's nice, man, but I'm going to get out."

"How?"

"I'm crazy. I was crazy when I signed those papers, and here it [the proof] is, man: non compos mentis. Now how are you going to tell me I'm with you?" When I came out of the hospital [Bellevue, 1958] I had crazy papers because I knew those guys existed.

"Man, you mean you tricked us?"

"I didn't trick you, I was just looking to not get with guys like you who tell me that if I dig a ditch you own my money. I may want to quit, I may want to retire and be a bum, you know? I got a right to do that."

It took a long time to beg my way into the hospital but I knew what I was up against. Now the only thing about it, I hate to tell you this, man, everybody got a little larceny in 'em, but the fact is you got to have them papers *before*.

GOODMAN: Before you sign.

MINGUS: But even if I hadn't have had the papers before, I would have got 'em dated before by the judge or somebody. I would have got 'em dated back. Only thing that bugged me in the contract—everything else was beautiful, man—three movies a year, not only to score but to act in three movies a year if I wanted to, but this was to score. Which do you think I'd rather do? I'd rather score.

GOODMAN: Damn right.

MINGUS: Three movies, a big band, dance halls—they were taking dance away from jazz, so we put that back in the contract. Plus, I was paid a salary, which I never had before, they took income tax out, unemployment, and all this for when I grow old, and paid me a salary. The rest was to go into stocks and bonds for a holding corporation. This was for my own business; their money was something else. If we got into tax problems they would set another corporation up—they called it a circle of corporations, three corporations. When one has to pay taxes, you give a loan from that one to the next one. That's how you make it.

So I had it covered with those good Gallo brothers. And I hope that they read this article and come back and get me, 'cause the blue bloods forgot me, the blue chips don't want me [*laughter*].

Al Ternoff didn't seem mad, but Max Kaufman said he wanted to kill me. Max told me something, "Look, Mingus, you taught me something," and he smiled. "Now, you're going to come back and you're going to sign again, and next time you won't get out like this."

And I might go back to them because I want a big band. When you asked me about the band, I thought, "You know, I should call Al. I'll get a better percentage now, I'm old enough, and will get a good deal."

GOODMAN: They're still around?

MINGUS: The brothers are still here, same guys. Joey Diehl took Joey Gallo's place, whoever that is.

GOODMAN: You want me to mention names in the article? It's a great story.

MINGUS: I don't care, man . . . if you make it look like I like Joey Gallo and look like only his accountants were rough. That'd be nice, man, just say Ternoff and Kaufman.

GOODMAN: You'll probably get a phone call.

MINGUS: I don't care, man, and especially say I might go back with them. Nobody from the bluebloods, the elite, has come to offer me a booking. They [the mobsters] know I've been more in their corner, and I never did anything to hurt them. And I kind of feel they been with me all along anyway. The last seven years I've been seeing these guys, but I can't explain how they show up.

GOODMAN: They come in the clubs or just see you in the street?

MINGUS: No, I won't lie to you, man, I'll tell you an incident happened some weeks ago, months ago. I was coming home, I had several thousand dollars here [*gestures under arm*]. I carry my payroll here, and this guy they call Karate Bobby followed me all the way and was talking to me. I sensed something was wrong, you know. He said, "I heard you know about the martial arts."

I said "When I was younger, I knew a little something about it. Can you pick that car up over there?"

He said, "Well, that's something else."

He called it some kind of tension or something.

I said, "When I was young I used to pick a car up with my back, things like that, but I don't know anything about karate. I know a little about judo, about getting out of the way, the gentle art."

He started to put his hands on me. "Don't put your hands on me." And this went on for about an hour. What was keeping me outdoors was I didn't want him to know what apartment I lived in.

Pretty soon here come three little Italian guys, like "Hey, Charlie." I only saw them in the bar across the street, and I know their names, little guys. They say [to Bobby], "Hey, man, do you know who you're talking to?"

[I said to them,] "Yeah, he's been talking bad, telling me he's black belt and how he could break boards with his hands, shows me his feet. I asked him if he could eat rice and climb a tree upside down. He didn't know I was talking about Charles Rice [see below]—better eat this rice before you mess with me."

He told me how bad he was, and the guys say to him, "Look, man, don't talk to us with your hands up ready to protect yourself. Be nice. Charlie's a friend of ours, he come to this neighborhood and everybody likes him—for six years. We believe in extrasensory perception, right Charlie?"

Now I hadn't used that word in twenty years, but there's a tune I'd written way back called "Extrasensory Perception," and I'd just pulled out the score to get it ready for a big band, so I [realized] these guys had come into my apartment and rearranged things. They're not the ones was robbing me, but they'd moved things around, just to let me know somebody's visiting, no matter what kind of locks I put on the door, so I know I been looked after, and it ain't the police department.

So anybody can come in through them kind of locks, especially the one I got now, a combination, they been in once. I got two doors, they still come in there. So I say [to myself], "Well, these are my friends, and I said some things I shouldn't have said about them in the book [the unpublished *Underdog;* see below], but they knew I didn't mean no harm." And here they come up and tell this guy to go away, man, and he made a couple of moves.

Then they say, "You know, you're a real tall guy and we're little. You know, one day the little people gonna take this world over, from the bottom, right up from your shoes." I feel they knew everything he was talking about [*getting excited*], 'cause the way he moved his hands, pointing like this . . .

GOODMAN: Is Karate Bobby a neighborhood guy?

MINGUS: Yeah, he's on television, least he tells how that he is, breaking boards with his hand. [He and] Charles Rice, those guys don't have no scars or nothing. He [Rice] teaches the police department, says to me, "Charles, you know I like martial arts too, but I like jewelry and women, you know, so I wear gloves." It's the same thing [playing bass], I use them on all the blisters. You're not going to hurt your hand anyway if you use them.

GOODMAN: So what did the Italian boys do?

MINGUS: They made him look like a fool, just with words. And they made me feel funny with knowing what was inside my house. Nobody knows what's on my piano. Either somebody's telling 'em what's on my piano—I suspected Sue, I suspected everything. For seven years I didn't know what was coming or going, but finally I got to the point where I realized somebody's coming in, but they ain't hurt me in seven years so they must be trying to tell me something else. I'm not dead yet.

GOODMAN: Are they your friends?

MINGUS: Evidently. See, in the original *Underdog* book I said that the Mafia has to integrate to save the society because the communists are getting to the black people. You guys—Joe Gallo, [Profaci]—got to get together because if the communists take the black people and blow the society of capitalism, they blowing you. You can't operate then. There's no better test for Biblical life than American society. Know what I'm talking about?

GOODMAN: No.

MINGUS: Well, everybody wants a chance to be good, so you have to have a world where there's bad in it. If you clean it up for them—if everybody gets fair employment, same salary, doctors, socialized medicine, everything you want, you got it—then it ain't no test for a little kid to grow up and say, "Man, I want to be a good football player." He's just another football player, and we're watching a bunch of dead people.

I say, "Wait a minute," and in my own head I'm figuring out that it ain't no fun living in a place like that. I want the challenge of life, man, even though it's been unfair and harder for a black man to make it. He got to be tough to make it, he got to be a champ. This is true in sports, and I think it's going to have to change in the business direction.

And if it doesn't, then everything else is legal, if they ain't going to change it. That means they want the black people to be criminals. If Rockefeller wants us to be criminals, that means the only way to operate is to join the Mafia, the black Mafia.

In my book I said—see I'd been listening to the black gangsters talk, this is way back—they say, "They took our numbers." (No, don't print this, 'cause I'd be dead.) "Mingus, they took our numbers but we gonna get 'em back. We'll hit them one after another, and they won't know who's doing it. [Because] they didn't just hit us in New York, they came at us in the South, they killed men, killed the big numbers rackets in Chicago, they hit all over. Our men are protesting this shit. But they [the Mafia] get writeups now, and we know 'em by name." Man, that's fifteen years ago I was told that.

GOODMAN: It's finally in the papers, about black people and the numbers.

MINGUS: I was playing in a club in Baltimore and we had to close because they killed the club owner. Few weeks before that he was a brave man, only black man in town who had the numbers. That don't make him no gangster. He carried a gun but he was just booking the numbers. My cousin started numbers in Chicago; he wasn't no gangster, he was a pimp, he was a lover. He said, "Mingus, look what they sent me, man, these cowardly cocksuckers. Why can't they just come and tell me?"

They sent him a brass coffin with his picture in it. "They're punks," he said. "Before they walk in with their gang, they have to send you some threatening thing to scare you. Well, I ain't going for it." They got him, though. This is way back, hell, it's more than fifteen years ago. I forgot I'm fifty; yeah, it's about thirty years ago. This innocent friend of mine—remember the McNeely brothers, Cecil? Got famous for a while in dance music.

GOODMAN: Jay? Big Jay?

MINGUS: Big Jay McNeely—well, his brother was in the band and they got the idea—there was no numbers in California but the "Chinaman," they called it, the "Chinaman," a lottery. So he started the numbers in California. He got rich, got sharp, took his family out of poverty. He was a musician, but he didn't know, man. Someone said start the numbers, so he started booking the numbers. He learned how to do it from the numbers in New York.

So one day some cats knock on his door, "Hey, what are you doing, man? Look at you!"

"What do you mean, 'Look at me'? You want to book? You can play. I'm a musician, man, trying to make a living, just like you."

They say, "Man, you didn't come to us and ask for this."

"I know, I went in the newspapers and figured it out. I'm looking at the horses. . . . It's a free game, right?"

Do you know what happened, man? They just took everything in his house, everything and said, "It's ours."

Then came the black thing. People said, "Wait a minute, man, what happened to Bobby? He's a good kid." Then [they] organized. In California some cats said we'll get it back. Now I don't know if they have or not. I'm pretty sure they could, 'cause [the Mafia] don't know Watts as good as these cats know Watts. Look, man, they don't give you no fair employment, so give us the numbers. Do you know, man, that the Mafia was even walking around to the pimps, taking their money from their black call girls? "You gotta give us a percentage of your money to live." We ain't that bad, man.

GOODMAN: And their percentage of the business can't be that much either.

MINGUS: Put this in the book, man: I knew a gangster once—and I flushed him down the toilet. I waited six months after he said he was going to kill me. And I got him while he was peeing, turning his back, and I flushed him, man. He didn't even know it was me, man, put his head down there and stomped him and flushed him. So when he came to, he didn't know who did it. Now, I'm a good cat and I would never hit anyone from behind. But when a guy says he's gonna kill me and says, "You won't know when it's coming"—so I saw this cat and figured, "Now it's my turn."

You can't play bass, you can't pimp, you can't do nothing.

GOODMAN: Were you pimping for a while, like you said in the book?

MINGUS: Sure, I tried. Well, put it like this. I didn't try to be no pimp, I tried to boost my ego. I get more kicks out of being with a broad who's gonna be the baddest hustler. "Hey, man, Mingus got Margo." (That's

Max's broad, but I won't call my broad's name.) "He got so-and-so, man, and she's bad, makes all kind of money." This broad wouldn't come home with less than a thousand dollars a day. Wouldn't come home with less than a thousand dollars a day! You get ten girls like that. . . . The guys I knew were bad cats, they wouldn't let 'em come home with less than a thousand a day.

People say that's bullshit, but it's not so, man. Police commissioner in Boston who worked for Harvard said it was impossible. He doesn't know, man. Those kind of broads would trick for [a minimum of] a hundred dollars, but they would also trick for fifteen, twenty, and ten, so they could come up with a thousand dollars—on a ten-day week. I don't know about now 'cause they made it a little tough with [cracking down on] these massage parlors. . . .

MINGUS: Joe Glaser used to have a map, he'd put a flag on it and then a flag on another flag, then when it got too tall for the poles, he put flags going *this* way—of *all* the clubs he had working in one town. I remember that cat, man, he was bad, baby. I said, "Here's one town there must be at least five hundred dollars in."

Joe said, "No, that's twenty thousand dollars."

I talked to him once about booking Louis [Armstrong], and he said, "Charles, he doesn't know it but I had a corporation set up for him. . . . This man is so beautiful, Mingus, I set properties up for him he owns 35 percent of."

Thirty-five percent? Except the management and all the production fees come off that, plus the salaries paid to the secretaries: Louis makes a good living for Joe's friends. Louis could have set the corporation up himself and employed the two people.

That was the message I was preaching. The Jewish people are already integrated; they have black people working for 'em, so I can say it in the story you're working on. But in those days, they didn't have no black people in the offices. That's what the original book said. I've gone through Joe's office, I've looked in Columbia, looked in this area—"No black men there?"

"No, Mingus, sorry. Oh, yes, we do have one."

Downstairs I found one, a janitor someplace, I usually found one. They got some in there? That's what the book [talked about], man. In the banks, there are some changes, the banks changed.

GOODMAN: So he [Joe Glaser] gave Louis 35 percent, eh?

MINGUS: Yeah and he put his name on the door—not on the door but up on the wall. His contract—go to Nat Hentoff, check with Nat—was 60 percent, sixty-forty—and expenses came out of Louis's money. I think there was a guaranteed salary of a thousand dollars a week. That's mainly what he got, a guaranteed salary. But that's good anyway. I wouldn't want no more than four or five hundred bucks myself—for the rest of the corporation, and that corporation is taxable—

GOODMAN: Right, but you don't want it in Joe's pocket.

MINGUS: That's right, but when one corporation is taxable, your goal is to set up a nonprofit organization. So you set up another company and give a loan, which is nontaxable, and first present your ideas of what you want to do—oh, man, I had this almost finished, opening my third corporation when I met Sue. I know who got my books, my checkbooks: she has a green one, I have a red one. Lotta bread went in that book, man [*unintelligible*].

See, the corporation can give a loan—if you give a loan of twenty thousand dollars a year in a corporation, you're taxed with 7 percent. That's a lot of money, a 7 percent tax. So you just give a loan of thirty thousand dollars, you almost break yourself. Start another company, they call it a circle. And your final one that you're looking for is a nonprofit organization. One that's gonna be set up for the welfare of the children of jazz musicians.[9]

It's gotta be jazz, because the classical guys are looked out [for] by the government. Until they free us, then I say give it to them, but right now my goal is to set up a nonprofit organization so that if a guy dies his family is looked after, same as a police officer. But these other cats, though, they are some bad cats.

CHAPTER 7 COMMENTARY

Dan Morgenstern on Mingus's Business Arrangements

MORGENSTERN: I think the closest I ever got to him was during a time in 1961 when he was having some problems. He had become involved with Joe Glaser, and if there were ever two people who were destined not to get along, it was Mingus and Joe Glaser. Around this time I was the last editor of *Metronome*, and *Metronome* folded. Mingus had been very friendly to me, and it was when we first got to know each other. I had written a thing about him which he liked. And we had a wake for the magazine which turned out to be quite an interesting party: lots of people came, he came, and there was lots of booze. A couple of days after that he called me and said he wanted to talk.

We went to a bar and sat in the booth and had a long, long talk. He was very concerned about what he should do, because Glaser wanted to sign him to some kind of big contract and it looked good, but there were things like control, artistic control, and so on, that Glaser wanted him to [give over]. He started talking about himself. During that time also the book [*Underdog*] was already in process and went through a number of phases, as you know. Bill Coss, who had been with *Metronome* prior to my being there, had been working with him on that.

And Charles also showed me the first couple of chapters. Through the years we've had our ups and downs. Once I met him on a bus quite unexpectedly, and he said, "Don't write about me anymore."

I said, "You're all right?"

"Yeah, but don't write about me." Apparently he said that to several writers at the time. Another time I reviewed a record of his, and I had ambiguous feelings about it but gave it a good review. And then when I saw him sometime after that, he said, "You know, the way you wrote about that, you made it sound like you were saying something, but you weren't saying anything." Which was very true.

GOODMAN: God, he picks up so quickly when people are unsure about things. He did that with Julius Lester [on television] last night, and it was kind of marvelous. I think he may have embarrassed them all a little bit.

MORGENSTERN: Well, he has a very good bullshit detector. He doesn't like any kind of insincerity. And he is very sincere himself, and he trusts making [*unintelligible*]. Have you talked to Max Gordon?

GOODMAN: I was going to go see him today, as a matter of fact.

MORGENSTERN: Well, Max can probably tell you a lot of stories. He went after Max with a knife once. Yeah, and Max was very upset about it but, you know, he took it in stride. He has probably worked more for Max than for any other club owner. They have a basically good relationship.

When the Thad Jones–Mel Lewis band was in Russia, Mingus did seven weeks at the Vanguard with the big band, seven Monday nights, and then when they came back he had a whole week with the big band there. This was undoubtedly the longest stretch that Mingus has ever had a big band. He enjoyed that tremendously. And there again, there were nights, I caught him about four or five nights, and sometimes it was beautiful— everything just going well, and when things go well he gets so happy that he just radiates, turns everybody on.

On the other hand, one night it was miserable because he was angry and some of the musicians were late, there were a number of substitutes, and things just weren't going right. "OK, you motherfuckers got it." And he walked off the stand, while everybody just sat there and didn't know what to do.

GOODMAN: Well, I hope he has success with this new Mercer Arts Center big band. I guess it's mostly the same people as the Vanguard group?

MORGENSTERN: Yeah, it would be great if he could keep it together because I think, in a sense, a big band is what Mingus really needs. As difficult as it is for him to deal with that many people, in a sense maybe it's better for him to have twenty people to deal with than just five, because you can't get as involved with everybody. And also, from a musical standpoint, it's really what he needs, a big canvas.

It's too bad that the economics of the business are such that keeping a big band together is almost impossible, unless he were to get some sort of grant. I hope he applies for [as] many as possible. If he can set up some kind of— I want to talk to Sue about that—because if he can set up some kind of regular program for the band, there are ways of getting money from the government. The only thing is there has to be a nonprofit element.

GOODMAN: Do I understand this right? He is trying to get together a twenty-two-piece band—and they are just going to split the gate among them?

MORGENSTERN: Yeah. That's the idea, which is not unprecedented. Gil Evans has been doing this for several months now. He just started again. Gil lives in Westbeth. Are you familiar with Westbeth? Westbeth is a housing complex funded by the city, for artists.

GOODMAN: Oh, in the SoHo area? Yeah.

MORGENSTERN: And there is a little area there which has a stage and lighting facility installed, which is just there for use by the tenants. Gil discovered this and had a twenty-piece band on weekends. It started out with three nights a week and then went back to two. And they have been charging admission and then dividing up the take. It usually winds up with Gil not getting anything. And some equipment was stolen down there. But it worked out all right.

GOODMAN: They drew pretty well?

MORGENSTERN: Yeah. So I think this is the same principle.

. . . Do you remember the Newport rebellion? The so-called Rump Festival? He was one of the instigators of that.

GOODMAN: What was that all about? I remember it occurred, but I don't remember what the flap was about.

MORGENSTERN: They decided George Wein wasn't hiring certain people, or he wasn't giving them enough money and not enough exposure. So they decided to put on their own festival. It was Mingus and Ornette Coleman and Max and a few others. It was very interesting because it came off pretty well. At Newport they siphoned off a lot of people from the regular festival. They even, I think, made a small profit—it couldn't have been very much—but it worked out all right.

But then they wanted to continue it, and they formed an organization, I forget what it was called . . . "The Newport Rebels," yeah. They put on a series of concerts on the East Side, a little theater there. That did not work at all. What happened was that one musician, who shall remain nameless, walked off with the cash box. Not for himself, but he said, "I've got five guys working here and they haven't been paid. Nobody had been paid." He just took the money and distributed it among his guys. It wasn't Mingus.

GOODMAN: No, that doesn't sound like him.

MORGENSTERN: But he's doing Mercer on his own, and he got other people involved, which is good, because it might work that way. Because in this other thing there were a number of leaders involved, Max and others, and that doesn't work. Too many ego conflicts. But I think Mingus can certainly count on musicians to help, you know, to work with him on this because, let's face it, it's one of the most challenging and interesting things a musician can do.

Max Gordon on the Vanguard Band

GORDON: So Mingus came in for a week and [he also] did very well on Monday nights. During the week [when they played every night], they did only fair, I should say. But that's because this is a business problem generally. Having them here once a week is a little stronger than having him here when you have to disperse all the customers [his fans] over a week's time.

That goes for every band, including Thad Jones–Mel Lewis.

But this was a good band, and it became a better band after playing here for a while. With all the rehearsals and playing, by the time they closed here they had a real good band. In fact, it's hard to see it break up because it's such a good band. I hate to see any good band break up and I wanted them to try—that is, I planned to do whatever I could do to keep them together. It was no use. I think Mingus said to me, "Well, I'm getting too old for this." To hassle with a lot of men, worrying about their losing their music, worrying about their getting here on time and all the rest, and he was real tired at the end.

I have no doubt that he regretted to see it happen because, hell, the only thing, the reason he put them together was because it interested him musically. He wasn't making much money with them. And I know Mingus well enough to know that this man is a musician, a jazz man, he has a great respect for music and wants to make good music himself. So, as I say, I am sure that he regretted seeing the thing go. And I wouldn't be surprised if he revives it sometime soon.

GOODMAN: Well, do you know about this gig in the Mercer Arts Center in June and July? A twenty-two-piece band or something. Probably the same people.

GORDON: No, I didn't know about that. He's going to be there for two months?

GOODMAN: Well, a month at least, June 15 through July 15. I understand from Sue Graham that they are just going to split the gate among them, and I guess they are getting some publicity out of the theater there. I hope it works for him. It's kind of an unusual way to do it.

GORDON: Yeah, I did not know that and I am glad to hear that. Glad to hear that it's going to happen. Wherever the music is, if you can't visit the Vanguard, if it's good music, I am glad to see it happen.

GOODMAN: Just from your observation, do you think he tends to get along better in a small group or big group?

GORDON: Well, yeah. I mean, he has violent tempers with the small band. Of course this isn't the biggest band he has had here recently. He has had bigger bands, and sextets and quintets. He once had a group of ten here. And a group of eight. That's why I always felt he wanted bigger groups. It was just a matter of economics and the problems of organizing and keeping those big groups together that prevented him from always having a big group.

That's why I felt when he had this opportunity [here] that he would take it. Besides, I always thought his music was better played with a big group. It sounds more like Mingus. The fullness and the thrust of his music comes through better, in my way of thinking, with a big band playing it.

GOODMAN: I heard that the big band played kind of irregularly, off one night and then up the next night. I suppose maybe because he didn't get things together with them, or what?

GORDON: Well, first of all his music is very difficult. More so than most jazz music and arrangements that you come up against. And therefore it requires a lot more rehearsing. Also, he has had problems with keeping some men. There were often changes in personnel and that was always a problem. And there is always, of course, the problem with men who are playing together: sometimes they are better than other times, let's face it. And also problems in the place where they're playing, sometimes [customers] would intervene, or intrude, let's say, on the execution of the music.

But I noticed, as he went along on the seven-week period of time here on Monday nights, that generally the music was getting better all the time. Sometimes he had high points, higher points than other times. There were times when people felt like he played better last week than this week. I have heard people say that. What the reason was is hard to say. I imagine the Philharmonic is better one evening than the next.

GOODMAN: Yeah. I heard John Wilson [the *New York Times* resident jazz critic] came one night—after the big flap about his review of Mingus's Philharmonic concert. Did Charles know he was here?

GORDON: I don't think he knew. He didn't know until afterwards. I told Mingus he was here and he was surprised that he came. But I don't think John had probably read the answer that Mingus had written in one of those little underground magazines [Sue Graham's *Changes*; see chapter 8]. I don't know—but I don't think it would have made any difference as far as John is concerned. John is a critic and his business is to listen to music and call the shots. And I know John. He has a certain integrity, and I don't think he would allow any personal matters to intrude on him. I don't think so. He didn't say a word when he came in here. He just came in. I saw him come in and I thought about it. I didn't say anything to him, naturally.

Sy Johnson's Writing for the Vanguard Band

I wanted to hear more about the Vanguard band and something about Sy's role in the band that was then forming to play at the Mercer Arts Center.

That Mercer Arts Center band was important to Mingus as an opportunity to get off the road, keep a big band together, and avoid the club scene (with all the problems that scene entailed).

"Number 29," which Sy mentions below, was one of the pieces Mingus played to illustrate musical points when he and I talked in his apartment. This piece never got recorded in his lifetime, surely for the reasons Sy discusses below. Finally, it appeared in a fine Mingus Big Band recording in 1996—as a kind of wild triple concerto (for alto, trumpet, and tenor), cut down to eight and a half minutes but clearly a Mingus masterwork.[10]

. . .

JOHNSON: Well, my part in the Mercer band is the same as it has been all along: just expanding the library. We're working on a major piece for Mingus which, at the moment, has only the title of "Number 29." That's the title in the book. We played this at the Vanguard, but it's such a long, broad piece that without extensive rehearsals, and everybody really knowing their role—the drummer, for example, plays a pivotal part. The spaces in the piece are drum solos. In other words, it's architectural, in a sense. The textures are broken by drum solos, and the drum solos are cue[s] for the next session to begin. The players have to act on a fantastic degree of understanding of the basic nature of the piece. If it was much shorter, if the thing was one-third as long, they could get it much easier. So it's difficult.

Mingus wrote it as a virtuoso piece for trumpet. And he deliberately exploited the trumpet from the very bottom, E-natural, all the way as high as a virtuoso player can play. The intervals in it—for example, there are places where it goes from the bottom of the trumpet to practically the top of the trumpet in one measure and back down again. It's just an awesome piece of writing. And, since it was obvious we'd never find a trumpet player to play that, I made the decision to reinforce that with other horns. Initially I was going to use tenor and alto and have a small-band unison sound going on in the middle of the orchestra, and orchestrate around that. And then eventually he wanted to use Lee Konitz and his texture too, so that we had two altos, tenor, and trumpet as a sort of small band inside the band.

But none of the trumpet players who played that—well, John Faddis did play his part, but the trumpet player playing before him was simply unable—you couldn't even hear the trumpet. It would sound like a saxophone in the music. And we orchestrated around that and then, at times for variety's sake, distributed the melody to the ensemble or other voices to give the players a rest. And we just had a lot of difficulty getting that piece to jell. We got through all the written part of it, but as soon as the solos started, then the players in the band—somebody would lose their place. It was just such a lot to understand. So suddenly everybody is lost and they can't—

GOODMAN: Well, who is going to play the trumpet part [in the Mercer Center band], John Faddis?

JOHNSON: I think John Faddis is going to probably play it. And it is going to take at least a couple of hours of concentrated rehearsal with everybody in the band. That's hoping that we don't have too many subs, or people coming in who are going to have to pick up on what's going on. It's not like Thad and Mel's band where things sound open, but are really very controlled. I mean, the average good jazz-oriented recording musician could get into that band and not get terribly fucked up.

Whereas with Mingus's things, he doesn't give you that kind of cues and the clues. I mean it's much more rambling and discursive and open, and people are not sure of their roles. Even people who are just playing the third alto part will frequently not know what's expected of them. Who are they playing with, what are they doing, you know. But I think it's going to be a major piece. There are times when it sounded absolutely devastating.

GOODMAN: How long does it run?

JOHNSON: Oh, it probably will run close to twenty minutes.

GOODMAN: The Mercer band: is it essentially the Vanguard people? Or—

JOHNSON: The bulk of the band will be the same people. And I'm sure that there will be a nucleus of those players, and then you will find section players subbing and taking off, and so forth, during the week, which is a problem that you face in any band that works like that.

GOODMAN: Do you think he's going to make it financially with this way of doing business? I guess the idea was to split the gate.

JOHNSON: I don't know how. If that's the way they are going to do it, then I don't think it's going to turn out to be a money-making proposition for anybody. The hope is that the music and the experience of playing in the band will be compelling enough so that good players will be willing to come down and play the book every night and begin to get into the music. Take it from me: I've been involved in the process of sorting that music out prior to the act of putting it on paper. Understanding it is not just a question of translating it to another medium. The understanding goes on before that: you just have to understand what Mingus had intended, and that frequently is the hardest part of dealing with these things.

Pieces like "Number 29" are so difficult to try to hear in your head when you are looking at the score. Leonard Bernstein would be confused by it. So the pre-hearing process is a very important one that I've had to go through. Nobody else is as aware of what's in that music, other than Mingus, or probably not even Mingus because he has not dealt with the orchestration of it. He's more into what he intended initially, and I've been more into what I intend the orchestra to do.

Frequently, even good performances only touch at the complexity and the richness and all the love seen and heard in that music. It's a fantastically complex, sonorous music. Even after the clarifying process that I was talking about, I've tried to clarify it so that it will be sonorous, so that it will sing and so that all the rich things in that tapestry will all be heard in the various structured layers.

GOODMAN: Yeah, get heard. Exactly.

JOHNSON: And it requires—I mean there are times, for example, in the orchestra, where somebody will be playing a part and you suddenly realize there are three players, or two players playing in unison somewhere, who simply don't understand what they are supposed to be doing. And sometimes you don't even have time to tell them. You can grab them during an intermission and say, "Gee, you guys, in that one section you got to lay back on it a little and make it sing against the time, so it will come through the texture. You have to sing on it a little, you have to do this and that."

I mean there are so many details in it that the business of getting the people in the band to understand their roles—I mean, even as you have understood to put it down—it is in a sense easier to understand when you are dealing with the whole totality of it than it is for some guy in the middle of all this confusion to know what he's expected to do.

GOODMAN: Max Gordon said the Vanguard band got better as it went along. Did you think so?

JOHNSON: Umm, I thought the high point came the second week. The band came in and Mingus assumed everybody had played most of the music at the [*Friends*] concert. He was going to try and get the same band, and no rehearsal was going to be necessary. And so the band came in the first night at the Vanguard, and it was a shambles. I mean this turned into a rehearsal with tempers frayed all around, people getting disgruntled and walking out, and Max Gordon pulling what little was left of his hair out.

They had a double concert scheduled in Philadelphia the following Saturday night, and it became apparent the only way the band could play a concert was to rehearse. So there were rehearsals scheduled on Tuesday, Wednesday, Thursday, and Friday and then another one Saturday. We just laboriously went over the music for the concert. We tried to convince Mingus to play fewer pieces, and he didn't want to do that. Eventually, at the concert, they did open the program up some.

GOODMAN: That's what I wished he would have done in New York.

JOHNSON: Yeah, I know. Well, he has all those people there and he wants them all to play. They're a natural resource, and he doesn't want to cut off any part of that.

GOODMAN: Oh, I meant the material more than just the personnels. It was too much.

JOHNSON: Oh, no question about that. It was just too much to understand in the rehearsal time we had for the concert.

GOODMAN: So in Philadelphia they did cut it?

JOHNSON: The Philadelphia concert was absolutely—particularly in the second concert—they just tore it up. They played so good that everybody was exhausted; they couldn't get anybody to leave Philadelphia. They all went into a bar and were just drinking and poking one another and saying, "How about that? Best fucking band I ever played in." They didn't even want to come home; they got on the bus and they still didn't want to leave. And then they came into the Vanguard, fresh from that experience, and tore the fucking place up.

Luckily, John Wilson came in that night to review the band again. He was flipping. He could hardly help it. The band was just singing. They had so much adrenaline going. And then the following week they lost some of that energy, and then we started rehearsing, and we got into a rehearsal problem because Mingus wasn't able to pay people to come down and rehearse every week before the gig.

So most of the people were willing to come down and rehearse free, but some key players bitched about not getting paid for rehearsals, and eventually the rehearsals got to be a half-hour or three-quarters of an hour long. The rehearsal would be called for seven o'clock and by 8:15

everybody would start to play. Then some people might not even show up, and it got to the point where the band went back to the workshop situation. There were things that would sound brilliant, and Mingus would stop the band and yell at people and start things over again.

They still had, under the circumstances, some very, very exciting nights, some nights when this thing would come alive and sound so fantastic. Then there were nights when Mingus was getting mad at people, getting at people whose egos needed babying somewhat and needed reassuring, and he was up there badgering and bullying them, and they would get all unsettled, and it was very difficult.

That's always going to be a problem with Mingus. Part of the volatility problem is that he's not going to make it easy for anybody. He claims that when things are going well, he's happy. He is, I've seen it demonstrated. That Monday night at the Vanguard I've never seen him so expansive. He was beaming—making long announcements to people, smiling at the band, carrying on. He was so elated he was waving to me all the time. He was beside himself.

So he does like it when things go well, but he also doesn't like to leave well enough alone. You know he's going to get in and muddy things up, keep everybody off their chair a little bit. He changes things spontaneously. He will suddenly decide he wants it to go another place, and he's like yelling, trying to get twenty guys who have the momentum—in one respect, it's not unlike a cement mixer. It just gets going in a certain direction, and to stop or change direction is not easy. So he wants to get everybody to veer off and go in another direction with a piece, and it unsettles people. But that's part of his creative process. And now that he's got the juices going, it's an awesome thing to see.

NOTES

1. A classic description of the club scene is Martin Williams's rendering of the Five Spot atmosphere during a Monk performance, "A Night at the Five Spot," *Down Beat*, Feb. 13, 1964, available at www.theloniousrecords.com/revanaly /M.W.%20Night%20at%20Five%20Spot.htm. For a good brief history of select New York jazz clubs (most of the famous ones), see Ashley Kahn, "After Hours: New York's Jazz Joints Through the Ages," *Jazz Times*, Sept. 2006, http://jazztimes .com/articles/17196-after-hours-new-york-s-jazz-joints-through-the-ages. For the cultural, legal and political context, see Paul Chevigny, *Gigs: Jazz and the Cabaret Laws in New York City* (New York: Routledge, 2004). The author's personal comments on the scene are valuable, and there's a story about Mingus turning on a radio in the middle of a performance (pages 50–51).

2. Max Gordon, *Live at the Village Vanguard* (New York: DaCapo, 1980), 101.

3. Mingus tells the full story in chapter 5.

4. First famous transgender person in the 1950s: www.biography.com/people /christine-jorgensen-262758.

5. According to Gene Santoro, Mingus's Jazz Workshop went into Café Bohemia in fall 1955; and Mingus did pack them in at the Five Spot in Christmas week, 1958. I don't know what club in Brooklyn he is referring to; it may be the Putnam Central. Gene Santoro, *Myself When I Am Real: The Life and Music of Charles Mingus* (New York: Oxford, 2000), 117, 144.

6. I think Mingus was talking here about Mike Cantarino of the Half Note, who did book Lennie Tristano. Mike and his brother Sonny ran the Half Note for many years. The original club was a bar-restaurant on Spring Street, just north of the Holland Tunnel. See Chevigny, *Gigs*, 49–50.

7. Lee Kraft was Mingus's producer at Bethlehem Records. See Brian Priestly, *Mingus: A Critical Biography* (New York: Da Capo, 1982), 89, 94.

8. This "Proficcio" is probably Joe Profaci. Copa City was a nightclub in Jamaica, Queens, and Mingus and the Jazz Workshop played there "several times" in 1961–62, says Gene Santoro, 177–78.

9. After Mingus died, Sue obtained a grant from the National Endowment for the Arts to set up the Let My Children Hear Music Foundation—first to catalog all of Mingus's works, then to enable repertory bands (now three) to keep performing his works. Since 2009, the foundation has worked with the Manhattan School of Music to produce annual Charles Mingus High School Competitions, wherein school bands compete nationally in playing Mingus charts. See http:// mingusmingusmingus.com/JazzEducation/LMCHMepk.pdf.

10. Mingus Big Band, *Mingus Big Band Live in Time*, Disques Dreyfus, 1996, two-CD set. See Sue Mingus's comments in the liner notes to that album.

8   The Critics

*"You stay away from my job and I'll
stay away from yours."*

One key to Mingus is that, for all his ranting about critics, he was indeed a perceptive critic himself. His comments about music and musicians cut to the essence of how jazz is made and how it should be made, what musicians are doing and how they do it. His essays in criticism reveal more about Mingus, by the way, than any interviews he did with jazz critics and more than most of the comments they made about him.

The major critical statements he offered in print were the two essays I've mentioned (see my commentary on the avant-garde in chapter 1): the liner notes to *Let My Children Hear Music* and "Open Letter to the Avant-Garde." There is one other foray into the open letter genre—a letter to Miles Davis that in a kind of fatherly way takes the trumpet player to task for his hard-ass critical attitudes toward himself and other musicians.[1]

Mingus's most complete statement of a critical position lies in his 1971 notes to the *Children* album, a defense of tradition and training in jazz composition. It's the single most important piece to read in understanding his approach to jazz, and it earned him a Grammy award nomination— even if the accompanying album didn't!

Out of print is the long blast Mingus published in Sue Graham's *Changes* magazine (March 17, 1972) attacking *New York Times* reviewer John S. Wilson, who had found the February 4 *Friends* concert in Philharmonic Hall "bland, colorless and all but anonymous."[2] I was there and, like most of the Mingus concerts, it was a mixed bag. But it had consistency and beautiful moments that Wilson didn't hear.

Here is the Angry Mingus at his noisiest and best. He leads off with: "The title of this article should read John Ass Wilson is full of shit." Among other things, he says Wilson (a generally reasonable, if bland himself, jazz critic) should be barred from any other Mingus performances . . . and fired.

He has no understanding of black music, art, or dance, and can't even acknowledge that the concert was a standing-room-only success for those who attended.

Mingus concludes:

> I've never sold out or tommed with my music, yet every move I make to better myself so I can survive this system, you fuck with me, comment on me with your opinion as though you are the all-knowing god who won't accept my music enough to allow me to earn a living by staying away from my music. . . . You drive the new fans away and you drive away the businessmen who must support the music. You stay away from my job and I'll stay away from yours. Unless one day you end up selling news copy on a street corner in Harlem at 12 A.M.

This is Mingus straight with no chaser, and beneath all the personal bitterness he makes the point that white critics haven't treated black music or dance fairly. And more, that their gatekeeper opinions have a real economic impact. This is surely true of any kind of arts criticism, and it's one of the factors that turned me away from writing music criticism years ago. As Teo Macero says in the interview that follows, "Wouldn't it be wonderful if we could turn around and sue them [the critics] for destroying our livelihood?"

In blasting Wilson, Mingus makes it in part a racial thing, which gives the piece its real bite, but it isn't a racial thing. The critic's authority is what is really called into question.

Mingus and I had an exchange about critics below, and he was in milder form, though he did say harsh things about Nat Hentoff and others selling out. I think what bugged him most about critics is that many have been so easily led astray from the music. At the time we spoke, the power of cultural and political issues was taking over much of what music criticism ought to concern itself with—the aesthetic realm—and cultivating controversies over foolish questions like what is and is not part of the canon. Jazz criticism, especially, has always contained more than its fair share of bullshit, as typified by most liner notes and reviews. I limit myself to one example.

Leonard Feather, once known as the dean of jazz critics, acted as producer for Mingus's groundbreaking 1960 *Pre-Bird* recording for Mercury (later reissued as *Mingus Revisited* on Limelight). In his album notes, Feather extols the fact that jazz has changed from an "occult, obscure pastime" to a music made by multiply-talented musicians, doubling on instruments and alternately composing, conducting, and playing—true Renaissance men: "These developments are part of the natural efflorescence that has characterized the jazz scene during the past decade. The jazzman, long made to feel unsure of his right even to call himself a legitimate musician, has moved forward into a brilliant new light in which he shines as creative artist, articulate spokesman for his music, versatile performer-writer, and symbol of a new social order."

Mingus of course "epitomizes these developments." What figment floating in his brain caused Feather to create this delusionary scenario? I wonder how he would have described Mingus's life a few short years later when he was broke, uninspired, doped out on pills, unable to perform, and, finally, evicted into the street?[3]

. . .

GOODMAN: That's another thing I wanted to ask you about: what are all those critics doing? Where have they gone? Does Bill Coss write anymore?

MINGUS: No, he's in Washington, DC, but I don't know what he's doing. Martin Williams doesn't write anymore either, does he?

GOODMAN: Somebody died who used to do jazz history—Marshall Stearns died.

MINGUS: Yeah.

GOODMAN: And Hentoff doesn't write jazz criticism any more.

MINGUS: No.

GOODMAN: There isn't anybody else, huh?

MINGUS: Couple of young kids.

GOODMAN: What was Sue telling me about Dan Morgenstern? That he's quit *Down Beat?*

MINGUS: Yeah. He quit for some personal reason with Chicago. He made some money, though not much.

GOODMAN: And you said you heard nothing about Barry Ulanov for a long time. . . . So you're left with Wilson, that's all you got.

MINGUS: John S. Wilson and Whitney Balliett.

GOODMAN: Well, Balliett's good, I like his stuff.

MINGUS: Yeah, I like his book. Lot of excerpts from the magazine, from the *New Yorker.*[4]

GOODMAN: Well, we've gotta talk about Wilson now in this book. What did he say about this *Friends* concert [February 4, 1972, at Philharmonic Hall]? I never saw his review. Same bullshit he said about the last one?

MINGUS: He didn't even tell about whether it was a success—I don't know if he writes for [about] the Beatles, or something like that.

GOODMAN: He doesn't review that stuff though, does he?

MINGUS: Well, the *Times* does. They tell how many people were there. Whether they like it [or not] you never know, they hide it. They've got so much to say about individuals, but they didn't mention John Faddis or Roland Kirk [in the *Friends* concert review]. They didn't say he played good or nothing. They said I tried to duplicate an old-fashioned battle of the saxes. That's never old-fashioned. We should have more battles and guys would improve.

GOODMAN: Nat Hentoff used to write some good stuff, used to know the music well, was very involved with it, very involved with you, I guess, you were friends with him—

MINGUS: Very good friends, I thought.

GOODMAN: I think what he writes in the *Village Voice* [on political and social issues] is not only bad writing, but—

MINGUS: Well, I'll tell you this, man, and you write this down, man. I'll tell you about Nat—he married a rich girl, a leftist. So to keep her interested in him, and to keep her job as a writer—

GOODMAN: And she's a better writer than he, incidentally.

MINGUS: To keep her job as a writer, and to keep his balls hard, here's a cat that leaves the guys and the thing he loves. And when you leave the thing you love, man, you ain't got much left. Put that in the book. The same goes for Leonard Feather, but he's [*unintelligible*] stuck hard. Ralph Gleason is a faggot.

GOODMAN: Ralph Gleason is a disaster.

MINGUS: Well, let *me* say it, 'cause we got to write this shit. [*Laughter.*] Ralph Gleason saw the hurricane coming, so he prepared himself; he looked for the safe spots. "Ah, my children love this." So he takes off his suit, puts on some Levis, puts a leather jacket on, and goes out and becomes like his children. He even goes and dances with 'em. I know this, I saw this. A hopping-around old man, and he's not writing the truth.

GOODMAN: I read the magazine all the time, and I mean his column is sad.

MINGUS: He still writes for *Down Beat*?

GOODMAN: No, *Rolling Stone*. When Ben Webster died, he wrote a nice thing about that.

MINGUS: He did? Well, he's still capable of rising from the dead.

GOODMAN: But it was like a voice out of the past. Like what he should have written is why Ben Webster is still important today, you know. Who cares about how great Ben Webster was twenty-five years ago? We all know that. I mean, we all have the records.

MINGUS: When you say "we," man, now you couldn't come to the gig tonight. But if my band don't cut the rock-and-roll band with all them kids there that never heard [this music before], then I'm drunk. 'Cause every night the public has come, they've dug our band. I dare [them] to put my band on the same bandstand with the Beatles. Without even saying nothing. Without the critics saying nothing.

GOODMAN: Did you know this was going to happen? That they would have the rock band on before you?

MINGUS: No, I didn't know that, no. That's what's killed the clubs, man. The club owners don't have anywhere to go, so they stiff the audience. Guy came last night and said, "Man, I thought at least they'd let you have the bandstand by yourself."

CHAPTER 8 COMMENTARY

Dan Morgenstern on the John Wilson Episode

MORGENSTERN: Mingus wrote [in *Changes*], "Even if you managed to get into one of my concerts you won't get any free tickets to my concerts. Even if you manage to get in, I'll have you thrown out bodily." Three weeks after that came out, Mingus was playing at the Vanguard and there was a big line outside and John Wilson came along and said to me, "How do I get in here?" I was waiting with a bunch of friends so I did not want to have a battle by using *Down Beat* [credentials], and all these people were waiting patiently. But John obviously was sent to do a review, and I was glad to see him there.

So I got him in the back way, through the kitchen, and after awhile we got in too. It so happened that John was sitting right smack in front of the band and Mingus was practically looking straight at him. I was sitting right behind him. I don't think Mingus really knows what John Wilson looks like; also, John had grown a beard. Nevertheless, he caught two sets and then wrote a very glowing review the next day, changing his story:

that the band had not been impressive at the [Philharmonic Hall] concert but this time it was more together . . .

I saw Sue that night, and after John had split Sue said, "Did you see who was here? Well, give him credit for courage anyway."

I said, "Do you think Charles knew he was here?" She said she had not told him yet but she did not think so. I think even if he had known it was John, he would not have done anything. Mingus got it out of his system by writing about it.

Teo Macero on the Critics

MACERO: After the [Philharmonic Hall] concert I told Mingus I thought it went very well. Of course we got a couple of bad reviews, but they always see it differently. You know, they march to a different drummer. I can't help it if somebody doesn't like what we're doing, puts us down for it or says it's old-fashioned. Let the record be the proof. You've got to be very careful these days when you start to criticize groups and so forth.

GOODMAN: Well, they are ultrasensitive and I guess they have a right to be.

MACERO: That's right. Look, Mingus has had a lot of hard roads to walk all by himself; from the early '50s, in the Charlie Parker days, it hasn't been easy for him. It hasn't been easy for any of those cats, the jazz players. They get up there to a certain plateau, and all the sudden they were looked upon as some bunch of evil creatures. They're not evil, they're highly emotional, intellectual machines, and they're people like anybody else. Those critics. I think the critics really killed the jazz thing in the '60s.

Look, you ask most of them [the critics] and they couldn't write a note of music if they went to hell. Alright, so some of them play an instrument, but that doesn't qualify them. They listen to records—alright, big deal, I listen to records too but that doesn't qualify me as a critic. At least I know a hell of a lot more music than they do. But these guys get out there and talk about the relationship of John Doe with somebody else and the relationship to somebody else, but they never talk about the immediate thing, which is the record, or the materials of the music. They always talk about something that's related in some strange way.

Suppose that you played a piece of jazz for the first time to an audience, to the critics—and we did play some new pieces after the first half—how can a man—and I am a composer-musician myself and I just barely understand the whole mechanics of it all—how can a critic sit back and say, "Man, this is a great piece of music" or "This is a bad piece of music"? You know, and evaluate it, not in terms of the material, but in terms of something else? They always have a different frame of reference, which drags me completely.

GOODMAN: To what extent do you think this is really affecting Mingus in his life?

MACERO: Well, I think it's not only affected Mingus but it hurts a lot of other people. Let's face it: here's a guy who has written a book. He's got a Guggenheim. He's got all kinds of prizes, he has written ballets, he's done movies, he's done everything. Now if you take a guy like that and you start beating him up in the press and say, "Man, this cat is not making it, his music is dull, his music is—" Well, all these years he's been making it with the right crowd, with the intellectual musical crowd. But with the so-called "other" crowd he hasn't been making it, the critics.

Now all of a sudden he pops back onto the scene in many different areas. Just think about that for a minute. I mean, it's amazing. I think it affected him, and it affected a lot of people. They just made it so difficult and so ugly for the guys to try to make a living. Mingus was strong enough as an individual to bounce back. And all the great jazz players are. They're strong, so they don't care what the critics say.

GOODMAN: Well, but they do [*laughs*].

MACERO: Yeah, but they do. Yeah, because it affects their livelihood. Wouldn't it be wonderful if we could turn around and sue them for destroying one's livelihood? This is in essence what they're doing. Right? I mean you go to a court of law and if somebody makes it impossible for you to make a living—if you're supposed to deliver something and if you can't deliver it, you lose money from it—then you can turn around and sue him, right? Well, this is what they've done. They've just destroyed these individuals, given them a meager living, a hand-to-mouth existence, with the exception of a few.

And here are these critics living off the fat of the land. They have nice palatial palaces, you can see them all over the university, lecturing here and writing a critique on this, and talking about politics. Yet the poor musician is living in a place in the SoHo district, or down in the slums, trying to make a comeback, and they don't permit it. [Musicians] ought to turn around and sue 'em. Mingus would probably agree with that [*laughs*].

GOODMAN: I'm sure he would.

MACERO: They could do a great service to jazz and find other ways of criticizing the music, not only from listening to it but coming to the concerts, coming to the rehearsals. I know it's a drag to do this, but they could talk to the composers, look at the score, say, "Gee, what do you mean by this? Was that right, did you play that really right last night?" But how wonderful that would be.

GOODMAN: Yeah. Get inside it.

MACERO: To get inside the music. They're on the outside; they never get inside. There are a few critics that did that: Barry Ulanov did it, and Bill Coss did, and a couple others, and Ralph Gleason. They try to get inside the music. But a lot of the critics just can't see it. The experimental avant-garde things were all destroyed in the '50s by the critics because they thought it wasn't jazz, but you turn around and look at what they're doing today in the twentieth century, 1972, in terms of jazz—let's put a label on it for the moment—they're doing the same thing today with the exception of a little difference in beat and some chords. The same thing that happened in the '50s.

But at that particular time, [the experimenters] were looked upon as some sort of idiots, musical idiots. Critics said, "Look, man, it's all a bunch of noise. What are those cats trying to do, man? There's no melody over there. Man, that cat's got a solo and he didn't even play the chord." Look at Ornette; look at the scuffling he had. I mean you could just go back and read the criticism of some of his records, and some of Mingus's and some of the rest of them.

. . . Music really shouldn't be put in categories. You go to a concert to hear *music*. There's so much cross-pollination nowadays that you don't know where the cats' groups are. And this is great. A lot of kids are digging jazz, jazz is digging rock, rock is digging folk, folk is digging classical music. You can just see it all around you. Everybody is trying to put it all into one kind of music. The critics, on the other hand, are trying to quickly pull it apart again and say, "No this is folk, this is rock. Man, this cat has a rock-jazz beat with a funk behind it." Right? They don't know what the hell they're talking about.

GOODMAN: Well, they've got to label it. That's one of the dilemmas of criticism because criticism has to put names on things. You have got to identify things. How the hell do you get language to deal with music properly anyway? Which is another discussion.

MACERO: Yeah, but you have to know what you're talking about. You can find the language but you have to know what you're talking about. You have to go see the group more than once. You can understand whether a performance is good or bad—if it communicates to you then it's good; it doesn't make any difference whether it's rock, jazz, classical, or pop. If it communicates, that's the important thing: *I got a message from that music.*

But critics go in with a negative attitude first. I've seen it happen. It's like going into the studio with a negative attitude about an artist who's standing out there ready to play and you say, "I hate that son-of-a-bitch." Can you imagine me doing that?

GOODMAN: Jesus, I hope not.

MACERO: I mean even if I thought that, even if I thought that and really wanted to say that, as soon as I walked through that door, brother, it's like somebody had just closed the trap door with me because it's all gone. We're there to create, and this is what we have to do.

NOTES

1. Mingus's open letter to Miles Davis was first published in *Down Beat*, November 30, 1955, and is reprinted online at www.mingusmingusmingus.com /Mingus/miles_davis.html, as are the full liner notes to *Children*, now entitled "What Is a Jazz Composer?" at http://mingusmingusmingus.com/mingus/an-open-letter-to-miles-davis.

2. "Mingus Concert Features Friends; Performance Is His First Here in Last 10 Years," *New York Times*, February 6, 1972; Mingus's reply in *Changes* was titled, "Charles Mingus Answers John S. Wilson of the N.Y. Times."

3. I am probably being too hard on Leonard Feather. All of us who have written about jazz have said stupid things at one time or another. Leonard wrote a brilliant essay for the liner notes to *Billie Holiday: Strange Fruit*, Atlantic, SD 1614, 1972, a reissue of her great Commodore sides.

4. Certainly the most literate (and often best-informed) of all the jazz critics, Whitney Balliett (1926–2007) wrote about Mingus a lot, mostly in the *New Yorker*, where he crafted exceptionally penetrating and lyric prose for almost fifty years. In many of his pieces, he had Mingus down cold and wasn't afraid to find substantial flaws in a musician whose music he very much enjoyed. A brilliant impressionist, Balliett was always a totally honest and penetrating critic of Mingus.

I recently picked up his *Collected Works: A Journal of Jazz, 1954–2000* (New York: St. Martin's Press, 2000) again and found an extraordinary summation (in "Late Mingus," 560–61) of Mingus's music, apparently written shortly after Charles died. Here is the opening: "Mingus's music was a distillation of Duke Ellington, gospel music, Charlie Parker, the blues, Jimmy Blanton, New Orleans polyphony, and fast small-band swing music. It was another weapon, another way of talking. At its best, it was a concatenation of voices, now solo, now in duet, now in quintet or octet—all shouting, laughing, exulting, announcing . . ."

9 Survival:
The Reason for the Blues

"Only time you drop the blues is when
you drop saying 'nigger' or saying 'black.'"

Toward the end of my 1972 time with Mingus, we did a long, loud, and uproarious interview in a Lower East Side bar with his friend Booker Tillery present. I never got to hear Booker's full story, but I knew he was an ex-con, now a tailor, and Mingus once or twice referred to him as "my road manager." In the opening pages of her book, *Tonight at Noon,* Sue Mingus talks a little about Booker, giving some of his history and describing his closeness to Charles.[1]

Later on, I asked Charles to pursue an idea we had talked about earlier: how the blues could straighten out black people, give them a music. We then got into various other aspects of the survival theme—everything from Cassius Clay to Mingus's war with the taxi drivers to sex and pimping. Mingus expressed his thoughts on the latter subject more succinctly, I thought, than he had in *Beneath the Underdog.*

. . .

MINGUS: Maybe it would be jazz but I think it is the blues. That was our music, and they took it from us. Who is that girl singer whose father's a preacher—?

GOODMAN: Aretha Franklin.

MINGUS: Aretha Franklin is part of that thing called "Without a Song" [the tune], which says what I'm saying. You take the Jewish people, they've got their race, their music. Everybody has their music. The Greeks have their sound, their sacred music, and their dance music. If you take that away from the people, then you separate 'em. Because black people were together on the blues at one point, and they knew they had the blues for a reason.

GOODMAN: I think you're onto something important. How do you define the blues? It means something different to everybody. It means maybe T-Bone Walker to you and—

MINGUS: It means more than that, man. The blues is a feeling you can also play and improvise on. It's a sound that you can't fool people with, when you're playing the blues. Guys can copy it and keep playing the way it was when they last heard it, but there are very few people left who can improvise on it and still play new things in it. You saw the band play in Philadelphia, man. They're just beginning to learn what the blues are.

GOODMAN: Some could do it, and some couldn't.

MINGUS: The blues is the language of a person moaning his feelings to someone else, [expressing] what he's feeling, the pain and all that.

GOODMAN: So you're talking about a style, a feeling, and forms too, right?

MINGUS: Well, see, you can play the blues with the classical form if you want. I'm talking about the original get-back-to-where-it-was blues, which has never left. People can't say because we got new hairdos and black is beautiful—which is of course [one of] the three biggest lies ever told. [*To Booker:*] You heard that one?

We got a lot of promises about new hairdos but no raises in salaries— the green ain't changed, you know? Everybody's free and everybody says "how beautiful," but nobody ain't got no more jobs. And some of the jobs they have, they been blown from, replaced.

TILLERY: You see what the president did—froze all the poor man's jobs, and the food and everything else went up. Nothin' changed, nothin'.

MINGUS: [*Eating.*] So that means, from where he [Booker] stands, and he's a street man too, the original blues would be just about the same, basically. Only time you drop the blues is when you drop saying "nigger" or saying "black." If you call us Americans, the blues might be gone.

But they came up with a new title for us that still makes us second-class citizens. They said, "Let's cut this shit out, man. Do in America like in England, call 'em freemen."

But then everybody said, "Let's stop this, 'cause these people *are* citizens. The freemen in England didn't have quite the same freedoms as a citizen."

When they start calling us *first-class* citizens—which will never be, I gotta figure—then there maybe won't be no reason for the blues. People [now] don't go nowhere where there's a meeting place, like a church or a bar where the blues was—which between the two I don't know where it started at first. They both had the blues in them. But there ain't no place for black people to meet now; they're separated.

TILLERY: Well how was the blues originated? Why did they call it blues?

MINGUS: Well, I was hoping that everybody knew that blue means sad—

TILLERY: Sad because they was in chains, y'understand what I mean? Slaves. They had to stop thinking about the position they was in, y'understand, they began to sing the blues, sad songs.

MINGUS: So some of them figured to make money out of it—T-Bone Walker and Big Joe Turner and Wynonie Harris. Their blues are the sexy blues. Now T-Bone did do some painful blues, but there's a cat— Rubberlegs—those cats will tell you a different story.

GOODMAN: You mean Blind Lemon and the real old singers, like Leadbelly?

MINGUS: Yeah, the pure blues. Gene Ammons is just playing the saxophone, he ain't no preacher, but they talk to him like he's a preacher 'cause they ain't got no churches. They done blew all their churches. He ain't singing no words but he must be getting something through to them.

GOODMAN: You think people are turning to the churches again, or not?

MINGUS: They mixed up the churches, man. Too many black Muslims, no, too many black movements. If they got it all together, get organized and stop fighting each other, then you'd get some customers.

TILLERY: Actually, the churches are on the decrease.

MINGUS: People don't go to church, and they don't go to bars too much, they're too expensive. That means they got to set up pot clubs, get some black legal pot clubs, like I played a couple of white pot clubs in Canada— they're all legal—then it's cool. Give the police their little cut or whatever they're doing, and let 'em run. They've got 'em legalized in Canada anyway, haven't they?

GOODMAN: It's not legal but they don't arrest people.

MINGUS: I met one [guy] on the street asking for a light, offers a joint up to me. Everybody, right on the street! "Hey, man, you want a drag?" But be careful after you take two pokes—*wee!*—I ain't gonna do it no more, man. [*Miles on jukebox in background.*]

TILLERY: I heard that Canada was very hip. They know all about being tied up, because they were in Canada doing time, you know, when

England kind of squeezed 'em. But now they got a freer mind, you know what I mean? They don't try to take and tie up their people. In the time of slavery, this is where the slaves ran to, you know, to Canada.

GOODMAN: And this is where the kids are running today, from the draft.

TILLERY: What's the name of that bad black cowboy? You don't even read about him in history.

MINGUS: Nigger Charlie? [*Laughter.*]

TILLERY: Something like that, Charles, but this dude was, man, you heard about these bad cowboys, the Dalton brothers and so forth, this sucker was so bad, man, it was a shame. And they couldn't catch him. I'll have my daughter check the library to get that book. And this dude, they never even printed nothing about him because the black cat wasn't supposed to be bad; he was supposed to be *meek.*

MINGUS: Well, he wasn't even carrying a gun!

TILLERY: Right, he was supposed to be the meek one. And then they took that choice and controlled him with that, y'understand? On the plantation they took one man and made him the overseer so that this man here, he had the whole run of the place, you dig it? And he lived like a few paces from the big house, but the slaves they lived in shacks. So this guy here, he was the overseer and the preacher combined and he preached fear into 'em. And the young people today, they won't go for that.

MINGUS: I'll tell you a funny story, and I can tell you straight 'cause the man is dead. He said, "I've been white, Charles, and the biggest fear of my life is to watch an Uncle Tom, not knowing he's an Uncle Tom, Uncle Tom to a white man."

I know that same man, the way he feels, feels towards me being part white—my father was very light-skinned—and I ain't going to expose nobody 'cause they ain't got many Uncle Toms no more—not really, them with the "yassuh boss" and all that.

I'll make another statement. Do you remember Richard Wright's book called *Black Boy?* Remember a guy in there called Red? Red was from the South and was an elevator operator, but at first he was something else, he always worked his way through. Richard was always trying to get out of the South. When he got to Chicago, the first thing he met was Red.

When he'd ride the elevator, Red seemed ashamed, like saying, "Hey, white man, want to kick a nigger in the ass—for a quarter? Kick me in the ass." And he said, he's the first one out of town. Get the message? A cat used to tell me that the man who'd say "Yassuh boss" to a white man, smile on his face, is more of a threat than the cat who'd say, "Look, motherfucker, you better let me alone."

TILLERY: Mm-hm, mm-hm. Yeah.

GOODMAN: Like Ralph Ellison's book [*Invisible Man*]. Ever read that? Same bit in there, a very true thing.

MINGUS: No, but it was in my book, the original book, too. The cat who's gonna walk around and kiss your ass and then, after you kick his ass for a dollar, let you kick it again—you betcha he's got hisself an army out there somewhere. Watch out for that cat, baby . . . .

MINGUS: Society itself, the bluebloods, Rockefeller blue-chip money doesn't want to accept anything the black man does, like jazz (they imposed the word "jazz" on our music). Since they don't want to back us in anything we do, the government doesn't want to back us, well, why not go with the Mafia? Why shouldn't the Mafia integrate—Italian, black, Puerto Rican, Jew?

Why shouldn't they get together and say, "Look, man, here's an empire, the only thing left. Somewhere somebody has to survive." Look at Louis Armstrong, they didn't leave any money for him. Yet I was told there was a building erected by his money alone on Park Avenue. Joe Glaser told me that himself: "I'm going to put Louis's name on it," and I looked and it was there on the [plaque]. He didn't leave any money for anybody that I know of. I imagine Louis would leave money to things like the Urban League, he was that kind of guy. I was told he did that, but he didn't like publicity.

But it would be nice to set up a school for the black kids to learn what he did, what he knew on trumpet, man—for the kids of tomorrow. At least that's one direction. Or find a medical thing so a kid could become a doctor, you know? Have all kinds of knowledge at their hands. All other races have that, man. The Jewish people have it. The Italian people go to Italian churches. The Greeks go to Greek churches. They have their meetings, folk dances. We need a place where we do our folk dances. When they broke us from the churches, split the churches—some don't like to all be Muslim, they got a right to be in Jesus if they want to be in Jesus. But the whole thing is, don't leave the church, don't leave the meeting place. They blew their meeting places.

I'm not talking about getting together to have a war, but to keep the spirit together, to get some ideas how to live, to laugh together, to dance together. You leave that and you're denying your heritage, man. For instance, Cassius Clay, he got the right idea but did it all wrong. You can't tell people "If you don't do this, then stay away." Invite 'em to come around, and say, "Maybe some of what you're doing is right, so let us absorb it."

Don't try to make us join and live your way completely. That's not religion, man. Saying you got to walk this path-line. Jesus Christ didn't say that. He didn't say you can't reach the kingdom of heaven if you break those rules. He did say you could come to the temple. Don't deny me the temple because I may not be as perfect as you are. Who is that, man? And he ain't that perfect anyway, or he'd still be champ. He wouldn't have got knocked out.[2]

GOODMAN: Yeah, what happened? He had it for a while but lost it, it's too bad.

MINGUS: Well, they killed him really, man. Face that, you can't beat a man down the way they beat him, and they were wrong. In a way, any black man has a right to protest and not go to war until he's free. Black man has the right to say, "Man, I won't compete in none of your things until you give all my people equal opportunities in every facet of life." He's right in that, and I back him all the way, and the country was wrong or they wouldn't have finally apologized by letting him fight again. And to hold a man down when he's in his prime when he could be fighting (and he might have never lost), they killed his spirit, that ego of his that made him win.

See, really, man, there ain't nobody stronger than nobody else: it's the mind. He was hypnotized into believing that, and they finally beat his con. He had conned himself: "Nobody's gonna whip me, baby." See, I know because I've been knocked out for seven years, and I know what they beat. They didn't beat my muscles—I was chinning and exercising, at three hundred pounds I could chin to the ceiling—but my spirit one day was struck dead, man, and I couldn't pick up nothing. I couldn't pick myself up . . . but I feel like I'm being reborn again. Plus that mild congestive heart failure—that really shook me into condition. That's something else.

How about them doctors taking the water off my leg in New York and not telling me what it was? Guy in the hospital said, "Swollen legs, that sounds like it could be the heart, or liver, or kidneys." Sounded very dangerous, so I was going to come into the hospital. I'm glad I went to Boston instead—Mass General. They didn't play around in Boston, man. Doctor here [in New York] told me to go to another hospital; I'm glad I didn't go to his hospital. They'd probably just took the water off. The knee

FIGURE 8.   Mingus in a wheelchair playing air bass at the 1978 Atlantic recording of *Something Like a Bird*. Photo by Sy Johnson.

was one thing, the leg was another. If I hadn't went to him, I'd have been dead probably.

[The doc at Mass General] said, "What's wrong with you is your heart. Come back in the morning and we'll know for sure."

I did and said, "What do you think now?"

He said, "Two things happened to you. Either you had a shock, or you got congestive heart failure. Did someone in your family die that you love? Like a child or something?"

"Not yet."

He said, "You been in love?"

I said, "A *long* time."

"Well, I'm not a specialist, but just from the signs I see—blood pressure, et cetera—it looks like congestive heart failure."

I said, "What causes that?" He starts running on, and I say, "Do me a favor. Write it all down for me. I want to be able to have that so somebody knows I ain't jiving 'em."

As soon as he told me this, I went home and my leg went down overnight, baby, and [the swelling] ain't come back yet. You know, 'cause the way I'm eating—the way I'm eating now is cool . . .

GOODMAN: Before the eviction, you said you had all that energy going. Were you living a fuller life then?

MINGUS: Put it like this: what I really meant is I've never felt physically no different than when I was ten, fifteen, twenty, fifty years old. I can play better now. I tire the young guys out. But I don't know if I want to anymore. I don't want to bullshit myself. I should take it easy, 'cause I am fifty. I didn't know that about being fifty, but the guys ask me if I feel different, which means I should be something else—to them. Although I know guys at fifty, right now, a coach friend of mine, he runs around the block, plays football all day. So I don't even know what they mean by that, you know.

I know guys in their sixties—Charles Rice is close to sixty, isn't he? He looks it, he's running around, walks several miles every day, teaches in a gym, karate. I mean, it's funny that I don't feel different than I did as a kid, except I got a couple of new pains—they call it occupational backache—but if I'm playing, doing something, I forget about it. So I don't know what it means about being old, yet I go home and see old friends of mine walking around on crutches. And I feel funny. I say, I hope it doesn't happen to me.

GOODMAN: I'm thirty-eight years old, and last year I did a lot of heavy physical work, construction work. You could do that shit fifteen-twenty years ago, but now I feel certain little pains I didn't feel before.

MINGUS: Construction. I always wanted to run a jackhammer. Well, sure, you gotta get your muscles trained. Age didn't do that. When I was a kid if I would start playing basketball, I'd get sore all over for three days. But Britt [Woodman] said keep playing, and finally the pain goes away.

I was playing basketball at 320 pounds with Sue's kid and broke my ankle and didn't hardly feel that.

MINGUS: I noticed this when I was in a cab recently: a cop comes up to a cabbie and he be talkin' like, "Shit, motherfucker, man, this is really a drag. . . ." You know, talkin' real street talk, but then he [the cabbie] said, "Me no savvy what you mean?" and some words in another language, it was West Indian. The cop came over at first with pure disrespect, saw a black face, then the cat ran the West Indian on him, got out of the cab, "Yes, officer," and they understood each other. Ain't that a bitch? And I'm laying back in there wondering whether the cop was going to shoot him, the way he was talking at first. He came up with his gun out, man. Yeah. There's some weird shit going in this country, man.

I just got busted recently coming out of Max's Kansas City, man. I don't like to talk about it, but I'll tell you, man, I came out and I was late for work at Slug's and I don't ride in small cabs if I can help it; I like to get the big ones because it's hard for me to bend down, I'm having trouble with my legs. So it's a little cab and I say, "Will you pull away from the curb, I can't get in your cab." Instead he pulled in closer, right in front of the joint. So then I couldn't even open the door, it hit the curb. So I just slammed the door and went away. I didn't slam it hard, I don't think I did, maybe to him I slammed it hard. He's well-partitioned in there, and I'm carrying a *lot* of money, man, lots of payroll—several thousand dollars—and some extra money I shouldn't have been carrying. Usually when I'm carrying that type of money, I have my knife out in my hands, in my coat or someplace because I don't want to be bothered. I got two knives, one in each pocket, and [I'd have] a gun if I could get one.

But this night, this cat got out of his cab, and I'm headed to the next cab in line looking for a Checker. He jabbed me in the back: "What the fuck you bothering me for?" Big motherfucker too, and I wasn't really feeling good—I had left Sue and was kind of unhappy and out of breath. So I turned around and this cat put his dukes up. I didn't know who he was; at this point I didn't even know it was the cabdriver. I thought he was trying to rob me, so I go and get my shiv out, you know. In fact, it's so dumb of him—I go in my pocket and it was locked, had a button on it. So I'm saying, "Oh shit" to myself and out loud keep saying, "Look, man, get away from me."

So finally I throw all my shit down, everything down. They stole a watch of mine, my watch is gone, the money in this pocket, I had about seven or eight hundred dollars, that was gone. So then he backs up and goes for the cab. He got to the cab door, and I said, "No more," the way he stood there and looked at me, didn't back no further. I said, "This cat's got a gun." So I picked myself off the street, went back to the next cab and got in, saw him standing in the street and said, "Fuck it, I don't care." I didn't even know my money was gone till I went for my watch.

Cops came up, say, "Get out of the car. You got a knife?"

"Sure I got a knife in my pocket, plus a payroll."

"Shut up."

I say, "Look, man, you better ask this man why he got out of his cab. I never even got in it."

They said, "Turn around or we'll shoot you."

Now for them to be like that, man . . . plus, when they put the handcuffs on, they hit 'em again to tighten 'em. My hand was dead; this finger still can't move. That means they think every black man's against them.

And if they think like that, they are against them. When they get a guy like me against them—if they gonna fuck with everybody black and hurtin' them—because they later found that first cab driver was a pusher. The cop himself didn't tell me this, another cab driver did.

GOODMAN: Did they catch him with a gun, the cops?

MINGUS: The cop got him for something else, a violation, and he didn't show up [at court] for witness because he was a pusher. So the cop said he didn't show up today, and we'll probably drop the case. I said, "Why didn't he show up, man?"
   He said, "Well, he violated section . . ."
   I said, "He's a dope pusher, that's why he didn't show up, because he knows I know that. His own buddy told me."
   Plus, people stood at the curb and watched it, and I told the cop, "Why don't you ask people what happened? First, you see the man is out of his cab. Why did he get out of his cab? I never got in it."
   No justice. He said, "Shut up or I'll shoot you."
   I said, "You sure will." And he shot me, man. I never felt this way about police in my life, and he shot me, man, that day. I never had nothing against no cops, man, but he showed me that they're prejudiced, two white cops.

GOODMAN: There is so much of that around.

MINGUS: Well, one thing made me feel a little better: I heard a TV program with a white attorney on and something similar happened to him. This cab driver asked if he could run it off the meter, and the attorney said, "No, I'd rather you not." Cabbie starts telling him he's a dirty motherfucker, a capitalistic son of a bitch. And the attorney who happened to be a good boxer says, "I'm going to kick your ass if you get out of the cab."
   The guy said, "I'll bet you can't." (This is on TV, man, with Art Farmer's wife, she had something to do with it.)
   And so he got out and knocked the cat out, you know. Witnesses and everything, the cat put his dukes up, so he caught his jab and the attorney knocked him out with his left hand. So the cops come up and beat *him* up. They didn't say "Who are you?" but here's a cab driver they was protecting. Every one you get in now is beating you out of money, man. Plus the cabs are too small—for me—it's ridiculous to ride in one of those motherfuckers. But the way they treat you, like you're a pig or something, man.
   They don't realize that I'm going to start a war against the motherfuckers. I know about a hundred cats who can just flatten every cab's tires

in two days, just put 'em on the line with flat tires [*laughter*]. If they not nice, they won't be no cabs moving in a few weeks. This is guaranteed, and it ain't even my idea. Cat said, "If this shit continues any longer, man, we'll line 'em up on the curb. They won't even be able to run." So they better start being nice to people, man.

GOODMAN: It's a fucking war, because the cab drivers, you know, all the assaults on them . . .

MINGUS: Well, we can't assault if they stay behind that glass now, man, and the glass is alright if they got a big cab, especially with the rate of kill like it is.

GOODMAN: You feel like you're in a goddamn cage in there.

MINGUS: Well, they lock you in. Oh, I got one the other night, it's ridiculous to tell you, but I got a cab to take Sue home, and the guy was a drag. He pulled away, and I asked him to let me out of the cab. I paid him and tipped him a quarter; he left me and I look for another. Got the other cab, and the driver said, "Do you mind if I do it off the meter?"

I waited and said, "Yeah, to tell you the truth, man, I do."

He still left it off, and when I think about it it's so petty—a couple of bucks—and I said, "If I was the cab owner myself, I'd find a way to catch you cats. I'd put a guy like me in the cab, or a shorter guy, and what I'd do, I wouldn't just have you fired, I'd shoot you."

He says, "Listen, motherfucker, don't lecture to me. I'll turn the meter on, but don't say another word. In fact, get out of the cab."

I say, "Tell you what, man, you turn right and go to the police station, right down on 5th Street."

He kept going straight, didn't turn right, so I know he's a little shook. So I got a little rough: "You call me motherfucker and say get out of the cab. How come you talking like that? I still say, and I repeat, 'I would shoot you.' As far as you know, I might be a cop off duty."

Then he gets a little more quiet, and I say, "Now turn right here at Avenue A, I'm down on 5th Street like I told you."

He said, "Get out of the cab."

"I'm not getting out of the cab, man, until you take me where I'm going. Told you the police station's on the same street, right on the block."

So he gets there, and I get my knife out: I was going to do his tires in. But I said, "Naw, he ain't done enough yet." So I walk around to pay him (I'm too heavy, at least right now, to go into my pockets in the cab), so I had to get out to get in my pocket and coin purse and pull out some bills. And

I'm looking for some change, and it's a dollar exactly—would have been more if he'd turned the meter on sooner—and I'm going to give him a tip.

He says, "I don't want your fucking tip," and he didn't say "nigger" but something else that referred to nigger.

I say, "OK, cabby, number 3G668 . . ." but he had his light off and I couldn't get all of it, and he must have heard me read the number wrong, and he snatched all the money out of my hand and drove away. I was robbed right in the street, about twenty-five or thirty dollars.

I called the police, and you know what they said when they came over? "It sounds like to me if you called the guy's number off it was somebody with a stolen cab. We'll send our detectives over and let you look at the pictures."

I said, "You guys think you're with the cab drivers. I want to see the man's picture while he's fresh in my mind. You know, thirty dollars is a lot of money to me."

"Well, the detectives will come by."

No detectives yet. I called them: "Oh, you're the guy got robbed the other night, Charles Mingus, right?"

He's a dirty motherfucker, that's where it's at. They some dirty cats, that's where it's at, man. They probably know who the cabdriver is up front, because I asked them, "Are there that many cabdrivers on at four in the morning?" I don't think there are in New York, man, not that many that they can't find who's on at night.

· · ·

And there was always sex to talk about. There was always a new wrinkle, and Mingus was constantly testing what he thought were the limits of Hugh Hefner's *Playboy* philosophy. We were discussing the infinitely varied ways the sexual marketplace works—which led him to explain what he was attempting in *Underdog* with all the various sexual exploits. Sex in its many forms was part of survival for Mingus.

· · ·

GOODMAN: Massage parlors—that's a whole new slant on it.

MINGUS: It is, but it doesn't offer the intellectual johns, the senators, it doesn't offer them any security. They ain't going where they can be photographed. I'm sure those places are still operating, they just found one on the East Side, in the Eighties.

GOODMAN: You can't stop that, it's a basic need.

MINGUS: Paris is built on come. (Can you print that? Say "come"?) You have your women's clothes made, and the woman who owns the shop is an ex-madam. Or her mother was an ex-madam. They end up owning Paris because sex sells better than oil [*laughter*]. Better than Bethlehem Steel.

I go there and find this shop where I have my clothes made. I had a leather jacket made, and at the end, she says, "You know, you can have my pussy. I found out who you are." And she owned fifteen shops in the town! And not just me—Max Roach had it happen, you would have too if you had your clothes cut there and been associated with Max and some of these cats.

Well, they thought we were like, something, like classical musicians when we go over there, they think that way about us. So that's the only thing besides baseball and hot dogs that America's got.

GOODMAN: That's a beautiful place, man. I love that city. Are you going this summer?

MINGUS: Yeah. I put out all this bullshit, but I'm really monogamous, man. I get hooked on one chick, and that's weird. When I'm not hooked on one chick I could have a million. But I've never had as much pleasure as being hooked. It's more painful mentally, being with one person, 'cause you don't know how to live with each other all the time. If me and Sue can get through this thing we're going through now, we'll have something. Or we should blow it before we're too old. That's difficult, man. I've done all those things I mentioned in the book and more. I'm ashamed but I'm sure all men have done it. Did I say [in *Beneath the Underdog*] that my drummer had seventeen?

GOODMAN: I think so, that's when you came on with having twenty-three.

MINGUS: I wasn't trying to sound like I was the exceptional man; I was saying, "This is how society makes the black man. . . ." Here we are as little kids—one of the Scottsboro Boys looked at some little girl and they said he raped her. So they say we got hot nuts, right? Down South you'll get killed for it, so you know they love it.

GOODMAN: Sure they love it—they need it, it's the scapegoat, man.

MINGUS: So you see when I put it in the book, they took it, pulled it out, put it up front, and it makes me look—

GOODMAN: It's wrong, the whole context of what is in the book is wrong. You were hitting out against that whole black image thing—the macho, hot nuts stereotype.

MINGUS: It's the phallic symbol, they made us the phallic symbol for the whole world and didn't even realize it. Every white woman, they think we got the hottest nuts in the world because here's a guy willing to die for it. That's what I wanted to say at first. I'd be so frustrated too, I'd go down to Mexico and line 'em up, especially with tequila. And now I found something better, man, it's Ricard or Pernod. But the difference is with that you can't come; with tequila you can come [*laughter*]. With Pernod you can go all day long. Now I know why so many guys used to like them licorice drinks.

GOODMAN: What about absinthe?

MINGUS: Well, I never had it, but I imagine it was better than Pernod. But it's got something to do with that licorice flavor and the alcohol combined.

GOODMAN: That whole scene with the black man and that hot nuts image, and now Eldridge Cleaver writes about that.

MINGUS: You know the black man had to provide a way to control the pussy in order to make a living. I'm not saying he knows it better, but he must have found some things. Now here's Brownie, a pimp, told me this recently (put this in the book). He said, "Take a little castor oil, Mingus, put it on your finger, don't even tell the broad about it, and make love to her and touch her clitoris with it. It does the same thing to her clitoris as it does to your bowels." I ain't tried that one yet.

He says, "Mingus, take away half your work, use castor oil. Everyday you come in here, I know you're coming around for something. Use castor oil, the word for today."

I say, "What do you mean, castor oil?"

He comes back fifteen minutes later and says, "Mingus, I tried this out today, it just came to me, I took some castor oil today to clean myself out, I'm old-fashioned, and I wonder what would happen if I put it on her clitoris?"

So he tried it and it worked on every one of them. They don't even know what's happening, they lose complete control—like they been holding back in their minds and all of a sudden it's just flushed down on 'em. They say, "Brownie's got me." [*Much laughter.*] I'm gonna try it.

GOODMAN: I'll try it too.

MINGUS: "Tasteless, odorless castor oil." Makes sense. It goes to the stomach, touches some organs, it's not a bloodstream thing. . . .

GOODMAN: Who was Billy Bones in the book? Was that Brownie or that Chicago cousin you talked about?

MINGUS: Billy Bones is Howard Blacktop McGee, who *wanted* his name called. He owned the Flamingo where Herb Jeffries and Dan Grissom used to sing. He was a pimp, sharp, slender black cat. I don't know why Nel [Nel King, *Beneath the Underdog*'s content editor] chose to change that unless it was because he was a gangster . . . a kind of hood, in with the cops, a bagman for the cops. But in those days I wouldn't have written that.

The feeling I had when I wrote all this is that someone went around and checked on me to find out if I was telling the truth. I was planning to take the names out, although Blacktop and Papa Collette said, "No, man, put my name in there." They were proud of what they did for their people. They called themselves liberators, man. They took property and built it up, made cheaper housing for black people.

They said, "Take your money and go out and see what your people [need] and set up companies with it. So you pay taxes on it and become citizens." I tried to go for that, because it really sounded right.

You can't be no senator but you know when your people are suffering, and they took their money and put it in that direction. My book was mainly on religion. See when I was writing this book, I was writing this thing on communicating with—how do you say?—the divine spirits. And, man, a million birds came to my window. I don't know what kind they were. But that was the funniest thing happened, with these birds. I felt we was on the same beam, man, tuned in the same . . . millions of birds, man [*makes their noise against the window*].

The subject I was writing on was that men will have the power—if this society keeps on hating, with war and destruction, white against black— the gods will give certain men the power of the animals, to go out and kill people. If you gonna have a war, it will be with the animals, with ants, man will communicate with spiders and birds and pick your eyes out. And, man, then these birds came to the window—you should have seen me close my window then! Call Judy my wife and ask her about it. She may remember that. And then a few years later, Hitchcock came out with *The Birds*. Well, he didn't steal that. McGraw Hill had my book by then. He wouldn't . . . it's just some thoughts. . . .

MINGUS: If I'd been playing the blues, I'd never lost a job. Gene Ammons never lost a job, because he played the blues. But I [always] tried to show what I know—damn what I know, I'm gonna get some money—and I know as much music as anybody living, just about, man, white or black. But I'm gonna start proving that, I'm going to go out and make me some money. I'm gonna get a blues band. And then you'll hear what the blues is. They ain't had no blues bands since the Savoy Sultans, way back. Those bands based on the blues. I can show the kids how to play the blues. All my friends could too but they forgot, they're in the studios, like Phil Moore. I'm gonna write a whole book of blues.

GOODMAN: Yeah, but it's a popular word now, and the kids are all picking up on it. Look at Al Cooper. "The blues, the blues!"

MINGUS: I'll call it something else, man, maybe the "black blues." Yeah. Blues is my music, man. I'm a blues player, really. I'll challenge any of the blues players. I can't sing 'em, but we do a blues with my tenor player singing the blues.

And the public does know, man, they know the blues are here. I can tell myself: if I follow somebody who's a hell of a blues artist in a concert, and if Charlie Parker had went up behind one of those blues singers, *he* would have died.

What's a very popular singer today? A very popular singer, a black man?

GOODMAN: Lou Rawls.

MINGUS: Go ahead, name some more. Jimmy something. He yells. No, don't look for Jimmy. Look for . . . He yells when he sings, screams and yells.[3]

GOODMAN: Leon Thomas.

MINGUS: That's one. Go ahead. California. Very important to find him.

GOODMAN: Is he kind of a jazz singer or a pop singer?

MINGUS: Kind of a jazz singer. How many can you name?

GOODMAN: Not too many. Joe Williams, can't think of any more.

MINGUS: He writes his own music.

GOODMAN: Keep talking, maybe I'll think of it.

MINGUS: I'm gonna get a list of all the guys I like, all the popular people, we need that list. This is wasting time. Anyway, James Brown is still laying his hysteria on the working people.

GOODMAN: But he's dying out, he had his big thing.

MINGUS: With the black people? Not where I live. Next door to my apartment, that's all they playing.

It's the working people, the laborers, the working black people who go to work in the morning, eight o'clock, come home five or six, really tired.

They have their entertainment—jukebox, record player, and TV. These are the people who I want to read this book. They've never heard jazz, never been exposed to jazz.

GOODMAN: Right!

MINGUS: They've heard this guy yelling [*makes loud, screaming sound*] like they feel. I don't blame 'em, they got no church, they got no nightclubs they can go to no more, they got just a single thing they do to stay related to themselves, man. That's their church; James Brown was their church, but they got a church in jazz [too]. As long as there's the blues, and without the blues they lost their church. That's the only hope there is.

 The blues used to be a music that people escaped on, man. That was their whole thing. The ones that drank and didn't go to church. You start the first two bars of a blues, and they yell. It's good that the kids haven't forgotten it—the black kids round here who start playing and start swinging.

GOODMAN: It will be a fad for the white kids, just another style. They'll get tired of that like they got tired of the Beatles. Do you feel as strongly as you did before, when we talked last time about that?

MINGUS: I still do.

 Duke Ellington's a blues band, man. Practically everything he writes is with the twelve-bar phrase. He doesn't have the old church feeling, I should say the old blues feeling. Duke has finesse, you know, but it's still basically blues. He's got all the fundamental sadness—

GOODMAN: But very sophisticated—

MINGUS: Sophisticated. And he has finesse, you know, but it's still basically blues.

GOODMAN: What do you think about his church music?

MINGUS: I like everything he does, man. It doesn't sound like church music to me.

GOODMAN: I call it church music ['cause he does] . . . and I don't have any other label for it. I've got mixed feelings about that—I don't know.

MINGUS: It sounds like the [earlier] music he wrote, "Black Brown and Beige." "Come Sunday" has a little church in it.

GOODMAN: But even that "Suite Thursday" he did not so long ago, it's beautiful.

MINGUS: Yeah.

GOODMAN: And it's a piece, a composition, a whole. Do you look at Ellington's music all as one thing?

MINGUS: All as one thing. I haven't heard nothing that didn't move me in some kind of way, even when he takes other peoples' tunes and arranges them.

GOODMAN: Well, Nixon likes him, that's one good thing.

MINGUS: Nixon likes Duke?

GOODMAN: Gave him some award, what was that? The Freedom Award or some bullshit.

MINGUS: Now I don't like Duke.

GOODMAN: Don't you remember that? He went to the White House in '69 or '70, they had him there for some big gala thing, with other musicians.

MINGUS: Who has the biggest prick in Washington? [*Pause.*] . . . We have. He [Nixon] should quit, man. He should just quit.

GOODMAN: No, I don't agree with you. I think he should not quit, the Congress should impeach him and get him the fuck out of there.

MINGUS: Yeah.

GOODMAN: Because if he quits, then he saves face, and the government still hasn't purged itself of all this shit.

MINGUS: I just can't see how he can go on. He might die, you know. Other presidents before him have had this happen to 'em. They go out on the road and try and convince the people they're alright. Like he was in Chicago when I was there.

GOODMAN: You know, I get the feeling that there's nothing much happening in terms of black people, man. They're just kind of cooling out, and nobody's doing shit.

MINGUS: New hairdos and no changes.

GOODMAN: Yeah. What do you think? Why is that?

MINGUS: I think the black people been separated too much, not together really. Before, they used to at least have church to get together and talk to each other, talk to the children, talk to the families, and have a purity thing going. Now they just have day jobs, and most of 'em don't go to nightclubs, just stay home and look at television.

GOODMAN: That's right, and who can afford to go out?

MINGUS: Yeah. They don't have any community things, except for the real out movements, which is the Panthers and—the ones who killed Malcolm X—the Muslims [the Nation of Islam].

GOODMAN: But the Muslim movement is very quiet now. I mean there's nothing happening, is there?

MINGUS: They just bought a million-dollar—one of their members did—a private club to play golf on.

GOODMAN: A friend of mine lives in the South Side of Chicago right near the Muslim temple, and he knows some of those people, and he says it's corrupt. It's just corrupt, like all those things after a period of time. . . . He drove me around one day and said, "Look at the homes these people live in."

MINGUS: They got a pleasure club, what do you call those clubs, the proper name? Rich men all belong to. Where you play golf.

GOODMAN: A country club. They're all into that, and they're big investors now. I suppose that's why they had to kill Malcolm, I don't know.

MINGUS: Yeah, too bad they didn't read his book, or they wouldn't have killed him.

NOTES

1. Sue Mingus, *Tonight at Noon: A Love Story* (New York: Pantheon, 2002), 10–11.

2. Boxer Muhammad Ali was born Cassius Clay and changed his name after converting to the Sunni Islam faith in 1975. Provoking much controversy, he aligned himself with Elijah Muhammad, leader of the Nation of Islam, and refused to fight in Vietnam. In 1967, he was stripped of his world championship title by the boxing commission and could not fight for more than three years. Arrested but not imprisoned for evading the draft, Ali appealed and in 1971 the U.S. Supreme Court reversed the conviction.

Ali was given to dramatic and controversial statements, à la Mingus. For example: "Why should they ask me to put on a uniform and go 10,000 miles from home and drop bombs and bullets on brown people while so-called Negro people in Louisville are treated like dogs?" And, "No Vietcong ever called me nigger." See the "Muhammad Ali Biography" at www.biographyonline.net/sport/muhammad_ali.html.

3. Jimmy Witherspoon's name came up later, and Mingus said he was the "very popular singer" he couldn't remember here.

10 Eviction and Laying Out

"Everything went against me, you know."

Here's Mingus talking to me and Booker Tillery about the dark time in the '60s when he simply laid out and couldn't function in music or in much else. It was a bad period for him and culminated in his eviction from the Great Jones Street loft, which Tom Reichman chronicled in his 1968 film and talks about in his commentary to this chapter.[1] Mingus also refers to another, prior eviction, from a place on Third Avenue, his so-called School of Arts, Music, and Gymnastics. Elsewhere Gene Santoro and Brian Priestly give rather rambling descriptions of these events, but Mingus himself spoke with feeling to Nat Hentoff about how he responded during that time and after.[2]

There is a lot of paranoia and pain in what he said to me and Booker. Some of it is self-serving and disconnected. It's also clear that Mingus had been setting himself up for a resounding fall, and I wonder whether he was not in a way somewhat conscious of this.

. . .

GOODMAN: What happened during the long period you laid out?

MINGUS: I was dead. I could still produce, but I was killed inside, [in] what made me function. I didn't know how to move, I had no reason to move. Had a couple of friends that looked out for me. I made friends with him [Booker], but I was very lonely. I had a woman, I had a bed partner, but I had nothing else.

There wasn't much I could do after [the Third Avenue] eviction. They stole things. I took my insurance money, I told you that, to buy that school. The floor alone I [installed to] originally start the school cost ten thousand dollars.

GOODMAN: You told me you took the insurance money to go to Tijuana with Dannie [see chapter 11].

MINGUS: No, used it for both. I'll get the address for you, it was Third Avenue and Twenty-eighth Street. That was when I started the first school. Then my attorney got me into a bad contract, a lease for ten years where I'd have to prepare the whole building. It was a sucker lease, really. But still I put that with the fact that I wrote in the book—that everything went against me, you know.

Then Judy, my ex-wife, got me a place to store my furniture. And when I met Sue, she's the one that said I shouldn't build a big school so I built a small school and opened that one up—I was just using that one to store stuff in really. And that's when I met Frank Mabry, around the same period too [see chapter 12].

So the City Urban Renewal League was supposed to find me a place. In the meantime, one of Sue's friends—named Claire Houghton, if you want a name—finds me the place of a guy who was gonna be movin', who was making a movie. I wanted a place with a high ceiling, like I'm still in now. So I go see the place [on Great Jones Street], and it's very cheap, they say ninety dollars a month, and the girl's name is Judy Nathanson, who I'm subletting from; she has an apartment as big as mine.

And she had a thing that she said I should leave my door open, so she can go in any time without my being there. So I'm sleeping with the door open, making love one night, and I hear somebody's banging the door to come in, a broad's voice, you know.

So this girl, she falls in nude in my room! Acts surprised, "Hey, what's this door doing unlocked?"

I say, "It's always open," and she walks in buck naked.

So I figured she wanted to have a party, but I didn't want to make the party though, man, I was in love. I didn't need no orgies—I had orgies when I was a kid, I didn't need no orgy.

So then she disappears, and they start asking for the rent. I said, "I paid it, I paid her six hundred dollars." So really I created this whole naked scene in the book anyway, the problem with my door, but I wouldn't have balled her either. I figure I was being set up by some guys, the gangsters I mentioned, trying to get me with my back down, with some broad they want me down with, you know, whoever the broad might be.

The point I made is that even the one I'm in love with might be one sent by them. Plus, the other one knocking on the door could be her buddy. I was rude and all that, but I just didn't want it to happen at that moment [*chuckles*].

Now, they ask me why I moved to the next floor in this building. Well, it's just what I wanted, had a hardwood floor—which I just lost—how they knew I lost the floor, I don't even know. Soundproof and all that. I went up and looked at it. It was nice, but I said, "If I move in here will you guys pay the movers to move the piano because that's a couple of flights up?" And I ain't paying seven hundred dollars to move my stuff again—with no money from the Urban Renewal League, which—they were supposed to give me two thousand dollars to move, plus find me a place.

Sold my pianos and my basses, and they evicted me because the woman [Judy Nathanson] who took the money didn't pay the rent. She split and they couldn't find her. During the eviction, one of the truck drivers said he was ordered to leave my stuff in the garbage. I got this on tape with the guy who was doing the movie [Tom Reichman]. He went around with his camera asking questions, "Why did you guys throw down the piano? Why is the piano apart?"

One of 'em says, "Well, I came to the stairs, and the guy told me to make it garbage, so I took the piano, shoved it slowly to the stairway, gave it a push and watched it go down."

"Hey, that would be a good piano for some kid to use."

"Well, they told me to make it garbage. That's what I did."

The next thing [he destroyed] was a bass, said he didn't know where he put it. I said, "That's one bass for the garbage, what about the four other basses?" That's how I knew my basses were stole. They took Ampex speakers and hi-fi equipment. I was building a regular studio, had most of the equipment I needed. I had gymnasium equipment from a Vic Tanney's gym that was going out of business—it was used but you can't wear out iron, so you know it was good. I had equipment for a steam room, ultraviolet light room for sun rays. It's all gone, all gone. My collection of pipes—six or seven hundred dollars, a couple worth two hundred dollars, a coin collection—they copped that. My payroll happened to be in a box—in Boston.

GOODMAN: Who is this, Charles? Who's doing this?

MINGUS: The city, man, the police and the city. Wasn't no gangsters in there. They were the only people allowed to be in there. They said they opened the door, or said it was open when they came in. When I came in, they were looking at my things. My music was on the floor and they were stamping it like it was carpet. They drug my mattresses—I only had one bed in there—but they claimed the papers and all my mattresses [showed] that I was running a whorehouse. But those mattresses were left by the guy who was making the movie.

I could prove the city was responsible, but I didn't have anything to do anything about it.

GOODMAN: Did you start any lawsuit?

MINGUS: I really don't need a lawsuit in a way because if I go to the Urban League they'll see I get my money to move, they're the ones that OK'd the lease, yet the woman who they paid the money to, they say they couldn't find her.

GOODMAN: So, no grounds—

MINGUS: Except the city, but I'll never go to the city. No doubt about it, man, I could make money so much faster if I forget about them people. The city is paying [people] to do this shit, and anybody'd take a job like that . . . That's what I feel: if you sue people like that, by the time I acquaint my mind with all that, I become a moneymaker in the direction I don't want to make money in! I don't want that bullshit because I can make some money in another way.

In the book, I said in 1965—and they took it out of the [*Underdog*] book—but I was a millionaire in 1965. I had planned it, I might have missed a couple of years and made it before, way it looks, but I knew what I was doing. You know, I ain't trying to brag but my wife [Celia], she's living in California and she's doing all right. I have her things to keep me from getting thrown in the street again—all the Debut record things [see chapter 11]. But if I had my publishing firm going, I'd be a millionaire today. You know, I had it mapped out. And I'm going to do it again.

GOODMAN: . . . Before the eviction, you had a rough time mentally, right? That's gotta be part of it too.

MINGUS: Before the eviction I was only worried about the fact that Louis Lomax [see chapter 13] had taken my book, which sacred friends of mine put on the fucking market and told personal stories in so that they would make you laugh. I wrote so the gangsters that I knew would say, "Goddamn, look at Mingus, here I am [in the book] but nobody knows it's me."

I was changing names, but the way they [the publisher] did it, it hurt my friends. I say gangsters 'cause you know they were into this—but "Why did he call my name? Hey, Mingus, why did you do that to us?"

And the way they said it, I knew they ain't going to hurt me. You read it in the book and say, "Man, nobody knows it but me." Yeah. And I even complimented them, made it look on the edge of flattery, I did that . . .

TILLERY: What about the time, after you wrote this book, later on they came and took pictures? Remember the movie they shot on Forty-second Street about you, evicted and so forth, they ran a whole movie on you, and you never want to rise nobody to that [*sic*].

MINGUS: No, no, that's [Tom Reichman's] film, that's the kid that discovered they were evicting me. He came to my house and they were tearing the studio down, throwing my stuff in the street.

Only thing about that, man, that was a setup too. I put that with the [Lomax] thing. In my own mind I tie it together. Reichman's brother passed away; he said he knew me. I remember the kid [*unintelligible*] was chastised a lot—about why he didn't study and learn, you know?—I kind of remember him, I played at his funeral.

But I always felt that his brother Tom—you put it down, man—he hated me, even though he did this film, I always felt it. The same as I felt about the man in the pocket book [reference unclear]: in his eyes and his heart he never really looked at me. As though somebody's brother must have told him—and I said, I know exactly what it was, it had to do with Jews.

And I told [the brother] he was in a good position—he was a rich Jew wasting his time where he was—to go and tell his mother and his father, why didn't they come out and book me [to play], something like that. A lot of life wasted. And then he finally told me he wanted to kill himself. And so I told my son the same thing, or very similar, because he wanted to kill himself.

But I didn't know [Reichman's brother] was one of those sick kids, he went to a special school. So I don't really feel guilty, but I told him, "If you want to kill yourself, I'll tell you the way to do it. Go to a whorehouse or go to a woman and make love to her—it's the way I would do it—and, you know when you come?"

"Yeah, I've come before."

I said, "The next time you come, don't cut it off." And that's how he died, fucking a woman—in Tangiers. That's what Tom was trying to tell me.

I tell him, "Your mind has control over your orgasm and you watch yourself, and you come just so long, right? And you cut it off. Next time don't cut it off. Just let it keep being good to you—and goodbye." And he was a big enough fool to do that.

GOODMAN: Who are you talking about—Tom's brother, the younger brother?

MINGUS: Yeah, his name is . . . I forget his name. And here's the other
story he took home.

Now here's how I discovered he was Jewish—and I don't know how to
tell if anybody's Jewish. Tom kept coming on about he's being white, and
he's taking up with all these whores, you know, at St. Mark's by the Five
Spot there, he's hanging out in a place close to the Five Spot, in a place
where the best whores were. And there was a good one there, a *bad* one
named Consuela, bad broad. Anyway—I'll tell you about that and Sue
sometime. Consuela ran in and said, "Charles, I just made fifty dollars; a
guy all he had to do was look at my legs."

Sue said, "Fifty dollars? Say, I'm gonna try that."

I'm saying, "Go ahead and learn. She'll show you, teach you a new act."
I give her a chance then, but she come on like she's just playing, 'cause
you know the girl's talking to me. That was Dannie's girl, Consuela, and
she looked out for Dannie.

But I was gonna tell you something more important. This kid [Tom]
was playing pool one time and he's talking about the white thing, and I
got tired of hearing the white thing. I said, "You know, I'll tell you
something. If you look at me and put your hand next to mine, you ain't
really much lighter, you know. You come out with 'nigger' and all this. I
don't know what race you are, but I know a kid named Elmer Holden from
Watts—he's in the [*Underdog*] book too—and he looks just exactly like
you and he don't call himself white. He can because everybody knows his
mother and father, and they know the insurance man who was his father.
Now what makes you think that your momma ain't making it with
somebody black?"

Now, you want to know what the facts really were? His momma *was*.
Put that in the book too, 'cause they showed it to me, the dentist she was
making it with. So, this is after the funeral, I met the guy [the black
dentist] at the funeral, and he didn't try to hide it. And the kid [Tom]
didn't look Jewish, he looked like a mixed breed to me, you know, and I
told him that.

And after the funeral, his mother was talking to me and says, "Charles,
you don't know what you meant to this family. I don't know if you're to
blame or who's to blame"—she skipped, stumbled, while she's sitting on a
chaise lounge, laying back on a golden pillow, beautiful teeth, money, and
she says, "My son just talked to me, and there's one thing I want to tell
you," and I know what she's talking about, "One thing I want to tell you
he told me, and I don't know whether I should tell you or not, but you
know the truth is the truth." And this dentist guy, he's at the party too,

the party after the funeral, good dinner. And I remember all that, man. I don't care what happens, but that's what happened.

GOODMAN: . . . I was up with Tom Reichman the other day to see the film, and he says he's getting hassled because he gave it to Grove Press, and they're taking it around to all the colleges and showing it. A lot of people have seen it, and he says they're ripping him off, he's not getting any money out of it.

MINGUS: He didn't spend any money, so why should he get any money?

GOODMAN: He says he's nine thousand dollars in the hole.

MINGUS: Well, who did he give it to? He didn't give it to me or the musicians. We didn't get paid for playing in it.

GOODMAN: Well, he said it cost him a lot of money to make it—

MINGUS: And I felt some kind of setup during this period, that someone was getting revenge on me for saying things about a trumpet player who I knew, who was written up in the newspapers, who made love to a little boy about twelve years old, or he raped a little boy and they let him go. Or the fact that Louis Armstrong was busted for pot. You know, little things like that—I was just saying how the government seems to accept it for certain people, and for others, they do a whole lot of time.

And I didn't think it was fair for a guy like Louis to go to jail [so briefly] when a guy like my son would go in for ten years over a stick of pot, and Louis will come and serve time every time he'd be in this particular town where he was busted at, he'd go and sit in the jail and smoke, drink, order beers for the cops, and have a ball. And he's spending [serving] time in there. So I said, well, that's alright, I dig where it's at, but there is or there ain't the law.

This was all in the original book that Booker's got at home, plus the thing where Frank Mabry was going to kill Joe Gallo, the accountants *and* Joe Gallo. And after that, I said, "You guys in the Mafia better watch out. There's a new gang in here called the real Black Hand, but they're tan." You know, the tall brown ones.

I wrote a little poem on 'em. I said, "You guys won't know 'em, you're so famous and get writeups all the time, you won't even know who they are because black is invisible—the real Black Hand."

TILLERY: Dig it, dig it.

MINGUS: So I'm walking down the street and here comes one of the cats I know and says, "What the fuck you doing, writing things like this? You got everybody upset. We know you're a good guy, so you just go away and hide someplace, or somebody might just kill you." I'll take you to him right today, man, walk you right in his face. He's the only one seemed like he was trying to tell me something.

So the more these things happen, the more it creates paranoia, you know. Too many things have happened since then. Lotta people asking for it [*unintelligible*].

CHAPTER 10 COMMENTARY

Tom Reichman on Filming and Working with Mingus

Tom was a sad-faced, skinny cat who lived in a cheap walk-up flat on the West Side. We got on well, and he screened his 1968 Mingus film for me—actually the first time I had seen it whole. His stories about Mingus had the ring of truth and really gave me a sense of how, from his point of view, both Mingus and Sue could occasionally use people for their own purposes.

When I heard he had committed suicide in 1975, I wasn't totally shocked. But his death underscored Mingus's words about his sad family: "There's some sick shit going on there." In 1970, Tom filmed and directed *How Could I Not Be Among You?*, a thirty-minute film about poet Ted Rosenthal, who contemplates his own death after learning he has leukemia.

Among the few comments extant about Reichman and his influence is this one: "Reichman, an impoverished genius best known for his stark 1968 film portrait of jazz legend Charles Mingus, dabbled in everything from low-rent porn to industrial gigs and sporting events."[3]

. . .

REICHMAN: I had shot most of the film that you've seen, but I felt the film needed some more insane caricature kind of things, which I could cut away to very fast. And Mingus had already been evicted and had moved up to Eighty-eighth Street between West End and Riverside Drive because that's where Sue, his girlfriend at the time, lived. And what he did is, he went up to—she lived on the fifth floor on the south side of the street. He went into a building on the north side of the street, directly opposite her window on the fifth floor, knocked on the door, and said, "Hello, I'm Charlie Mingus and I'd like to sublet your apartment so I can keep an eye on my girlfriend."

And this girl who had the apartment said, "Oh, you're Charlie Mingus! Sure, you can sublet my apartment." So he moved in. Anyway, he made an arrangement with me to meet at eight o'clock in the morning one day to shoot some more scenes, and I had been blowing a lot of film but had the equipment rented and I was at Mike Wadleigh's [the cameraman's] studio, which was around the corner. At eight o'clock in the morning, I went over to Eighty-eighth Street.

It's kind of like a heavy number every time you commit yourself to a day's shoot because you have people tied up and equipment and film and since we had no money to start with—anyhow, I get there and there is a note on his mailbox. "Dear Tom, I have left the country. I cannot continue with the film. There is a letter for you at Sue's across the street."

So I was a little upset and went across the street to Sue's and here was a note on her door. "Dear Charles, I am having the painters in and I won't be in today. Sue." So I went back to one of these studios and sat around for a couple of hours and the crew was really pissed off. "Where the hell is this guy?" And, I somehow felt that he would explain himself.

Around twelve noon, he showed up and said, "Tom, you've got to read the letter."

So I went with him to Sue's house and he opened the door and there was this very thick envelope there. The letter was on the outside addressed to J. Edgar Hoover, and on the inside it was addressed to [Mayor] John Lindsay, but he was giving it to me to read. It was all about a pimp in Los Angeles in 1941, about twenty-eight pages or something like that, and it was totally surreal. I read the whole thing, and Mingus was just totally relieved when I finished reading it. He said, "OK, let's go shoot."

Meanwhile, my crew was totally flipped out. They were really turned off on this whole thing. So we got in Wadleigh's truck and started going downtown and Mingus said, "What do you want to film?"

I said, "Look, I just really want to—whatever you're going to do. We just want it to be really natural."

He said, "Oh, this is a cinema verité and everything? I'll tell you what I was going to do today. Tell me if you want to film it. I was going to go down to O'Henry's Steak House because three years ago I ordered three lamb chops and they only gave me two and I want to get the third lamb chop today."

And that's exactly the kind of thing I wanted to film, so I said, "Beautiful." So when we get down to O'Henry's, he says, "Look man, I was just putting you on. That was a lot of shit. What I was really going to do today is, I was going to go see my lawyer."

I said, "Fine." So we went down to Wall Street, the whole film crew, camera and everything. He had a wireless mike on, an FM radio mike, and we went up with a camera and sound man and Mingus to his lawyer's office. Well, we got there, and it turns out that Sue had been there all day having the lawyer draft a contract for me to sign away all rights to the film. So he had tricked me into bringing my film crew in to film me signing away the film.

And I was about to start crying. I just went insane. That was just it. So, he came out and said, "Look, man, I just had to do this because of Sue. Sue told me to do it. Wait downstairs for me. I'll come right down in ten minutes."

We waited downstairs for about an hour, and he never showed up and we went upstairs and they said, "Oh, Mr. Mingus left about an hour ago." So we went driving around all of lower Manhattan trying to pick him up on the receiver because he still had the radio mike on. And finally, Mike Wadleigh had to go shoot another film in the evening, and he said, "Look, the [other] film is for the Mobilization to End the War Committee [National Mobilization Committee to *End the War* in Vietnam] and some Sioux Indians are coming in from South Dakota, so if you do run into Mingus you can bring him down and we can do both things at the same time."

So I went back to Wadleigh's office and Mingus was waiting for me. He had shaved all his hair off and he had painted his head blue. And he said, "Man, I'm really sorry. Let's go have some Chinese food. I look like Buddha."

So we went and had Chinese food and I told him about the Indians. He said, "Oh, man, real Indians? Shit, let's go down and do the Indians."

GOODMAN: Why did he shave his head?

REICHMAN: Oh, he does that from time to time.

GOODMAN: This had no connection with the Indian thing?

REICHMAN: I think it had something to do with the whole day, but I really don't know. I can't get into analyzing his motives at all.

We went down and waited around, and then the Indians came out and he introduced himself, "Hey, man, I'm Charles Mingus and my great-grandmother was a Navajo and I'd like to invite you for some fire water." So we went down to this bar, and we're shooting this. The Indians were sitting there with their pigtails, exhausted from the trip in from South Dakota. Most of them couldn't speak English anyway, and they're just downing bourbon after bourbon, just sitting there, with the fire water, you know?

And Mingus is like totally opening up to them and talking like for hours and saying, "Man, all I want is to find the perfect squaw and go up and get myself a teepee on a hill and smoke the peace pipe and really do it." He's just talking for hours.

All of a sudden, the doors of the bar open up like in a Western, and in walks this short guy who is the producer of the other film that Wadleigh was shooting. His name was David Weiss, and he stands there in the door and says, "You goddamn bastards, you used my Indians in your art film." And then Wadleigh had to split. Now Mingus spent the rest of the night jumping over parking meters and making like an Indian.

Anyway, that was one incredible day. . . .

When the film was finally finished, I had another very paranoid experience. Mingus was very frightened about the whole editing process. In other words, during filming, it was beautiful. But during the editing he felt that I had this incredible power to distort what he had been saying and show him shooting the gun and talking about sex and all these sensational things, and not really let it run out.

GOODMAN: The record business is the same; he's very sensitive about that.

REICHMAN: That's right. So when the film was finally finished, I invited him to a press screening, and he refused to come but instead sent a huge committee. I mean, like he sent his kids and ex-wife and Sue and three ex-managers and lawyers and Red Callender, the bass player, somebody named Louis from Los Angeles. Nel King came. Two Hollywood editors came in. It was like, lawyers, accountants—it was just huge. It was really paranoid, and I was scared shitless.

After it was all over, they all came up to me and kissed me and they loved it, and they called up Mingus and told him it was OK. And then he spent the next two weeks at the theater, day and night, bringing us food, going out to the lobby and inviting people, "Come on in and see my story." That was really great. It was an incredible screening.

[*Pause.*] But I think I've kind of repressed a lot of the stories. Forgotten them.

GOODMAN: Yeah, and why not? It's very hard to deal with him on any kind of a regular basis, I'm sure.

REICHMAN: The thing is to get in, do it, and get out. There were a lot of guys who really had long relationships with him, like Nat Hentoff and those people.

GOODMAN: Well, he hasn't spent much time with Hentoff for quite a while, apparently. Mingus is a tough man.

REICHMAN: The film was kind of interesting in that it was also Mike Wadleigh's really first attempt at shooting.

GOODMAN: Yeah, that's one thing I wanted to ask you about.

REICHMAN: I think it was his first whole film. He had done a lot of little things for A and T [reference unclear] and he was at NYU Film School. And he only shot the jazz stuff. He didn't shoot the interior stuff. The interiors were done by Lee Osborne, who is actually a sound man who ended up doing the sound for *Woodstock* and the album [of the same name]. But Wadleigh was just an incredible, natural cameraman, as you can see. Some of those shots are just—he just picked up the camera and instantly became the best hand-held cameraman in the world. It's all hand-held and rock steady.

GOODMAN: Did he do all the *Woodstock* film?

REICHMAN: Well, he directed it and he was the main cameraman. There were twelve other cameramen. Hasn't done anything since, which is unfortunate—because of *Woodstock*, he's kind of stopped working. It kind of priced him out of the whole market. He's trying to put together his next film.

GOODMAN: Who's the little girl [in the Mingus film], Karen? What's her name?

REICHMAN: That's Mingus's daughter by his third wife.

GOODMAN: Yeah? Judy?

REICHMAN: Yeah, Caroline. Caroline is the daughter's name. He really kind of brung her because when it came down to it, when it came down to actually shooting that night, he was very camera shy. She was fantastic. He got his hair cut and he was drinking a little wine to get loosened up. What happened was I had planned the film very differently around his eviction. I wanted to bring in, like, all the main people in his life: Miles and Duke and his wives and all these people and have them coming and going and make it kind of look like one long day and then have the whole thing build up to the eviction. But what happened was the city moved the date of the eviction way up, so we had to rush in at the last moment just to get this last night. They'd already cut off the electricity.

   Then the actual day of the eviction, I was on my way down to court to try to have the thing postponed, and on my way down to court, I just stopped at his house to make sure it was OK. When I got there, they had already started the eviction. This one guy grabbed me and said, "Mr. Mingus, you're getting evicted."

I said, "I'm not Mr. Mingus." And I said, "You have no right to evict him until he gets here."

So I called up Mike Wadleigh, and I said, "It's happening. Get Mingus. Get Sue." And a friend of mine was there and called the press and all the press came down, which was good for the film, and good for him.

GOODMAN: What do you know about the whole background of that and why the city went after him?

REICHMAN: The eviction?

GOODMAN: Yeah.

REICHMAN: He was living this very complicated [life], I never really understood it thoroughly, and I didn't really care to, because the eviction really was a symbol in the film. A lot of people complained that I didn't explain the specifics, but I didn't think it was necessary. But as I understand it, he was living up near Bellevue Hospital in the Twenties [in his Third Avenue loft], and they were expanding, and the city had to move him out. Under some kind of artist residence program, they found him this new loft, which is on Great Jones Street.

Actually, when he signed the papers [for Great Jones Street], it was a subcontract, a sublease, and technically on that particular lease there was no subleasing allowed. But the landlord was going to go along with it and the person who was subletting it was obviously going along with it. Mingus was going along with it, or he didn't even realize [any problem] at the time. Then, he moved in with all his really paranoid setup, so that place had, you know, the gun over the door. He had had all the windows electrified, the fences electrified, so if you touched them, you were electrocuted. He had tear-gas bombs all around the place, shotguns all over the place. It was really insane.

And of course he was making a lot of noise playing music. He had his white girlfriend or whatever. Anyway, the landlord wanted him out of there. And he was doing things like shooting holes in the ceiling. So the landlord started pulling the illegal sublet thing. "You've got to get out of here. Illegal sublet." When Mingus heard that, he stopped paying rent for about four months. Ultimately, I think they got him for nonpayment of rent.

When the cops arrived—there was a car wash around the corner for police cars, so they all swarmed in when they saw the eviction. And they found a hypodermic needle, they found handcuffs, and they found a shotgun. And he was arrested.

GOODMAN: And the pills.

REICHMAN: Right. And, he got out of jail about a half an hour later. He walked out of jail carrying the hypodermic needle, handcuffs, and the shotgun, and he had licenses or prescriptions for all of it. And he said, "I think I'm the first man black man to ever walk out of jail carrying this shit." It was incredible.

But I think, this may just be my interpretation, but it wasn't really a case of the white society taking on the poor, black artist. It was a hell of a lot of dramatic masochism involved. He likes to blow up these things that are going to happen anyway and really call attention to the whole thing in order to stop it.

GOODMAN: He still reads it that the city was out to bust his ass because he was trying to start a school and they accused him of having a lot of bad-ass black people around, junkies and, you know, that kind of thing. That's the way he tells it.

REICHMAN: The cops were so friendly to him that I thought it was going to ruin the picture. They were so goddamn nice. And, one interesting story that happened was, it turned out that I really needed NBC's footage because they had their sound going and I was kind of wanting to make fun of the interviewer, and I asked him if I could have the footage, and he said, "Sure. Call up so-and-so at NBC."

So I called the guy up and he said, "Well look, as it turns out, we have to use about twenty minutes of this on the six o'clock news tonight 'cause there's no news."

GOODMAN: Twenty minutes!

REICHMAN: "And we'd like you to set up another interview with Mingus in a couple of days so we can find out what really happened." So, I went through the trouble of doing that, which wasn't that easy at the time. They asked him, it was Thanksgiving evening, and they said, "Well, Mr. Mingus, on Thanksgiving evening, do you think you have something to be thankful for?"

And he said, "Yes, that I'm not a crackerjack." And he got up and walked away.

Then I went to NBC and I said, "Look, you got your second interview. Can I have the footage now?" And they didn't want to know me from Adam. It took me eight months to get that footage. And I really needed it.

Finally, through every means possible, everybody in the film industry I knew, they just wouldn't give the footage. And finally, through a lawyer I knew who knew people at NBC, they arranged for me to be able to—

GOODMAN: Did you sell them this interview or give it to them?

REICHMAN: I set it up. For the news. And I was willing to pay for the footage. And I gave them the original news story. So, finally, they would allow me in the editing room up in NBC just to view the footage on a viewer. The minute the film can came in, I grabbed the can and knocked over the guy, ran down ten flights of stairs and ran all the way uptown to Thirteenth Street and . . . it's in the film. It's really kind of interesting because the eviction scene is with two cameras—Mike Wadleigh and NBC—and they get into a fight. When Mingus is getting into the police car—

GOODMAN: What cameraman do we see on the film?

REICHMAN: Well, you see both of them, kind of, but they shoot each other. Wadleigh was kind of a short-haired, skinny guy with a tie on. What happened was, Wadleigh was following me off the street and the NBC cameraman was backing up with him and Wadleigh backed around to get him [Mingus] going into the car and he backed into the NBC cameraman's shot, and there was a fight.

GOODMAN: So that's what the fight was?

REICHMAN: Yeah, and the NBC cameraman is saying, "Where's your goddamn press card?" And Wadleigh's saying, "Get out of my way, you idiot." And I've got both shots. And Mingus meanwhile gets out of the car three times to make sure he's been photographed getting in. And I'm screaming for Mike to get the shot and forget about the fight. Then when the car pulls out, the cameramen shoot each other, and I have both shots, of them shooting each other. It was really kind of funny. It's kind of an inside joke.

GOODMAN: That's incredible. Did you ever give the film back?

REICHMAN: Oh, no. My cut in the film. They [NBC] showed up at the opening night at the New Cinema Playhouse with lawyers and everything. And then when they saw the film was drawing about five people per showing, they just left it alone. If they could've made any money, they probably would have tried to sue me. And I think I would have had a good chance of winning. Unless they own the courts, I don't know.

GOODMAN: Mingus last night was talking very briefly about you and the filming, something about his piano being pushed down the stairs? Do you remember anything about that?

REICHMAN: Do you mean during the eviction?

GOODMAN: Yeah.

REICHMAN: Well what happens during an eviction—I was evicted myself about six months after I made the film because this landlord was just trying to get me out so he could raise the rent and he kept sending me eviction notices, and if you don't respond in five days, they automatically show up, and I had missed one of them. So I had the same thing happen to me, which I thought was rather funny.

And the guys who threw me out in the street remembered the Mingus thing. Ultimately, I had a screening of the film for the sanitation department. So I'm kind of familiar with the laws. And what they do is, they load up one garbage truck full of stuff, and then they split. And everything else inside that remains in the apartment is declared legal junk. So what they always do when there's a lot of stuff like in the Mingus loft, they take all the shit and put it in the truck so he can reclaim that [later]. And then all the good stuff they leave inside, and they steal it, sell it, or whatever.

I don't specifically know what happened to his stuff except that we went down the next day and got some stuff in Mike's truck.

GOODMAN: Yeah, just stuff they had hauled away.

REICHMAN: Yeah, also he had moved out the really important stuff a couple of nights before. But he still had a lot of stuff. I don't think he had a piano there. But I'm not sure. I mean, on the night of the eviction.

Sy Johnson on the Eviction

Sy began by telling about meeting Mingus in the street during the years after he had quit the band at the Showplace in 1960, and then he talked about the eviction and the man's health.

· · ·

JOHNSON: Yeah, he was wearing a hat. And he would be strolling around on Third Avenue and we would chat. He would keep saying, "The city's trying to kill me, man" or "The government is after me. The government is trying to fuck me up, man. I'm trying to make a school and teach young

kids how to play jazz, and they are doing nothing but fucking me up."
And he was right, they were.

GOODMAN: Do you know anything about that? What was all that
business about the [Great Jones Street] loft?

JOHNSON: Well, I know what finally closed it down. It was the building
department. He had replaced all the flooring in that loft and spent about a
thousand dollars putting a new floor in and trying to get it up to building
code standards. But they evicted him and said it was not fit for the use he
wanted to put it to. That was just a bureaucratic thing. I mean, they were
just out to get him. I suppose some official in the city administration
imagined sort of a Fagan turning out jazz musicians and drug addicts on
the street, and all kinds of creepy people scratching themselves would go
out on the street and infect the city, you know.

So in a righteous attempt to save the city from this, they closed the
whole thing down. Even though that's the kind of thing that creative
people have to contend with anyway, but Mingus was such a frightening
figure, and so misunderstood, largely through his own efforts, that people
were scared.

GOODMAN: You know, he opens himself up to this.

JOHNSON: Right. He's paranoid and suspicious and all, and he doesn't
help his own cause in any way. So I would see him occasionally at the
Village Vanguard, go down and hear him play and we would chat a little.
He goes in and out of those periods frequently—where he gets defensive
and uncertain and his productivity goes down and he pretty much is
reduced to playing old music and he gets docile and fat usually. Then he
begins to get going again.

GOODMAN: Do you see it more like a cyclical thing?

JOHNSON: It's a cycle. It's a cyclical thing. I'm certain of that. He would
do that just before the big band thing started. I mean, he was coming out
of another period like that. And the [*unintelligible*] said he was just getting his momentum going at the time of the recording of the [*Children*]
album. That's one reason I think he delegated as much responsibility for
the album to Teo and myself as he did. Because he didn't have the juices
flowing in to the extent that he had. He was just building up his head of
steam again.

To some extent, the condition of Mingus is a natural phenomenon, like
the weather. Which you get from some agency or another—whether it's one

of the musicians in the band, or Sue, or a combination of both—an input into this private little network that revolves around the sun. In a sense, Mingus is just large enough to be a sun. So all these planets and various celestial bodies are revolving around Mingus but, of course, some people revolve around him to a much greater extent than I do. You know, Sue and Dannie, for example, are much more closely connected to Mingus than I am. . . .

But there's an analogy to the music: when I first started going over to Fifth Street and working with him, he had a big pot of soup going. I mean, when I say he had a pot of soup, I mean he had a pot like *this* [*gesturing*] going on the stove the whole time, simmering. He was tasting it constantly.

And he would say, "Needs another carrot." He would like chop another carrot and then go back and taste it about fifteen minutes later and say, "It needs an onion." I mean, it was a process that was going all the time. And it's the same with the music. And Sue has told me that pot of soup frequently would be on the stove in a continual state of simmer for a month. Finally he would throw two-thirds of it away, having been sampling it, adding water to it and adding things to it all the time. It was always in a state of becoming something. And the music is frequently like that.

The other thing—now he's on a health food kick. You know, in a typical gargantuan way, he ordered a whole bagful of health food carrots which turned out to be twenty-five pounds of carrots or something, eighteen dollars the bill came to for the carrots. He called Sue, "What am I doing to do with all those carrots?" But anyway, he constantly has that bowl from his juicer-blender half full of something, all the time. He's always walking over to it, he looks into it, peers into it and says, "It needs another apple." And he's telling Sue that he's going to lose a lot of weight because he's eating nothing but health food.

GOODMAN: He's worried about his health now.

JOHNSON: Yeah, well, usually it's about his health. And he eats enough to stock a small vegetable store in raw vegetables every day. *But he also eats everything else.*

GOODMAN: Yes, I noticed that the other night.

JOHNSON: So in addition to all this, which is taking care of his health, then he eats because he's hungry. He likes to go to an Italian restaurant and order everything he sees walk by the table. "What's that? Well, why don't you bring some of that to the table?" So he has gargantuan appetites and abilities. There's nothing about Mingus that's small in any sense of the word. Have you ever seen him when he was skinny? When he was lifting weights?

GOODMAN: No. I saw him when he was thinner than he is now. I've never seen him when he was skinny.

JOHNSON: Oh, there was a time he walked into a club and I didn't even know him. He walked in and was so compact, and so small—he's not a tall man really. He looked like, [*pause*] it's hard to imagine, he looked like the stew that he boiled for ten days and skimmed all the fat off and what was left was just nothing but meat and muscle. He was fantastic and so compact. The bulk of him had simply disappeared. I think he said he weighed 185 pounds at that time. That must be 125 pounds less than he weighs now when there's another person grafted onto him, you know, in a sense. He was small, compact, and hard. Like a very large vegetable, or something like that, that had this hard kernel in the middle and all this stuff around a hard core. It's all just extra; the nut is still in there, you know.

GOODMAN: People tell me he's happier when he is fat. He gets very irritable and nervous when he's thin.

JOHNSON: He can't get much more irritable and nervous than he is when he's fat. He is the way he is. He probably is more expansive when he's not on a rigid regimen of some kind. I mean, he's not naturally given to discipline in the sense of lifting weights every day and all that. That isn't his natural way of living, and so he's probably more uptight than he would be normally.

NOTES

1. You can see Reichman's 1968 fifty-eight minute film, "Charles Mingus," posted by Rick Stolk, Dec. 20, 2010, www.youtube.com/watch?v=VKuwFVDmt5I.

2. Gene Santoro, *Myself When I Am Real: The Life and Music of Charles Mingus* (New York: Oxford, 2000), 256–57; Brian Priestly, *Mingus: A Critical Biography* (New York: Da Capo, 1982), 169–73. The interview with Hentoff appeared as Nat Hentoff, "Mingus: 'I Thought I Was Finished,'" *New York Times,* Jan. 30, 1972.

3. The quote comes from a bio [undated] of filmmaker Lech Kowalski, who was much influenced by Reichman. See www.lechkowalski.com/kowalski_bio.html.

11 Mingus Women

"They won't admit it, but the women got all the money, man."

Lately there seems to be a growing consciousness, among jazz scholars at least, of the highly sexist, macho culture of jazz—in everything from gross "hypermasculinist" talk to the dearth of women in jazz bands.[1] That said, the history of jazz as a mostly male art is what it is, and bringing a new, liberalized cultural awareness to the table—a good thing—cannot change how the music's creators have historically asserted themselves, both on-stage and off.

Everything about Mingus's upbringing created and reinforced his macho attitudes about sex and women. His feelings about women also related to his thoughts about race, protest, and money. As I've said earlier, he was a consummate romantic, a melodramatic one at that, who had to have women in his life constantly, sex twice a day (he said), and total openness and honesty from a partner. You hear the evidence in these conversations.

Mingus also loved to reminisce about women. He begins here with one from his younger days, when he and Buddy Collette had just started to play together: Mary Campbell, who is briefly mentioned in chapter 2. May Libby, who comes up later in this chapter, was also heiress to a soup fortune. I don't want to speculate about what that pattern of attraction means.

. . .

MINGUS: During my younger days—I must have been about sixteen or seventeen, and she's in her twenties—I met a broad named Mary Campbell. Me and Buddy Collette, and Oscar Bradley [on] drums, Spaulding Givens [piano], John Anderson, trumpet player, Britt Woodman [on] trombone—we had a group, played in a hotel, and during intermission I'd go down the hotel halls to find a room with a piano in it. Went in to play, and she was walking by—almost made her on sight [*laughter*], almost got her to back my bands and everything. This is with the piano, I didn't say a word. She's talking with me and I'm playing the piano, man [*laughs*]. Gotta get a little sex in this [book], can't do without sex.

GOODMAN: We're gonna have a whole sex section there or something—

MINGUS: Well, this is the sex section. It was really nice. But she was very helpful; to begin with, the conversation was about what she could probably do through her family, contacts. I said this is no pickup group, she should come down and hear it.

I talked fast but not a lot. I'm pretty handicapped now for talking, but in those days I had the gift of gab, a hell of an imagination about life eternal—I knew I was going to heaven—not heaven, but I knew there was life eternal, that I'd never die, and that's what I was pushing to her. I'd always talk that to most girls, even the whores, and that would amaze them, man, to hear this kind of conversation from a funny black guy.

GOODMAN: That's the secret of your charm? This reminds me of the party scenes in the *Underdog* book—and we should talk about why the young white chicks keep coming on to the black musicians.

MINGUS: Well, let me call it this way: they don't come on no more. It's funny that my drummer—you and I got to do an interview with him because it would help in the history of my life, 'cause he can talk about that better than I can. I ought to go get him now, really.

GOODMAN: We'll get him later.

MINGUS: Just the other night Dannie was saying, "Man, where are all the girls?" And it's funny, we notice that the rock bands draw [different] girls. They draw the ones who walk up to get your autograph or pull on your clothes, but they don't draw the ballin' chicks. There were very serious romances in this band I used to have, very serious romances, man. Each one in its own was the greatest thing ever happened because I've always been aware of—I don't say always, I'm not as aware now as when I was younger—but to watch yourself weave a little net, that has to be quick—

GOODMAN: Ah, you bastard.

MINGUS: You got to be quicker because you're not white. If you're white you're always surrounded by girls. So, you've got to cut everything she's heard before. Tell interesting stories about whatever you tell her. And my thing was always the Bible. Always got into the Bible and religion. How about that? I preached to 'em [*laughter*], telling 'em how to live right.

Yeah, Mary Campbell is probably one of the most beautiful women I've seen, and in my day we were taught in those hotels not ever to look at a white person, always look down, look at the floor. The hotel didn't tell you, the musicians told you, the guys who were older and wanted a job, didn't want to get fired with some young negro bass player making eyes at a white woman.

And so when she came in the room, I just acknowledged her and went back to my playing, which wasn't as good until I got my sexual urge to play for her. Before that I was playing for God, or I thought I was. The tunes I wrote were to the Immaculate, to God, to the Master Wife. But when a woman came to the door, I hadn't been out with a human being, and I would look at her from the side of my eyes and try to figure out what kind of life she's been living.

. . .

There's a famous story, or set of stories, about Mingus in Tijuana, drinking tequila with Dannie and screwing multitudes of women (the numbers varied with each telling). Except for the *Underdog* versions, I had not heard any of this in 1972, so I asked him about it.

. . .

GOODMAN: How did you get the Tijuana thing going?

MINGUS: Every time I would go anywhere in California, I'd go to Tijuana, 'cause I imagine if there's something missing in your life, you go there and check it out—and get yourself together. And my drummer, he felt the same way. I didn't have no wife, was single then. Let me see, something made me do something very strange.

This second time we went I had a limousine, and we started from California. I put my man, my drummer Dannie, in the back and put a chauffeur cap on. And we got a police escort from San Diego. We'd stop, I'd go in and buy him things, he had his turban on, you know. This is a beautiful story, man.

Niggers driving a Cadillac in, you're immediately suspected of narcotics—especially the kind I had—had a police sireen [siren] on it. The one I got was a judge's car: he had ordered it and he didn't pick it up, then he passed. And they told me they would give me a deal, so I bought this car. It had a sireen and a red light that flashed in the back, and in fact I used it once and the cop stopped me, so I knew it was a bad light: "What? Are you carrying guns? Who are you?" But I didn't have my chauffeur cap on, I had it in the back window, so I learned to put the cap on.

So I'm with Dannie and I say, "Let's have a ball, man." And I laid the turban on him. He's always sharp. I don't dress sharp: I wear Levis to let the white man know that I'm protesting against this society until my people are free. That's before Martin Luther King came up with it, and I've always been like that. In night clubs I always dressed in dirty clothes. But I'm changing now, I'm gonna get very hip.

Anyway, Dannie thinks it's a good idea. And all along people say, "Who's that? Who's that?" With the cap on, I'm playing the sharp chauffeur. Didn't use the siren. If necessary I would. But I was sharp, baby, the sharp chauffeur.

We'd walk in someplace and they'd ask "Who is he?" and I say, "Prince Amamingo from Africa. I'm the only one who can interpret the language."

I lay it on you, man, me and Dannie would talk: "Summa coola cow."

"N'goo koo?"

"Sing geelavah."

"Five dolla."

"Oh, five dolla? Soong moongolah."

I say, "Look, man, he wants to know, can he get that girl for five dollars?"

"No, no, she's not a whore, she's just a dancer."

But I'm skipping something, man. Going in, I set the thing up so that when we came out they escorted us out through the customs—in *and* out. He was a prince and he never spoke one word of English in there. So they got this African prince—and this Dannie Richmond he is a sharp mother-fucker, man. He knows how to dress, and with that turban he looked like a cat trying to be an Americanized prince. Legs crossed, sitting in that car, baby. We had six broads that would dance for him, and I made them all with Sue [apparently on another trip!].

First of all now, I carried the money. If he wants money he has to come to me. He had some, but I had to handle the money because I was the bodyguard too. So, fuck 'em, man, he say, "I want a girl," and I say to him, "You can't have her here."

"Ong soomuckalah, no good." I'd say enough English so that they would guess what we were saying. So we cut out to a place in the hotel, and the prince he wanted some more, and we got some more.

Everyone came to our room. The scene in the book where I came with the broads was years before that, but this scene I didn't put in that book, it's not in there. Dannie Richmond'll tell you the same way, man, because I just put the two things together. With my broad [Sue] we didn't do twenty-four,

I did twenty-four with Dannie. And Dannie was so polite. After I did about twenty, he finally found two girls he liked—we was having an orgy in other words—and he said, "Look, Mingus, I'm gonna split."

"What do you mean you're gonna split? We got all these broads, man."

Listen, the police came up, and I was giving out hundred-dollar bills. I say, "Ding, baby, we having a party, you want to come in or you want to go? Here's a hundred dollars, you go."

They say, "We go, we go, baby."

I say, "I don't want to go to your jail, your jail stink, man. I don't want to stay in your jail overnight. All we want is some pussy."

"You don't want no marijuana?"

"Fuck marijuana, man, all I want is some tequila and pussy."

"Pussy and tequila nice, no marijuana, no dopey."

"No dopey, baby. Just pussy."

See, I rented a suite, the best they had, and the police were wondering where all the hundred bills were coming from. That was my thing—I would bust hundred-dollar bills to get recognition, to get respect, 'cause, see, when I first went there I couldn't get the good pussy, the fine broads. You'd get the sailor stuff. They give you twenty-dollar bills. What is that shit? I want a fine broad! I know a fine broad when I see one.

So the pimp thinks, "Here's a bad motherfucker, dealing hundred-dollar bills in front of us."

So he says, dig this shit, "Look, Mingus, don't you know we could kill you? You down here in the fucking whore neighborhood. We could kill you and take all your money."

I say, "Man, did you see what they did to Watts? You fuck with me, they'll come in here and burn your place down—it's all wood shacks—in five minutes. That's my men, they'll burn your shit down in five minutes. All I got to do is snap my finger and one of my men is watching me. You think I come down here alone with this much money flashing like this? I ain't alone, baby, I got an army with me, right here."

I'm crazy, but I had a lot of fun, me and Dannie, man. But I learned something, man, and I'll tell you real quick—about lock picking. I left my keys in the car, and I told the cop I was locked out, gave him a dollar or two, and [told him] everything was in there, clothes and all.

He says, "I can't open it, but you turn your back and I'll find out how to open it."

I turned my back—and just that quick, man—he had to do it, so I know cops got keys. Did I tell you about my apartment? Anything they want to open, even probably a safe deposit box.

GOODMAN: They've got keys to a lot of things. That's a funny story, man.

MINGUS: Anyway, let's see now. We'd do things like this: always protesting—I'm not saying I didn't suck no pussy. I dig it, but I didn't then, especially no whore's pussy, but the girls would be dancing, and Tijuana's very open . . .

GOODMAN: What time are you talking about? The last time?

MINGUS: This is 1972, so it's . . . 1962–63.

GOODMAN: Not true anymore, is it?

MINGUS: When I went with Sue it was a little closed up. But they know me there now, man. I come in the gate, and they say "Clean it up," probably because I'm with a broad. Next time I'll go in disguise and check it out because it can't be that closed up, man. It's just moved somewhere else, but it used to be all over town. You'd go right down in the heart of Tijuana and we'd go to this restaurant where they had the finest dancers—I mean bad, baby, bad. *Playboy*'d have trouble with this club. In fact, one broad I could tell I could have her without the money, one of the dancers. They weren't all whores.

Now, what did I want to tell you? Oh, good point. Oh yeah, we went back to see the girl dance. And she come up to the rail, pull her dress up, pussy hair, titties bent out—and all these young college kids would kiss it. And I guess that's all right but they was doing it up right there for free while the others was waiting to pay to do it. I wanted to come, you know, to fuck her but not behind the cat kissing her. You want to make money, you could blackmail their families: "I've got a picture of your son kissing Mexican pussy—in public." You want to make some bread? [*Laughter.*]

So me and Dannie got a thing going to the boss and said, "Look, they all *kiss-kiss*, right? We want *hanh!*" And we had every Mexican in the place doing it. With the elbow, the Italian thing [*laughs*]. So I had to get Dannie, 'cause he's my prince, you know, and he don't talk—still in the prince disguise, never came out—he talked to the Mexican man and he said, "Me no likee kissee-kissee pussy. Me want hochee-hochee."

So this cat goes around saying, "The prince, the prince, everything for the prince." I could see the people in there, sailors, everybody, they'd look at Dannie and they really couldn't tell: "These niggers are pulling some shit here."

I say, "No, baby, there ain't no shit. Just you and me and this whole place will go if you fuck with my prince."

'Cause they thought I had some iron, and you could get some iron in Mexico, but I didn't have no iron. But I could have had everything: hand grenades, pistols, machine guns. That's why I said, "Don't fuck with my prince." If a woman would walk up close, the waiter got in and said, "No, no, take her away, nobody comes near the prince."

Ooh, it was beautiful. We set it up so that everybody in the joint would be a bodyguard, not just [for me] but Dannie too, nobody got to him, and they knew he had all that money, or at least they knew it had to come from somewhere, but nobody knew who had it: we would get together and come up with some hundred-dollar bills. Man, the first few bills they said, "Wait a minute, man, this is counterfeit. What are you doing to us? You know we don't see that kind of money all the time."

I say, "Well then, we won't pay for the drinks. That's all we got. We'll find somebody who'll take them, you don't pull that shit on us." They were worried about the bills.

They don't know that I took my insurance money, saved that shit up and just blew it all at once. See, I was in an accident—the one where this motherfucker didn't take this cartilage out of my knee—and I [got some money from it and] just decided to live like a rich white man for one time. I wanted to see what it would be like, you know. You can't blame me, man.

GOODMAN: Blame you? I want to do it.

MINGUS: And I think I outdid him, especially with that. . . . See, it's a little different: anybody can have money, be rich, but when you're with somebody that's royalty, from another country, that's another feeling, man. He didn't talk no English and *oooh* those girls loved him, baby. And he finally found two. This cat sure liked titty—he's a *Playboy* boy—'cause I noticed the two he walked out with had great big titties [*laughter*]. Yeah, Dannie's a lover.

So you clear that up in the book: I wasn't just braggin', man. I had twenty-four true and I masturbated later 'cause my glands is just like that. I didn't feel love. But Dannie had seventeen, and he ran out of money. What I mean by that, I gave him advances but we'd have had to have a whole lot of jobs before I could give him any more. And we weren't booked after that: that's what we were getting drugged about. He's like my brother: any time I got some extra money, no matter how I got it, I'd say, "Come on Dannie, let's go." Five hundred dollars, whatever, I don't care where we working. He'd pay me back with his love. No, that's my brother.

Of course we fucked, man, but we don't think that's wrong. We felt maybe if we were married or something, maybe it would be wrong to go to Tijuana fucking without your wife, but we never felt we were doing anything wrong. And especially we felt we were helping to free our people that way. It may sound funny, but I been to Tijuana with the Mexicans walking around looking down on you, man.

So I say, "I'm going to give these cats another dose. How about an African nigger—one with a turban on, motherfucker?"

And I made those motherfuckers bow, man, and they bowed not just to money but to the superiority of another tribe. "He ain't no ex-slave, he don't talk that shit language, what you say how you feel about me. I may talk like that but I [also] talk to him a little bit in his language." And I learned that if you speak another language in this country, you're free.

. . .

The discussion about women continued, and I told him a little about why I had moved out of New York—the violence, drugs, expense of schooling, the typical litany of charges that expats were coming up with in the 1970s.

This led him to a discourse on the pill and "women's lib"; then we got into the subject of Mingus's legendary attraction to women with money, that is, to young women from old-money families; then it was on to Sue, then Teddy Charles and his conquests. Mingus would rather talk about women than just about anything.

. . .

MINGUS: See, New York has a tendency to exaggerate everything. You go to Europe, and you see a little pussy in a film where they got pornography, you know, maybe two at most. But if pornography's legal in America, then every theater's got it, I mean super-pornography. My kids deserve a chance for more than that shit. Because when that shit's around, all the freaks in the world are walking the streets and the kids don't stand a chance, man. My kids look alright, better than most kids I see. How many of the kids are supposed to have a chance, man? If they don't get it, I got to find out why.

That's the society I'm looking for. That's my Mafia. In the other one they'd kill the kids if the daddy did something wrong. In mine, I kill the daddy if the daddy do something wrong. Not the kids, 'cause if the daddy do something wrong, it hurts the kids. That's the guy that should go down, not the kid, man—the kid is the future.

If the birds can have babies and get along, if we could learn how to do that, there must be something right about it. The pill's blowing it anyway, man—nothing to worry about now, the pill's going to cover it, 'cause all the mothers are giving their daughters the pill at twelve years, fourteen years old. The rich people are going to have babies when they want to; the poor people gonna blow their glands. They'll be out fucking and won't have nothing left.

GOODMAN: They can't get the pills to the poor people; there's no money for that. I love New York City but I still want to throw up on every street corner.

MINGUS: I feel the same way. Let me ask you something. How would you feel if you came home with your wife, and your daughter's sixteen, maybe seventeen, and she's got a man sleeping over? How would you feel about that? Would you let her do it?

GOODMAN: I don't know, but I think, no, I would not.

MINGUS: Here's why I wouldn't. Let me tell you where I'm at. Now here's a mother, her daughter's probably going with the pill since she's fourteen. Well, so what? I saw kids shooting dope at fourteen, but, dig, here's what you do. I say: don't give her the pill; tell her, go to a doctor and get a prescription, and tell her this, most important, that people on earth are very funny—they believe in love and they look for love. And especially girls, they get tricked. A guy will tell her he loves her to get her body only. And he goes to bed with her, and then he's through. So in case she may be fooled into thinking he loves her and he's gone, here's the pill—in case. Not that she's going to have a baby the first time she knew the guy loved her, but if she wants to have a baby and she knows she's safe and she's loved, don't take the pill.

Well, mama didn't do that. Mama just said, "Here, darling, here's your pill." That's some weird shit, beyond me, man. If it's women's lib, I hope the other women are happy, the rich ones who dig inheriting their husbands' money, who really run this society. I hope they can cope with them kind of women, 'cause that's what they're raising with women's lib. That's some weird shit.

If it ever happened to me, I'm not sure what I'd do. My position, you know, with my stepdaughter, I would be trying to raise the kid to look for love. Plus, get an education first. And it might even be better if she slept out in the park and made love a few times before mama said, "Come on home and lay in bed." If he loved her and asked to marry her, said he loved her, then they could do that sometimes and sleep over there—with a board between them like in the olden days, right?—but he didn't even say that. He was just her boyfriend.

So I'm saying that if that's being lib—especially when women's lib is so lib already . . . anyway, the men in America are just the guards of rich women's money, the bodyguards of the women who own the money. Since I was seventeen years old I knew that—aside from Peggy Hitchcock telling me.[2]

She says, "I know gangsters; I know rich men; I know Miles Davis; I know you, Mingus; I know Allen Eager; but I know one thing: that we, that is, my mother, is the boss bitch of this country, she and about seven other women. If she don't like that guy over there, she says, 'Move him over this way so I can see a little clearer,' and somehow he'll move over that way and we can all see clearer."

The world's richest women in America were listed in this one book, and a woman named May Libby wasn't listed. So she wrote a letter protesting that [so-and-so] may have the money, but we have the class. [She was] from Massachusetts. "We didn't work for this, we were born with this." I read this in an article. When I went to play at Smith College, the president of the class was named May Libby. The daughter was the one who wrote the letter. Ain't that a bitch? I'm eating this soup and tomato juice, and they bought that [company] just to keep life interesting, not to make a living. Eighteen billion dollars.

Peggy was born with three million—that was her thing. Each birthday—I'll tell you the Hitchcock side, not the Mellon side—she got another million. This is for taxes.

Finally, she married a nut, the guy who owns the *East Village Other* [newspaper]. That's my broad, man, that's my broad. She was in a car with Miles and me at Newport once, and I didn't know who she was. But Miles did and was putting her on, acting the pimp.

An attorney later told me how stupid I was, not to know who the mother was. "You don't know who the Hitchcocks are?" I didn't know who they are. "She's a Mellon."

I said, "What the fuck is that, a watermelon? Maybe she owns watermelons?"

He says, "No, man, she's the Mellon family, all the steel in Pittsburgh." "Well, ain't that a bitch."

And I wouldn't kiss her 'cause I thought she's a whore. I said, "If you stop your trade and be my woman, I'll kiss you, because you out sucking them dicks every night." [*Laughs.*] I said, "Jazz is so big that you don't need to sell yourself no more, baby. I can make it. We can take a little money you got already and start a record company, a publishing firm and make it ourselves. You don't need to sell your pussy no more."

And she didn't say anything but "Yes, Mingus? Yes?" Dirty bitch, dirty bitch [*laughing*]. She really got me there.

But one thing she can't deny, man, she knew one motherfucker who dug her, and I dug her so much. I gave her a charm bracelet for friendship—nothing on it—then I gave her a telephone and ring charm 'cause I had a thing going where if I couldn't say anything good, I'd just say "ding"—meaning, I'm thinking about you—and hang up. I'm not saying she got every message, but I gave her a couple of things. "I'm gonna give you the last charm"—finally she put my pieces on when I found she was rich—so I was gonna give her a tenor saxophone, which meant Allen Eager. I would give her that and say goodbye, your farewell present, you know.

But anyway, I got with Sue as her husband-to-be, and we [Sue and I] couldn't say a word to each other, man. So if you print that thing about the daughter and the pill, that's what's happening now. This women's lib thing is so weird, man, I can't believe it. That's what led my mind back to Peggy. Even though she was women's lib, she would discuss it with me, we could talk about it.

GOODMAN: I'm hung up with my wife, and we can't talk about some of these things.

MINGUS: They ain't telling the truth, man, because, see, the point is this: I admit that it seems like it's a man's world, but it really ain't 'cause it's a woman's world. They won't admit it, but the women got all the money, man. The men walk around, "My woman's ass is home with the family." And, *ugggh*, he has a heart attack. And the wife inherits some money 'cause he has worked his ass off all his life.

GOODMAN: They outlive the men anyway.

MINGUS: That's why though, man. If the men laid back, it'd be cool.

Well, how's the daughter feel about me? See, and her mother never invites me to spend the night, you dig? I don't sleep at the mother's house. But the mother can invite in a boy to sleep with her daughter. That makes it look kind of weird to me, man.

The reason I was telling you that story is that I'm just wondering if I didn't make a mistake . . . because at that point whether Peggy meant it or not, she said, "Why is it that you and I can talk? And why is that you feel you gotta make a million dollars before you can ask me to marry you?"

And this was something I never knew, man. Having been raised to be a pimp, I thought, I [have to] rely on myself. So I know if I had it made, then she would know I loved her. And man, you know how many years I blew on that? Twenty years. But I didn't blow 'em because when they blew me in 1965—see, I saw a way, you know, that life could become commercial.

Although after I done some wrong things, like joined with a pimp and got some money, I saw what I had and went complete legit and made a million dollars—by transferring my corporation, having three of them going, even when I was with the Gallo brothers.

I had a publishing company and a record company. Everything I gave my ex-wife Celia—she's a millionaire right now, over a millionaire. She has Fantasy Records. I gave her all my [rights], couldn't afford to keep 'em so I gave her everything I had. Her exact words when I talked to her last: "You think I'd cheat you now, with royalties? When I was poor I didn't cheat and you know it, so you think I'd cheat you when I'm a millionaire?"

I said, I don't know, but I think maybe her company might cheat. Because I'm being cheated. The old Massey Hall tapes with Charlie Parker, Dizzy Gillespie. . . . See Fantasy is collecting my money—they're not even supposed to be—collecting my money in Europe . . . And Sue's just finding all this stuff out.

They don't mean to . . . [*fumbling a little here*]—see, I can't count nails, so I was always with a woman who could count nails. Sue don't do that either. So I left my wife, which I shouldn't have, I should have just went and made love to Sue and had a ball. That's all she wanted. But I needed somebody to keep my business going who wasn't drawing a salary. 'Cause they [Fantasy, Celia] knew that if it ever happened, that if I left her, she'd have the company, 'cause I wouldn't take it—we've got kids, and Celia would be a millionaire, have it all. And I'd start again, that's what I've always done.

But see, I blew what I was doing. I told Peggy I'd be back in a year, and I was going to make it in a year, but something happened that I couldn't control. Then I met Sue and I didn't want to go back after that, even though it seemed like Peggy did. And dig this: my ex-wife introduced her [Peggy] to the guy she married—and you know what kind of guy she married? This guy came in—see, I used to dress my ex-wife like Peggy [dressed], like Jackie Kennedy, you know how they dress, Saks Fifth Avenue clothes and shit, have them made a certain way—and so Celia's wearing one of them damn suits one night, she went to some party where artist people were at—and this guy walked in with Levis and sandals on and says, "You're a rich girl, I need you to back my newspaper, I'm going broke." She says, "You think I'm rich? I'll show you a rich girl—right over there, Peggy Hitchcock."

"She's rich? Then I want her."

And he walked over and said, "Hey, baby, you rich?"

"Well, yeah."

"Well, I want to marry you." And they got married—not that quick but soon.

Before I left Rusty [Celia], I was getting tired, and I met Judy—I mean, I met Sue—and I was trying to meditate and feel what I was going to play. Me and Peggy had a communication, and I went out with this broad [Sue] because I thought maybe I could get communication with her—'cause I felt like fucking in other words, and I had stopped fucking, man. I have to fuck every day, and I'm not trying to brag, but *Playboy* should write about guys like me. I've got to come twice a day or something's wrong, it hurts, my balls swell up. So that means I gotta jack off if I don't [fuck].

So I even prayed, "Dear God, everybody thinks I'm a bad guy, but I know I'm not, I've been loving purely, this new woman I'm in love with her, and we fuckin' so I hope we can tie in our minds." There was always hope [with Celia] it would be that way, yet I turned my wife off, I wouldn't fuck her. She wanted me to move out, but then she found she wasn't happy that way.

Then finally I told an English girl about it: I brought Sue by and introduced her, told her I was in love. The girl said, "You're not in love." She finally got married, very happy, living in England. And she said, "When you come to England, go fishing in our lake. And if you like to shoot, we've got a little shotgun; come and kill the pike in our lake—the pike eat up all the healthy fish." So I assume she must have a little room to have a lake.

MINGUS: You know, if Sue and I don't make it, it means that every black man that meets a white woman, they're all whores. All I know is black guys with white whores. Only good marriage I know is Lena Horne and her husband [Lennie Hayton]—and their bass player said she thinks, "I'm not his whore, but I am his musical whore." What's his name? Lennie somebody, married her.

Dorothy Dandridge, who killed herself—and I tell you where the book is at, man—she came to New York and an agent told the prostitute I was going with, or that I knew, "I know you're German but (he knew she liked girls), how about going with a colored girl?"

And she said, "All depends who she is." She figures going with a black man who is clean as I am and she'll be all right, you dig? But that's how she got turned on because she was a prejudiced white woman. I'm serious, man. That's how she turned on: Nazi, stone Nazi. So she's telling me, "Charles, you know who she was? Dorothy Dandridge."

So they met together to see if they would like each other. You know who the agent was? Joe Glaser. Joe wanted to sit not even in the room with the girls: he sits in the toilet with the mirror on the door open, they're on the bed sucking and fucking, and he jacks off. He didn't even want to touch it. You know what's so funny, man?

That case was in the book exactly the way I just said it, with Diane and Donna, Donna Lee. That was Donna Lee, Joe Glaser, and Dorothy Dandridge. Nobody believes that shit. Dorothy Dandridge wasn't my woman, but I was so shocked because I knew Dorothy Dandrige as a kid. Lee-Marie, that's Mary Ellen. Mary Ellen would have made Dorothy Dandridge and Lena Horne both look like homosexuals. Man, if you saw Mary Ellen`... Do you know who the white girl was who looked like Donna Lee and Lee-Marie together?[3]

GOODMAN: The college girl at the end [of *Underdog*]?

MINGUS: Yeah, that's Susan Scott, [of] Scott's toilet paper. Fuck it, print it, I don't care. But that broad had a color of olive, suntan all the time, she was tall, which never bothered me too much (lotta guys ashamed of a tall broad). Long legs, she had good breasts, everything, baby, she was bad. She used to go with a lesbian-type girl, you'll meet her, named Ann McIntosh.

And they both came to my party, the party was for real, but that party [in the book] is mixed with two things: a scene at the Bandbox (next to Birdland where Art Tatum was playing), a party I had with Nat Hentoff and some guys when I was with my ex-wife; and then it was mixed with a party I had when I was living with Donna Lee and a girl named Diane at 8 East Seventy-sixth Street. Diane had just left me and so I brought 'em over, had a house full of lesbians, they were dancing together, didn't think nobody was there but each other.

Then I brought this schoolgirl lesbian [McIntosh] in with this rich girl [Scott] and later found she's richer. This Scott girl tells me, "Look, she's richer than we are, if you just want my money. I thought you wanted me."

"Well, then it's obvious: of course I wanted you . . ." It's just like that scene [in *Underdog*]. Teddy Charles was there, ask Teddy.

GOODMAN: Well, the Teddy Charles bit comes off very well there.

MINGUS: [*Imitating:*] "My yacht, my yacht, my yacht . . . My daddy's got an eighty-foot . . ." I said, "Ding, baby, let's dance." When I heard him [Teddy] say, "Well, that's a thousand dollars a foot," and she says,

"Yes, my father has that" and when she said, "Schooner," *ooowee!* [*Laughter.*]

But then I looked at her, and she's like a board, stiff. There's a thing in an old dance, where you put your knuckle in the back on the spine, all the pimps know it—massage while you're dancing—she's like, I drop my arm to the side, dancing with no arm, and then I put it on her shoulder, and she was all over me.

And that was for money but, man, the broad was something else, man. Teddy was there. In fact, just recently I found out who his attorney was, somebody gave me a message, and he called me and he hasn't called back yet. Teddy's lost a lot of money, and he's thinking about coming back to music. He's a great vibe player, ain't nobody better than him, believe it. Ain't nobody on earth no better'n Teddy Charles. In fact, on the four hammers, he cuts everybody. Red Norvo was the best, but Teddy cuts him, man.

GOODMAN: The Debut record he did with you and Miles—in fact they did "Nature Boy."

MINGUS: I got Miles out of jail, ask my wife, she's a millionaire—she got Monk out of jail, she. . . . It was Miles's date, and he hasn't fulfilled his contract yet.

GOODMAN: It's a goddamn good record.

MINGUS: Damn right. Teddy wrote [arranged] "Nature Boy"; I wrote "Alone Together." Wrote the arrangements. We was just jammin', but that was arranged music. That's what gave Miles the idea of pedal points, my tune, "Alone Together" [*sings*]—I had Britt Woodman on trombone.

Miles said, "One chord? Fuck one chord."

I said, "Man, come on and try it." Now he's doing that only. Check it out, man. Miles used a lot of chords before that. Elvin Jones, Miles Davis, Teddy Charles. Teddy wrote the music, I wrote one. I always write one. I mean an arrangement, 'cause you know, see, when the guys write a tune, they write guitar chords, and they leave out a whole lotta things on the bottom, so you add things around it.

Teddy has always been less commercial than I was . . . and a lover of pussy. He could do something I could never do: we'd be on an elevator and he'd say to me, "See that blonde? You like it?"

And she'd smile. I say, "Yeah, she's nice." (I'd be shy.)

Teddy: "Just like the one on the photograph upstairs, what's her name? Bette Davis." And by the time the elevator's down, we talking to her.

He says, "You should come back up and see this woman, just like you, Bette Davis when she was young."

"Really?"

"Yeah, she's posing in the nude—oh, those breasts, *mmm.*" Oh, man, that fucker could do it.

There was a United Airlines pilot he used to hang out with, and they swore that any woman you brought they could hypnotize her into doing the whole house up. And they never failed.

He used to start by saying, "Damn, man, why are people so inhibited by clothes?"

He'd take his shirt off. "I bet she feels like this. Isn't it hot?" And you're not supposed to say nothing; this is your woman. You sit on the dime.

"Yeah, it's hot, to tell the truth." She looks at you a couple of times.

When it's over, man, everybody's fucking. I'm not saying I can do it, but I can get it done for you! Unbelievable, man.

When Teddy had a number—like the one on the elevator—he'd say, like, "I want to photograph you because there's big money [in that] and I know we're all poor. If I can get the right photograph into *Playboy,* that's it, for both of us. Let's go up." *Quick* too, man. "I'll show you the picture of Bette Davis, and if you don't think you look better than she does when she was young . . . and I think you look better, you're a winner."

Upstairs in five minutes, titties out: "Mingus, what do you think?"

"Well, you know what I think. They look good, but I wonder how they feel, Teddy?"

GOODMAN: Are they real, man? [*Laughter.*]

MINGUS: Any more plastic in that boob? You bet. "Can I kiss one of them?"

"Oh, no, I can't do that."

All the clothes off. Man, Teddy is the inventor of *Playboy,* man. The inventor of *Playboy,* man.

GOODMAN: Where is he? West Coast?

MINGUS: Teddy's here, man. He's got a yacht, everything he's dreamed about. His daddy passed. His daddy, he didn't even know it, his daddy owned some junk yards. So Teddy took his part and got boats, takes people out on pleasure trips—I know he gives some pleasure, baby—but . . .

GOODMAN: Does he play at all? Get him to play in your band, for Christ's sake.

MINGUS: Yeah, this big band thing. I'm gonna call his attorney and find

his address, 'cause the phone number he has, says you can't call me. . . .
See, his boat got wrecked and the insurance company collected a lot of
money on it, and he said, "Mingus, I made a mistake and put it right back
in the boat." So he's probably out on the water somewhere, 'specially in
the summertime.

Yeah, the boy's a lover. This same girl I'm talkin' about—I didn't tell
you this story, this is way before Sue, man—by the time she had her
clothes off, kissing her titties and all that shit, and she had nice tits, he
says, "Mingus, what's that thing you were telling me about that two men
can do with a woman?"

"Well, I figure to make a woman happy, they want to see a guy fucking
her while she's sucking."

She says, "Sounds all right. I never tried that."

I said, "Well, you got two dates."

Teddy says, "OK, she sucks you and I fuck her, but only from
behind—baby, I want you to bend over. Gimme the butter, where's the
butter? No Vaseline, we need some butter, baby." And he's buttering his
dick, ready for her ass, the *whole stick* [*much laughter*]. She's sucking
my dick, and he goes way over on the other side of the room and runs
up—*bappp!*

He runs up to it, and man, he's a little guy. Yeah, he hit that ass from
behind: *bappp!* "Hold still, hold still, I got it. Don't put your hands on it;
it'll get in there." And she was happy, ain't that something? A happy broad.
I shouldn't say this, man, but I don't care if you print it: to look back and
say, are all women like that? Well, all I've met were like that, man.

GOODMAN: Yeah, how do you figure?

MINGUS: Well, I put it like this: we're not trying to let them be free
sexually, because women's lib will outdo us, it'll embarrass us. If you talking
about women's lib, they'll make you sorry you ever asked for a woman who
wanted to be free. They can think up more things . . . when we got through
with this broad, she said, "Now you do this. Here's what I want *you* to do."

And Teddy is telling her things like, "Pretend this is your last chance to
be free." And we ain't high—this is sober. "Here's your chance to be free,
and you've got five minutes to live on earth, you know you're gonna die
and you're in bed with a guy: what would you like to do?"

First she says, "Well, I'd pray."

"Well, aside from that, what would you do? You got ten minutes, take
five to pray." Teddy's smart. "What are you gonna do?"

"Well, I might tell the guy . . ."

CHAPTER 11 COMMENTARY

Mingus on Pimping, from Beneath the Underdog

Pimping was a complex subject for Mingus, one which Eric Porter has covered well.[4] Mingus used pimping and its essential ambiguity, for him, as a kind of shifting rationale throughout *Underdog* for his behavior and his feelings. Women were tools to use for pleasure and profit; they were also objects of worship and distraction from his real life—creating music.

In the beginning of the book, Mingus uses the device of talking to his psychotherapist. The doctor asks him why he practiced pimping, at least for a time:

> "Well, it's true I tried to be a pimp, doctor, but I wasn't really making it 'cause I didn't enjoy the money the girls got me. . . ."
> "If you didn't want the money, what was it you wanted?"
> "Maybe just to see if I could do what the other pimps did."
> "Why?"
> "That's almost impossible to explain—how you feel when you're a kid and the king pimps come back to the neighborhood. They pose and twirl their watchchains and sport their new Cadillacs and Rollses and expensive tailored clothes. It was like the closest thing to one of our kind becoming president of the U.S.A. When a young up-and-coming man reaches out to prove himself boss pimp, it's making it. That's what it meant where I come from—proving you're a man."[5]

Later in the book, we meet Billy Bones, "the Black Prince of Pimps," elegant and tall, who "lived a kingly life, like a man on a continuous vacation with interruptions to see his florists or talk to his chef or instruct his brokers." Billy is lecturing Donna, a prostitute he sent to service a very rich john, and segues into a lecture to Mingus about the morality of pimping and playing jazz. How seriously we are to take these views is never clear, like so much of the posturing in *Underdog*, but it's good posturing:

> Those people [the very rich johns] own the backbone and some of everything else in this country—even this chump Mingus's profession, which might be said to make whores out of musicians. . . . [*ellipsis in original*] Now, Mingus, here's how to save yourself from depending on what rich punks think and critics say about jazz, true jazz, your work. By my reckoning, a good jazz musician has got to turn to pimpdom in order to be free and keep his soul straight. Jelly Roll Morton had seven girls I know of and that's the way he bought the time to write and study and incidentally got diamonds in his teeth and probably his asshole. He was saying, "White man, you hate and fight and kill for riches. I get it from fucking. Who's better?" That's what Jelly talked when we hung out, and I want you to do likewise . . .[6]

NOTES

1. See, for example, Eric Porter, *What Is This Thing Called Jazz? African American Musicians as Artists, Critics, and Activists* (Berkeley: University of California Press, 2002); and Alex Stewart, *Making the Scene: Contemporary New York City Big Band Jazz* (Berkeley: University of California Press, 2007).

2. Heiress to the Mellon fortune, Peggy Hitchcock lived a rather wild life. She was a friend of Timothy Leary's and a participant in his psychedelic experiments. Mingus also had adventures with the Leary crew, though not in drugs. Leary spoke of her as "an international jet-setter, renowned as the colorful patroness of the livelier arts and confidant of jazz musicians, race car drivers, writers, movie stars. Stylish, with a wry sense of humor, Peggy was considered the most innovative and artistic of the Andrew Mellon family. . . ." See Leary's *Flashbacks: An Autobiography* (Los Angeles: J. P. Tarcher, 1983), 126. Her father was Tommy Hitchcock, Jr.; her mother Margaret Mellon Hitchcock was the daughter of the founder of Gulf Oil. The "*East Village Other* guy" was Walter Bowert.

3. Mingus is not clear here about the names of his characters. In *Underdog*, his major loves were Donna, who was white, and Lee-Marie, who was based on his boyhood sweetheart Mary Ellen. He coalesced the two into "Donnalee," which also happens to be the name of a Charlie Parker tune. Diana (maybe based on Diane Dorynek, his onetime partner, referred to below) enters as a yet another lover.

4. Porter, *What Is This Thing Called Jazz?* 141–46.

5. *Beneath the Underdog: His World as Composed by Mingus*, ed. Nel King (New York: Alfred A. Knopf, 1971), 6.

6. *Underdog*, 267–68.

12 Mingus on Sue

"If we don't make it now, we ain't gonna make it, man."

The summer of 1972, when I got to know Sue and Charles, was a time of great stress in their relationship—which translated into arguments (one or two of which I witnessed) where nothing got resolved. Mingus was feeling rejected because of what he saw as Sue's abiding failure to communicate.

I was sympathetic and ended up being more involved in his revelations than I wanted to be. His need to talk about Sue also dominated many of our conversations in 1974; a portion of one (with Booker Tillery present) follows here.

I trusted Mingus but never fully understood his perceptions of Sue until I read *Tonight at Noon,* her extraordinary book about meeting and getting hooked on Mingus, their off-and-on relations, his crazy behavior, and the people, parties, and events they shared—until his terrible illness took hold. At that point the book transforms and becomes much more than a mere chronicle of a relationship. Sue finally opens up.

In the beginning of *Tonight at Noon,* she attributes her conflicts with Mingus and with her first husband Alberto to a somewhat petrified upbringing as a society girl in Milwaukee and an irrepressible need for self-protection. When she should have been open and accessible, Sue admits to being remote, distant, controlled, and too lofty—as in a candid passage in which Alberto complains about virtually the same behaviors as Mingus had.[1]

The assertions about Sue that he made in these interviews now have a different context, and the only reason for reporting them here is to explain a side of Mingus that few ever got to know. Angry, hurt, and deeply in love, he held nothing back. The plot always thickened. And some of the plot was very likely fictitious, as when Mingus accused Sue's husband of threatening to kill him. Even in pain he was still a great fabulist.

· · ·

MINGUS: So I'm saying, I'm still with Sue, and we ain't communicated yet, man, outside of . . .

GOODMAN: Bullshit, you've been with Sue a long time, you've gotta communicate. Somehow.

MINGUS: Well, if we don't make it now, we ain't gonna make it, man. It's a disbelief because if she's with her daughter, she can't talk to her son. She turns on and off; if she talks with her son, the daughter feels neglected. Everybody knows she's like that but why does she have to go off alone with everybody . . . to communicate?

GOODMAN: Because some people are like that. It's like a camera, you know, you focus up close and the rest is not in focus.

MINGUS: Well, they got it, man, I don't dig it. And that means to me that they haven't found the right person to go off with, to communicate with.

GOODMAN: It's just her personality, maybe.

MINGUS: No, no good. Before Sue's husband Alberto died, he said, "Mingus, you know I'm Italian, don't you? I'm not even American, I'm Italian, and you took my woman. And I'm gonna kill you in a way that you won't even know until the last minute, and you'll think it's too late but what can you do about it? Then you'll know it's me."

So I never forgot them words, man. So when she said he's dead, I said bullshit, he ain't dead—'cause if I go for that *I'm* dead. He ain't dead. I look for him in my shower. I'm prepared to find his ghost, man, because he told me, "I'm Italian, and you know what I mean." If he hadn't said that, I would believe everything she was running on me. "I'm Italian and you know what that means."

I said, "Yeah man, it means you're the Mafia." He didn't say no but he said, "You know what I mean."

She told me another story . . . I got to tell you the opening. One day there was a misunderstanding, and she says, "Charles, we probably won't have much understanding because I got to tell you something. One day I was dying. I had jaundice, and the man who was supposed to love me, I told him I was sick and I wanted to go to the hospital.

"He kept saying, 'Oh you're not sick, you're alright.'"

And she told me this thing way back in the beginning, and we used it like seeds. So it made me susceptible about anything she'd do 'cause if I say here's a woman who's dying and nobody believed it . . . So they finally took her to the hospital and they found she had jaundice and they saved her life. Well, here's the woman I love, and in some things she can't express herself. So I believed her story.

GOODMAN: Or the man was an idiot.

MINGUS: Yeah, so I went that way. Well, that's the way she tells it now but she made it sound—she used him as an example, but there were other times when she was misunderstood. She didn't say, like, this guy was an idiot.

. . .

The difficulties with Sue kept coming up, and Mingus mentioned them in our talks more than almost any other subject. He was—I think the right word is "obsessed"—with thoughts of Sue's betrayal, her real or imagined unwillingness to communicate, even the fact that she might be tied in with the mob. Our conversations show Mingus testing out his every suspicion and, at the same time, confessing how he loved her. The man was in great turmoil. Yet he would immediately shift gears into stories about ribald sex and pimps.

The following conversation with Booker present was in a Lower East Side bar. On several occasions I had heard talk about a slippery guy named Frank Mabry who seemed to have some sort of malign power over Mingus, or over Mingus's imagination. In real life, they had a long association, and Mabry sometimes helped Charles out of present or impending troubles.

But Mingus had tied Frank in with Sue in some surreptitious, threatening way, and a lot of what follows can be seen as Mingus's so-called paranoia speaking. The man was suspicious of many people, and who is to say whether such suspicions were without cause? Mingus often saw night where others saw dawn.

. . .

MINGUS: That football robbery movie, remember that?

GOODMAN: What? Train robbery?

MINGUS: No, about a colored guy who played the lead, Jim Brown. Check it out. Well this guy was acting on Frank Mabry's style. He was black but Frank's a light-skinned nigger. Jim Brown had no class to him, really, but he's in that Frank Mabry bag: walk in and knock cats down. He [Frank] got his jaw broke one night and it took ten guys to do it. That's what he tells me, but I don't believe his jaw's broke—Frank can't lose. He got me down by the Village Vanguard one night, says, "The Village Vanguard is out against us, Mingus."

"How do you know?"

"Well, that's where they got you and Sue that night." Six guys did jump on us when I was with Sue one night.

GOODMAN: We got to get him in the magazine.

MINGUS: Oh, definitely a lover. And he lives in a house with seventeen girls, ain't no doubt about that. Got whips and everything you'd dream about in a book—he got that covered. Plus some other houses. He's definitely a playboy.

TILLERY: You got to say this for him: he's a hell of a pimp, a hell of a pimp, and he's so fickle, don't know how—

MINGUS: [*Excited*] That's what's wrong with him, that's what's wrong with Frank. In the book I said Benny Bailey was the baddest pimp that ever lived, and that's why Frank went crazy about him. 'Cause Benny maybe had nine girls—and Frank's probably got more, but I didn't say that, so he got drugged. See, I thought he only had Margo.

TILLERY: You know what he used to do? I went into his house, y'understand, and he got the four girls there—all of 'em is his, y'understand—and just to emphasize something he told her, "Look, you do so-and-so," and "You do so-and-so," and "How much money you got?"

GOODMAN: Display of power, eh?

TILLERY: And I said, "Now, what did you call me up here for? You want to talk business with me, or are you calling me up here to show me how you giving these girls orders?" I say, "You come down to my shop, and you can see how I give orders too."

MINGUS: [*To me:*] He's got a tailor's shop, that's beautiful [*laughter*]. Come to my shop, same thing, it's your office. Put that in the book, what he said there.

You know, this guy came into the club one night—you brought him to my house, that drummer—

TILLERY: Oh, Sonny.

MINGUS: Well, Sonny had broke seven chairs on my body—[first he] went to get a butcher's knife but the chef had just put 'em away. So he came out, I happened to have a chair [in my hand] 'cause I didn't follow him but I knew what he was doing. So he saw me with a chair, picks up one himself, and I laid mine down—I didn't want to hit the cat. So he broke a chair on my body, and I don't know what it was but I didn't feel nothing. So I saw it didn't hurt the way he was doing it, so I just kept letting him break chairs on me until he stopped breaking chairs.

So Charles Rice [Mingus's friend, a martial arts man] is sitting at the bar, he came over and said, "You know, you scared the shit out of Frank Mabry."

I said, "Frank's not here."

"He was, but you scared him. He's gone home, he's practicing with chairs now."

"You trying to tell me that he's out to get me, he's practicing to get me?"

"I don't know what it is, he says he's going to practice with chairs."

A week or so later I'm invited to Frank Mabry's house, and every chair in the house is broken. He had somebody beat him with chairs—[*pause, while this sinks in*]—Booker, honest. Every chair, every chair, and everything was loose, and these were *heavy* chairs, not ballroom chairs like this. This cat had them other kind—house chairs—

TILLERY: Heavy duty—

MINGUS: Like you couldn't break 'em hardly, but the glue was all loose, to sit on one, you got to put the leg back in it [*much laughter*].

GOODMAN: Where is this great man? I want to meet him.

MINGUS: You want to meet him? Booker, I used to think this: either the Mafia is after me, when the book came out; or they had hired Frank Mabry to run me in, run me crazy; or my psychiatrist was trying to heal me. I even thought they might have hired him in this thing. Or my wife. I had to figure that nobody could do all this, and spy and find so much time to be evil with me. I mean all the time.

I came up with Sue one day, man, he [Frank] had a thing where he was wearing one of those bags on the shoulder, something like you doing now, they were all carrying these bags, and they were all tall—and all light-skinned. You hear the guy say that the most prejudiced guys in the world are all light-skinned negroes? Have you dug that?

Three that I knew were together, standing across the street and watching, they fold their arms, same old style. Plus they called and said they gonna kill Joe Gallo, which I think they're scared to do. They ain't the ones to do it. At least they said on the phone they were [going to do it], but they could be calling their brother. I ain't gonna be the one to say, "Let me see the number, let me talk to Joe Gallo."

They're cops, man, nothing but cops. Frank—he's some kind of cop.

TILLERY: He told me, "With all these kids you got, you come with me. I go to the government store"—some place in Brooklyn—"and I'll buy all your food."

MINGUS: Commissary—right. So he's a cop, man. Some kind of special cop. He's got to be, the things he gets away with, man. We went through Canada with Judy many years ago. He drove my limousine up to the gate of Canada, showed the papers. And I didn't have nothing for my bass, and I'd been through that before: you had to call the club owner where you were gonna go to work, and he [had to] sign the papers and all that; it takes hours.

Frank says, "What kind of shit is this, man? You got no papers? Look, take my passport." And he talks bad [tough] to the customs, and "See this? We're going through." And just drives through. I don't know what he showed the guy. It was crazy, man. And he and Charles Rice are together too, Booker, some kind of way. We better turn [the tape] off.

. . . I mean, middle of last week a hand comes through my window, "Here, take this, Mingus." How did he know I'm there? I might not be there, I'd be waiting for somebody else's hand [*excited*]. If the hand come in, from the top of the window—that's why I put bars in—and it's a hand full of Coca-Colas.

GOODMAN: What time did all this happen, what years?

MINGUS: It just stopped last year, ain't nothing happened this year except once I saw him on a very weird night when Sue disappeared.

We'd been having a fight that lasted for a week, and one thing she said I'll never forget: "I wonder why men like to go places and see nude women and things, and yet they never want to take their girls where there's nude men."

So Trude Heller [club owner]—she's the one that started [the trend of doing] the twist with the titties hung out, and she's got a new thing going now: she's showing the men's dicks hanging down—but not out—you can see the impression. So I ran it on Sue, you know, and she couldn't stand the joint, man. And I didn't want to fight with her.

So she disappears and comes back, and she's still acting this funny way that makes me a notorious person who would do anything, no respect, so I said, "Let's go."

And I'm about to snatch her but I don't; we're out front [of Trude Heller's], I say goodbye, and here come Frank Mabry, *zzzooop*, "Hello, Susan and Charles. Can I take you home?" And she gets in the back seat, no questions. We drive around to her house, say goodnight, and he says [to me], "I'll take you home" and I say, "I'm not going home, I'm going to talk to her."

So I get out, talk to her for a few minutes, it starts to be a fight and gets worse, and I'm talking to make things better when she starts to run across the street. And I can't run, I ain't never run after a woman in my life. Even if I could run, I'm too heavy, so I let her go and stood there thinking, "Why the fuck did she run that way that quick, and disappear?" I couldn't even see her after two or three cars. And then my heart gets broken, 'cause I think, "That's where it's at; she's going with Frank."

I walked down the same street, and there's a guy laying in the street like he's drunk, and a cab comes and picks him up. He gets in like he's, well, like he's bleeding. And kids are on the corner shaking up somebody, saying, "You bitch, you phony bitch. We got ours now, we [*unintelligible*]." I looked to see who it was, if it might be her. So I just took my knives out, 'cause she told me that the block was bad with robberies. Practiced a little bit and walked home.

[*Mingus listens to jukebox, now playing "Porkpie Hat":*] My man Bluiett playing my tune. Baritone.

I know when there's a real fight, and I wasn't even ready for a real fight, you know. Like she'd been picking this for days. I see it now, she does it every now and then, and she just disappears every now and then too. It's clearing up now, man, she's making it more obvious.

I'm serious, man. If it's been a game, I'm in the final period. . . . She plans these little [*unintelligible*] and walks away, every now and then, she just disappears and leaves me all twisted.

You know, she used to go with some cat and I said, "You tried to convince me you never been with no black man, right? And yet here you talking about a Brazilian, and he was a black Brazilian, in Paris."

I'm just trying to say where she's at. Every white girl I meet they say I'm the first black guy. Why is that? I never say you're the first white girl. It's obvious. Why do I have to be the first black guy? [*To me:*] Why do they always say that, man? What is that dumb shit? Put that in the book.

GOODMAN: That is really dumb shit. That's an old twisto on the prejudice bit, man.

MINGUS: It is, it is. "You're the first . . . and the last. I'll be true to you."

TILLERY: Mmm-hmm, yeah.

MINGUS: In fact every white girl I had, except Judy, said that. Like, "You're the first black man I ever had." In fact she was dancing one time with a cat, and I said, "There's one thing about you I like, Judy, it's that you don't care if a cat's black at all, if he's black you'll dance with him, you don't care whether he has class or no class."

I was really putting it on, 'cause these black cats—some have class, some have no class, right? I said, "You'll dance with any of 'em, 'cause they all look alike to you, *don't we?*"

She says, "Yeah, you all do," and she kept right on dancin', man. "You all look alike . . . *pretty!*" [*Laughter.*] She's crazy, man. Good chick, Judy.

TILLERY: Judy is beautiful, man.

MINGUS: It's so funny, man. You know I'm not normal, but I still got some normality left, and it's because Judy didn't tell me nothing about herself—what she would do or not do—but yet I believe everything she's doing. There's no mystery. She got a guy and calls me, "Charlie, I got the crabs. What'll I do about it?"

"How did you get 'em?"

"I don't know, some guy, I finally went to bed, you wouldn't come home, and it's a drag. I got the crabs. How do I get rid of 'em?" I forget the stuff I told her about—some purple stuff, and in ten-fifteen minutes it's all over.

MINGUS: I met a woman in Canada looks exactly like Sue, and I didn't go with her because Frank Mabry sent her. That's where I'm at. [*Mingus and Dolphy music in the background.*] .

It was a stone setup, Booker, stone setup. She had a big dinner for the whole band. McPherson was the first guy who told me about Sue, how beautiful she was, and he says, "[The Canadian] has got more soul than Sue, she's nice, she's warm. Sue's cold. And she's pretty as Sue, prettier," he said. I felt all along that McPherson, he was setting me up with Sue. I was happy with a woman who wasn't as pretty as Sue.

But she needs somebody—I need somebody.

. . . You know what McPherson said to me, man? That I had more chicks than anyone in the joint, except I wasn't balling them.

"Mingus, I just dug something about you: you enjoy just talking to broads, 'cause you know you can get 'em. And you keep us from getting 'em 'cause you can talk to 'em [but] don't want to go to bed with 'em. Why don't you be cool and become a stately gentleman, 'cause you don't want to chase broads all night, and let *us* go get some pussy?"

I say, "Man, you know every day I'm really looking for the woman I want, 'cause I must be talking to 'em wrong, but I'll keep talking till I find one that don't just want to fuck." Print that.

I'll tell you something, I'm not trying to brag [about what I said] in the book about the twenty-seven girls, but put it like this: I think any man could do that, and they didn't point out that my drummer had made seventeen and was trying to do more but he ran out of money and I didn't have any money to give him 'cause it was an advance at that. I don't want to make the white people think that I was . . . a phallic symbol to the American tribes.

I meant that the white man had forced us to look that way by saying that every nigger in the South was out to rape a white girl. Or be a Scottsboro boy. Clear that up in the book. But another thing I will say is that I do have to make love at least twice every day, either with . . . a woman who loves me, or someone else. I enjoy it. I'm not saying I'm the *best* at it; in fact, I'd like to learn how to do it better [*laughter*]. They got some good teachers, I'd go for that.

GOODMAN: There's an idea for a school, man. You should start one.

MINGUS: Why don't the girls come teach us, women's lib? I'm one of the guys who wants to learn; I don't know how to do it, but all those guys who are lovers got it. I see 'em with all the girls, it makes me jealous. [I think,] I can't do as good as he can do, I can't beat chicks up with whips and all that, get pussy willows and whip 'em on the back or tie 'em up. I know a guy got a swing he puts 'em in, a chain swing hanging up. You know about that?

GOODMAN: I've heard about it.

MINGUS: He swings them to it, and if he don't want any, he pulls the swing to the side until they go crazy and beg him to stand up and give it to them. I want a girl who'll show me how *she* wants to do it—put *me* in the swing [*much laughter*]. This is *Playboy* magazine, right? We can discuss this properly, change the names so no one and their families would be hurt—except those who know who they are. That's how I feel, man. I know I ain't too good at it, or I'd be married by now.

TILLERY: See, I think the same way you think, man.

MINGUS: Or else I gotta go home to Judy, 'cause I can't be too good at it, the way it look to me. Ain't no broad saying, "Come on, get in my Cadillac." Or, "Don't buy me no fur, daddy, here's a diamond ring." Or, "Here, take this twenty [dollar bill]. . . ."

Here's a guy last night, owns a little club, and he said, "Man, check out this four hundred dollar tie." A four hundred dollar tie?! Golden threads woven in it. He didn't tell nobody except me. He had it made [for him] with golden thread, man, and you know there's something happening or I wouldn't have asked that question. Plus he's got another little gold thing hanging over that. It was something else.

So they were talking about Dizzy Gillespie (that was how the tie thing came up) going into some club, some hotel, the Palladium or some big hotel, and Sweetback—what was his name? The guy who wrote that—

TILLERY: Melvin Van Peebles—

MINGUS: He had just got in with his shirt off, his Levis on, and barefoot. So he got in, he's sitting there. But Dizzy goes in with an ascot and a suit on, sharp, and he couldn't get in. So they're saying, what a drag that Dizzy—prominent person, and they wouldn't let him in because he didn't have a tie on.

GOODMAN: Just recently, this is?

MINGUS: Yeah, they wrote about it in all the columns.

GOODMAN: So you got to get a four hundred dollar gold tie.

MINGUS: No, I don't want that.

GOODMAN: That's terrible shit, man, who wants that?

MINGUS: No, but these guys must be doing something to them girls. I wouldn't buy no tie while my kids need school books. I'd buy some scholarship to a school. I want 'em to go to school.

But the cat must be doing something right, something I don't know how to do, man. I want one of his girls to put me in a room, put me in the swing and show me how to do that, take her whips out and whip *me* so I can go back and find me a girl like he got.

'Cause I want to send my kids to school, man. I want them to get an education. I'd do anything to get that done, man. Not anything, I won't kill nobody—but I ain't gonna run from no killer either.

TILLERY: That's my whole thing, my kids.

GOODMAN: Tell me about your kids. How old are they?

MINGUS: Eric's seven, Eric D.—for Dolphy—Mingus. And Caroline is twelve. Booker and I tried to get Columbia to advance us some money to set up a publishing company so that, you know, when I pass away, anything in my music that would continue my kids should have. We only asked for twenty thousand dollars, that's not much, especially under a contract with eight albums on it, that ain't no money. They give that to newspapers—

GOODMAN: That's an advance—

MINGUS: Advance on royalties. If they got me down for eight albums, it seems like twenty thousand dollars, that's only a regular advance on four of 'em. Only they lying, you know.

GOODMAN: Is that the deal, eight albums?

MINGUS: That's what Sue says it is. I haven't read the contract. I don't know how she got it like that: they said only two, but she said I've got it for eight. And either they come up with this advance, or when I go to Europe I'm recording with every company I come across. I'll tell 'em [*unintelligible*] if you get your book out in time.

   If they can't come up with some money so I can support my kids—I can't leave 'em anything else, the companies don't pay no royalties when you're dead, you dig? So if I have a company going, my kids can run it, and when they're dead, [their] kids can run it. When I'm dead, you dig?

· · ·

The next day Mingus and I met alone at Chick & Chock's bar near Mingus's place on East Fifth Street. He brought up the Tijuana business again, adding more details and telling me to be sure to refer to Sue as a "society lady, not to be confused with anyone I know now," and to emphasize that the whole episode was many years ago. Then he wanted to talk about some kind of abortive orgy.

   After that, it got serious.

· · ·

MINGUS: I didn't belong at no orgy. I was sacredly in love with this girl. To me, our love was sacred, and I didn't want sharing that shit with nobody. She seemed like she wanted to do it, man, but she didn't make it clear. She said, "Well, I read in your book how you used to be a pimp and all that. That's what I thought you wanted."

   But she's never committed herself to really what *she* was. We were playing guessing games, and it's all over, far as I'm concerned. Except trying to find out what the truth ever was with her.

   It's the same old paranoia shit that's [*unintelligible*], that's gonna lay on my life. So, mix me up about Sue, make me confuse this Sue I'm with now with my manager or with someone else in the past who went to Mexico with me, you know what I mean?

   . . . She must have some attitudes on that, but she won't comment. So it makes her look guilty, man. See, I wrote her a letter, and she hasn't even

FIGURE 9.   Sue Graham and Mingus, seated, talking to Sonny Rollins at Norman Mailer's fiftieth birthday party, 1973. Photo by Sy Johnson.

answered, but since I am hooked on the broad, if she did answer, we'd at least have something to talk about. The way it is now, what stops us is we have nothing to talk about because there are so many questions.

I mean doesn't she think it would affect me if a guy is saying she's Frank Mabry's old lady? I mean she must have some attitudes on that but she won't comment. So it makes her look guilty, man, to think it's not going to affect me that somebody's playing a game with me and the game is working. You saw it working [when the three of us were out the night before]. I didn't tell the people to mention his name but it's continually going back and forth.

CHAPTER 12 COMMENTARY

Sue Graham on Mingus

In 1972, when they were having their difficulties, I asked Sue to comment on Mingus's personality. It was the best analysis I had then heard of Mingus as a person, and I think it still stands as such. Her detachment about him was extraordinary. Which may be a clue as to why they had, at this point in their lives, such a difficult relationship.

. . .

SUE: Charles is not an easy person to—uhh, he is a giant of a person, really in every kind of way. A very complex person, and there is a moment where you have to look ahead and see what he's getting at and put up with things along the way that can be extremely difficult. Certainly, all his musicians know this as well as I know it. There are moments that are utterly impossible. I mean extremely difficult moments, when people are just ready to throw in the towel and say, "That's it, I can't work in these conditions," or "I can't get along this way."

Most of the people who have stuck it out with Mingus have just felt that it was worth it in the long run. Because he is a very exciting, very deep, beautiful person. And his emotional structure is a very complex one. He considers every possibility all the time. You know, everything is always possible, and his head is filled with so many alternatives and so many maybes and his imagination is so immense that, what might seem very simple to somebody else, he's looking at on more levels than you can imagine.

You know, there is a paranoia sometimes. It's in there, he certainly has had an extremely difficult time in his life, in his childhood. And then he will use any method to get reactions out of people. He does this on a personal, human level, and he does this musically. He will infuriate people, humiliate them, insult them, beg them, love them, hate them, and he gets this tremendous response from people. I mean he gets musicians playing at the top of their ability, sometimes out of sheer fury or because they are just so goddamn mad that they are going to do it.

Or out of love. It depends. He runs the gamut of emotions. He uses every technique there is on people. If it doesn't work with love, he will try threats, or violence, or humor or whatever. But he will try every single thing to get that response reaction that he wants. You know, I have seen musicians practically in tears, musicians who were never going to speak to him again, and they always come back because—

GOODMAN: Yeah, very few people seem to stay angry at him.

SUE: And then he has this huge respect, that he should have, from musicians that are [*unintelligible*]. It's a very exciting thing to play with him. But, you know, you have to be tough, you have to be able to stick it out. Because he gets people to do things that other people don't.

See, his motives are right. This is the whole thing. See, the means he uses can be outrageous. If you were to just look at the way that he does a lot of things you might say, "What the hell, this is impossible. You know, you can't deal with people on this level." But his motives are always right, and I think that's what people respect about him; and they understand that maybe he doesn't handle things the best way, but they know it's from the heart and they simply put up with it.

. . . See, what he does is, he lives out all his—most people don't live as full a life as Charles does. He is inhibited about very few things, and he lives out his feelings, he lives out his doubts, he lives out his angers. See, most of us have learned to curb certain things, to control certain things.

And [*pause*], that's partly what an artist does anyway. You know, a lot of art is simply really being a loudmouth. Saying everything, spitting it all out, getting out all your feelings, examining them—and eventually certain truths become apparent. You know, most people don't expose themselves all the time, but that's how you do find art. You know, it can be at the expense of a lot of people around you when you're doing this, but this is an artistic need.

· · ·

Things between them did not improve during the summer of '72, which Sue in 1974 referred to as the "summer of scenes, the last time we three were all together." Mingus did a European tour and returned to have a breakdown in Central Park, very briefly described here. Mingus, Sue, and I next got together in March 1974 to discuss the idea of doing a book, and Mingus, mostly silent, sat on the floor while Sue and I talked. I was trying to catch up on, among other things, their rocky relationship, but felt that was risky territory after Charles's breakdown and hospitalization, and Sue moved deftly away from the subject.

At the end of this session, we got into discussing some of the angry and humorous things Mingus had done (running after Ted Curson, hitting Jimmy Knepper, throwing down Max Gordon's door), and the situation was defused.

Never were two people more emotionally divergent than Charles and Sue. This discussion, with Charles mostly on the sidelines and Sue analyzing his problems in the third person, was an epitome of that split—but also of their respect for one another. Their love was another, private matter.

· · ·

SUE: [When Charles got back from Europe,] it was a very angry, upsetting period, and it culminated about two days after he returned from Europe, after about two months in . . . uhh, I don't know how we could describe it, Charles.

MINGUS: When I went to the hospital?

SUE: Just a breakdown, a crisis that happened in the park, and Charles went to the hospital, the same hospital [Bellevue] where he had spent about two months, two years earlier. He spent only a week, and this was partly because there was a pyromaniac in the bed next door to him who set fire to the room twice. They finally figured that whatever problem Charles was having, he was going to be safer outside the hospital than in the hospital. And then this doctor put him on a lot of medication. As had happened once before, he was about a tenth there, just really not involved with anything. He suffered, and his music suffered.

GOODMAN: Did you keep playing?

MINGUS: I kept playing.

SUE: But his hands started not reacting, he had the feeling that it was all over, that he was just too old, and I said, "Look, Duke Ellington is, what, in his seventies. I mean Charles is hardly over at fifty." And I knew it was the medication, and in fact his hands again, in the last three or four weeks, have started to come back to what they were before, as the medication got out of his system.

MINGUS: This medication caused a crust in my mouth. Either that or cigars, I don't know which.

SUE: I think it might be the cigars, Charles [*laughs*], considering the quantity. Charles smuggled in a whole box of Cuban cigars in his stomach when he came back from Europe last week.

GOODMAN: In his stomach?

SUE: Yeah, in his belt. That's one advantage of being heavy, they don't notice when you carry—are you a cigar smoker?

GOODMAN: Oh, occasionally.

MINGUS: I'll tell you a cigar story—when he [John] lit up, the way he was waving it around.

SUE: That's a great compliment [*laughs*].

GOODMAN: I enjoy it occasionally. . . . Again, [I remember] George Wein dropping some innuendos that day I talked to him—I'll put it in a delicate way—that Charles has certain problems, certain kinds of psychoanalytic difficulties, or certain things that Mingus has had in his past that can never be told. I'm wondering, "What the hell is he talking about?" When we get to that point, we have to decide whether to broach that subject in a book like this.

SUE: It might be interesting to go into it, with more explanation. This whole sense of paranoia and so forth . . . people always said Charles was [paranoid]. But the more I know Charles, the more everything becomes very understandable, if not always justifiable. But certainly you can see that this is not particularly the reaction of a crazy man. When for the first twenty years of your life, you've done a certain thing and people have reacted in a certain kind of way. Later on, when maybe everyone isn't quite so awful and so ugly, you've been so used to a certain kind of response so that you continue acting the way you always had to act in order to defend yourself or go on living at all or get anything done.

You know, if Charles had not been so exaggerated from the very beginning—or if [he hadn't been] in other people's eyes so exaggerated—he would have been beaten down, he would have never done what he achieved. And he did it by simply fighting against every obstacle. Now there were times when, from the point of view of the outsiders, this kind of fighting was very exaggerated or it wasn't justified by whatever set it off, but if you go into it and examine it, it usually was and it was usually not so paranoid. . . .

As far as understanding the person, there are a lot of things Charles did that I think would certainly not be justified, a lot of the methods he used were maybe absolutely unjustifiable. But it's certainly easy—

MINGUS: What you talking about?

SUE: I mean just a lot of things, Charles, a lot of angry things that you did.

MINGUS: Name some.

SUE: A lot of screaming and yelling and punching that went on because you felt very strongly about things, and it seemed the easiest way to react. I'm saying a lot of the things that you did, if you examine them individually, maybe weren't justifiable. But the reasons that you did them are certainly understandable. . . . I mean, I can't think of any, now that you asked me, but there must be hundreds of things. I mean your methods were always very dramatic and very strong.

NOTE

1. Sue Mingus, *Tonight at Noon: A Love Story* (New York: Pantheon, 2002), 86–87.

13 The Real and the Fictional Mingus

"Finally I believe I'm violent; I read it enough."

This session started in Chick & Chock's bar, around the corner from Mingus's apartment at Fifth Street and Avenue A, talking about dope. Later in our conversation, he invited me into his place for piano music and more talk. Some of the best, most telling comments Mingus made to me about his music were in that apartment, where he illustrated his points on the piano. That discussion covered his new composition, "Number 29," Bach, Thad Jones, and Sue. There was also the ever-present answering machine (a big focus in Mingus's life) and some marvelous piano interludes and musings.

I put this short piece here to illustrate the difficulty of separating fact and fiction in Mingus at times. Dan Morgenstern vigorously denied the Weinstock story, which doesn't make it false, however; and Mingus's thoughts on Charlie Parker may have been just a way to express a contrarian point of view, which he often did. I mean, *Down Beat* didn't get Parker busted for being a junkie, as Mingus claims here.

But much of this has the ring of truth—even his confession that he first tried dope with Benny Harris, which to my knowledge he had not revealed before. And the pain he had been feeling with Sue was entirely real.

· · ·

MINGUS: Yeah, all Bob Weinstock [head of Prestige Records] had to do was find a good pusher, bring him to the [recording] date, keep the guys happy, and get some music out. He paid Charlie Parker, he paid Sonny Rollins, he paid practically everybody who was using dope that way. He got better dope than they got, white dope.

GOODMAN: Weinstock Enterprises, eh? Was Sonny Rollins into that?

MINGUS: Yeah, he was a junkie.

GOODMAN: Oh, that's right, now I remember.

MINGUS: Well, he [Rollins] beat it, beat it the hard way, man, with the Rosicrucian thing. I was into [dope], everybody was into it at one time or another, in some kind of way.

GOODMAN: You told me you never were.

MINGUS: Yes, I did, I told you I did. You misunderstood me—I tried it once, man, with Benny Harris, one of the greatest trumpet players ever lived.

GOODMAN: Right, Dizzy's "daddy."

MINGUS: I was with the Red Norvo trio then, just visiting, and me and Benny got high. I can see how it can happen, because if you like somebody who plays with it, if they do it, you'll do it. "You shouldn't be afraid of this," they say. But Benny's kicked [drugs] too, and he had to leave the country to kick. Because the same pushers keep coming back.

GOODMAN: I wanted to ask you about Bird and particularly when he was all strung out at the end. Were you with him at all then?

MINGUS: I never saw Bird act like a junkie; he never seemed strung out. I've seen him drunk—at Birdland a couple of times.

GOODMAN: Really? He's the most famous junkie in the world.

MINGUS: I know. You know who did that? Jazz magazines made him famous. Stan Getz, they made him famous.

GOODMAN: But all the stories about his habit though, man.

MINGUS: Bird was never busted for narcotics. That's what *Down Beat* did to him, man. They talked about that, and Stan Getz was busted. I never knew if Bird was a junkie or not, 'cause if he was, he was a heavy junkie. I think in the olden days when he was very young, starting in jazz in California, with Norman Granz and all that, he was thin then: I'm sure he was a junkie then. That's when he went to Camarillo [State Hospital].

But he told me himself, his words, he said, "Mingus, I can't afford that stuff. I got six mouths to feed—my wife and her two children, my daughter and son and my dog"—and he called the name of the dog.

GOODMAN: If the stories are anyway true, the way he was into it would be expensive as hell, man, hundreds of dollars a day.

MINGUS: Sure, and he sure wasn't making that.

GOODMAN: What happened with the iodine business [his attempted suicide]? You know anything about that?

MINGUS: Iodine? I remember something like that, but . . . well, if Bird wanted to kill himself, he knew how to kill himself.

GOODMAN: But he didn't want to. It reminded me of your story about Bellevue—he said he took the stuff to get out of a contract.

MINGUS: Oh yeah?

GOODMAN: Because if they accused him of having suicidal tendencies, then he could get off the hook. Something like that. I'll find it and send it to you.

MINGUS: I didn't know that.
    How about Billie Holiday, she was never busted. But they watched her all the time, as a big connection, for the FBI to close in.

GOODMAN: Right, they made her life hell, a horrible story.

MINGUS: One negro who can consume maybe one hundred dollars a day. . . .

GOODMAN: But Bird was so goddamn careful, you know.

MINGUS: Bird was so . . . recognized. He wasn't as famous as Billie Holiday.

GOODMAN: Well, by 1950 or '51, he was sure a goddamn star.

MINGUS: I can't understand how they stay junkies, man, 'cause that sickness is so long, so much longer than being high, and then you go and get high again. Your high is three-four-five hours, where your coming down period is days. So I can't understand where if a kid is on junk . . . I wouldn't want it, man.

GOODMAN: Do you think it's a big thing today? Are people in music as hung up with the dope scene as they were in the '50s? Maybe that's a dumb question.

MINGUS: No, it's not so dumb. I see a lot of cats, even in the avant-garde, who are junkies. I see that there's more of them than was in modern jazz, before avant-garde.
    Now they're in it now, man, to where they don't know they're junkies. They say it's a health kick. But when you get high, the last thing you want to do is see some food. So most of 'em are thin, drawn-out skull faces, so

it's hard to say if they're using junk or not. But when I see their eyes, I know they're using drugs. Then if they have enough brains about it, they use belladonna, which opens your pupils up. Real junkies got that down.

GOODMAN: Forget the smack, some just eat the stuff.

MINGUS: They do everything, man. They do everything now. They don't just get high, they use LSD. Friend of mine, my baritone saxophone player [Hamiet Bluiett], said he heard Ornette Coleman was in a movie [*Chappaqua*, 1966]—this is how they exploit musicians to goof their own life—so he went to the movie to see Ornette, and all they did was show Ornette in the movie in a teepee with a peace pipe, smoking the pipe. He's with the Indians.

GOODMAN: Well, people do a lot of things for money. If you're going to be exploited, if I were in his shoes, that would be the last thing I'd ever do. Sit my ass in a teepee and smoke a pipe in a movie.

MINGUS: Yeah, peace pipe. Maybe he needed the money so bad he couldn't make no choice.

GOODMAN: Right, this could be.

MINGUS: [*music under*] . . . And that thing you were hearing [me play] is a kind of blues ["Taurus in the Arena of Life"], but now I want to take this into [the idea that] the blues is for everybody. I was gonna move into that. It's really a suite, this thing I'm doing, but a suite with a little story to it.

The section I'm in now is more like a funeral blues, like a funeral march blues. I've been hearing that, why I don't know. I'm not here to die. I'd like to live, but the last seven years all I've seen is sadness, having no actual reality as to how my existence is in relationship to my friends and my love. The person I'm in love with—I don't get any, uhh, assurance that it's really there.

The only assurance I get is to call my wife [Judy] and say, "Look, you know it's funny every time I get with Sue, I go to [*unintelligible*] and she ducks." Like she did last night when I'm leaving the club.

GOODMAN: Maybe she's scared of you.

MINGUS: But this is her act, she's not afraid of me, man. Judy says, "That's very funny because you get cuddly when you get drunk. You get violent when you're not drunk." Me and Judy have no fights anyway. So how is it that when I fall in love with someone, she [*unintelligible*] me and Judy?

FIGURE 10.   Mingus composing at Sue Graham's Tenth Street apartment, 1974.
Photo by Sy Johnson.

She just got bored and wanted to leave. We're two good friends, like brother
and sister. You can't live with your sister. We had sex, it was agreeable sex,
she came and I came—but it wasn't enough to see us through it. I mean, I
went to the piano after that, writing music.

But here I've got somebody I really dig—put that in there—and would
like to have more than just the piano, and there's nothing: we have sex
and it's all over. And the very reason that there's nothing to talk about is
that she hasn't shown who she is. Or where she stands at. And since she's
pushing this angry act, that I'm violent—she kept telling me that I'm like
my articles say.

The critics have done that; I haven't done it. They're the ones that
say, "Well, he hit so-and-so." One guy wrote something, like, I hit two

guys. I mean, Tommy Dorsey and his brother [Jimmy] used to fight all the time—nobody said they were violent. Yet people end up naming me "violent Charles Mingus." Finally I believe I'm violent; I read it enough. Have to learn to protect myself because people think I'm violent.

. . . You know, Christ came to save cats who didn't believe. They may not give 'em what *they* want, but don't become the way the killers are, the real killers. Be able to defend yourself and kill if they attack your people, even though he said "Thou shalt not kill."

This cat, beautiful black man, my cousin, my blood cousin, he said, "I'll tell you something, man, you can tell all the pimps with the best money and whores in town because they can teach."

CHAPTER 13 COMMENTARY

Dan Morgenstern on Prestige and Dope

MORGENSTERN: Did you see him on television last week?

GOODMAN: Yeah, I was there in the studio with him. It was good.

MORGENSTERN: Yeah. Well, there are several things he said on camera about a certain record company executive that—

GOODMAN: Oh God, wasn't that wild?

MORGENSTERN: I am sure Bob Weinstock never did that. A friend of mine was involved in working with Prestige at the time they recorded Mingus and it seemed very unlikely to him. He was quite shocked, not that he particularly likes the guy. But Mingus says things like that more or less because at the moment he is mad at someone for no good reason. I think Weinstock is actually out of the record business. He sold the label and it has been bought out.

They just brought out a three-record set of a thing that Mingus did a year ago [*The Great Concert (1964, Paris) of Charles Mingus*]. He called me when it came out last week, furious, and wanted to know how to get ahold of Weinstock, and I said I first needed to see the record. I had not seen it yet but did know it was out. I said, "Charles, Weinstock has nothing to do with Prestige anymore. He sold it outright, he is retired and lives in Florida." But he did not want to hear that. I could not get through to him.

GOODMAN: Yeah, but he repeated what you just said to me last night. So you did get through to him. We had dinner after the show and he expanded on this whole thing.

MORGENSTERN: Well, ten minutes after he hung up, Sue called me and I explained it to her.

Regina Ryan on Publishing Beneath the Underdog

Regina Ryan was the editor at Alfred A. Knopf who worked closely with Mingus on *Underdog*. When we spoke in 1972, she had some special insights into how the book finally came to be published, the history of their relationship, and Mingus as a person.

. . .

RYAN: Well, it seemed like one of those crazy publishing stories. It was a most unusual thing and quite a coup in a way to me. I didn't know much about him but somebody told me about this book, somebody who really loved his music, one of these fanatic people that just adore him. He said, "Buy that book. You could make yourself such a name in publishing if you could ever get that book. It's been around for years. Everyone has tried to get it; you ought to see what you can find out." I didn't know where to begin, really.

I couldn't find out anything about it, and Mingus had dropped out of sight. Suddenly a friend called up nine months later and said, "I just bought this record of his that I've been trying to get for years, the *Mingus at Monterey* concert." And there was a flyer in it saying, "No one will publish my book. The publishing industry's against it; I need money to publish my book; send money to P.O. Box XXX."

GOODMAN: Right, I'd forgotten about that.

RYAN: So I wrote him a letter. And Sue Graham Ungaro answered. He wouldn't meet me for months. But we talked about it, and he was interested. I couldn't believe it, and it got to be crazier and crazier, more bizarre as time went on. But finally he agreed to let me read it. It had been all over publishing from one house to another, but people felt it was too wild at the time. But people were apparently Xeroxing parts of it, or he felt they were. He said people would walk up to him on the street and say, "Why did you say that about so-and-so?" because he used real names [in the draft manuscript], even though he didn't intend to publish it that way. So he wouldn't let us see it.

Finally, it came to a compromise that he would let us see it if Sue Graham was present. We had one day, and she brought this thing in—in PanAm bags, I mean dripping with paper, you just couldn't believe it—and for about four hours I sat there and read. He doesn't know this, but I put her in another office, and she did her business. I mean she couldn't sit there and watch me for hours while I read. And then I would grab up a handful and I'd run into our editor-in-chief and say, "Look, this is pretty exciting stuff. What do you think?"

You could tell right away that he had this tremendous poetic ability. There were great lunges, and some wonderful stuff in there.

So anyway, on the basis of that, we said we wanted to do something. But we had to get an outside person in there; it was just too unshaped, just a mass of papers with lots of good writing. Then we had to get into an option deal—and it was so complicated, I cannot tell you—and an arrangement with Nel King to do it [the editing]. He knew her from the movies, and he'd apparently been after her to do this. Then we found out that he had a contract with McGraw Hill years ago, seven or eight years ago, and Louis Lomax was supposed to do it [the editing]. And I don't know what happened, but I gather that Louis Lomax took the money and ran and never did anything.[1]

You can understand that you had to find just the right person to do this. Charles is so distrustful, he's been so hurt by so many people, and he's difficult. Anyway, he trusted Nel, and she had the kind of talent to penetrate through all the stuff.

It's weird but he's convinced that half of the best part of the book isn't there—that we cut it out. The thing is too he would come up with stuff he found in a suitcase, you know it was years of writing. I've run into people now who told me, "Oh, I held his manuscript, two boxes of it, for three years" or something.

It was the most difficult emotional and psychological and every other kind of publishing involvement you could imagine.

GOODMAN: How long did it take from when you first looked at it to get to print?

RYAN: I heard about it in '68, I guess, and then I finally got the address in '69, and it came out last year [1971]. Finally, once we had the contract, or the option, then we met, he and I. And of course he was so sweet and dear and like a little lamb. I expected this raging terror, I didn't know what to expect. And it went well. I think it meant a lot to him in terms of getting himself back together and getting into the public eye.

I've hardly seen him since the book came out. But it seemed to me that it meant a great deal to his . . . [*pause*] well-being. Then he suddenly began to write music again, which he hadn't done for years, and started appearing. It just seemed to be a turning point.

I think when I wrote to him he was in some hospital or something—really in pretty bad shape at the time.[2] Frankly, he was very difficult to work with because he was so . . . he was very tranquilized. But all of a sudden you'd get a sense of the wit that's in the book, and gradually you began to sense that he was back, back to being himself. So I think it was perhaps just fortuitous, but it seemed to do a great deal for him. And of course it attracted all sorts of attention to him again, which could only help.

We paid a lot of money for it, and the paperback sale, and all the publicity we did for the book, although that came a little later. It just seemed to give him a new start.

GOODMAN: Can you tell me more about what precisely you had to do with Nel King's version? What was the process there?

RYAN: Well, I worked almost every day on it. After a certain point we [Nel and I] went over it, and we discussed the language—for instance, to give it continuity, we might have, she might have felt it needed a few sentences to set the scene. So she did some writing, a little writing, and we would discuss that language, or whether a thing made sense, whether something else was necessary. We went over it line by line, word by word together.

GOODMAN: And structurally too?

RYAN: Yeah, pretty much. I really worked with it closely, but what she did was, first, get it back in some kind of sensible order. We never wanted it to appear to be a straight autobiography at all, and he had a lot to say about that too. And he didn't want to write about his music. It was very odd.

GOODMAN: Yeah, I know, and everybody's commented about that too.

RYAN: But as someone said in *Down Beat,* people are so wrong to think this should be about his music, because this was about the man. The music is about the man too, just another facet, but, as he kept saying, "How can I write about it? What can I say?" But we did get him to write about the people he played with. This book to him was about finding God . . . because he was convinced he had lost him, again [*chuckle*]. He sees this as a very religious book, a truly religious, spiritual thing.

GOODMAN: Some parts of it are very clear and strong that way.

RYAN: Mingus is such an interesting combination of things. There's a sort of childishness about some of his ideas and then this almost sophisticated mysticism and philosophy, you know. It's very, very interesting. But that's what he told me: this book was about finding God.

And also he wanted forgiveness. I have a letter where he said he wanted forgiveness for some of the things he'd done, some of the people he'd hurt. And of course it's not true, an awful lot of that book [isn't true].

We put that in the beginning but I don't know if people believe it or not. It's fantasy, almost more true than true, those characters like the pimp in San Francisco. Well, there was a real pimp there but I don't know that Mingus was involved with him quite the way he saw it. But we had plenty of problems about the legal things, you know, the pimps and who was going to sue.

GOODMAN: Like what? Because of naming names?

RYAN: Or because they might be recognizable. I'd say, "Well, you say so-and-so in the band was sleeping with this one's wife and that one's wife," or something like that, and he'd say, "Oh, he'd love it. He'd just love to have that said about him." And we'd say, "Well, yeah, fine, until some smart lawyer tells him he can make a million dollars."

But Mingus couldn't understand that. Also, he made some woman a whore—that was really interesting. There was a whole thing with this girl that he couldn't marry when he was a kid, or he'd run away to marry when he was a kid—

GOODMAN: Donna Lee, no, Lee-Marie.

RYAN: And he introduces this whole thing about her becoming a whore, and of course it's not true at all, but it was like, working out his anger. I said, "Well, you can't say that about somebody!" His defense was just that she wasn't, that it was not true. And that went to the heart of the libel problem, and it was quite interesting to try and untangle all that stuff. But the point was that this was really a psychic autobiography more than—

GOODMAN: I think most people took it that way.

RYAN: I guess so, I would think. But he has such a gift for making it seem so real. He's really very talented as a writer—wonderful scenes that he did mostly through dialogue, not much description. But you just know that [any] scene, it's more real than real.

Did I explain enough about how the book was worked on? He worked very closely with Nel King, and then I worked with her really after. But he was very involved, every inch of the way.

GOODMAN: They had a falling out, huh?

RYAN: Yeah. . . . it [money] was the cause of most people falling out.

GOODMAN: Somebody said in a review that he was pleased, that he thought what she did with the book was fine.

RYAN: He was, oh, absolutely. Oh yes, he really liked it. No, he was delighted, thrilled. I think sometimes out of self-defense, he'll say, "Oh, well, the best part of it's gone," or that kind of thing. But it's not. There were a couple of scenes he wanted in that just didn't seem to have anything to say, repetitive, so we cut them.

GOODMAN: Did you watch him on Channel 13 the other night?

RYAN: No, I didn't know he was on.

GOODMAN: And there was a thing about the book—Julius Lester gets up there with a copy and starts talking about it.

RYAN: We were trying to arrange that for a long time.

GOODMAN: So you got some nice publicity out of it. And Charles says, "Well, of course, this book is only one of my autobiographies. I gave Nel King one thousand pages, and there's a great deal more here. This is just the surface of Mingus," or words to that effect.

RYAN: I know, he often says that, or something like that. But I got so annoyed at these reviewers. Man, they should know better. Some of them would say, "The publisher's ripping him off," or something, and I never worked so hard in my life on a book, trying to get every ounce out of him to use. But a lot of the reviewers would say, "What has this awful publishing company done to this man?" Not quite that simplistic, but almost.

GOODMAN: Really?

RYAN: Yeah, a lot of the black reviewers. They also got mad about having Nel King work on it, you know, some white person. In England it has gotten a much better reception. It has really been treated the way it should have been treated here, as a genuine work of art, as genuinely fine writing, as a fascinating work of a very talented, complex, peculiar, unusual man. And here, people just couldn't see beyond the blackness, the anger, the sex. Very interesting.

GOODMAN: . . . Somebody told me it was going to be translated— or not?

RYAN: Into French, they're publishing very soon, I think. Of course it was published in England, to great acclaim. Not that they said it was the greatest masterpiece ever written but it got wonderful and serious critical attention. It's been bought, I believe, in Holland. They haven't sold it in Germany, but the Japanese have bought it. They [the Japanese] love him, you know.

GOODMAN: I went to a Japanese restaurant with him last night. God, he loves that food. Sushi and everything.

RYAN: He gets into these kicks. I remember one night he really wanted to go out and eat calf's head or something. He wanted to go to a Greek restaurant where they served this thing, and he called up all over the place to find it. And of course his weight problem is terrible for him.

GOODMAN: He's scared of it now. The doctors have scared him.

RYAN: It's a terrible problem and it comes through in the book too, how sad it is that he's so tormented—that wonderful scene where he describes his father and how he can't cross his leg. And you can see it: I mean he goes up and down, and sometimes you just wonder if he can actually walk. He toddles.

One story I didn't tell you is that David Siegel, who was one of the famous editors who came here [to Knopf], died last year, a young man, and he had had it [*Underdog*] under contract at McGraw Hill. He couldn't believe the book was finally being published when he came here. It had gone around eight-ten years ago. He said even if they had signed it up he didn't see how they could have published it then.

GOODMAN: How was the contract business finally worked out?

RYAN: No, the only difficulty was how they were going to split the money. It's spelled out in the contract but it is a bone of contention. I mean, Nel King thinks she's getting screwed. . . .

Yeah. Gee, when we had the publicity party Max Gordon took this forty-five-foot poster of Mingus—he wanted it and he was going to put it up in the Vanguard. He kept trying to put it up and it kept falling down. I think he must have covered the walls and the ceiling with it. But he wanted that thing on his wall. It was funny.

GOODMAN: Well, how was the party?

RYAN: The party was sensational. Yeah, that one night was really wonderful. And of course Charles was so thrilled, it was so nice, it really was, for him. We haven't sold as many copies as we had hoped but I think it's going to be really big in paperback. One of the problems was a lot of the TV people were really afraid of him. His reputation had preceded him, unfortunately. They were just afraid to give him national attention—live, or any other way, I guess. Although they did do some.

John Goodman on the Real and the Fictional Mingus

The fictional Mingus is best seen in *Beneath the Underdog,* a series of poses that reflect the roles Mingus sometimes chose for himself in real life. I frankly don't like the book that much and find that, as others have said, the best parts occur when he lets the various masks drop and talks about the music in dialogues with musicians. The Fats Navarro passages and his talk about Watts and its people (e.g., Billy Bones the pimp) come from real, genuinely felt, not fictionalized, experience.

One way to look at the book is as a wholesale critique of the jazz industry, with the artist as victim of a corrupt capitalist society (see, for example, the Fats passages). It also presents a story of "pimp or be pimped," in which the party scenes and the narrator's sexual preoccupations dominate everything else. His women seem little more than objects of rabid desire.

Music wins out over pimping, predictably idealizing the narrator's "creativity" over earthbound concerns about women and sex. He comes out for "racelessness" in the end, which ideal is best expressed in the monologue with his father. But finally, it's hard to believe in the narrator's conversion from pimping because that too seems like just another pose—taken so as to come out on the right side of creativity.

I know the book has had lots of praise, much of it from people who didn't know Mingus or his music. Anatole Broyard, writing in the *New York Times* on May 3, 1971, apparently did know the music, but he punted on the book, implying that it didn't fulfill its promise. Elsewhere, the critical responses were pretty predictable. Derek Jewell, writing in the *London Times* on March 10, 1971, heard in the book "a gigantic, baffling, obscene, and innocent cry from the soul." Though out of balance and too reliant on sex, it is however a work "upon which a WASP can scarcely claim the right to pass any judgment at all." Mingus did intimidate a lot of people.

The *Village Voice* reviewer—Felipe Luciano, writing on July 22, 1971—ranted at length about the evils of Christianity, racism and the political system, black genius, the importance of fucking, and whether or not Mingus is/was a nigger. It surely brings back the spirit of the time to read this stuff again. Richard Freedman in *Book World* on June 20, 1971, saw the book's obvious flaws but found passages "of great power, a power more associated with fiction than autobiography." Mingus, indeed, could have been a writer. But he was not, at any rate, an editor.

His editors had plenty of problems with those "bags of papers," as Regina Ryan referred to them, and it's hard to criticize her or Nel King without knowing just what they had to deal with. Still, I find the result to be much like the 1962 Town Hall concert, a halting rehearsal with some brilliant moments. There is a consistent voice, yes, but a voice which isn't always Charles's, as his talk in this book can attest. *Underdog* is a stew of Mingus wannabe roles, all of them in conflict with his search for God and a true self. And maybe that search was just a role for him too: in all my talk with Mingus, I never had the sense that he was on any kind of religious quest. Spiritual, certainly, but not religious.

I still don't know what is in all those boxes that Sue gave to the Library of Congress—including the material that Charles called the "original book." It's surely anticlimactic and redundant to think about a revised *Underdog*, but likely there is valuable stuff there beyond what Gene Santoro used in *Myself When I Am Real* and Eric Porter revealed in *What Is This Thing Called Jazz?*

That original *Underdog* manuscript meant a great deal to Mingus, and I think to a large extent he discounted the published version. He felt that his disordered, unpublished manuscript would set the record straight on many issues, including his life in music, besides explaining himself to the world and answering his critics. *Underdog* doesn't really succeed in these endeavors and, to be fair, it doesn't attempt them.

Like his posthumous *Epitaph* in music, the original *Underdog* was going to be his last word and testament on life and finally, as he told Ryan, his attempt to find God. At one time, I had notions about how I might be his literary Gunther Schuller, but could not follow through for all kinds of reasons. By shopping the manuscript around, showing it to too many people, Mingus turned out to be his own worst enemy. It seems as though some who had to do with the original book either had solely their own interests at heart or tried to screw him over—the latter was his conclusion. More probably, it was just too much disjointed stuff to contend with.

He did, however, appear to get a good screwing from Louis Lomax—as he made clear to me in one of our 1972 conversations:

. . .

MINGUS: Most people don't know I paid Louis Lomax—he asked me how much I want to edit my book. He said, "Well, your book's not worth anything [as is]. You know, I get a lot of money for doing a book—they pay me four or five hundred dollars for doing a book."

And I say, "I'll pay you five hundred." That sounded cheap to me. Not that I'm rich, but to edit a book?

He said, "Let me think about it," and he goes and tells his wife, "This guy's got some money."

Then he says, "My wife was reading the book, and it's not really that bad"—and he probably hadn't even read the book—"so I'll edit. It'll take a lot of writing and rewriting. Then I'll give it to you and we'll take it to a publisher."

"No, I'm gonna publish it myself." Be sure and print that. "I have my own record company and I'll have my own publishing company for books."

He said, "Well, that's all right, but I can probably get you a good deal because I know a lot of publishers."

He calls me up months later and says, "Man, I got you a deal—sell your book for seven hundred, more than I ever got for a book."

"Man," I says, "kiss my ass. Seven hundred dollars? Look, I get fifteen thousand dollars for a record date—what are you talking about, seven hundred dollars? What kind of book are you writing?" I saw him on television, and I thought he was something, you know.

So then this Lomax calls back and says, "It's too late, man. We might get more money, but the book is in McGraw Hill's office right now, and they want the book."

I say, "You tell them to call me, or get my book to me, or I'm going to kill you." That's my exact words. "I'll send a cat to see you right now, Frank Mabry, and you get my book right now so he can have it."

I was planning on three writings of that book, edited by an educated man, because he's educated. I saw him on TV, that's how I got to know him. I accidentally called him on his phone and he hung up in my face: "I'm watching my show! Call me back!" and hung up. So I waited and called him back after his show was over, told him I wanted to see him about editing a book.

No shit, man, because I wanted to put that book out myself. Edit it after he'd do it, plus he didn't take the names out—I was gonna do it myself to be sure. I thought we'd use him just to clean up my ideas, then we'd go and put me back in there again, 'cause I ain't no writer, but I know how to use a writer.

. . . I made some mistakes [in the book], but you never saw so many changes in the book that [actually] took place. If you read the book, which you need to do, you'd tell if I'm lying. You'll find evidently I must be a mind reader of the country, 'cause I predicted white people would have long hair. Six years before it happened, it was in the book. I didn't predict it, I said they should do it. And I never said "black is beautiful," but I used to straighten my hair with my momma's hot comb, so I would get my people to accept me, but when I washed it out, it would kink back. I later made my hair beautiful kinky, beautiful black.

· · ·

There are wonderful flashes of insight into the "real" Mingus throughout *Underdog*. Besides the Fats dialogues, such scenes as Charles's imaginary harangue to his father about racism and the great put-down of prominent jazz critics at a party resonate for me as the real Mingus talking. For better or worse, *Underdog* is the representation Mingus has left us. As his editor Ryan said, he had his hand in everything that saw print. The book was very much his fiction.

In another sense, Mingus was fictionalizing and role-playing through most of his life, when and as it suited him: the Clown, the Baron, the King Pimp, and so forth. The real Mingus is finally as indefinable and inimitable as his music. A man whose ego sometimes overran his conscience and good nature, Mingus moved his friends to love, anger, and performance of the impossible—just as he moved his musicians. The urgent needs he manifested constantly and sometimes acted out to his detriment were often tempered by a warmth and openness that were not always on display. Mingus was "the easiest person in the world to love," said Bobby Jones, who frequently had formidable fights with him.

In my interview with Bobby, he talked about Mingus the contrarian, about getting to know and understand him over time and, particularly, about his mastery of theatrics. I think Mingus loved to put people on, but there was also a side to him that was quixotic. Like the dour don, Charles was quick to take up his sword against perceived injustices to his person, his notions of fairness and justice, or his pursuit of musical truth. Like Don Q., this got him into all kinds of troubles, which were mostly seen as the fault of others. His contests with the cab drivers (see chapter 9) and the evictions (see chapter 10) are examples. Charles was also in love with the idea of love: he was a true romantic in every sense of the word, and a real scrapper for the things he believed in. Dannie Richmond was forever his Sancho Panza, a notion which struck me the first time I heard the Tijuana tales.

The parallel only works so far, of course. There were many Minguses, not just the three he suggested in *Underdog*. Here are a few that I saw: the gourmet-gourmand, the hedonist, the racial activist, the social critic, and the great manipulator. Sometimes he conveyed the sense that he was very consciously playing these roles, that he assumed them with an almost ironic involvement, for example in his flirtations with pimping.

You could say that Mingus never really decided who he wanted to be, so he kept trying on all these different suits of clothes. It's probably more legitimate to claim that the many Minguses were just facets, layers on that hard kernel of a man that Sy Johnson talked about.

What matters is that this multiple experience, together with much study and natural talent, combined to produce some of the greatest musical stories a jazz musician has ever told. Mingus was a teller of multilayered stories, as you've heard here and as his compositions testify.

NOTES

1. See Simond Griote, "The Life and Times of Louis E. Lomax," *Gibbs Magazine*, www.gibbsmagazine.com/Louis%20E%20Lomax.htm; and http://en.wikipedia.org /wiki/Louis_Lomax.

2. After the 1966 eviction, Mingus had a very bad time for a few years and indeed ended up in Bellevue again after a naked romp in Central Park. See Brian Priestly, *Mingus: A Critical Biography* (New York: Da Capo, 1982), 173.

Chronology

This chronology represents selective milestones in my work with Mingus, such as when we did our interviews, and events that have significance in this book, such as concerts and publications. It is not in any sense a complete chronology of all important Mingus events for these years.

1972

February	*Let My Children Hear Music* released by Columbia
February 4	*Mingus and Friends* concert, with Bill Cosby as MC, Teo Macero conducting, at Philharmonic Hall, New York
March 15	Mingus's "John Ass Wilson" piece ("Charles Mingus Answers John S. Wilson of the N.Y. Times") appears in Sue Graham's *Changes*, March 17, 1972
March 20	Mingus big band starts its seven-week run at the Village Vanguard, New York
May 30–June 2	Mingus appears on Julius Lester's PBS TV show, *Free Time*; *Mingus Speaks* interviews in New York
June 3	Mingus's band plays at Gino's Foxhole in Philadelphia; *Mingus Speaks* interviews in Philadelphia
June 14–15	Bradley's and Mercer Arts Center band rehearsals; *Mingus Speaks* interviews in New York, including music colleagues, Booker Tillery, and Mingus in his Fifth Street apartment
June 15–July 15	Big band booked at Mercer Arts Center
July 4	Mingus performs in Newport in New York festival
August	European tour, booked by Sue Graham
Fall	Mingus college tour

Late October	European tour, booked by George Wein
November 17	*Playboy* turns down my proposed Mingus feature piece

1973

January 19	Mingus Carnegie Hall concert, with quintet and Dizzy Gillespie

1974

January 19	Second *Mingus and Friends* Carnegie Hall concert, with Roland Kirk et al.
March	*Mingus Speaks* interviews with Mingus and Sue in New York, over dinners at Max's Kansas City, Bradley's, and elsewhere
March 23	Second series of *Mingus Speaks* interviews in Philadelphia, including the "Pernod interviews"
May 15	Book proposal sent to Doubleday
July–October	Mingus on tour in South America, Europe, and Japan

1979

January 5	Mingus dies of ALS in Cuernavaca, Mexico; Sue cares for him
May	Sheldon Wax (*Playboy* managing editor) dies in plane crash in Chicago
July	*Playboy* grants license to reprint their material—from February 4, 1972, *Friends* concert review and my obit for Mingus
November	My *Playboy* obit for Mingus appears

Acknowledgments

It must be sometimes boring and pro forma to write a list of people to whom your book is indebted, but of course it's traditional. In this case, with a book perhaps thirty years overdue, it's a belated pleasure for me to acknowledge those who contributed in so many different ways.

There is no one to whom I'm more indebted than Sue Mingus, who has been helpful with all kinds of advice over the years, some of it critical but all of it accommodating to my delays and changes in approach.

All the other commenters, living and dead, who have spoken herein made the book far richer than had it been simply a record of conversations between Mingus and myself; my particular thanks go to Sy Johnson. Their differing points of view have been invaluable; their contributions enabled me to attempt finally to present Mingus whole.

The New York Foundation for the Arts (NYFA) sponsored the project when it was conceived as a multimedia venture in 2008, and I am most grateful for their confidence and help, especially that of Marina Gonzalez. Attorney John Edozie of New York City gave me valuable advice on rights, procedures, contracts, and more. Bob Connolly of pdfPictures in Toronto was extremely influential in helping me conceive how these Mingus materials could make a successful e-book.

Regina Ryan, my agent, was incredibly helpful to me in drafting a proposal and finding a first-rank publisher.

When I was living in Maine four years ago, I got ideas for contacts, content, funding sources, and Mingus lore from several people. I had good talks with jazz trumpeter Don Stratton. He put me in touch with Richard Nelson, professor of jazz at the University of Maine in Augusta, and with saxophonist Dick Hafer in Los Angeles, who once played with Mingus. I still haven't been able to follow Don's recommendation to hook up with

Justin Di Cioccio, chair of the Jazz Arts Program at the Manhattan School of Music, but we will.

My best Maine source for talk and support was invariably jazz fan and counselor Chris York, the man instrumental in finally getting me on track to finish this book. Another spiritual advisor along the way was Dr. Dan Josephthal of Charlottesville, Virginia, who helped me face down some of the delays and denials that kept me from writing.

Over the course of time, I used the services of several off-the-tape transcribers—two in particular when I lived in Virginia: Cathy Gentry and Elizabeth Hart. Readers can't imagine what it's like to transcribe somebody who talks like Mingus. There would have been no book without their help.

When I was writing for *Playboy*, I got much encouragement, wisdom, and support from then–managing editor Sheldon Wax, the man I worked for for nine years, who died in a tragic plane crash five months after Charles passed. Shel was the prime mover for jazz at the magazine, and he was gracious to let me have my shot at Mingus. Others at the magazine researched, pulled and copied articles, pored over multiple sources, and helped greatly with my research.

Finally, friends and family have examined and remarked on various portions of this manuscript (and its approach) over time—and, naturally, made comments ranging from carping to helpful. One of the most helpful friends was Rusty Hassan, Washington, DC, disk jockey and the city's biggest jazz enthusiast. My sister Boo Hubbard, lately passed, was my greatest booster. I thank all the others for their forbearance and urge them to write their frank, penetrating reviews on Amazon or elsewhere in order to tell me at last what they really think.

Thanks, everyone. I needed your help.

Index

Page numbers in italics indicate illustrations.

Gordon, Max, 3, 126–30, 187, 206, 208–10, 213, 214, 215n2, 296, 310
gospel music, 1, 8, 9, 68, 225n4, 242
Gould, Glenn, 31
Graham, Sue. *See* Mingus, Sue Graham
Grammy Award, 217
Granz, Norman, 135, 144, 300
Green, Benny, 164
Greenberg, Clement, 38–39
Griffin, Johnny, 148
Grimes, Herman, 144–45
Grissom, Dan, 240
Guggenheim Award, 184, 223

Haden, Charlie, 96n4
Hadi, Shafi, 25–26
Hadnot, Gil, 64
Half Note club, New York, 19, 187, 195, 216n6
Hamilton, Chico, 139–40, 193
Hampton, Gladys, 162
Hampton, Lionel, 18, 19, 110, 132, 144, 147, 148, 162, 189–90, 191
Hancock, Herbie, 181
Handy, John, 96n3, 135
Harlem Renaissance, 12
Harris, Barry, 29
Harris, Benny, 299, 300
Harris, Wynonie, 146, 228
Hawkins, Coleman, 35, 57, 125, 136, 141, 144, 146, 154, 169
Haynes, Roy, 96n4
Hayton, Lennie, 276
Heath, Percy, 48, 62n5
Heifetz, Jascha, xii, 15, 17, 18, 30, 98
Henry, Ernie, 137
Hentoff, Nat, xiii, 37, 157n3, 205, 218, 219, 220, 245, 255, 263n2, 277
Herman, Woody, 115, 175
Hess, Myra, xii
Hillyer, Lonnie, 5, 28, 29, 156
Hindemith, Paul, 56
Hines, Earl, xii, 125
Hinton, Milt, xiii, 70, 74, 77, 96n6
hippies, 19, 109, 195
Hitchcock, Alfred, 240

Hitchcock, Peggy, 273–76, 282n2
Hite, Les, 60, 144
Hodes, Art, xi
Hodges, Johnny, 174
Holiday, Billie, 11, 225n3, 301
Horne, Lena, 276, 277

improvisation, 28, 47n9, 54, 55, 101, 134; collective, 39, 40
Indian music, 21n4, 22n8, 27, 30, 32–34, 59–60, 98
Institute of Jazz Studies, Newark, 94
intellectuals, black, 5, 9, 12–13

Jackson, Calvin, 144
Jackson, Mahalia, 8, 101
Jackson, Milt, 153
Jacquet, Illinois, 111
Jamal, Ahmad, 186n6
Jazz Composers Workshop, 40, 58–59, 62, 81, 96, 151, 186n3, 188, 216nn5,8
jazz poetry. *See* poetry
Jefferson, Blind Lemon, 228
Jeffrey, Paul, 78, 87–91, 119–23, 152, 155–57
Jeffries, Herb, 240
Jewell, Derek, 311
Joffrey Ballet, 62n2
Johnson, J.J., 164
Johnson, James P., 143
Johnson, Sy, xiv, 40–46, 47n13, 65, 66–79, 93, 94, 95n1, 96nn2,3,6, 111–15, 130n6, 137, 180, 210–15, 260–63, 315, 319
Jones, Bobby, xiii, xiv, 5, 7–8, 68, 79, 91–94, 95, 115–19, 122, 124, 156, 168, 314
Jones, Elvin, 193, 194, 278
Jones, Leroi. *See* Baraka, Amiri
Jones, Philly Joe, 62n5
Jones, Quincy, 9–10, 101
Jones, Spike, 30
Jones, Thad, 184, 206, 208, 212, 299
Jorgensen, Christine, 191, 216n4

Karate Bobby, 200, 201
Kaufman, Max, 197, 199

305, 312, 317, 318, 319; interviews with, 18, 65–66, 177–85, 294–98
Mingus Orchestra, 46n4
Minton's Playhouse, New York, 134, 135, 146, 157n4
Monk, Thelonious, xii, 1, 27, 87, 88, 89, 90, 121–22, 146, 150–53, 155–57, 159, 186n3, 191, 195, 215n1, 278
Monkees, the, 99
Monterey Jazz Festival, 69, 81, 96n3, 160, 181–82, 183
Moody, James, xiii, 69, 93
Moore, Kermit, 17, 55, 176
Moore, Oscar, 144, 148
Moore, Phil, 10, 21n5, 50, 51, 105
Morgenstern, Dan, 94–95, 123–26, 154, 185, 205–8, 219, 221–22, 299, 304–5
Morton, Jelly Roll, 3, 40, 281
Mulligan, Gerry, xiii, 65, 77
Muslims. See Nation of Islam
Myers, Marc, 157n2, 186n7

Nash, Ted, 70
Nation of Islam, 244, 244n2
Navarro, Fats, 131–33, 137, 148, 311, 314
Neilson, Celia Germanis, 21n6, 48–49, 147, 151, 163–66, 186n4, 191, 248, 275, 276
Nelson, James, 157n2
Nelson, Oliver, 139. See also Nelson, James
Newport Jazz Festival, 13, 26, 55, 81, 141, 143, 168, 169, 171, 173, 175, 180
New Thing, 17, 20, 23, 24, 32
New Yorker magazine, 191, 219, 225n4
New York Foundation for the Arts, xiv
New York State Council of the Arts, 184, 185
Nixon, Richard, 243
Norvo, Red, 18, 35, 56–57, 105, 149–50, 151, 173, 177, 190, 278, 300

O'Hara, Frank, 56, 62n4
Olatunji, Babatunde, 33

Oliver, King, 16
Overton, Hall, 90

Parker, Charlie ("Bird"), xii, xiv, 2, 11–12, 14, 16, 18–19, 24, 25, 27, 28, 35, 47n9, 49–50, 57–58, 59, 62nn1,5, 101, 104–5, 108, 123, 131–32, 133, 134, 135, 137, 139, 140, 142, 145, 148, 154, 157n2, 164, 190, 222, 225n4, 241, 275, 282n3, 299, 300–301
Patchen, Kenneth, 194
Payne, Rusty, 80, 82
Peter, Paul, and Mary, 183
Peterson, Oscar, xii
Pettiford, Oscar, 16, 129, 190
Philharmonic Hall concert, xiii, 8–9, 79, 82, 84, 86–87, 176, 217, 219–20, 222, 317. See also Mingus, Charles, albums by: Mingus and Friends
pimping, 147, 203–4, 226, 274–75, 281, 293, 308, 311, 315
Plater, Bobby, 148
Playboy magazine, xii, xiii, xv, xvi, xvin2, 52, 93, 123, 160, 182, 237, 269, 270, 276, 279, 291, 318, 320
Plugged Nickel, Chicago, 167
poetry, 8, 46n4, 194
politics, xvi, 5, 7, 23, 24, 38, 96n5, 223, 243
pop music, 21n2, 39, 41, 47n6, 68, 83, 101, 158, 161, 181, 225, 241
Porter, Eric, 46n1, 186n3, 281, 282n1, 312
Powell, Bud, xii, 2, 26–27, 123, 131–34, 135, 164, 166, 186n6
Powell, Richie, 131
Prado, Perez, 132
Prestige Records, 58, 62n5, 163, 165, 186n5, 299, 304–5
Preston, Eddie, 26, 168
Priestly, Brian, 21n2, 216n7, 245, 263n2
Prince, Wesley, 144
Profaci ("Proficcio"), Joe, 197, 201, 216n8

Text:	10/13 Aldus
Display:	Aldus
Compositor:	IDS Infotech, Ltd.
Indexer:	Andrew Joron
Printer and binder:	Sheridan Books, Inc.